LOST
ON THE
FREEDOM
TRAIL

A Volume in the Series
PUBLIC HISTORY IN HISTORICAL PERSPECTIVE

Edited by
MARLA R. MILLER

LOST ON THE FREEDOM TRAIL

THE NATIONAL PARK SERVICE
AND URBAN RENEWAL IN POSTWAR BOSTON

SETH C. BRUGGEMAN

UNIVERSITY OF MASSACHUSETTS PRESS
Amherst and Boston

ISBN 978-1-62534-623-0 (paper); 622-3 (hardcover)

Designed by Deste Roosa
Set in Centaur and Avenir
Printed and bound by Books International, Inc.

Cover design by Sally Nichols
Cover photo by Della Huff / Alamy Stock Photo

Library of Congress Cataloging-in-Publication Data
Names: Bruggeman, Seth C., 1975– author.
Title: Lost on the Freedom Trail : the National Park Service and urban
    renewal in postwar Boston / Seth C. Bruggeman.
Description: Amherst : University of Massachusetts Press, [2022] | Series:
    Public history in historical perspective | Includes bibliographical
    references and index.
Identifiers: LCCN 2021022886 (print) | LCCN 2021022887 (ebook) | ISBN
    9781625346223 (hardcover) | ISBN 9781625346230 (paperback) | ISBN
    9781613768983 (ebook) | ISBN 9781613768990 (ebook)
Subjects: LCSH: United States. National Park Service—History—20th
    century. | Historic sites—Massachusetts—Boston. | Heritage
    tourism—Social aspects—Massachusetts—Boston. | National parks and
    reserves—Social aspects—Massachusetts—Boston. | Collective
    memory—Massachusetts—Boston. | Urban
    renewal—Massachusetts—Boston—History—20th century. | Boston National
    Historical Park (Boston, Mass.)—History. | Freedom Trail (Boston,
    Mass.)—History. | Boston (Mass.)—History—Revolution,
    1775–1783—Historiography. | Boston (Mass.)—Race relations.
Classification: LCC F73.65 .B78 2022 (print) | LCC F73.65 (ebook) | DDC
    974.4/61—dc23
LC record available at https://lccn.loc.gov/2021022886
LC ebook record available at https://lccn.loc.gov/2021022887

British Library Cataloguing-in-Publication Data

A catalog record for this book is available from the British Library.

For Paul Weinbaum,
who helped me get started

CONTENTS

PREFACE

Lost on the Freedom Trail is, in essence, a rearticulation of an argument I've already made for the National Park Service (NPS). The argument lived its first life as an administrative history that I wrote between 2015 and 2020 for the agency under the aegis of its cooperative agreement with the Organization of American Historians, an agreement conceived of some years ago toward involving professional historians in the work of history within the parks. That version of my argument, however, will be inevitably lost amid a federal bureaucratic apparatus that has no obligation to circulate my findings beyond a very small group of readers. I know this because my first administrative history, which I wrote about a decade before the current one, suffered the same fate, and was never in fact certified by the agency. The version of it I later published did ultimately get my argument into broad circulation and, within just a few years, *did* have a very real impact within the NPS.[1]

What was my argument back then? I argued that, despite its progressive potential, the agency's New Deal Era history program ultimately succumbed to partnership dynamics, economic pressures, staffing protocols, and a tangle of nested chauvinisms that reduced public history making to an endless resuscitation of white male supremacy. What is my argument now? Having revisited the story as it played out at a very different park in a very different place, and having drilled down rather deeper into the late-twentieth century, I've discovered that, despite its progressive potential, the agency's New Deal Era history program ultimately succumbed to partnership dynamics, economic pressures, staffing protocols, and a tangle of nested chauvinisms that reduced public history making to an endless resuscitation of white male supremacy.

This is not to say that *Lost on the Freedom Trail* recycles an old argument. The sources, methods, and historiography are all very different from that first project. And yet, the difference that really matters is me. Since that first encounter with the NPS, I have spent more than a decade doing public history in a city and at a university wherein the degradations of systematic racism are inescapable. The experience has taught me, above all, how powerfully our frameworks for doing public history are bound up at the intersection of whiteness and capital, and how even more powerful is the inability of white people to recognize it.

The distance between books is thus the measure of my own awakening, a period of coming to terms with my positionality in the nation's heritage landscape. As a result, my argument is more pointed this time around, and certainly more urgent. Some readers may be surprised by positions I now take that I did not a decade ago. I am no longer, for instance, an easy advocate for historic preservation. I am suspicious of all monuments, and most museums. I cannot champion public history in quite the same way that I once did. It does not seem to me that much of the change heralded in recent books by public historians and preservationists amounts to the kind of systemic trans-formation that is essential for dismantling white privilege or redistributing historical authority. My work now, as I see it, is to help other white historians and heritage professionals understand why they, too, need to break old habits of mind. *Lost on the Freedom Trail* is for them.

To that end, I've had several goals in mind while writing this book. I've sought to amplify, for instance, the findings of another report sponsored by the Organization of American Historians, its 2011 *Imperiled Promise: The State of History in the National Park Service.* It was that underappreciated study that first laid bare the depth and complexity of the National Park Service's history problem. *Lost on the Freedom Trail* is intended, in part, to illustrate his-torically how the problems outlined in *Imperiled Promise* took hold in Boston and resulted in millions of Americans being encouraged to understand the past as a parable of white male entrepreneurial accomplishment. It is a story about entrenched privilege, the calculated devaluing of historical knowledge, the allures of profit, and the costs of all of this for Americans who toil in the history trades, and for those whose claim on prosperity is most deeply eroded by cultural amnesia. It is, ultimately, a warning to public historians that, to regain control of the agenda, we must reclaim our own labor and invent new structures to carry it forward.[2]

I've sought here also to show my university colleagues how inadequate graduate training in history has been for people who've wanted to make a difference within the bureaucracies that produce so much of our public history. Researching this book made palpable to me the enormity of the failure of our system for training historians to intervene in the decades-long struggle against the kinds of narcissistic nationalism that, just as I sat down to write this preface, coursed through the 2021 insurrection on Capitol Hill. I see us as having unwittingly lost that struggle some time ago in places like Boston. Much of the fault is our own. This project has reinforced my sense that historians' sequestering of themselves from one another—across specialties, professional settings, and networks of prestige—has long obscured how common our lot really is. And how fragile our accomplishments are. Historians' opportunities for making real change appear to be vanishing amid the collapsing into one another of organizations that teeter at the balance of private capital and public funding. *Lost on the Freedom Trail* tells the story of how the collapse began in one corner of the NPS history program.

Finally, a few thoughts on an issue that I've struggled with mightily. One of this book's wonderfully astute anonymous reviewers captured it well in characterizing my expectation that the park service could ever be guided by historical inquiry rather than profit as "chimerical." I think that's probably right. Researching this book all but convinced me of it, even after years of writing and teaching about the NPS and wanting to believe that it could be more. What propelled me all of that time was a sense of possibility that the agency could articulate a brand of American nationalism not defined by war, violence, or hatred. It seemed to me, too, that the NPS had done uniquely important work over the decades toward empowering women and people of color despite persistent obstacles for both throughout the agency. And, of course, I had been inspired as a kid by history programs that I now know were born decades ago of the agency's mercurial flirtation with the then-new social history. Since then, I've grown leery of any brand of nationalism, violent or not, and I've seen how what appears to be empowerment can be just the opposite. Still, I've clung to Verne Chatelain's vision for a "new kind of technician," as a model of what progressive history training might achieve when universities work together with the NPS.[3] But that hope too seems chimerical in light of the structural deficiencies embedded within both institutional contexts. I'm left with an aching awareness that my faith in the National Park Service was always an artifact of my own white manhood.

I raise the point here to clarify that this book does not propose solutions to the problems that undermine the agency's capacity to do responsible history in Boston, or anywhere else. Historians more than anyone should understand that truth is a precondition for reconciliation. Before the agency can do better, its problems must be laid bare. I contend that chief among its problems is a deep and abiding structural whiteness. I too am a product of whiteness, a power construct from which I cannot reasonably hope to extract myself. For me, as a historian, it is a critical weakness, and thus leading with it is a way of being honest. But it is also a provocation. I want readers to understand immediately why I am not the best person to write this history, even despite being the only one who likely ever would. *Lost on the Freedom Trail* is my attempt to document one critical expression of the problem and how it has denied Americans an honest reckoning with their past.

ACKNOWLEDGMENTS

Doing public history, I tell my students, is often—maybe always—about answering other people's questions. This book responds to questions first put to me in 2011 at a two-day scholars' visit in Boston hosted by a crack team of National Park Service (NPS) staff and their fellow travelers. Key among the NPS folks were Inez Wollins, Celeste DiBernardo, Louis Hutchins, and Martin Blatt. Susan Ferentinos, who served as the Organization of American Historians' (OAH) public history manager back in those days, was in that group, as was Paul Weinbaum, who came out of retirement for the chance to work with old friends. I first met Aidan Smith, Sue's replacement-in-training, at that gathering. It was the start of a friendship that would be cut way too short. Paul Revere House executive director, Nina Zannieri, made an important cameo too. I was an anxious junior professor back then, with a baby on the way and tenure still looming. Two days away somehow felt like a risky use of my time. And yet, working with so many smart compassionate people inspired me, and renewed my commitment to doing history beyond the university. What a delight to reconnect with several of them for this project, even if only by way of telephones and interviews.

I didn't know then, of course, what two days in Boston might lead to. I was reluctant, when Aidan first asked me, to take on the park's administrative history. He convinced me, in part, by assuring me that Christine Arato would lead the project team. I had worked on several other projects with Christine, who was then chief historian of the agency's northeast region, and so I knew that her fierce commitment to critical history done well would create the space I needed to do the project right. That it got done at all, and was made into a book at that, is very much a tribute to her vision. Also on the project team was, once again, Marty Blatt, another fantastic historian who despite having just retired, graciously shared his expertise and memory with the team and his humor and encouragement with me. Two other team members had responsibility for keeping me on task in the archive. David Vecchioli spent many hours with me in the Charlestown Navy Yard sorting through records, making copies, and tracking down this or that along the way. And Steve Carlson, who knows the park's history better than anyone, watched patiently as I tried to figure it out on my own. All of these folks read drafts, provided feedback, answered questions, and otherwise led me through the daunting complexities of a uniquely complex national park and the often-baffling federal agency that manages it.

The years encompassing this project witnessed what likely amounted to the most overtly hostile attacks ever waged against the National Park Service from within its own government. The agency was not strong before Donald Trump became president, and so keeping this project alive during his administration required careful interventions by key chaos managers. Chief among them within the park service was April Antonellis and Bethany Serafine, who pulled whatever levers needing pulling to keep my work on track. Aidan, of course, moved mountains to sustain this project, but once he was no longer with us, Paul Zwirecki stepped in at the OAH and helped me navigate the difficult last phases of writing and review. Helping him was Derek Duquette, who also did heroic work toward moving this project to completion. Derek had taken the job fresh out of Temple University's MA program in public history. Seeing him thrive cast a bit of light onto some otherwise dark days.

Others at Temple too played an important role in making this work possible. Jay Lockenour, who chaired the History Department during much of this project, helped me convince those who needed convincing that a research fellowship with the National Park Service really does constitute scholarly activity. How dispiriting it is to have to make that argument, and to have to make it repeatedly. Jay's support made me feel like the work I do actually does matter, something for which I am deeply grateful. Senior Vice Dean Kevin Glass also helped considerably by working directly with the OAH to manage financials and otherwise remove obstacles that I wouldn't have even known needed removing. College of Liberal Arts Dean Richard Deeg approved two course releases, without which I would not have been able to initiate the project. Finally, in the College of Liberal Arts, Gina Barnes and Yvonne Muchemi helped manage the National Endowment for the Humanities summer stipend that allowed me to translate my administrative history into a book. I am grateful to them, and to the NEH, for supporting this project.

It is my conviction that all research projects, funded through or with universities, should provide some measure of training for students. And since I already have a decent-paying day job, I try my best to distribute as much project funding as possible among as many students as possible. On that front, this project was particularly successful. Bits of funding from this work gave Steve Hausmann a crash course in harvesting data from federal records in the park's navy yard repository. It allowed Temple's Center for Public History to support Abby Gruber, who advanced this project in many ways, including by digitizing a huge stack of park newsletters. And it helped our department make sure Gary

Scales got to serve as its first digital history fellow, which gave me plenty of opportunity to chat with him about mapping memory in Boston. All of their work appears in these pages, and I've done my best to highlight it wherever possible. Other students too have made important contributions whether they know it or not. At Northeastern University, Rebecca Bryer provided research assistance in the very early phases of this project. Students in my spring 2019 Introduction to Heritage Interpretation endured having to act out "We've Come Back for a Little Look Around" (see chapter four), just to help me understand what the play would have meant in Bicentennial Boston. And I can think of several advisees—especially Joanna Arruda, Devin Manzullo-Thomas, Ted Maust, and Alaina McNaughton—who've had a profound impact on this project by way of *many* conversations about the National Park Service, and also by inspiring me with their kindness, hard work, and intelligence.

Elsewhere I relied on a corps of archivists, curators, administrators, and data professionals to help me piece together the story in Boston. They include Judith Adkins (NARA–Washington), Beth Carroll-Horrocks (State Library of Massachusetts), Marta Crilly (Boston City Archives), Bob Cullum (Dugmore & Duncan), Sean M. Fisher (Boston Department of Conservation and Recreation), Michael Frost (Yale University Library), Julia Howington (Moakley Institute, Suffolk University), Kathy Kiely (Boston Ad Club), Kate Monea (USS *Constitution* Museum), Danny Pucci (Boston Public Library), Suzanne Taylor (Freedom Trail Foundation), and Nathaniel Wiltzen (NARA–Boston). What bits of information I could not find in their collections, I sought out in interviews with several people to whom I owe special thanks, some of whom I've already mentioned. Marty Blatt, Steve Carlson, Louis Hutchins, and Paul Weinbaum were all kind enough to be project supporters and oral history narrators. Nina Zannieri too served in both capacities, and also kindly helped me after our interview to understand some of its key points. Richard W. Berenson made a generous gift of his time at a particularly busy moment, to reflect on his family's remarkable impact on the Freedom Trail over the years. And Hugh Gurney fought off a bad cold just to share with me his powerful memories of being the park's first superintendent, nearly half a century ago.

In the background during all of this were the many voices of valued colleagues—people I encounter daily on social media, sometimes in conference halls, once in a while via email, occasionally on the phone, and all too rarely on the street—who gather at the intersections of public history, preservation, National Park Service history, memory studies, and urban history. A few whose insights found their way into these pages include Richard Anderson, Teresa D. Bulger, Lizabeth Cohen, Ken Finkel, David Glassberg, Patrick Grossi, Mitch Kachun, Theodore Karamanski, Perri Meldon, Charlene Mires, Whitney Martinko, Michelle McClellan, Sara Patton, Bryant Simon, Angela Sirna, Cathy Stanton, William S. Walker, Patricia West, Anne Mitchell Whisnant, David Young, and Joan Zenzen. NPS Bureau Historian John H. Sprinkle Jr. enriched this project with his own excellent research. I owe him a debt of gratitude, too, for fielding countless research questions and procuring all matter of hard-to-find sources, often at a moment's notice. I am grateful also to the organizers of the University of Delaware's History Workshop Series for inviting me to discuss this project during fall 2016, back when I was still trying to find the trail. I send special thanks to Jay Driskell and Laura Miller for providing skill, expertise, historical insight, and labor when I most needed it. Their professional paths are models for historians looking to make a difference beyond academia.

The funny thing about making books is that, just when you think you've accrued more professional debts than any person should, a whole new cast of characters comes along to make your work just that much better. So it is at the University of Massachusetts Press, whose dedicated staff has now been through this process twice over with me. I've been chatting about this project with Editor in Chief Matt Becker for a long time and am grateful for his patience in waiting to see it through. Marla Miller, who edits the powerhouse of a series that is *Public History in Historical Perspective,* has been a guiding light for so many of us who've come up through the field over the last decade or so. I am entirely confident in saying that without her, and without her book series, there would be considerably less space for public history in American universities today. My debts to Marla extend well beyond this book. Thanks go also to Courtney Andree, Rachael DeShano, Sally Nichols, and no doubt many others at the press who kept this project on the tracks. Several others beyond the press helped me get to the finish line. How wonderful to learn that Sue Ferentinos, who witnessed the very beginning of this project, would return at the very end with her deep knowledge of NPS history and keen copyeditor's eye. Kate Blackmer, who is a true collaborator, worked patiently with me to make gorgeous maps. And, finally, Andrew Lopez produced yet another excellent index despite my truly atrocious email habits.

It's hard to even begin sorting through all of the many changes and challenges that I, my family, and really everyone the world over has had to contend with during this last decade. I measure them by the rapid-fire sequence of spaces wherein I remember having had to work on this book: a dusty basement, hospital waiting rooms, a construction site, aboard a sailboat, in a sweltering hotel room above the Charlestown YMCA, atop my mom's old couch, so often in the parking lot of a turnpike rest stop, on campus and then suddenly off. I'd be lost to those spaces were it not for Hilary Iris Lowe, whose deep and sustaining love makes everything possible. And, of course, nearly every single word in this book I've written during the morning twilight, knowing that soon Juniata Gladys Bruggeman would be waiting to recount her dreams. How glad I am to hear them.

LOST
ON THE
FREEDOM
TRAIL

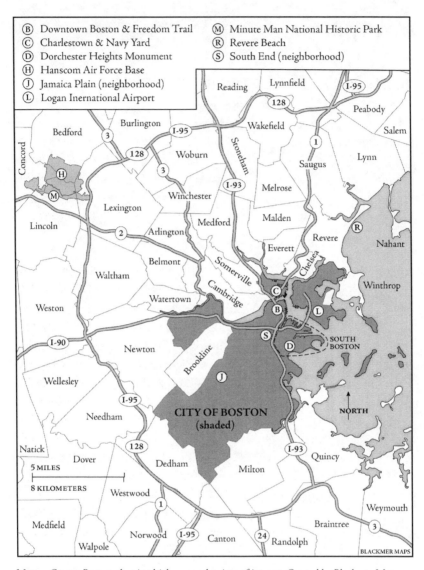

MAP 1. Greater Boston, showing highways and points of interest. Created by Blackmer Maps.

INTRODUCTION

Lost on the Freedom Trail

I drove north out of Boston over the Mystic River Bridge with the top down on my car. On the right was Old Ironsides at berth in the Navy yard and to the left of the bridge the Bunker Hill Monument. Between them stretch three-decker tenements alternating with modular urban renewal units. One of the real triumphs of prefab design is to create a sense of nostalgia for slums.
— Spenser, in Robert B. Parker's *God Save the Child* (1974)

It's Monday afternoon in Boston, the last bit of a hot muggy day in late July. I am vacationing with my wife and our seven-year-old daughter. We left our home near Philadelphia this morning and are driving north to Maine. Boston is the perfect layover. It's far, but not too far. It's walkable. There's plenty to keep all three of us interested for a few hours of sightseeing. And, of course, it's easy to get to. Interstate Highway 95, which threads together all of the eastern seaboard's big cities, delivers us directly to Boston. We've followed I-95 all day, lulled by the ebb and flow of its hypnotic sameness, a rhythm interrupted only by the tangle of expressways that announce New York City. We prefer side roads, but with our travel trailer in tow and a rack of kayaks above, it's easy to appreciate I-95's predictability. Easy, that is, until we arrived in Boston, about an hour ago, when it suddenly appeared that there might not be anywhere to park this rig. But it's a slow day, and we find a spot in a marina lot reclaimed from the long-shuttered Charlestown Navy Yard. With that, we check in at the hotel, wipe the sweat from our brows, and turn toward a setting sun to discover Boston on foot.

But where should we start? I want to stretch my legs, but it's late and everyone's hungry. We need to eat, but we've come too far to settle for fast food. And wouldn't it be great if we could see some of Boston's famous historic sites near wherever we're going, or maybe on our way? I explain to my daughter that Paul Revere's actual house is just blocks away. She shrugs, but I know that, if nothing else, she'd love Boston Common at dusk. We need a surefire way to make this work and to make it work fast. We're only here for a night, after all, and who knows when we'll be back?

Fortunately for us, and for the millions of others just like us who've repeated this ritual over and over since the middle of the last century, Boston has just the thing: The Freedom Trail.[1] The Freedom Trail is a two-and-a-half-mile-long "heritage trail," literally a line drawn onto Boston's sidewalks—with red paint, inlaid brick, and a phalanx of sign posts—that leads tourists past the city's most iconic historic sites. At one end is the towering Bunker Hill Monument, rising high above neighboring Charlestown, and at the other, in the heart of the old city, is sprawling Boston Common. In between, the Freedom Trail cuts a meandering path through Boston's gentrified North End and past its imposing Government Center. Each of the trail's stops corresponds with a place, a building, or a burying ground associated with, as boosters put it, "the story of the American Revolution and beyond."[2] And, sure enough, it works. We pick up the trail in Charlestown, near *Old Ironsides,* and before we know it, we are ticking off the stops: Copp's Hill Burying Ground, the Old North Church, and, yes, Paul Revere's House. There's no time to linger, of course, but it's all right because just following the trail—and guessing where it might take us next—is somehow deeply satisfying. And, besides, the day is wasting. The sun dips, and the evening crowd emerges amid bars and cafés that mix seamlessly with the heritage chic that prevails here. A neon sign catches our attention, and soon we're in line for dinner at a historic restaurant, content to pay far more than we need to for a so-so meal in Boston.

Such is the magic of the Freedom Trail. Within just minutes, this simple red line creates an itinerary for us, guides us on our way, and even shows us where to spend our money. We trust the trail. It's safe. "People stick [to it] as if it were a magnet," observes Annette Miae Kim, who once pitched a Freedom Trail concept to authorities in Vietnam's Ho Chi Minh City.[3] Boston's is the original, however, and its name, well, says it all. The trail frees us of our reliance on smartphones and tour guides. It makes us feel adventurous, leading us down narrow streets and around ancient corners that, in twilight, are tinged with mystery. It gives us a sense of time travel, mingling our footsteps with the nation's founding dramas: the Boston Massacre, the dumping of the Boston tea, Paul Revere's ride. And yet, there's a sense of timelessness here, too, accentuated by the buzz and hum of a modern city. We do eventually make it to Boston Common, where the tourists have already begun their retreat and the occasional whiff of pot smoke signals that we too have reached the end of the trail. My kid runs for a playground, but she's exhausted and will spend most of the walk back dozing on my shoulders. In other words, our vacation is off to an excellent start.

Except that, for me, this leg of it is not entirely a vacation. Just moments after arriving in Boston, we pulled over along Third Avenue in the old navy yard just long enough for me to jump out and deliver a package. The package contained old newsletters, about a hundred of them, produced over a span of forty years by the staff of Boston National Historical Park. Yes, there is a national park in Boston, and though many tourists never notice it, the park encompasses several of the historic sites that line the Freedom Trail. The newsletters belong to the private collection of Steve Carlson, who came to work at the park shortly after Congress authorized it in 1974. Today, Steve is the park's preservation specialist and de facto keeper of its institutional memory. I find him in a small office on the second floor of the massive old Navy Yard Building #107. This is one of several structures remaining from the years when people built war ships in this sprawling complex. Though its exterior is preserved to appear as it did a century ago, Building #107 has been home since the late 1980s to the park's Cultural Resources Division and the vast museum and archive collections it stewards. It's a massive space, rich with treasures, and yet, entirely invisible to unaware passersby. It is, in other words, a perfect metaphor for Boston National Historical Park.

I have been picking through Building #107's treasures for the last several years, and digging through scores of other archives too, all toward writing what the National Park Service (NPS) refers to as an "administrative history." Administrative histories are detailed accounts of how national parks—and other kinds of National Park Service units—get made and how they have been managed over time. They are, in essence, institutional histories. And they tend to be big hulking studies that, though intended to guide management decisions, more often than not end up collecting dust on shelves in places like Building #107. The Boston project is my second administrative history. The first one had been a life changer for me, back in graduate school, when my prospects— for a dissertation, for a career, for a future—seemed dim. The assignment then was to write an administrative history of George Washington Birthplace National Monument in Virginia. I did, I got paid for it, and the book that resulted ended up being my ticket to a tenure-track job at a good university. In fact, that book had been so successful, it got some people thinking that maybe administrative histories don't have to always end up collecting dust. It's precisely the notion that got me invited back to work on the Boston project. And it's the same idea that I had in mind as I returned the last of my research materials to Steve and headed out with my family to take one last look at a place wherein, despite my research, I still felt entirely lost.

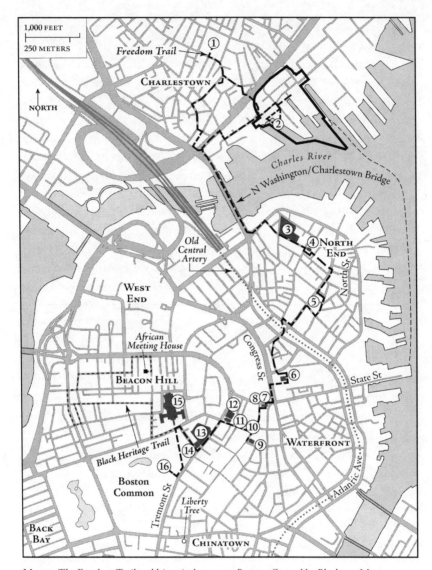

MAP 2. The Freedom Trail and historic downtown Boston. Created by Blackmer Maps.

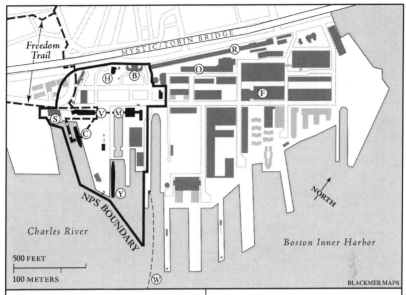

THE FREEDOM TRAIL	CHARLESTOWN NAVY YARD

THE FREEDOM TRAIL

1. Bunker Hill Monument
2. USS *Constitution*
3. Copp's Hill Burying Ground
4. Old North Church
5. Paul Revere House
6. Faneuil Hall/NPS Visitor Center
7. Site of the Boston Massacre
8. Old State House
9. Old South Meeting House
10. Old Corner Bookstore
11. Benjamin Franklin Statue & Site of Boston Latin School
12. King's Chapel & Burying Ground
13. Granary Burying Ground
14. Park Street Church
15. Massachusetts State House
16. Boston Common

CHARLESTOWN NAVY YARD

- ■ Open to the public
- ▦ Historic structure
- ▢ Non-historic structure

WITHIN THE NATIONAL HISTORIC PARK

- B Marine Barracks
- C USS *Constitution*
- H Commandant's House
- M USS Constitution Museum
- S Hoosac Stores
- V NPS Visitor Center
- Y USS *Casin Young*

OUTSIDE THE NATIONAL HISTORIC PARK

- F Chain Forge
- O Building 107
- R Ropewalk
- W Ferry to Long Wharf

* * *

Lost on the Freedom Trail is, in the simplest terms, a history of Boston National Historical Park and its indelible bond with the Freedom Trail, which predates the park by over two decades. More broadly, it is a chronicle of loss. My first instance of feeling lost on the Freedom Trail occurred early on during this project, as early, in fact, as its first day. It was the first time I encountered Building #107, where in 2015 the project team gathered to discuss project logistics. I arrived with memories in mind of my first administrative history start-up meeting, about a decade earlier, during which park rangers mounted a feisty argument with NPS historians about what was more important: George Washington "the man," as they put it, or how we've sought to remember Washington over time.[4] It was that fascinating question that ultimately framed the entire project.

Now, though, years later, the mood within the National Park Service had shifted. There was no feistiness, no spirited argument, and no weighing of provocative contrapositions. Instead, there was a dire sense that if this project didn't get done soon, it would never get done at all. The agency's federal appropriation, after all, had stagnated during the interim and was barely keeping apace of inflation. Newspapers reported on the impossibility of national parks ever contending with a multibillion-dollar deferred maintenance backlog. It was, of course, just one facet of a much larger decline in public funding for federal, state, and local arts and culture organizations, a decline that had roots in the 1980s but had reached a crisis point during the 2000s.[5] Worse yet, the NPS was still recovering from the devastating government shutdown of 2013 and the gut-twisting indignities of budget sequestration. Scandals seemed everywhere. Accusations of sexual harassment roiled leadership, as did suspicions of corruption and ethical lapses in the Director's Office. The agency's chief historian appeared to have vanished; rumor was that he retired abruptly while on vacation in Europe. And, in Boston, the park's new charismatic leader—its first Black superintendent, the person who had argued for funding my administrative history—had just announced that he too was moving on. It seemed to me, in that moment, that the NPS—or, at least, its history program—was on the verge of collapse and that I was, in some inevitable way, one of a last few desperate breaths.

My second instance of feeling lost on the Freedom Trail came about four months later, when I sat down to write a summary of what I learned from hours spent sifting through papers in Building #107. Things just didn't add up. I expected that this administrative history, like my last one, would pivot on contests of memory. At least, that was the impression I gleaned from another meeting in Boston, a "scholars' visit" hosted by the park back in 2011. The goal then was to solicit opinions from historians about how well the park grapples with key historical themes concerning the Revolution and its legacies. Memory was a concern too, which explains why I got a seat at the table. What seemed to worry the staff most was the problem of contending with the Freedom Trail. Back when the trail was created, they explained, the city gave responsibility for managing it to the Freedom Trail Foundation, an offshoot of the Chamber of Commerce. The foundation's historical vision had thus always tracked with the chamber's concern to generate tourist revenue. The park's goal, however, was not to make money, at least not ostensibly, but rather to do good history while protecting the park's resources and making them as broadly accessible as possible. Maintaining the right balance between preservation and access is a tricky business, which is why the law that created the NPS way back in 1916 has long been regarded as a "contradictory mandate." And it hasn't helped that lurking just beneath the outward-facing progressivism of so many NPS boosters over time has been the back-room profiteering of politicians, developers, industrialists, and xenophobes who've always had a hand in setting the agency's agenda.[6]

The problem in Boston, then, seemed to be an old, familiar one that had everything to do with memory: one group wanted to remember the Revolution in an affirming way that would encourage visitors to spend money; the other group wanted to remember the Revolution in a critical way that might prompt tough questions about who, over time, actually benefited from the Revolution. With all of this in mind, then, it seemed clear to me that my administrative history would have to address this unresolved contest of memory. It would have to show how the Freedom Trail had always been a fault line between two ways of thinking about the past.

But that wasn't the story I discovered in Building #107. Sure, it was clear from the park's papers that, since the 1990s, there had been real tensions between the foundation and the park's historian concerning how best to plumb the past along the Freedom Trail. But the sides weren't as clearly drawn as one might suspect. The foundation, after all, functioned independently of the heritage organizations that for at least a century had individually managed the trail's various constituent sites. And each of those organizations had its own ideas about how to do history. What's more, the park's own interpretive programming varied considerably across time and even across different sections of the park. Some of it was progressive, but much of it was not. In fact, a good bit of it seemed just as uncritical and hagiographic as what the foundation pedaled in its trail guides.

What I found most startling was that, the deeper I dug and the further back in time I looked, the more it appeared that what defined the relationship between the foundation and the park was not difference, but similarity. The same people who had bankrolled the Freedom Trail, it turned out, had also played key roles in planning the park. And the very person who pioneered the foundation, the man who had become synonymous with the Freedom Trail in Boston, had also chaired the park's influential advisory commission for its entire ten-year run. My assumptions had been altogether wrong. The Freedom Trail wasn't a fault line at all, at least it hadn't been until recently. On the contrary, it was—from the outset—a through line. And that through line, I started to realize, led directly to urban renewal.

One need not scratch too deep beneath the surface to discover that every facet of the entwined histories of the Freedom Trail and Boston National Historical Park is caught up in the story of how politicians, real estate developers, business leaders, urban planners, and a whole cast of pundits sought to re-engineer Boston into a city that could harvest wealth newly distributed among white Americans, especially after World War II. Redevelopment projects—including the clearance of so-called slums and their replacement with public housing—had begun in and around Boston during the 1930s and, as we will see, played a key role in shaping the world views of the park's progenitors. It was a shift during the 1950s toward new federal policies of "urban renewal," however, and especially the privileging thereon of private developers, that guided the National Park Service's work in Boston.

It is impossible to separate the history of modern heritage tourism in Boston from the story of urban renewal, in part, because it was urban renewal that created the canvas on which today's touristic experience is drawn. This was precisely the notion that mystery writer Robert B. Parker captured back in 1974—and at the outset of this introduction—when his hardboiled detective, Spenser, recognized the "nostalgia for slums" conjured by the juxtaposition of old and new along the bit of Freedom Trail that winds up through Charlestown. Recall, too, my family's own trip to Boston. Even before we arrived there, we followed highways designed by postwar planners and funded with redevelopment dollars. And, just as those highways chose our route for us, so did the renewal-era expressways that recall decisions made long ago about which neighborhoods to destroy and which to preserve; about which residents to protect and which to displace; and about which pasts to remember and which pasts to bulldoze. All of these choices made for us during the postwar years silently condition our experience of Boston's history today.

They even decide who we, the tourists, are. Indeed, the same vectors of prosperity that urban renewal sought to reinforce also explain why my white family can afford to travel, why we feel safe on the Freedom Trail, why we care about this history at all, how I—of all people—ended up writing about it, and why most of the people we see along the trail look just like us. The Freedom Trail is at once a hallmark of urban renewal and a monument to white privilege. It and the park are ostensibly about the Revolution. But, as we will see, in Boston most of what we learn about the eighteenth century was imagined for us during the nineteenth and then repackaged during the twentieth by people eager to aggregate wealth and influence long into the twenty-first century and beyond.

FIGURE 1. A couple strolls past Faneuil Hall and toward the Freedom Trail in a promotional video. © 2020, Historic Tours of America, Inc., used by permission, all rights reserved.

Insomuch as this book is a history of Boston National Historical Park and the Freedom Trail, then, it is also necessarily a book about how the National Park Service fashioned itself after World War II into an agent of urban renewal in American cities. The peculiarity of the urban park is not a new story. Authors including Charlene Mires, Hal Rothman, and Cathy Stanton have weighed at length the processes by which Americans have—in cities such as Philadelphia, San Francisco, and Lowell—sought to negotiate the terms by which federal park stewards reimagined urban landscapes into natural and cultural resources during the twentieth century.[7] What is less clear is how the NPS positioned itself in relationship to the array of federal redevelopment programs and new currents of private capital that together conspired to fundamentally reorganize life in American cities. As we will see, the Freedom Trail and Boston National Historical Park share common ancestry in urban planner Ed Logue's postwar vision for a "new" Boston as well as real estate developer James Rouse's efforts to reorient American retail around the "festival marketplace." But we will learn, too, that, even before the war, NPS planners imagined possibilities for Boston within the framework of urban redevelopment. In fact, though the war years often figure as a critical fulcrum in NPS histories, the Boston story prompts us to reconsider that periodization. It also forces us to recognize how key facets of urban renewal's intellectual scaffolding—especially its admixture of public and private capital and its figurative and sometimes literal erasure of Black Americans and other working people—became deeply embedded within the mission of the postwar National Park Service.

This book, then, is about the history of a national park and the history of the National Park Service's relationship with urban renewal. But because the park in question is one of the nation's most prominent historical parks, a place where millions of Americans have traveled to learn about the past, this book is also about how our nation's history gets made. And, in that regard, it corresponds with a third instance of loss along the Freedom Trail. More surprising to me than discovering that the park and the Freedom Trail had been cut from more or less the same cloth, was learning that the organization most vocally opposed to establishing Boston National Historical Park in 1974 was, incredibly, the National Park Service. As we will see, the agency had many reasons to resist expansion during the 1970s. But at issue in Boston was the sense, expressed in retrospect by one of the park's key planners, that the NPS had "lost control of the agenda."[8] Politicians that is, not historians, had come to decide what history parks would be about. That these were, of course, the very same politicians who sought to create economic momentum in Boston through urban renewal suggests that the National Park Service's planners had lost control of the agenda long before 1974.

This realization—that the NPS tried to kill off a historical park that it had been eagerly developing for nearly thirty years—troubled me more than anything when it came time to write up my findings. It did so, in part, because the NPS staff I met in Boston were so proud that their park was the first of the agency's "partnership parks." By this, they meant that it was the first park to demonstrate on a large scale that numerous historic properties could be managed through cooperative partnerships rather than through outright ownership and, in some cases, land condemnation. It's an idea that, since the 1980s, has justified the agency's sponsorship of what it calls "national heritage areas," more than fifty of which now exist to protect natural and cultural landscapes in a way that many consider to be more sustainable and more community-positive than the old park model.[9] But what did it mean, I wondered, that this new approach had caused so much worry among planners a half century earlier? And what did it mean that the Boston experiment had become an inspirational touchstone for a generation of park planners since? Did those early concerns get ironed out along the way? Had the model changed somehow during the intervening decades to ensure that the park could do good meaningful history? Certainly, it must have, since the historians that I knew who worked at the park were fantastic. But then again, if that were the case, why was there so much concern among the staff about the difficulty of contending with the Freedom Trail?

These questions get at the core of a concern that I suspect lingers in the minds of anyone who does history for or with the National Park Service and, perhaps, anyone who identifies as a public historian. Plainly stated, the question is this: can we really make a difference? That we can has become a matter of faith promulgated by a field of professional practice and by a body of scholarship that depends for its legitimacy on the assumption that we can. And yet, some of our field's most highly regarded scholarship, including books that are now mainstays in public history seminar rooms, suggests exactly the opposite. Consider, for instance, historian Amy Tyson's contention that front-line interpreters are endlessly bound to a system of labor that neutralizes their capacity to make historical impact, precisely by exploiting their desire to do just that. Even more germane to my study is anthropologist Cathy Stanton's account of the progressive historians who brought considerable influence to bear at Lowell National Historical Park, despite ultimately being limited by precisely the same networks of capital and privilege that, as we will see, stymied NPS planners in Boston years before. These authors suggest that, though not all hope is lost, our possibilities for making a difference—for really intervening in how Americans learn to make sense of their pasts—are deeply curtailed by circumstances that inhere in modern capitalism. In other words—words familiar in today's political landscape—we historians are snared in a rigged economic system, of which we are both product and victim.[10]

What follows is my account of coming to very much the same conclusion vis-à-vis the history of Boston National Historical Park. In fact, readers might sense in this account something of a prequel to Stanton's book. However, mine is not at all ethnographic and is rather more concerned with exploring particular historical moments wherein the NPS made clear choices to follow the logic of capitalism—by way of urban renewal—rather than the logic of historical inquiry in defining the terms by which visitors would engage with the Revolutionary past in Boston. Whether or not history and capitalism can even be conceived of as discrete phenomena is an old question, but one re-posed here in terms that I hope will have meaning for public historians who are struggling everywhere today to stake claims in professional settings that, for the most part, are run through with systematic inequity. Indeed, one goal of this project is to urge public historians to ask, regardless of their professional settings, whether or not they have been able to retain control over the agenda, as it were. History workers, it's worth pointing out, have been noticeably slower to unionize than their counterparts in, say, art museums.[11] That is, they appear to be less likely to insist on retaining control over the agenda. Is there a reason for this? Is there something special about the work of historians that predisposes them to labor vulnerability? Are they more broadly subject to the emotional labor that Tyson describes, or less able to recognize and respond to it? These are the kinds of questions that administrative histories can help to answer, and the story in Boston, I think, is a particularly useful example.

* * *

Congress authorized the establishment of Boston National Historical Park on October 1, 1974. The park's purpose by law is to preserve and interpret "certain historic structures and properties of outstanding national significance located in Boston, Massachusetts, and associated with the American Revolution and the founding and growth of the United States." These include the Bunker Hill Monument, the Charlestown Navy Yard, Old North Church, the Paul Revere House, Faneuil Hall, the Old State House, the Old South Meeting House, and the Dorchester Heights Monument. Nestled too within the park's oeuvre are the fifteen contributing sites that constitute Boston African American National Historic Site, wherein interpreters recount the dramatic struggle for freedom that continued in Boston after the Revolution. Tying them all together is Boston's iconic Freedom Trail. In most instances, the National Park Service neither owns nor independently manages the various sites that constitute the park. The NPS is, rather, a cooperating steward, one of many organizations in Boston that contribute money, labor, and expertise to protect the city's historic resources. Few of the park's more than three million annual visitors, however, are either aware of or necessarily interested in the distinction. To most, amid the noise and bustle of Boston's summer tourist season, the NPS's presence—backed by nearly one hundred employees—is most immediately evident in the scores of ranger tours that wind through the city on paths blazed by memories of the Revolution and its legacies.[12]

I've sought in the pages that follow to recount the park's story while capturing some sense of the difficulties that inhere in managing a history park that seems everywhere and nowhere in Boston. My goal in every case has been to understand the institutional contexts in which the National Park Service and its staff have, over time, made decisions about how to grapple with the past in an American city. In other words, this is a mostly one-sided history. It does not contend with the histories of all the agency's various partners in Boston. Nor does it capture any full sense of how individuals and community organizations in Boston responded to the NPS and its various initiatives over time. Much of my analysis, moreover, is top down insomuch as it relies on the archival records of park administrators, rather than on insights gathered from rank-and-file staff. In some instances, these limitations are by design, and in others they reflect the exigencies of federal record keeping. In all cases, they reflect my intent to recount in some detail how a federal history park actually gets made. Others who have written histories of national parks have captured rather more dramatic moments of public encounter.[13] In Boston, however, the most profound contests over historical meaning unfolded within the monotonous and mostly unseen grind of federal bureaucracy. We find their traces in seemingly inconsequential choices about, say, how to record meeting minutes, who to include in those meetings, and where even to meet. Buried within these gray zones, wherein power so often operates and is so readily obscured, are explanations for why one of the nation's foremost history parks never fully devoted itself to doing meaningful history for all Americans.

My research methods and my concern throughout this study with institutional contexts speak to this project's former life as an NPS administrative history. What an administrative history should and should not be has become a matter of considerable debate in recent years.[14] What everyone can usually agree to, however, is that the purpose of an administrative history is to dwell in the proverbial weeds, to dig in and really detail how a park comes to be. Administrative histories are management documents, and so they are also almost always written for use by a very small subset of NPS staff. The point is typically not to intervene in scholarly debates or otherwise make a historiographical contribution. And yet, administrative history is rich with possibilities for doing just that. This book, for instance, fits well within a large body of work concerning the American Revolution in public memory. And though it is not conceived of as urban history per se, it should nonetheless be useful for people who study the course of American cities over the last century, and particularly the impact of redevelopment and renewal therein. *Lost on the Freedom Trail* joins a longstanding debate concerning the legacy of postwar renewal by considering its particular impact on Americans' ability to think historically about race, power, and citizenship.[15]

This book also engages with several conversations ongoing in scholarship concerning historic preservation. For instance, it joins a shelf of books that trace the history of historic preservation in cities such as New York City, Charleston, and Philadelphia. More specifically, *Lost on the Freedom Trail* can be read alongside histories of preservation that foreground intersections with economic and community development. At issue in that conversation is whether historic preservation ever could, as some proponents have and still hope, stimulate economic growth in ways that might benefit Americans across categories of race and class difference. Questions like these, especially as they pertain to race and power, roil preservationists during these days of toppled monuments, particularly as it becomes clearer that diversifying heritage professionals and shifting interpretive themes are simply not enough to root out structural inequity. It is this "reckoning" among preservationists, as Erica Avrami terms it, that *Lost on the Freedom Trail* aims to advance.[16]

Finally, as I've suggested in the preface, there is much to learn in *Lost on the Freedom Trail* about how whiteness functions within the NPS, and in that way this book joins another vein of scholarship that has as its purpose a weighing of race and power in American life. For my purposes, "whiteness" refers both to the belief that white people are normal and everyone else is not, and to the strategies used to make real that belief.[17] To be certain, I did not begin this project in search of whiteness. And yet, I found within every facet of Boston National Historical Park's story—from its embeddedness in Revolutionary memory to the decisions its managers made about who to hire—deep currents of corrosive structural whiteness. Contending with whiteness within the constraints of an administrative history presents real methodological obstacles, not the least being an agency that is notoriously averse to confronting its own demons.[18] More problematic is the extent to which the endemic absenting of nonwhite voices from park records has created an archive that is itself a monument to whiteness. *Lost on the Freedom Trail* thus dwells in whiteness rather than interrogate it from the margins, as have so many important recent studies.[19] There are real limitations to this approach, but my hope is that Boston's story will resonate for those among the nation's majority-white heritage corps who care to change.

I divide the story into six chapters. Chapter one considers the earliest expressions of three ideas. The first idea is that there is value in remembering the American Revolution. One function of collective memory is to render preposterous the notion that there are other ways to remember. Such is the case in Boston with regard to the American Revolution. But as scores of historians have illustrated, how we have come to remember the Revolution was deeply influenced over time by people for whom neither history nor even the Revolution per se were primary concerns. I summarize their impact in Boston throughout the nineteenth and early-twentieth centuries, toward con- textualizing the emergence of a second idea: that there should be a national park in Boston to help us remember the Revolution. This idea can be traced to the 1930s, amid the sudden expansion of the National Park Service, and in response to desires among some residents of South Boston for their Irish ancestry to be officially bound up with American nationalism. The third idea, which gained steam just after World War II, is the notion that Boston's heritage tourists might get lost among the city's unseemly places if not led— literally, by the Freedom Trail—from one historic site to another. Each of these three ideas, I argue, had at its core common assumptions about race, power, and profit. And each gained strength with successive waves of urban redevelopment and renewal.

All three ideas coalesced in the work of the Boston National Historic Sites Commission, which had as its purpose the task of imagining a national historical park for Boston. Chapter two explores all facets of the commission, from Representative John W. McCormack's 1951 proposal to Congress that it be constituted, to the writing of its final report by NPS historian Edwin Small in 1961. We discover that, from the outset, the commission's goals were deeply influenced by the logic of urban renewal and Cold War Era anticommunism. We find out too, that the commission was divided over key issues such as whether or not historic preservation merited destruction of landscapes not considered significant by the National Park Service. Most importantly, we find in the commission's minutes a prevailing concern with making the past profitable in Boston. Among all of its challenges, none troubled the commission more than the unlikely question of whether or not Boston's butchers should be allowed to sell meat in Faneuil Hall. It was this question, above all, that revealed just how little national park building in Boston during the 1950s had to do with doing history. I explore the commission's response to the meat market dilemma toward making sense of what mattered most to the people responsible for reinventing the National Park Service and its mission after World War II.

The Boston National Historic Sites Commission proposed the rough contours of a national historical park for Boston in 1961. We learn in chapter three, however, that a series of events delayed those plans for an entire decade, during which ideas about urban renewal and historic preservation shifted dramatically. These were the years during which Boston's renewal strategies changed course under charismatic city planner Ed Logue, a man whom newspapers described as a "gladiator," a "master rebuilder," and "Mr. Urban Renewal."[20] Despite sharing common goals with Logue, the NPS seems not to have sought any partnership at all with him, which explains in part why the agency and its political supporters failed throughout the 1960s to get traction for a national park. But then two events simultaneously fast-tracked and transformed the national park concept in ways that the NPS could not have anticipated. News that the federal government would shutter its historic navy yard in Charlestown, just across the river from Boston, and that Boston would have to compete for funding associated with the nation's Bicentennial celebration, sent city planners into a tailspin. Their solution: an expanded national park concept that would include the Charlestown Navy Yard, generate Bicentennial funding, and also revitalize a local economy flagging amid deindustrialization. It was not at all what the NPS had planned for, however, thereby leading the agency into a tense showdown with its partners in Boston and with politicians in Washington. In the end, as we will see, the agency could not overcome the entwined politics of urban renewal, heritage tourism, and Revolutionary memory that it had itself been complicit in promulgating from the very beginning.

When Congress finally authorized the creation of a Boston National Historical Park in 1974, it did so amid turmoil both within the city and within the agency. In Boston, violent collisions over the desegregation of public schools occurred alongside proto-gentrification of the city's historic core by young affluent white people. It was a moment of stark contradiction, most famously captured in Stanley Forman's Pulitzer-Prize-winning photo of a young Black lawyer named Ted Landsmark being assaulted with an American flag by white thugs just feet away from the Freedom Trail (see Figure 7, page 117). Part one of chapter four lays bare these parallel worlds of race and affluence as they existed in Boston at the time of the park's authorization. It also explores how the agency itself changed, at the same time, in ways that rendered it fundamentally incapable of grappling with the complex reality of lives lived in Boston during the late twentieth century. To make the point, part two of chapter four details precisely how the park's planning team set about its business amid the tumult on Boston's streets. Though committed to creating a community-positive park, the team—consisting of professional planners flown in periodically from the agency's planning office in Denver, Colorado—could barely make sense of who the park's neighbors really were, let alone intervene in the fraught battles over race, memory, and power everywhere evident in Boston during those years. Although park staff fared somewhat better, I contend that the park's formative moment ultimately amounted to a lost opportunity.

That opportunity seemed to drift even further away as the park built up its staff and established daily operational routines. Chapter five begins with yet another instance of atrocious racial violence within the park's boundaries. And though this time staff openly discussed what to do about the problem of racial discrimination, records reveal a workaday park consumed almost entirely with operational concerns: how to sustain staff on a shoe-string budget; how to get visitors from one point to another; how to preserve everything from warships to centuries-old churches. Although, as I show, the problem of racial violence was itself an operational concern, not to mention an important facet of the history Congress charged the park with interpreting, not once during those years did the agency deploy qualified historians—scads of whom lingered in Boston, especially during that era's academic hiring crisis—toward making sense of the problem. That it did not reveals a deeply rooted conundrum within the NPS, exacerbated by its investments in urban renewal and historic preservation, about the meaning and purpose of history. In Boston, as elsewhere, the NPS conceived of historians as primarily valuable in supporting the work of preserving historic buildings. When an opportunity arose in 1978 to intervene in the parlous history of the Dorchester Heights Monument—an epicenter of racial violence in South Boston—the park sent police. Conversely, when Congress unexpectedly authorized the Boston African American National Historic Site just a few years later, its Black stewards insisted on building up public programming around historical research. I weigh these contrasting approaches to the past and suggest that the park's history problem and its race problem have always been, in essence, the same problem.

Boston National Historical Park struggled throughout the 1980s. A quick decline in Bicentennial fever alongside Ronald Reagan's new conservatism created desperate challenges for a park and an agency now expected to do considerably more work with substantially less support from Congress. All of that seemed to suddenly change, however, with the arrival of a new superintendent: John Burchill. Within months of Burchill's arrival, it seemed, new management strategies, new public initiatives, and even new revenue streams had reversed the park's fortunes. By all measures it was a boon for Boston's national historical park. By all measures except one, that is. Chapter six considers the fate of history making during the park's 1990s renaissance. It turns out that, though Burchill was remarkably successful at winning congressional funding for the park, his success relied entirely on old ideas about Revolutionary memory. These were the same ideas, in fact, that garnered interest in the park concept way back during the 1930s. They were the same ideas that activated the Freedom Trail and that echoed throughout postwar urban renewal. Burchill's ideas were, simply put, that history should turn a profit and that the American story is the story of white prosperity. Those ideas had always lingered along the Freedom Trail, but it took a charismatic superintendent and the happenstance of yet another economic transformation in Boston to lock them into the park's *raison d'être* at the turn of the millennium.

It took other catastrophes too. Burchill's unprecedented fundraising success occurred amid a precipitous decline in federal funding for all national parks. It would be the park's last bout of funding on a scale capable of creating real change. It also occurred immediately before two national traumas that, together, would divert most of what remained of the park's appropriation to managing the threat of terrorism. Federal response to the attacks of September 11, 2001, and the Boston Marathon Bombing of 2013 created such impossible security demands on the park and its staff that Burchill's imprint—and nostalgia for it—lingered amid thin resources and a revolving door of staff and superintendents. Agency records from these years are a mixed bag, and oral history alone cannot complete the picture. I grapple with this recent past in an afterword that considers the work of history activists in Boston today and ponders why the park has not, and perhaps cannot, join them in asking hard questions about the past. Those questions, unsurprisingly, concern race, urban renewal, and the purpose of a historical park whose own history is precisely the problem.

CHAPTER I

Remembering the Revolution in Old and New Boston

One gets the sense today, walking along the Freedom Trail, that Bostonians have always lived in quiet partnership with the past. Allusions to the American Revolution are so ubiquitous that, in some sections, little sense lingers of what happened before or after the two decades we typically associate with the nation's founding drama. Indeed, histories of the Massachusett people, Boston's Puritan past, its abolitionist saga, and especially the struggles of working people and generations of immigrants, all take a decided back seat to the prevailing narrative of Paul Revere and his exploits. But why is that? Boston National Historical Park is obligated by its authorizing legislation to preserve properties that are "associated with the American Revolution and the founding and growth of the United States."[1] It's a wide-ranging mandate, but one which—with important exceptions— has invariably settled on the late eighteenth century and a few years beyond. As we will see in chapter two, the people charged during the mid-twentieth century with imagining a national park for Boston considered, albeit briefly, casting the unit's interpretive net much wider. The park's commitment to the Revolutionary past, therefore, is a choice, one bound up with a very particular way of remembering the American Revolution rooted in habits of memory with a history all their own.

My purpose in this chapter is to understand why it was that people came to believe in the first place that Boston needed a national historical park to safeguard its Revolutionary past. It's a simple question, but one that requires we grapple with several other questions along the way. Why, for instance, have Bostonians so consistently chosen to favor Revolutionary memories above all others? To find out, I survey the early history of historic preservation and heritage tourism in Boston and discover that Revolutionary memory became particularly profitable there well before World War II. How, then, did the federal government end up doing history in Boston, or anyplace for that matter, during the first half of the twentieth century? This question requires that we consider dramatic changes in the National Park Service during the New Deal years. Along the way, we meet the park's earliest protagonists—U.S. Representative John W. McCormack and NPS historian Edwin Small—and see how their formative encounter in 1938 reflected both change in the NPS and considerable resistance to change in South Boston. And finally, the question that roiled my research early on: which came first, the NPS or the Freedom Trail? Although possibilities for both in Boston emerged more or less concurrently, we'll see that it was the trail and its progenitors that set the terms by which subsequent generations of tourists would experience Boston's heritage landscape. This fact had everything to do with urban redevelopment and renewal at mid-century, the emergence of a so-called New Boston, and the aspirations among some to determine how and what the rest of us get to remember.

REVOLUTIONARY MEMORY AND ITS USES IN NINETEENTH-CENTURY BOSTON

The history of remembering the Revolution, of course, long predates the first stirrings of a national park concept for Boston.[2] Historians tell the story in three acts. First was a brief, though intense, period of remembering just as the war came to a close: memorial sermons and battlefield tours in Lexington and Concord; blockbuster Fourth of July celebrations in Philadelphia; the careful editing of George Washington's wartime papers by his assistants at Mount Vernon.[3] Subsequent decades, however, introduced a second phase, a period of commemorative uncertainty that reflected tensions persistent throughout the war. The American Revolution was, after all, "the first American Civil War," a long and costly ideological conflict that pitted friends and families against one another, often in murderous violence. And for what? The first government it created succumbed in less than a decade to the radically different vision of a few elite statesmen. And clearly, given the persistence of forced labor and landed patriarchy, the ideals of liberty set forth by the founding generation had very obvious limitations. Historian Michael A. McDonnell notes that, to move past the Revolution's problematic legacy and to build a functional nationalism, Americans set out after the war to forget its most troubling contradictions. But "forgetting," as he puts it, "was a political project and it took time."[4] It wasn't until the 1820s that the politics of forgetting produced something resembling a national consensus about how to remember the Revolution. But not even during this third act, as we will see, could Americans entirely ignore the fierce claims made by many that the Revolution's legacy was incomplete.

Each of these acts played out in Boston with such vigor that it, alongside Philadelphia, may fairly claim to be a birthplace of American Revolutionary memory. It was Boston, for instance, that generated the epoch's earliest and most durable iconography. Paul Revere's *The Bloody Massacre, Perpetrated in King-Street, Boston, on March 5th, 1770* (1770) "was almost immediately turned into a site of American cultural and national memory," and also famously omitted the mixed-race Crispus Attucks, who later became a hero of abolitionists.[5] Theatrical performances, including Mercy Otis Warren's tribute to the massacre, *Adulateur* (1773), repeated Revere's themes toward encouraging outrage against the British.[6] Similarly, John Trumball's *The Death of General Warren at The Battle of Bunker Hill* (1786) inspired a painterly genre all its own while, again, erasing race—Peter Salem in this case—from the nation's memory of its founding trauma. And, of course, Charles Bulfinch built the first Revolutionary monument, a towering column, atop Beacon Hill in 1790, though it would remain there for barely two decades.[7] So, although the war's first commemorations, like the Revolution itself, showcased a variety of perspectives, some Bostonians—and others who looked to Boston for symbols of the Revolution's legacy—had already begun to sketch out a more staid memory of white entrepreneurs and property owners in earnest struggle against the imperial excesses of a distant monarch.[8]

The War of 1812, and the United States' second victory against the British, intensified the nation's commemorative mood. Nostalgic nods to the Revolution, and particularly to George Washington, appeared high above Baltimore and deep within rural Virginia by 1815.[9] Washington's adopted grandson, George Washington Parke Custis, completed his Arlington House by 1817 and created there a veritable theme park of Revolutionary memorabilia and costumed performance.[10] It was amid this acute period of Revolutionary nostalgia that Boston's 1822 city charter, its first, included a provision tasking city council with the protection of two historic sites: Boston Common and Faneuil Hall.[11] Only three years later, builders set to work on the iconic Bunker Hill Monument.[12] And, amid all of it, as historian Whitney Martinko describes, a nascent interest in the adaptive reuse and rehabilitation of Boston's oldest buildings flourished alongside a trade in print guides to the city's historic landscape. Although historians have long looked to the 1853 restoration of Washington's Mount Vernon in Virginia as the real beginning of the nation's heritage industry, it is clear that Bostonians had trod the path at least a generation earlier.

This facet of Boston's early fascination with its own past is particularly relevant to our story. It reminds us, for instance, that although Bostonians have long cherished their Revolutionary heritage, it's not the only history they've valued. Consider, for instance, the city charter and its proto-preservation mandate. Although Americans may have associated Faneuil Hall primarily with the Revolution by 1822, Boston Common conjured a much deeper past hearkening back to the city's Puritan forebears. It wasn't the only site valued for associations beyond the Revolution. The Old Feather Store (1680) and the Province House (1679), for instance, typified other sites that, though significant for histories predating the Revolution, inspired the city's collectors and would-be preservationists.[13] And this is to say nothing, of course, of early efforts in Boston and its surrounding communities to commemorate Puritan notables including William Bradford and Cotton Mather.[14] Backward-looking Bostonians could—and did—follow any of several paths into the city's deep and rich history. One of those paths led to the Revolution; others did not.

Why then did Boston's heritage gaze shift precipitously toward the Revolutionary past by the 1830s? It is true, as others have pointed out, that the Revolution weighed heavily on the minds of Americans after the War of 1812. Just as Americans today lament the passing of World War II veterans, vanguards of the so-called greatest generation, Americans during the 1820s valorized the lives of a vanishing generation of Revolutionary War soldiers.[15] The triumphant return and nostalgic national tour of General Lafayette in 1824–25 reinforced the tendency to think of veterans, including Lafayette himself, as relics of a bygone era who might endow those near to them with special powers of retrospect.[16] Interestingly, for years after the war, veterans remembered it in decidedly unglamorous terms. Soldiering was monotonous, they recalled, punctuated only occasionally by treacherous combat and more often by unprincipled recruits scavenging the countryside for wine and adventure. Pension records reveal more soldiers propelled to enlist by boredom and churlish in-laws than by conviction.[17] Written accounts of the war shifted significantly, however, by the 1820s, and increasingly "featured common themes, individuals, and tropes," many of which would become staples of modern Revolutionary memory.[18] It was a shift, incidentally, that coincided too with the deaths of the Revolution's last remaining political icons, including Thomas Jefferson (1826), John Adams (1826), and James Monroe (1831).

It was precisely that generation's unfinished business, ironically, that intensified longing in subsequent decades for its supposed virtue. The congressional machinations required to sustain slavery in the young republic, typified by the Missouri Compromise of 1820, created anxieties everywhere and always present in the United States. Contestants on both sides of the slavery debate invoked Revolutionary forebears in their claims to republican virtue. And, increasingly, the argument against slavery issued forth from Boston. Abolitionism had, of course, been present in American political discourse since before the Revolution, but its terms had been largely defined by the staid and legalistic Quakers of the Pennsylvania Abolition Society. By the late 1820s, however, the balance had shifted to Massachusetts. Historian Richard Newman explains the change as owing, in part, to the intensity of revivalism in Massachusetts during the Second Great Awakening and a greater openness there to the grassroots politics that accompanied the presidency of Andrew Jackson.[19] Also unlike their Quaker counterparts, who advocated for gradual abolition, Massachusetts abolitionists demanded immediate abolition—for which William Lloyd Garrison became the nation's leading advocate. Garrison, by organizing abolitionist societies in Boston and headquartering his newspaper, the *Liberator*, there in 1831, ensured that any nostalgia for the city's Revolutionary past would have to contend with the specter of its greatest failure.

And yet, as concerned as some Americans in the early republic may have been with the past, many were also squarely focused on the future. Boston was no exception. Reverence for Bulfinch's monument to the Revolution, for instance, did not exceed desires to clear the view from his majestic new State House, itself a monument to the potential of American republicanism. The monument's removal in 1811 prefigured widespread change throughout Boston's landscape. As Martinko points out, Boston Mayor Josiah Quincy initiated a period of what we would later term "urban renewal" in the years after the 1822 charter. Key among his accomplishments was construction of Quincy Market in 1826.[20] The market's iconic Greek Revival edifice conjured the hazy grandeur of classical republicanism while imposing order on Boston's generations-old commercial district. The market's retro republicanism thus constituted a new way of imagining Boston's past and future, in immediate juxtaposition with nearby Faneuil Hall, wherein Boston's leading patriots famously excoriated British rule. Urban renewal thus put old and new into sharp contrast. In some cases, owners concerned with protecting their properties from demolition sought, amid Boston's burgeoning cult of Revolutionary memory, to reimagine their homes as historic relics by way of advocating for their survival. These proto-preservationists, Martinko contends, perceived in urban renewal more than just a shift in aesthetics. In their eyes, renewal prompted a battle to determine which portions of the city would be public, which would remain private, and who would profit most from Boston's new political economy.[21] Simultaneously backward- and forward-looking, early concern for Boston's historic buildings thus mingled Revolutionary memory with some of the 1820s' leading preoccupations: power, profit, property, and party politics.

The folding of Revolutionary memory into American political culture is particularly significant for explaining why it was that Boston's historical gaze focused increasingly on the Revolution during the 1830s. It is an argument made most famously in Alfred F. Young's classic 1981 essay, "George Robert Twelves Hewes (1742–1840): A Boston Shoemaker and the Memory of the American Revolution," which was reprinted in 1999 and since in *The Shoemaker and the Tea Party*. Young makes the point that Boston's working people—even folks largely uninterested in ideological matters—found as great a stake in the Revolution as any of its patricians. His example is George Robert Twelves Hewes, a workaday shoemaker who participated in the Boston Tea Party and who became famous for it shortly before his death in 1840. Young shows us that Hewes, and probably the Tea Party too, would have remained unknown to us had the obscure shoemaker and his Revolutionary memories not been repurposed during the 1830s by an affiliation of Whig politicians in their campaign against labor activists, abolitionists, and others who struggled to make real the promises of American liberty. As Young puts it, "Hewes was taken over by such conservatives [who] tamed him, sanitizing him and the audacious popular movement he had been a part of."[22]

Boston's fascination with the Revolutionary past, above all other pasts, thus stemmed from its political expediency during an era of radical change, when it fell to a new generation of leaders to sort out the aspirations of their predecessors. That new generation was anything but unified, but because the Revolution's legacy was so ambiguous, its memory could be populated with no end of contradictory meanings. At one end of the spectrum, as Young shows us, Whig politicians managed to transform war veterans into symbolic endorsements of an economic system that bred inequality. At the other end, Boston's abolitionists pitched Revolutionary memory in support of their efforts to ensure equality for all Americans.[23] In the years preceding the American Civil War, the contest between these two distinct visions raged within the walls of Revolutionary Boston's most iconic building: Faneuil Hall. Beginning in

1837, when abolitionist Wendell Phillips scathingly criticized Massachusetts Attorney General James T. Austin there for claiming that the murder of another prominent abolitionist invoked the legacy of Boston's patriots, Faneuil Hall became an epicenter of antislavery oratory. By the 1850s, according to historian Donald M. Jacobs, abolitionists had succeeded "in transforming the building into a temple of patriotic Bostonian resistance to slavecatchers."[24]

It was the powerful interweaving of abolitionist sentiment and Revolutionary memory on view in Faneuil Hall and elsewhere in Boston that inspired what has since become the most persistently influential vision of the city's historic landscape. Henry Wadsworth Longfellow's *Paul Revere's Ride* (1861) has long passed as a staple of patriotic Americana, a poem to be memorized by school children and presidents.[25] It made a national hero of Paul Revere, whose notoriety had previously been limited to New England.[26] And, for generations of readers, it transformed the Revolution from a vague concept into a palpable event wherein real places—the Old North Church, Boston Harbor, Charlestown, and all "the roofs of the town"—carried the action. What its ubiquity has obscured, however, as scholars have dwelled on at length, is that Longfellow's most famous poem was crafted in the moment to raise up northerners against the terrors of chattel slavery.[27] It is a masterstroke of abolitionist writing, which relied upon the prevailing imagery of its time, namely nostalgic invocations of the American Revolution, to warn of a lurking evil that threatened to destroy the nation if not defeated. Just as the Whigs claimed Hewes during the 1830s, Longfellow claimed Revere for the Radical Republicans a generation later, a decade after the Whig Party had folded over the fate of slavery. How and why Boston has remembered the Revolution, then, has always pivoted on politics and, for much of that time, the problem of slavery.

The interweaving of Boston's Revolutionary memory with nineteenth-century struggles over race, class, and power is perfectly illustrated by the story of the Bunker Hill Monument.[28] From the standpoint of commemorative history, the Bunker Hill Monument easily ranks among the most significant monuments in the United States. Designed in 1825, it is one of the earliest expressions of American monumental nationalism. Its distinctive obelisk—a commemorative form popularized throughout Europe during the Enlightenment—inspired thousands of subsequent American monuments, including the Washington Monument in Washington, DC. It is a truly impressive monument, which, during its creation, was judged an awful inconvenience. Not complete until 1843, its neighbors complained about long years of disruptive construction. Fundraising was harder than anticipated. To pay for the thing, the association sold off most of the old battlefield that it had been seeking to commemorate. All may have been lost had not *Godey's Lady Book* editor Sarah Josepha Hale spearheaded a last-ditch fundraising campaign, which—apart from saving the association's reputation—anticipated the central role American women would play as caretakers of the nation's memory. The monument's difficulties suggest that, during the 1830s, Americans were significantly less eager to celebrate the Revolution than we might guess from the monuments they left us.[29]

Perhaps their reluctance, in this case, had something to do with how little the Bunker Hill Monument memorial had to do with remembering the American Revolution. Like all monuments, the one at Bunker Hill reveals the desire of its sponsors to enshrine themselves above all else. An earlier Bunker Hill monument actually commemorated Joseph Warren, renowned for setting Revere on his path to Lexington and Concord and rendered iconic by painter John Trumbull. The 1825 monument cast its commemorative net more broadly, but never fully expunged Warren's memory. A grand lodge was erected next to the monument during the late nineteenth century to accommodate a growing tourist trade and showcased a large statue of Warren who had, by then, grown in significance with Longfellow's popularization of Revere's ride. When Boston's leading citizens pooled their efforts to form the Memorial Association, they hoped to burnish their own reputations through a symbolic affiliation with Warren's. Building on such an unprecedented scale on the Charles River's far side certainly ensured "a highly visible display of civic and patriotic pride" for the people of Boston.[30] It also suggested that national memory did not belong to the lowly or disenfranchised.

It is worth pointing out that the monument's dedication ceremony in 1843 appears to have garnered considerably more local interest for a scandalous racial *faux pas* than its tribute to the American Revolution. Historian Margot Minardi describes the outrage of Boston's radical abolitionists after President John Tyler, invited to speak at the monument's dedicatory ceremonies, appeared to have brought along an enslaved man to hold his parasol. Although Tyler was not, in fact, accompanied on stage by an enslaved person, Boston's abolitionist press leveraged the nonincident in its indictment of the federal government's complicity in the national crime of slavery.[31] Like Faneuil Hall, the Bunker Hill Monument assumed powerful symbolic meanings during the nineteenth

century, which, although rooted in memories of the Revolution, had everything
to do with their own historical moment.

PRIVILEGE, PROFIT, AND HISTORIC PRESERVATION

Unless they linger in the park's museum, few visitors will ever comprehend the
Bunker Hill Monument as a paean to antebellum Whiggery. Indeed, although
our memory of Boston's eighteenth century was largely invented for us during
the nineteenth century, a host of factors conspired by the turn of the twentieth
century to naturalize its myths. For one, there were few historians, at least
not as we know them today, to propose credible counternarratives. The first
historians to chronicle the Revolution did so toward shoring up nationalist
sentiment. George Bancroft, for instance, typically thought of as the father
of American history writing, wrote the foundational *History of the United States
of America* between 1834 and 1874. A wealthy politician and scholar, descended
from one of Massachusetts' first families, Bancroft unsurprisingly portrayed
the Revolution as an inevitable stride toward liberty by visionary men (his
own ancestors!) who were heir to American exceptionalism. His celebratory
account and others like it, which plagiarized a well-known loyalist account
of the war, prevailed well into the early twentieth century and came to be
known as the Whig interpretation of Revolutionary history. When American
universities began training professional historians during the 1870s, it was
Bancroft's understanding of the Revolution that set the standard. It wouldn't
be seriously contested until the 1910s.[32]

Even beyond the small orbit of American intellectual circles, the Whig
interpretation of the American Revolution found tacit expression in the pan-
oply of activities variously associated with the so-called colonial revival.[33]
Colonial revivalism is typically understood in terms of Americans' consumer
passions, particularly between the Civil War and World War II, for colonial-
themed homes, gardens, furniture, and all sorts of bric-a-brac turned out by
men like Wallace Nutting, who produced nostalgia-inspired prints and furniture from his studio outside of Boston.[34] Beneath all this, however, lay the
same ideological strains of patriotic nostalgia that had percolated in Boston
since the 1820s. In fact, that impulse had sharpened in the years after the Civil
War, as white Americans perceived increased threats to their longstanding
patrimony. Boston was, once again, a bellwether. The collapse of antebellum
trade networks, the shifting of industry south and west, and growth among
the city's immigrant communities made anxious patriarchs out of those who

remained of Boston's first families, the so-called Boston Brahmin. Faced with dwindling fortunes and a shifting social and political landscape, these people turned further to the past. Joining a historical society, celebrating old-house days, or buying a Nutting dining room set all figured as expressions of yearning for an imagined era of supposed simplicity.[35]

Colonial revivalism flourished in Boston early on, owing in part to celebrations associated with the one-hundredth anniversary of the Revolution. Boston's centennial celebrations, however, revealed just how entwined Revolutionary memory still was with matters of race, power, and identity. Between 1870 and 1876, as historian Craig Bruce Smith puts it, a remarkable cast of Bostonians challenged the proclaimed "blood ancestry" of the city's first families by proclaiming their own "symbolic inheritance" of Revolutionary ideals. Black Bostonians, for instance, enthusiastically celebrated Crispus Attucks Day in 1870 toward leveraging memories of the Boston Massacre in support of racial equity. In 1873, suffragists chanted "no taxation without representation" in Faneuil Hall during centennial celebrations of the Boston Tea Party. And throughout these years, Boston's sprawling Irish Catholic population sought to demonstrate its claims to the American saga by monopolizing participation in celebrations such as that in 1875 at Bunker Hill. In each of these cases, however, others turned to genealogy to refute the claims. Genealogical research emerged as a craze among colonial revivalists who, buoyed by a belief in social Darwinism and the delusion of racial purity, sought legitimacy in heredity. Boston's New England Historic Genealogical Society (1845), the first of its kind in the United States, became a base of operations for white people who sought to, for instance, cast doubt on Attucks's racial purity, or refute claims that George Washington was part Irish.[36] During the late nineteenth century, then, memories of the American Revolution were much less a matter of history than a matter of context for Boston's simmering culture wars. Revolutionary memory was the stage on which Bostonians vied for social power.

That stage became less figurative all the time thanks to changes in Boston's heritage landscape. As historian Whitney Martinko notes, Bostonians had demonstrated an abiding interest in their city's historic buildings and landscapes for many decades. That tendency intensified after the Civil War owing, in part, to the same anxieties that accelerated colonial revivalism.[37] But other factors, too, convinced many among Boston's nascent preservation set that the city's historic landscapes faced imminent threats. Fire ravaged Boston's downtown, for instance, in 1872, thus revealing woeful inadequacies in the city's infrastructure. Elsewhere, such as in Back Bay, developers built on reclaimed land at a break-neck pace, effectively creating a city that couldn't have existed a generation before. Against this backdrop, the successful campaign to save the Old South Meeting House from demolition in 1876 was, according to historian Michael Holleran, "the greatest American preservation effort of the nineteenth century," and consequently, the spark that lit Boston's preservation movement.[38] In its wake, the Bostonian Society coalesced in 1881 around the campaign to preserve the Old State House. A few blocks away, up on Beacon Hill, architects and patriotic organizations including the Daughters of the American Revolution fought to save the Bulfinch State House throughout the 1890s. And descendants of Paul Revere organized a memorial association in 1907 to restore what remained of the building that Longfellow's hero called home. The project of restoring Revere's home was particularly significant insomuch as it launched the career of William Sumner Appleton Jr., whose Society for the Preservation of New England Antiquities would soon set a standard for historic preservation throughout the United States.[39]

The preservation ethos filtered into other aspects of Boston's turn-of-the century commemorative landscape too. In 1902, for instance, Bostonians gathered in South Boston to celebrate the unveiling by the commonwealth of a one-hundred-foot commemorative marble shaft erected atop Dorchester Heights in Thomas Park. The monument was built with funds appropriated in 1898 by the Massachusetts State Legislature, known by locals as the General Court. Designed by the Boston firm Peabody and Stearns to commemorate Washington's preemptive defense of Boston against the British, and their subsequent evacuation to Nova Scotia, the monument exemplified colonial revival architecture. Henry Cabot Lodge, Massachusetts' powerful Republican U.S. senator (and a trained historian), headlined the event. Lodge recalled being fascinated early on by a cannonball half-buried in the side of the old Brattle Street Church, which, he noted, had since "fallen before the march of trade." That cannonball, tradition held, had been lodged there by Washington's cannons. "The historical event," he continued, "that thus came out of the past and made itself real to me" was the fortification of Dorchester Heights. Lodge's paean to Dorchester Heights was, in essence, a tribute to the power of Revolutionary memory and the old church, "which I wish might have been spared and preserved."[40] In his estimation, the new monument was a proxy for both.

Boston thus led the nation in protecting historic buildings and landscapes and making them more or less accessible to the public. And yet, at the same time, Boston is also notable for its early efforts to support the preservation of private properties, including entire neighborhoods. As Holleran points out, the campaign to protect the Bulfinch State House had made policy activists out of Boston architects, particularly those inspired by the City Beautiful movement and its fascination with the White City, built for the 1893 World's Colombian Exposition in Chicago. It was their efforts, for instance, that resulted in a commonwealth ordinance limiting building heights to about eleven stories, the first law of its kind in the United States.[41] The height restriction enlivened a nascent effort among wealthy homeowners in the adjacent Beacon Hill neighborhood to reverse what they perceived as architectural and economic decline among their neighbors. Rather than tap into the Progressive Era's public-spiritedness, however, these individuals pooled their private wealth to buy, renovate, and then sell choice properties to other wealthy Bostonians. The Beacon Hill Association thus formed in 1922 "to keep undesirable business and living conditions from affecting the hill district."[42] Key among the association's early activities was advocating for zoning policies, which took effect in Boston in 1924. Thereafter, the association worked diligently to defend against any proposed zoning variances—especially any favoring low-income housing—which might conflict with its notion of what constituted an appropriately historical streetscape.[43]

Private investment in Beacon Hill's preservation mirrored a growing awareness after World War I of the possibility of profiting from the past. Historians frequently cite John D. Rockefeller's Colonial Williamsburg (1926) in Virginia or Henry Ford's Greenfield Village (1929) in Michigan as indices of a rising heritage tourism industry during the 1920s, but Boston was in many ways at the leading edge of the trend. It was the Boston firm of Perry, Shaw, and Hepburn, after all, that Rockefeller hired to manage the Williamsburg restoration. And it was their landscape architect, Arthur Shurcliff, who'd return from that project to design historic Sturbridge Village and, later, as we'll see, what would become Minuteman National Historical Park, just west of Boston. Shurcliff—along with other prominent colonial revivalists with Boston ties, including Appleton and DuPont heir Louise Crowninshield—had seen history and profit tied together early on in places like Nantucket, which offered its historical landscape as an enticement to wealthy vacationers since the turn of the twentieth century.[44] And they learned there that the key to making history profitable was giving customers what they wanted: simple affirming stories of American enterprise in charming places that seemed unchanged over time. Accordingly, the historic house museums and heritage attractions that these three helped to preserve during the 1920s engaged deeply in the cultural politics of anticommunism and American nativism, which proliferated during the interwar years. Although Appleton died before he could have a direct hand in planning Boston National Historical Park, we'll see in chapter two how Crowninshield factored in the conversations that produced the site.

THE NEW DEAL ORIGINS OF A POSTWAR PARK

By the 1920s, Bostonians had built a sophisticated heritage infrastructure that projected a patriotic vision of Longfellow's Revolution onto city streets. But even as they did, significant changes anticipated challenges for history making in Boston and beyond. It was throughout these years, for instance, that New England's textile industries gradually collapsed amid the flow of industry into the nonunion South.[45] Boston's economic base, though cushioned by its capacity to serve other regional industries, had nonetheless already been weakened by the time the Great Depression settled in during the 1930s, taking with it much of what remained of the city's traditional labor markets, including its once-ubiquitous waterfront jobs. At the same time, Boston's Mayor James Michael Curley's four terms of leadership—intermittently spanning a period from 1914 to 1950—created their own set of challenges. Curley poured resources into white working-class neighborhoods surrounding Boston's urban core, thereby destabilizing the already wavering political and economic power of its downtown elite. By prioritizing the periphery, however, Curley neglected Boston's central infrastructure, so much so that even the *Boston Globe* characterized it as "a hopeless backwater, a tumbled-down has-been among cities."[46] At the same time, Curley's notorious machine politics worried federal relief administrators who, during the 1930s, delivered considerably less New Deal funding to Boston than to other cities of comparable size.[47]

These were the circumstances that put into motion two people who, though moving on separate trajectories, collided with one another around the possibility of creating a national park in Boston. They were Edwin Small, a young historian recently employed by the National Park Service, and John W. McCormack, a Democratic politician from South Boston recently elected to the U.S. House of Representatives. The fateful moment occurred sometime in 1938, when McCormack conveyed to Small his wish that the federal government take possession of the Dorchester Heights Monument in South Boston and recognize it as a national monument. Privately, Small doubted the site's significance, arguing in a report that "it does not appear that the occupation of Dorchester Heights . . . made very much difference in the final outcome of the Siege of Boston."[48] Nonetheless, Small dutifully submitted the proposal to the National Park Service Advisory Board—which Congress had only recently constituted—wherein it promptly stalled and remained stalled for over a decade. After World War II, when it became clear to McCormack that the advisory board likely would not endorse his plan for South Boston, he upped the ante by proposing a full-scale federal commission to investigate an even bigger possibility: making the entire city into a national park. McCormack's strong-arm tactics worked. Boston would get its national park, though it would take a quarter century for it to happen.

But what was it that sparked the idea in 1938? One answer has to do with the NPS and its meteoric growth during the 1930s. The NPS famously benefited from New Deal Era largesse. It was the Civilian Conservation Corps (CCC), after all, that built much of the agency's early physical infrastructure. And it was the Works Progress Administration (WPA) that filled those new parks with tours and exhibits and other bits of what today we call interpretive programming. But these were only the most visible signs of growth in the NPS during those years. What had truly transformed the agency was Executive Order 6166, President Franklin D. Roosevelt's sweeping reorganization of the federal government that, in 1933, lumped into the agency's management dossier all national monuments, battlefields, parks, and even public buildings in Washington, DC. The NPS, which until that point had been a fairly small agency concerned with protecting iconic landscapes out west, had suddenly become a truly national organization with responsibilities for managing natural and cultural resources everywhere, even in eastern cities like Boston.[49]

The notion that the National Park Service could play a role in those cities followed the path of urban renewal. In St. Louis, for instance, a 1935 partnership between the NPS and the Jefferson National Expansion Memorial Association leveraged private and public monies to replace nearly forty blocks of aging buildings with the towering sculpture known today as the Gateway Arch. As historian Tracy Campbell recounts it, the project immediately thrust the NPS into controversy. Massive election fraud, it turned out, allowed a coterie of white St. Louis power brokers to advance what amounted to a sham real estate deal, conceived of to rid the city's waterfront of rental properties and the Black laborers who relied on them for affordable housing. Even after newspapers revealed the fraud, the NPS forged on, "willingly ignorant."[50] Similar plans for a national park took shape in Philadelphia prior to the World War II, though wouldn't be implemented until 1948, with the authorization of Independence National Historical Park. There, too, the city displaced working people for the sake of renewal, demolishing six blocks of "non-historical" buildings in order to create a more appropriate setting for Independence Hall.[51] Closer to Boston, the National Park Service worked with private investors to acquire Derby Wharf and other properties it hoped to isolate from signs of economic collapse in downtown Salem, Massachusetts. Boston, too, was on the precipice of a new bout of urban renewal, signaled by the debut of preliminary plans for its new Central Artery in 1927.[52]

Within the NPS, there was also a brand-new impetus to do history, though what that meant wasn't entirely clear. Conceived of as a steward of wilderness, the NPS had wrestled ever since its founding with how to appropriately manage the bits of human history, such as old buildings and archeological artifacts, that appeared all throughout its parks. Longtime NPS operative Horace Albright pushed hard for history, but suffered a humiliating first go at it as director when the agency inadvertently enshrined the wrong house as George Washington's birthplace in Virginia.[53] Only in 1931, with the establishment of its branch of research and education, did the NPS really get serious about history. Historian Denise Meringolo describes how the man hired to lead that office, Verne Chatelain, insisted that the agency develop historic sites systematically, with regard to context, narrative, and other facets of "historic mindedness" that he found wanting in federal history work. Some within the agency, however, pushed back against Chatelain. Foremost among them was Charles Peterson, a historical architect who favored data gathering over storytelling. Peterson won an important victory for his approach in 1933 by securing congressional funding for his Historic American Building Survey, a wildly successful program that still documents threatened historical structures today. It was Chatelain's vision, however, that ultimately framed the Historic Sites Act of 1935, which brought coherence to the agency's history mandate. It tasked the NPS with surveying the nation's historic sites and taking stock of particularly interesting ones. And it created the National Park Service Advisory Board, with authority to recommend which of those sites deserved federal protection. But it also institutionalized Peterson's documentation program, thus setting up a longstanding tension in NPS circles between historians and architects.[54]

It's the Historic Sites Act, too, that activated one of our story's key protagonists: Edwin Small. Small, who grew up in Goshen, Connecticut—a place lodged within the crucible of New England colonial revivalism—had only just earned an MA in history from Yale University when the new law went into effect.[55] He was precisely the kind of young historian that the agency was looking for in 1935 to fulfill the Historic Site Act's mandate that the NPS compile detailed inventories of America's historic landscapes. In fact, it was Chatelain's hand-picked successor, Ronald F. Lee, who hired Small under authority of the CCC. Small bounced between offices in Springfield, Massachusetts, and Washington, DC, before landing at a new district office that opened in Boston in 1936. When the office relocated to Salem a year later, Small followed and began work on a survey of New England historic sites for the new National Park Service Advisory Board.[56] He made an impression: only a year later—barely two years out of graduate school—Small became superintendent of the newly established Salem Maritime National Historic Site, the first NPS historic site in New England.[57]

By the time Representative McCormack contacted him, then, Edwin Small's stock was already on the rise. Preservation historian Charles Hosmer described Small as "a most efficient and diplomatic emissary for the National Park Service in a region where the federal government was not trusted."[58] He had to be. Salem was a crossroads for some of the early twentieth century's most important preservationists. It was in Salem that George Francis Dow, head of the venerable Essex Institute, introduced the period room to American museumgoers at the turn of the century. William Sumner Appleton had a keen and longstanding interest in Salem's historic houses. And Louise DuPont Crowninshield, who kept a home in nearby Marblehead, had married into a family of Salem descendants and eagerly involved herself in all things preservation there. Even more locally, businessman Harlan P. Kelsey and Mayor George J. Bates were determined by the 1930s to restore the Revolutionary-era Derby Wharf, intending to cash in on WPA funding and, they hoped, make a claim on an emergent heritage tourism industry. A tangle of private interests, all variously involved through ownership of Salem's historic structures, added to the mix of those invested in the town's historic landscape. Once the NPS resolved to stake its own claim at Salem, and to assert there its new commitment to historic preservation, it fell to public servant Edwin Small to negotiate this complex and powerful network of private interests.[59]

Small managed it all by taking a pragmatic approach to partnership and an aggressive approach to preservation. He worked cautiously to earn Appleton's trust, despite the Boston preservationist's deep and well-documented distrust of the federal government.[60] In this task especially, he found an important partner in Crowninshield, who, though ensconced within the nation's elite preservation set, had also become a powerful public partner to the NPS by helping it clean up the mess at Washington's Birthplace.[61] Small worked vigorously to align the agency's preservation interests with the concerns of his community partners. He assured them that NPS involvement would "draw people to this section of the country as never before" so that "New England [can] keep pace with other parts of the country as a vacation land."[62] To make sure it would, Small relied on a constant stream of technical support from the regional office, including from Assistant Architect Stuart Barnette. When Barnette drew up a preservation plan for Salem in 1937 that recommended widespread demolition of buildings deemed nonessential to the agency's preservation mission, Small supported it entirely. In one case, Small defended the proposed demolition as "desirable not only as a slum clearance proposition, but also to widen the perspective of the waterfront . . . and could also be effectively utilized in connection with solving the parking problem."[63] As early as 1937, it seems, Small had already begun developing strategies for managing collaborative preservation in urban settings with an eye toward heritage tourism, economic development, and, of course, urban renewal.

By 1938, then, a perfect set of preconditions existed for federal heritage work in Boston. There were new laws, new money, new people, and new ideas about cities and citizenship that all predicted McCormack's fateful encounter with Small. But what was it exactly that prompted that encounter? What was it that compelled McCormack to take such a powerful interest in Dorchester Heights in 1938? We probably cannot know for sure. McCormack's papers are regrettably partial and reveal almost nothing at all about his interest in history or historic preservation. Archivists at Boston College's Gottleib Center, where McCormack's collection is kept, intimate that his people likely "cleaned" the collection before donating it.[64] So, what made Dorchester Heights special? Where might we look for answers?

McCormack's career in federal government certainly gives us some clues. By 1938, McCormack was ten years into what would be a distinguished forty-three-year run in the U.S. House of Representatives. He was a committed New Deal Democrat, and deeply loyal to President Roosevelt. At the same time, McCormack railed against so-called un-American activities. On any given day back in his home district, newspapers might report on McCormack's advocacy for federal employment on one page and, on another, his concern that fascist operatives might seduce unwitting Bostonians. The late 1930s thus confronted McCormack with two entwined crises: the rise of fascism in Europe and declining support for New Deal policies back home, especially after the failure of Roosevelt's Supreme Court-packing plan in 1937. In this light, it's easy to speculate that McCormack reached out to Small in 1938 toward building support for New Deal heritage policy and also to shore up American nationalism in the face of perceived threats from abroad.[65]

We also may find clues by looking deeper into McCormack's political life. McCormack had come up, after all, amid the fisticuff ward politics of interwar Boston. He was a poor Irish kid raised up by a single mother in a tenement just blocks from the Dorchester Heights Monument. At least, this was the story McCormack had to invent to survive in Boston politics. It is true that he grew up poor in South Boston, but his absentee father had actually been Canadian, a fact of birth that would have stalled McCormack's ascent had his family not agreed to obscure it. They did, but as biographer Garrison Nelson makes clear, McCormack's genealogy was a source of lifelong insecurity for a politician who sought ways throughout his career to prove his Irishness. And if ever it was in doubt, McCormack could always refer to his older brother Edward "Knocko" McCormack, whose exploits as a streetfighter and bootlegger seem to have earned a seal of legitimacy for the entire family. Whereas the younger McCormack sought political fortunes beyond Boston, Knocko established himself as a fixture in city politics by becoming a key operative in James Curley's notorious machine. Knocko's claim to Irishness was so complete, in fact, that for years he served as grand marshal of South Boston's annual blockbuster March 17 Evacuation–Saint Patrick's Day parade.[66]

And it is in the parade wherein we discover a critical clue concerning McCormack's encounter with Small in 1938. At least since the 1890s, South Bostonians had celebrated Saint Patrick's Day together with Evacuation Day, the anniversary of the day in 1776 when British troops fled Boston Harbor in fear of what Washington's troops might achieve from their position atop Dorchester Heights. Scholar Anthony Bak Buccitelli speculates that the conflation of these events owed to the determination among South Boston's dwindling Yankee power elite to stymie their ethnic Irish neighbors.[67] If that was the plan, then it backfired spectacularly, as South Boston's Irish majority leveraged the coincidence of the two holidays toward making even greater claims on American memory. And 1938 was the year the convergence became official: the Commonwealth of Massachusetts officially declared that

March 17 would, thereon, also be celebrated as Evacuation Day, so that "the
first major military victory in the war for American independence . . . may be
perpetuated."[68] It was in 1938, then, that Massachusetts legally bound Irish
heritage to Revolutionary memory.

This declaration marked a significant victory in a decades-long campaign
among Boston's ethnic Irish to claim a place for themselves, not just in Boston,
but within the nation's historical saga. Historian Thomas H. O'Connor suggests that, by the turn of the last century, Irish Catholics in South Boston vied
for power in Boston's political milieu by mingling their immigrant ancestry
with the nation's patriotic memory.[69] The Dorchester Heights Monument
achieved just that by reminding Boston that its Irish community safeguarded
the spot where colonials sent the British packing. An 1891 public sculpture of
the vaguely Irish Civil War Navy Admiral David Farragut in nearby Marine
Park made a similar claim more directly, as did the building of South Boston
High School in 1901. At the center of efforts to create all of these was the South
Boston Citizens' Association (SBCA).[70] It was the SBCA also that organized
and hosted South Boston's annual Evacuation-St. Patrick's Day parade, the very
event that by 1938 had elevated Knocko McCormack to new heights of local
celebrity. And, as the *Boston Globe* reported, it was the SBCA that was working
hard to convince the "Federal Government [to] create a national memorial at
Dorchester Heights . . . it has been known for some time that Congressman
John W. McCormack is ready to sponsor the national legislation." Indeed,
additional reports suggest that McCormack had met regularly with the SBCA
and the mayor's office all year toward building the case for federal protection.[71]

The campaign to establish a national historical park in Boston thus
began neither as a paean to Paul Revere nor amid a prevailing concern with
Revolutionary memory. Rather, the earliest stirrings of what would become
Boston National Historical Park emerged of a powerful investment in Irish
American nationalism by a politician deeply concerned about his own claims
to political power. McCormack understood perfectly how memory and power
worked in South Boston. And he certainly understood that, by 1938, his most
fervent constituency perceived new threats to its mnemonic claims. Consider
that the WPA's 1937 guide to Boston dismissed the city's "legend of ethnic
homogeneity" as "so much pernicious twaddle." The notion that "Boston is
an 'Irish City,'" it proclaimed, was just a "modern fable." Among immigrants,
Canadians outnumbered Irish, with Italians and Russian Jews close behind.
What's more, it noted, a historically small segment of Boston's population had

begun to grow: "there are also in Boston 20,574 Negroes."[72] Though Boston's Black population did not expand significantly until the 1940s, an interwar wave of immigration from the West Indies and the Cape Verde Islands had already triggered visible change. White Bostonians responded immediately, and in 1934, Boston's Irish political machine gerrymandered Roxbury's Ward 9 to prevent a concentration of Black voters.[73] Making Evacuation Day a state holiday, pouring energy into the annual parade, and seeking federal protection for Dorchester Heights all similarly expressed a desire among some Bostonians to keep history Irish, which by 1938 equated to keeping history white. McCormack asked the NPS to help the SBCA do it; Edwin Small agreed.

In the short term, at least, the plan seemed to work. At McCormack's urging, Small submitted the proposal to make the Dorchester Heights Monument a national memorial to the advisory board for consideration. In the meantime, McCormack secured authorization in 1939 from the Commonwealth of Massachusetts for Boston to convey the Dorchester Heights Monument to the United States to be managed under authority of the Historic Sites Act.[74] The advisory board seems to have dragged its heels on the matter, but by spring 1940 agreed that Dorchester Heights was indeed eligible, according to the agency's new guidelines, to be designated a national historic site. Deciding whether it actually would be designated, however, would require yet another round of deliberations. McCormack's people submitted a second-round nomination in 1941, but only just before the United Sates entered into World War II.[75] For the time being, at least, the campaign to create a federal monument in South Boston was on hold.

A FREEDOM TRAIL FOR NEW BOSTON

A federal monument to the city's Revolutionary past in South Boston was a truly novel concept in 1938. Not only did it challenge a century-long local tradition of private heritage stewardship, it also challenged Beacon Hill's long-standing claims to historical authority. This is not to say that McCormack's historical vision was any clearer than the Brahmins'. It relied on the same tropes that had made Revolutionary memory politically expedient ever since the 1820s, and played into yet another facet of Boston's deepening racial anxieties. It is clear, though, that the possibility of asserting itself in Boston raised for the NPS the specter of even greater possibilities. The agency's so-called park résumés, kept secret by the director for fear of stirring real estate speculators, indicate that by 1947, Small's old survey of New England historic sites had reemerged in conversations about a new national park, as had Concord and Lexington.[76] These were old plans, but now that the war had ended, opportunity awaited history-minded NPS planners in Boston.

They were not the plans, however, that would drive Boston's new postwar heritage economy. A "New Boston," as historian Jim Vrabel puts it, was born on November 8, 1949, the day that Mayor Curley lost his last bid for reelection to John Hynes.[77] Hynes, who had been voted in alongside a new city charter that granted him unprecedented power, set out that year to repair the considerable rifts that Curley had cultivated, especially among Boston's Irish majority and its downtown financiers. Growth, Hynes posited, would hinge on building a coalition of government, business, labor, and media, particularly Boston's impressive corps of newspaper publishers. His plan for accomplishing this coalition was urban renewal. As we've seen, urban redevelopment was well underway in Boston before World War II. It was after the war, however, that new federal housing laws subsidized "slum clearance" in cities that devised redevelopment plans in partnership with private developers. What's more, the Federal Highway Act of 1956 subsidized construction of new highways and granted state and federal officials considerable authority to determine their routes. It was after the war, then, that Boston's new political leadership and new federal policies coincided in ways that would result in a fundamental reconfiguration of modern Boston.[78]

Postwar renewal had very different impacts in different sections of the greater Boston metropolitan area. Beyond downtown, renewal opened Boston to the meteoric economic growth that seemed everywhere in the years after World War II. Cold War military spending especially swelled Boston's universities with federal military funding and, thanks to the GI Bill, welcomed thousands of returning veterans into their classrooms. Hanscom Air Force Base, built just outside Boston during World War II, became an epicenter of military spending during the Cold War, thus spurring the development of a high-tech industrial corridor along nearby Massachusetts Route 128. New technologies and new industries, alongside large-scale federal public works projects (including highway construction), pumped money into the economy and, thanks to powerful labor unions, distributed it across a broad cross-section of American families. And with war and depression behind them, young Americans celebrated by having more kids than ever before.[79]

Back in downtown, however, Bostonians struggled amid a very different set of circumstances. Following the new federal guidelines, Hynes constituted a Boston Housing Authority (BHA) that drafted a 1950 city plan with particular emphasis on updating transportation systems and removing pockets of "blight" from around the downtown business district. When construction on the Central Artery finally began in 1950, residents of Boston's historic North End suddenly realized that, not only would the project cut them off from the city, it would destroy hundreds of buildings and businesses throughout their community. Residents of Boston's Chinatown even convinced the city council to oppose plans for a portion of the artery that threatened their part of the city. None of this, however, stopped construction, which continued through 1959.[80] At the same time, Hynes and the BHA advanced renewal projects in Boston's South and West End communities that resulted in the displacement of thousands of working-class Bostonians, many of whom were immigrants, people of color, or both. In the West End alone, over three thousand families lost their homes, with up to half being relocated to lower-quality housing at higher costs. By the late 1960s, urban renewal displaced over ten thousand families throughout Boston, and about one-third of those were families of color. The election of Mayor John F. Collins in 1959, as we will see in chapter three, would shift renewal away from demolition and displacement. For many Bostonians, however, the damage had already been done.[81]

Tourism boosters, however, saw within these downtown disruptions new opportunities to profit from the past. In myriad ways, the postwar years created national demand in Boston for precisely the Revolutionary memory its local heritage brokers had promulgated for over a century. Historic sites beckoned to newly prosperous white middle-class families whose kids had memorized *Paul Revere's Ride* in school, and maybe even heard it on the TV or radio—perhaps on the DuPont Company's *Cavalcade of America.* A trip to Boston was educational, but it also encouraged the kind of Cold War patriotism befitting a young generation charged with protecting democracy at home and abroad. And getting there would be easier than ever before, or so claimed proponents of the Central Artery. Hynes's encouragement of new partnerships between government and business made a prominent place for Boston's Chamber of Commerce, which eagerly sought ways to turn a profit on heritage tourism.[82] In fact, it was the chair of the chamber's Committee on Historical Places, a plastics magnate and history enthusiast named Mark Bortman, who would eventually lead the effort to develop a national park concept for Boston. How, though, would Boston's new heritage coalition translate a nineteenth-century story about the city's eighteenth century into the language of twentieth-century heritage tourists?

What few accounts exist of the Freedom Trail's founding impulse situate it firmly within the postwar years. A deeper look, though, points to a longer history of retrieving Boston's past on foot. And, remarkably, doing so has often been bound up with urban renewal. Way back in 1837, for instance, Mayor Quincy's own son Edmund critiqued the excesses he perceived in his father's renewal campaign by describing a figurative walking tour, a "solitary walk through those streets of our city which have suffered least from the levelling hand of modern improvement." His itinerary included old homes already demolished and some still standing: the Old Province House, the Old Brick, Governor Hutchinson's mansion, the Sir William Phips House, Ben Franklin's boyhood home.[83] Nearly a century later, the Boston Tercentenary Committee of 1930 proposed a heritage walking tour "to venerate [Boston's] many shrines."[84] The *Boston Herald* proposed its own historical walking tour of the city in 1935. Henry Moore's "Trudging over Hub's Historic Loop Makes

FIGURE 2. Boston's West End redevelopment project, sometime between 1959 and 1964. Photograph by the Boston Housing Authority, item WE_0021, Boston Redevelopment Authority photographs (4010.001), Boston City Archives, West Roxbury, MA.

Leisure Profitable," points to the eagerness among Boston's first-wave renewal boosters to link history with profitability.[85] It also suggests that the contours of what would become the Freedom Trail had already become clear in Boston prior to World War II. Accompanying Moore's proposal is a map of a walking tour drawn by Old North Church Rector Robert M. Winn connecting twenty historic markers in a circle covering Boston Common, Beacon Hill, and the North End.[86] "No other city in the country," Moore assured his readers, "has so many historic spots within such easy walking distance of each other."[87]

Neither Moore nor Winn, however, seem to have been able to make the idea stick on their own. Credit for that accomplishment goes to *Boston Evening Traveler* Editor Bill Schofield, who beginning in March 1951 focused his daily "Have You Heard" column on the problem of lost tourists in Boston's North End and the need there for a "liberty loop."[88] As the story goes, Schofield—a self-described "Swamp Yankee descendant"—hatched a plan in conversation with Winn to "mark out a 'Puritan Path' or 'Liberty Loop' or 'Freedom's Way' or whatever you want to call it, so [tourists] know where to start and what course to follow" in their pursuit of Boston's historic sites. Mayor Hynes or Chamber of Commerce President Harry Blake, Schofield suggested, could "do the trick on a budget of just a few dollars and a bucket of paint" if they were to simply put up a few signs designed "to guide a visitor from one shrine to the next along the most convenient foot-route." Schofield and Winn had even worked out a rough itinerary. Beginning at the State House, tourists would follow fanciful markers (featuring a figurative "Colonial, striding onward") to the Granary Burial Ground, King's Chapel, Old South Meeting House, the Old State House, Faneuil Hall, the Paul Revere House, Old North Church, and then Copp's Hill Burying Ground, near where they could catch a ride at North Station to points beyond. The whole thing could be done in "no more than a moderate walking jaunt," and a more ambitious motor route might be conceived of along similar lines for those eager to venture beyond the city. "THE PEOPLE would like it," and "it would add to the looks of the city."[89]

Schofield and Winn's nascent plan for what would become Boston's Freedom Trail is remarkable for many reasons. On one hand, it reveals the powerful and persistent imprint of Boston's nineteenth-century heritage brokers. Schofield's proposed itinerary, after all, amounts to a walking tour of Longfellow's historical imagination. And yet, on the other hand, Schofield's vision made the old narrative accessible to modern audiences, particularly vacationers whose postwar appetites for consumer patriotism sent them hurtling

across the nation's new web of highways. In other ways, too, the plan spoke
specifically to Boston's postwar circumstances. The trail that Schofield and
Winn envisioned, history notwithstanding, was conceived of in terms of
economic development for a city struggling amid industrial decline. Time
spent searching for historic sites, they argued, meant "that much less for
pleasure and incidentally for spending money." The broader contours of this
argument are on display in additional essays Schofield dedicated to the trail
project in 1951. In one, Schofield detailed Winn's eagerness to make space for
more tourists and their cars by redesigning "the whole North End peninsula
[with] all the occupied buildings moved out of the way" of its historic buildings.[90] A week later, Schofield argued that the overwhelming response to his
column predicted a time soon when "fewer visitors who start out looking for
Copp's Hill Burying Ground [will] wind up at a Salem street salami counter."
None other than Lenox E. Bigelow of the Massachusetts Development and
Industrial Commission, Schofield intimated, expected that "such a plan would
pay dividends almost beyond belief."[91]

   Cast in these terms, what appears on the surface to be a commonsensical
solution to the problem of lost tourists, reveals itself to be more complicated.
Schofield and Winn's plan was complicit in a brand of mid-century urban
renewal that sought to accommodate privileged white consumers by margin-
alizing those who were not. As Schofield's quip about salami counters hints,
the section of the North End that Winn was so eager to clear out was, by
1951, the center of Boston's working-class Italian community. Since the middle
of the preceding century, Boston's cramped and commercial North End had
been a frequent terminus for immigrants, first Irish and later eastern and
southern Europeans. After World War II, the North End's majority Italian
population—as well as its stock of historic properties—was effectively cor-
doned off and, in some cases, displaced by construction of Boston's Central
Artery. The colorful street life and frolicking children that urban reformer
Jane Jacobs observed there during the late 1950s worried the suburban tourists
that Schofield spoke with, who complained of being "greeted with mobs of
urchins at Paul Revere's House. We were so irritated we left in a hurry."[92] They
wanted the *historical* North End conjured by Longfellow, Schofield believed,
not the ethnic ghetto made notorious by Sacco and Vanzetti.[93] Other sites
remained completely off limits. None among the trail's early planners ever
attempted to route tourists past the site of the famous Liberty Tree, which by
1951 abutted Boston's bustling Chinatown. Even a decade later the Freedom

Trail Foundation, which had been requested to include the site on its path, remained "reluctant to do so due to the deplorable condition of the area and obvious problems of bringing tourists into that section."[94]

For Schofield, at least, the problem of ethnic and class difference in the North End was just one facet of what he and others perceived to be the corrosive influence throughout Boston of an increasingly "deviant" urban landscape.[95] The trail, Schofield argued would ensure that a tourist could find Bunker Hill, for instance, unlike his "cousin who used to say: 'Nope, I started for Bunker Hill but somehow I wound up at Revere Beach.'"[96] Schofield's reference to Revere Beach, the nation's first public beach and, by the 1950s, a summer retreat for Boston's working class, underscored his concern that the city's historic places were being sidelined by coarse amusements.[97] Directional signs would, he suggested, "prevent [the tourist] from getting lost somewhere among the hamburger stands."[98] The possibility that respectable tourists might encounter the actualities of daily life in postwar Boston so rattled Schofield that he continued to dwell on it over two decades later in the foreword to his book about the Freedom Trail: "It was not unusual for a safari trying to track down Faneuil Hall to get lost in the tattoo shops and burlesque dives of old Scollay Square . . . It was chaos."[99]

Mayor Hynes agreed. Schofield reported that the mayor had called him and expressed his intent to "go along with the Freedom Way plans." The Boston Chamber of Commerce and the Junior Chamber of Commerce too, Schofield added, "are plugging the plan." "More people," he predicted, "will get to the Old North Church and Paul Revere's House this season than ever before, and fewer lost visitors will wind up wondering how to get out of Scollay Square."[100] Schofield had succeeded. In the following months, the city installed painted plywood signs "along 30 prominent street corners pointing toward Old Boston's most famous historical shrines." Mayor Hynes officially dedicated the "Freedom Trail" on June 11, 1951.[101] Schofield described a not-so-modest victory lap around the new Freedom Trail. "City workers are busy . . . cleaning up the rubbish scatterings," he observed, "a very good sign indeed." "Youngsters of the neighborhood" still clustered "around the sightseeing busses . . . for pennies and dimes," but overall Schofield found the city streets "cleaner than they used to be, except in the North End." As it turned out, the trail "is a comfortable and convenient way to see the sights of Boston," and could be enjoyed in forty-five minutes of leisurely walking.[102] Boston's heritage tourists seem to have agreed. By 1953, an estimated forty thousand visitors had followed the trail. The city considered it such a success that, in that year, it commissioned a new series of permanent metal signs to replace their dilapidated and, in some cases, vandalized predecessors. With a nod to Longfellow, each one prominently featured—in gold—a silhouette of Paul Revere on his horse.[103]

* * *

Whereas the advent of Boston's Freedom Trail might be seen as the starting point for a history of the city's modern heritage landscape and, later, the NPS's role in managing it, my hope in this chapter has been to illustrate how the Freedom Trail actually represents the culmination of a two-century-long contest over the meanings and uses of Revolutionary memory in Boston. Understanding that contest, and the motivations of those who joined it, is absolutely critical for making sense of the challenges that planners encountered in Boston when they arrived during the 1950s to rough out the contours of a new national park. It shows us, for instance, that by mid-century, Revolutionary memory was already highly politicized in Boston, and deeply entwined with struggles for social justice. Urban renewal would soon stir old passions among claimants to the Revolution's legacy. It shows us too that, by the 1950s, Boston had devised a sophisticated heritage infrastructure reliant upon private investment, complex zoning laws, and the considerable influence of decades-old historical societies. All of this was bound up in efforts to assert white affluence along the trail, even in matters of faith. Historian Devin Manzullo-Thomas shows, for instance, how the stewards of Boston's Park Street Church used their position along the new Freedom Trail to legitimize a nascent vision of white Protestant "evangelical heritage."[104] And, of course, we've seen how Boston's heritage saga produced a coterie of preservationists deeply nourished on an earlier era's cultural politics and the notion that history could and should turn a profit. Their involvement with the NPS in Boston and beyond would bear significant influence on Cold War Era public history.

In fact, what is most striking about the Freedom Trail, as it was conceived, is how vigorously it mapped nineteenth-century ideas about the past onto Boston's twentieth-century streets. Schofield pitched the trail as a beacon to lost tourists. But what really got lost on the Freedom Trail during these years was any possibility of recognizing that the trail had almost nothing at all to

FIGURE 3. Bill Schofield follows the Freedom Trail past the Paul Revere House in 1974, photographer unknown. Photograph reprinted with permission from Boston University Photography.

do with the Revolution. The Freedom Trail, rather, as had been the case with Revolutionary memory in Boston for over a century, was always about the future. It was always about making choices about whose pasts would be remembered and whose would be erased. It was always about imagining an America in which business paved the way to freedom. And it was always about enshrining Paul Revere, the perfect icon of American white male entrepreneurship, so that people who fancied themselves as inheritors of his legacy might come share the fruits of their own entrepreneurial success with Boston's struggling economy. Remarkably, tourists who glom on to the park's popular ranger-led tours of the Freedom Trail learn very little if anything at all about who it was who drew the line that they follow today, or even why it goes where it does. The Freedom Trail has thus become its own claim to historical authority, the most powerful and problematic object within the park's collection, and yet the one the park is least able to contend with.

CHAPTER 2

Imagining a National Historical Park for Boston

The year 1951 was a watershed in the course of events leading to the creation of a national park in Boston. The debut that year of Boston's Freedom Trail, as we've seen, distilled generations of Revolutionary memory into a simple story of American exceptionalism ready-made for postwar visitors. At the same time, the start of construction on Boston's Central Artery promised to funnel more and more of those visitors directly downtown. Its path through Boston's historic North End also threatened to divide the modern city along old class lines and displace ethnic communities roiled by protests, foreshadowing a generation of conflict associated with urban renewal. That year, Boston also implemented a new city charter, which granted unprecedented power to Mayor John Hynes, who handily won reelection against a spate of candidates—including his rascally predecessor, James Michael Curley. Armed with a new city plan and a mandate to reinvigorate downtown, Hynes set out to unite a coalition of public and private interests in realizing a new modern Boston, just as his mayoral compatriots had done in Chicago, New York, and Philadelphia.

And it was in 1951, amid all of this, that U.S. Representative and house minority leader John W. McCormack—a devoted supporter of "historic and patriotic matters," according to National Park Service (NPS) historian Edwin Small—first introduced a bill proposing to authorize a Boston National Historic Sites Commission to study the possibility of creating a national historical park in and around Boston.[1] A similar kind of group, though not a federal commission, had helped to establish Independence National Historical Park in Philadelphia, where the NPS officially assumed control of Independence Hall, also in 1951.[2] That project demonstrated how powerfully the NPS could figure in postwar urban place making and, as we will see, its example became a template for possibilities in Boston. Federal park building in Boston, however, presented a very different set of challenges, owing in part to the existence there of a deeply established heritage infrastructure.[3] As we discovered in chapter one, a web of organizations staked a claim on Boston's mnemonic landscape by 1951. There were, of course, the dozens of private heritage societies that had proliferated there during the previous century and that managed several of Boston's most iconic historic sites. The Metropolitan District Commission (MDC), a state entity, had charge of the Bunker Hill Monument ever since 1919. Boston's Chamber of Commerce also exerted considerable authority in heritage matters through its sponsorship of the Freedom Trail. In coming years, the commonwealth would involve itself even further by way of the Boston Redevelopment Authority (BRA) and, beginning in 1955, the creation and management of local historic districts.[4] Indeed, most of the historic sites that the NPS might manage in Boston already had managers, a fact that raised real concerns in Congress about the necessity of a national park in Boston.

How then did McCormack convince lawmakers to endorse a project that appeared, in most every regard, unnecessary? We find out in this chapter by sifting through congressional debate over McCormack's proposal. Not everyone, it turns out, was convinced. In the fever-charged atmosphere of Cold War policy making, however, the rhetoric of urban redevelopment and anticommunism won the day. Once it did, and once McCormack's commission went to work, the baton passed backed to Edwin Small. Small had returned to Salem, Massachusetts, after World War II only to get tapped for the assignment that would make him a critical architect of the agency's postwar history agenda: chief of party for the Boston National Historical Sites Commission. It was the commission's task to imagine what a national historical park in Boston might accomplish. Thanks to Small's punctilious record keeping, the commission produced detailed meeting minutes that reveal just how unfocused its members were on matters of history. Economic development proved far more alluring, so much so that the commission even became embroiled in a factious public dispute over where and how Boston's butchers should do business. These were the very people, it's worth noting, who worked alongside the NPS to establish expectations for federal history making in the United States after World War II. Indeed, what makes this story so important is the extent to which it was a dress rehearsal for system-wide changes that transformed the National Park Service during the 1950s. Boston was a rough draft, as it were, for a new modern National Park Service. And that rough draft, as we will see, looked very much like the Freedom Trail.

THE CASE IN CONGRESS FOR BOSTON

World War II could very well have derailed hopes for a national historical park in Boston. Most immediately, it scattered the park's key protagonists. McCormack, of course, retreated into the abyss of wartime politics. Small joined the U.S. Navy Reserve, where he conducted historical research, first in the Office of Naval Intelligence and then for the Director of Naval History in Washington, DC.[5] More critically, the NPS suffered drastic dislocations during the war years, including a temporary relocation of its headquarters from Washington, DC, to Chicago, and crippling reductions of staff and funding. The situation was so bad, in fact, that Congress temporarily suspended authorization of new parks. And for some years after, it was far from certain whether the agency could ever rebound from its losses. What saved it was Mission 66, a massive ten-year program conceived of by NPS Director Conrad Wirth to rebuild the national parks in time for the agency's fiftieth anniversary in 1966. Congress funded Wirth's plan on the order, in today's economy, of nine billion dollars. Mission 66 fundamentally reinvented the NPS in the likeness of Cold War America. By the end of the 1960s, its visitor centers looked more like spaceships than frontier outposts. Its expanded parking lots welcomed waves of newly mobile highway travelers. Its rangers put on costumes and spun wool, all toward making good on a belief that "ideal interpretation implies . . . re-creation of the past." And, more than ever before, Mission 66 encouraged the NPS to organize itself around private capital.[6]

The NPS did not implement Mission 66 reforms until 1955, however, and so efforts to create a national park in Boston continued on their own trajectory during the immediate postwar years. Recall from chapter one that, during the late 1930s, McCormack had convinced Edwin Small to propose to the National Park Service Advisory Board that the old Dorchester Heights Monument in South Boston be made a national monument. The proposal stalled during wartime, but by January 1951 it was back before the NPS.[7] Again, however, the advisory board stalled, noting that among the dozen other sites in and around Boston it had also ranked as nationally significant, Dorchester Heights was not the most remarkable. The board suggested additional studies, but neither the city nor McCormack would hear of it. Instead, McCormack forced the board's hand by drafting H.J. Res. 254, a bill to establish a historical sites commission for Boston. With that the Department of Interior agreed to a memorandum of agreement with the City of Boston designating Dorchester Heights a national historic site.[8] The board finalized the designation that spring and, until 1979, the NPS and the Boston Parks Department jointly managed the monument and surrounding Thomas Park as Dorchester Heights National Historic Site.[9]

But what now concerned the NPS in Boston was not the matter of Dorchester Heights' significance, but rather the possibility of creating there an entirely new historical park. That spring, Assistant Director Ronald Lee and Chief Historian Herbert D. Kahler encouraged Chief of Interpretation Rogers W. Young to make a preliminary field survey of Revolutionary-era historic sites in and around Boston. Kahler proceeded by calling on none other than Edwin Small, who had compiled his own survey back in 1937. Together they agreed that the Old State House and Faneuil Hall should become federal property. Several other sites, they resolved, should be recognized as national historic sites in nonfederal ownership by way of cooperative agreements. Dorchester Heights had conveniently become a model for just this arrangement. Other sites considered for inclusion in a national historic park were the Bunker Hill Monument, Old North Church, the Paul Revere House, and the site on Cambridge Common where George Washington became commander of the Continental Army. Sites between Lexington and Concord associated with Paul Revere's ride and the British advance should be marked, they suggested, though the "conservative attitude of these old established Town Governments may make this task a formidable or even impossible one to overcome." The commission might succeed, Young and Small decided, if its membership included "public spirited citizen[s] of the highest type," who "represent the best in the old tradition of public service, peculiar to New England." It would need an "outstanding" architect as well, and "representatives of the highest type from the political life of the city, the State and the Nation [sic]." Lee suggested that perhaps even someone from Philadelphia's Independence Hall Association, perhaps Judge Edwin O. Lewis, "should be considered for appointment."[10]

The only problem, of course, was that there was not yet a commission for which to consider appointments. McCormack's bill did not move through Congress as quickly perhaps as the agency suspected it might. When the Subcommittee on Public Lands of the Committee on Interior and Insular Affairs met in August 1951 to review H.J. Res. 254, McCormack stressed that precedent for such a commission was evident in connection with several national memorials, including Mount Rushmore and the Jefferson Memorial (now Gateway Arch National Park), and especially the Independence National Historical "project" in Philadelphia. The Boston commission would enable Congress, he argued, "to keep in closer touch with the study . . . which in the final analysis must be enacted into law if the project is to be a success." "A commission stimulates more interest," he added, "in the community itself." McCormack emphasized the Interior Department's conclusion that Boston and its surroundings constituted "one of the greatest historical regions of the nation," though he cautioned that, if established, a commission would have to "obtain the permission of the proper local authorities" before venturing beyond Boston's city limits. He assured the subcommittee, however, that "the local authorities are interested," including Mayor Hynes from whom McCormack "not only obtain[ed] his consent but his approval."[11]

McCormack's pitch hit its mark. Arizona Congressman John R. Murdock, who also served as chair of the House Committee on Memorials, expressed his support, given the similarity of McCormack's proposal to what "we are just giving attention now to [at] another cradle of liberty up here at Philadelphia." Colorado Representative Wayne N. Aspinall wondered what, specifically, McCormack meant by "Boston and the general vicinity." McCormack explained that, in his mind, Boston's "vicinity" included Cambridge, Somerville, Quincy, Newton, Everett, Malden, and Revere, or towns within approximately ten miles of the Massachusetts State House, "which is more or less in the heart of Boston." The subcommittee's chair, Texas Representative Lloyd M. Bentsen Jr., inquired whether state and city governments had begun working on the project. McCormack answered "no," prompting Bentsen to note that "we do not feel on this Committee that this is a local matter because all of America feels that it has an interest in these historical sites."[12]

The notion that all Americans had a stake in Boston's history pervaded the hearings. McCormack took up the topic in a comment concerning Evacuation Day, "the biggest day in the year in my district." "A significant part of the exercises of this year," he explained, "was the signing of the necessary documents which made Dorchester Heights a national historical site." But, McCormack followed, "that is piecemeal." The proposed legislation would encourage a broader coordinated effort worthy of Boston's national significance. The theme continued in a statement made by NPS Assistant Director Ronald Lee. Lee emphasized how "the historical properties of the nation are one of its most important heritages which contribute to the national welfare." "In times such as the present," once again invoking the social and political anxieties of the mid-century United States, "it is important to focus national attention upon the basic traditions of our historical heritage."[13] With that, the subcommittee unanimously voted to present McCormack's proposal to the full committee.

Several days later, the full Committee on Interior and Insular Affairs convened to consider H.J. Res. 254.[14] This time, however, the bill met resistance almost immediately. Texas Representative Kenneth Mills Regan noted the many memorial proposals he had heard while serving on another committee, including those regarding the Louisiana Purchase Exposition in St. Louis and "many bills doing something for Columbus and Franklin Roosevelt, and probably 25 to 50 others."[15] All those bills, he noted, "we have postponed this year in the interest of economy." "If we pass this bill . . . it is contrary to the policy we have been following on similar memorials." Representative Wesley A. D'Ewart of Montana wondered why the National Trust for Historic Preservation couldn't manage the Boston project. Toward turning the tide, Chair John Murdock recalled from the subcommittee's deliberation "the similarity between this proposal and that carried out by the Committee and Congress at Philadelphia." "In these times," he continued, "when we have to fight ideologies which are so dangerous, we ought to further our own ideology with its roots and backgrounds as much as possible." C. Norris Poulson of California agreed. He recalled touring Great Britain during World War II and marveling at how its historic sites "create the love and admiration and respect for the past." "It certainly had a great tendency to fight Communism," he argued, "which is to destroy all those things and bring in new ideas." It was the appeals to anticommunism that made the difference. Despite some continued debate about the purpose of the National Trust, the committee voted and agreed to report the bill favorably.[16]

Although H.J. Res. 254 passed the House, it failed to arrive on the Senate floor before adjournment that year. It did, however, reemerge two years later when reintroduced by D'Ewart as H.J. Res. 122, though this time with a reduced appropriation of $30,000, no doubt intended to appease budget-minded congressmen.[17] Once again, D'Ewart noted a precedent for the bill in the legislation that, in 1936, established the Philadelphia National Shrine Park Commission and that eventually led to the establishment of Independence National Historical Park in 1948. A preliminary committee vote on advancing the bill resulted in a narrow 10-to-9 victory. After roll call, however, New York Representative James G. Donovan inexplicably changed his vote to "no," thus spelling defeat for the bill in committee. McCormack returned to the Subcommittee on Public Lands on May 4, 1955, to pitch the commission once again. Importantly, although McCormack hit several of the same notes as before—including the national significance of Boston's local heritage—he led this time with a different theme: "[Boston's] historic sites are perpetually threatened by . . . destruction by the bulldozers and steam shovels of progress." "If Paul Revere's house should collapse," he continued, "or if the highway authorities were to build an elevated expressway over Boston Common, that would be the loss, not of Boston alone, but of the Nation."[18] Managing urban renewal now joined with anticommunism as key rationale for shoring up Boston's heritage infrastructure. And it did so with evident success. Without any further debate, the subcommittee voted favorably to report the bill to the full committee wherefrom it advanced expeditiously.

THE BOSTON NATIONAL HISTORIC SITES COMMISSION

Congress established the Boston National Historic Sites Commission (BNHSC) by joint resolution on June 16, 1955, and outlined its charge in Public Law 75. On paper, at least, the BNHSC's task seemed straightforward: to investigate the "feasibility of establishing a coordinated program in which the federal government may cooperate with local and state governments and historical and patriotic societies for the preservation and appreciation by the public of the most important of the colonial and revolutionary properties in Boston and the general vicinity thereof which form outstanding examples of the United States' historical heritage."[19] The year of establishment, 1955, was a "critical period," it suggested, one during which "the inspiration afforded by such prime examples of the American historical heritage and their interpretation is in the public interest." "It is proper and desirable," therefore, that the United States preserve for public use "historic properties that are intimately associated with American Colonial solidarity and the establishment of American independence."[20] This was very clearly the language of anxious postwar lawmakers buoyed by the mid-century notion, promulgated by consensus historians, that Boston's Revolutionary holdovers recalled a bygone era of American "solidarity." In the hypercharged atmosphere of 1955—a year during which the Cold War filled headlines—Public Law 75's nostalgia for an era when political unity supposedly prevailed over a virtuous enemy aimed to manufacture consensus where little existed.

Despite all this, or perhaps because of it, the commission's mandate was riddled with quandaries: Which historical and patriotic societies ought the commission engage? What are the most important colonial and Revolutionary properties? What exactly does "general vicinity" mean? And what counts as an outstanding example of American historical heritage? To make matters more confusing, Public Law 75 allowed for consideration of "architectural merit" in addition to historical significance. Seven people would be chosen to settle these questions. They would include one member of the U.S. Senate, one from the House, one person appointed by the secretary of the interior, and four presidential appointees, including at least one from Boston. Together, these seven people would focus on completing four tasks outlined in the legislation: make an inventory of historic properties, including real estate costs; document the "existing condition" of the properties in its inventory; recommend mechanisms by which state, local, and federal governments might work with cooperating associations toward preserving whatever properties the commission considered "in the public interest;" and, finally, summarize all findings in a report and transmit it to Congress within two years. Congress granted the commission authority to hire expert advisers, if needed, only so long as its budget did not exceed $40,000 (about $360,000 today).[21]

The first matter of business, of course, was to assemble the commission. For its part, the Senate appointed Massachusetts Senator Leverett Saltonstall. Representative Thomas P. (Tip) O'Neill represented the House. As for the remaining four presidential appointees, NPS Director Conrad Wirth—the architect of Mission 66—recommended eight men, including himself. Most of his recommendations had made notable contributions to mid-century preservation, including William Graves Perry, whose architectural firm managed the restoration of Colonial Williamsburg. Others included wealthy Bostonians with antiquarian bents. Mining executive and bank president Seth Thomas Gano, for instance, served in numerous heritage organizations, including as treasurer of the Lantern League of Old North Church. Mark Bortman, a plastics and textile magnate, also held leadership positions throughout Boston's heritage landscape, including as chair of the Greater Boston Chamber of Commerce's Committee on Historic Places.[22] President Eisenhower endorsed Bortman, who would become a personal friend to the Eisenhower family in later years, but opted against Wirth's other recommendations in favor of individuals recommended through other channels: Boston attorney John P. Sullivan; Charles H. Watkins, president of the Old North Church Lantern League; and stalwart NPS ally, Louise DuPont Crowninshield. Finally, Wirth himself represented the Department of the Interior.

The commission's first meeting, at Salem National Historic Site in September 1955, foreshadowed tensions that would reemerge periodically over the course of its life. Senator Saltonstall had let it be known before the gathering that Watkins should be appointed commission chair. But because neither Saltonstall nor Watkins could attend the first meeting, O'Neill—who did—immediately nominated Bortman for the job.[23] Crowninshield responded by nominating Watkins on Saltonstall's behalf and then seconding the nomination herself. Sullivan seconded Bortman, thereby leaving Bortman with the deciding vote. Bortman, of course, endorsed himself, thereby winning the appointment.[24] A second vote, this time split three to two, made Sullivan the executive secretary.[25] NPS Northeast Regional Director Daniel Tobin attended the meeting in place of Wirth. As presiding officer, he could not vote, but later explained to Wirth that the meeting went "somewhat different from what had been anticipated [and] I am not at all sure but that it is an advantage to the National Park Service."[26] Crowninshield later recalled of the first meeting that "the Irish politicians . . . voted me down every time."[27] Word of the cantankerous first meeting spread throughout Boston's preservation community. In a letter to Wirth, Walter Muir Whitehill—Boston's arch heritage advocate and, eventually, a transitional figure in the commission's story—expressed his "hope that something useful will come out of this Boston Commission even though in many senses it has started off on an awkward foot."[28]

For its second meeting, just two weeks later, the commission gathered in its new headquarters in Boston's Post Office and Courthouse Federal Building. It appointed an executive committee—Bortman, Sullivan, Watkins, and Wirth—charged with sustaining "the proper conduct of the work of the Commission." It also made NPS Regional Director Tobin a designated alternate for Wirth, thus forming a core group that would meet regularly throughout the commission's life, with Crowninshield, Wirth, Saltonstall, and O'Neill joining only periodically.[29] Chief of Interpretation Young, who had surveyed Boston with Small in 1951, joined the meeting to discuss the steps taken in Philadelphia. Young also provided the commission with NPS criteria for the selection of historic sites, its inventory procedure for a historic sites survey, the National Trust's criteria for evaluating historic sites and buildings, and portions of the report he and Small had compiled in 1951. NPS Assistant Director Lee had cautioned that "inasmuch as this is a confidential report, our thinking here is that possibly [a few pages] might be released to the Commission." The report's suggestions concerning how to staff the commission and what sites to engage through cooperative agreements would thus be redacted, leaving just fieldnotes for the commission.[30] With that, the commission voted to define "Boston and vicinity" in the same terms that the NPS had: Boston and twenty-seven surrounding cities and towns.

It also voted to host its first public hearing. Park planning during the first half of the twentieth century had primarily been a top-down affair. In response to the remarkable expansion of federal bureaucracy during the New Deal years, however, Congress had sought to ensure a stronger public voice by passing the Administrative Procedures Act in 1946. The new law required that all federal projects solicit public input and that all federal meetings be open to the public.[31] The commission, working with a mailing list provided by Boston University History Professor Robert Moody, thus invited historical and patriotic organizations to gather in November so that it might "explain the objectives of Public Law 75."[32] Minutes from the gathering do not appear to exist, possibly because the commission had yet to hire a stenographer.[33] The *Christian Science Monitor*, however, reported that the "lively meeting made plain that plenty of New Englanders are eager to preserve their historic landmarks." Their hopes for doing so evidently ran the gamut, from ridding Faneuil Hall of meat vendors to restoring West Roxbury's oldest standing school.[34]

Meanwhile the commission still struggled to get its own procedures in order. Although Wirth had granted Tobin authority to appoint personnel and spend whatever money was necessary, correspondence reveals constant confusion concerning the commission's spending authority, how to obtain office supplies, and even whether or not the government would pay for its postage expenses.[35] The commission's sole action at its November meeting, after the public hearing, was a unanimous vote that Sullivan write to the secretary of the interior "for assistance in expediting the appointment of a stenographer."[36] Bortman explained to Saltonstall's office that "at this moment we are completely stymied . . . because of the lack of efficient co-operation from the proper bureaus in Washington."[37] The situation was so dire that Tobin recommended to Wirth a decrease in the commission's 1956 fiscal year operations fund given that "delays . . . and lapses" had resulted in "considerably lesser need for funds . . . than was originally programmed."[38]

By spring 1956, however, the commission had hit its pace, partly as a result of appointing a trusted hand as chief of party: Edwin Small. When Tobin first approached him about working for the commission, Small worried that the assignment might jeopardize his tenure at Salem. But with adequate assurances that his appointment at Salem would remain for him, Small signed on as the commission's principal researcher, writer, and agency liaison.[39] It was a crucial turning point that, in many ways, determined the direction of the commission's work. Indeed, years later, Small recalled that he "actually did all the work [of the commission]," adding that he even "initiated and presented the ideas." Before his arrival, according to Small, the commission "had a couple of public hearings, but nobody knew quite what to do so I came in. I got a hold of things and got 'em going."[40]

A BIG ROLE FOR EDWIN SMALL

The commission formally appointed Small, in fact, at the very same February meeting wherein it hosted a second public hearing, this time for officers of state and local government concerned with preservation in and around Boston.[41] Not unlike the November 1955 meeting, during which the commission heard from representatives of historical and patriotic organizations, the February 1956 gathering of state and local government representatives generated lively conversation among over fifty participants. Many of the participants, like the city historian of Quincy, came to advocate for consideration of particular sites, such as the two Adams birthplaces and the site of the first railroad in the United States. Not all the participants belonged to governmental organizations. A representative of the West Roxbury Historical Society, for instance, again petitioned the commission to consider the neighborhood's first schoolhouse. The matter of Faneuil Hall's meat markets emerged again too. George P. Donaan of Boston's Real Property Department asked that the commission advocate for "a more dignified environment for Faneuil Hall," along the lines of "Independence Hall in Philadelphia." The city, he indicated, hoped that the commission might particularly help with Faneuil Hall, "where it has been suggested that the markets be eliminated . . . and cleaned up." The suggestion encouraged others to voice similar concerns about Faneuil Hall, and fore-shadowed a debate—as we will see—that would return with a vengeance in following months.[42]

A topic that particularly interested Commission Chair Bortman was the potential profitability of Boston's heritage landscape. Lenox E. Bigelow, representing the Massachusetts Department of Commerce, volunteered that "his agency was looking at the Commission's work in a little different way—they were looking at it in a commercial sense." Bigelow reported that his department had surveyed vacation travelers and found "very definitely" that "visitors want to 'see' history." He estimated that vacation travel could earn Massachusetts $425 million each year, but that "we have failed in a great degree by not publicizing." Bortman wondered if travel might be increased "if we put on a show similar to Williamsburg." "Our historic spots are there," he added, "they just needed pointing out." Bortman's concern with profit, like worries over meat markets in Faneuil Hall, would become a recurrent theme in the commission's deliberations.[43]

By March 1956, having gathered community input and with the vital addition of Edwin Small, the commission finally hit its stride. It did so, in part, by tasking Small with much of its work. He managed contact with interested Bostonians, including local artists eager to sketch out what a new national park might look like. The commission largely dismissed the artists, though Small viewed their work anyway, toward insuring "against any possible criticism that the Commission was disinterested in the cooperation of the public."[44] Small also reached out to the Boston City Planning Board, directed by Thomas E. McCormick, which had worked up a preliminary plan to redevelop the North End waterfront and create a park for the USS *Constitution*. Nobody on the commission, however, expected the city to pay for the project and, besides, Small thought the planning board "has done very little work . . . and has nothing to offer that would be of any interest to the commission."[45]

It is difficult to overstate the extent to which Small's opinions about preservation, historical significance, and community engagement—shaped over long years of working in New England—framed the commission's deliberations. They did so, in part, by merit of Small's copious list making. At the commission's sixth meeting, for instance, Small submitted the first of his surveys of historic properties, what was in essence a first draft of what would become the commission's final report. In it, Small identified ten properties with potential for inclusion in a national park, including with each entry an assessment of each building's "survival value"—how much of its eighteenth-century fabric remained—its relative significance to the commission's period of concern, and whether or not action by the commission was needed to ensure the building's preservation. Four properties in particular garnered the most conversation: the Old State House, Old North Church, the Bunker Hill Monument, and Faneuil Hall.[46] Small presented the Old State House as vitally significant, though poorly restored inside and mismanaged besides. The commission resolved to approach the Bostonian Society, which managed the building, and the city, which owned it, about paths forward. The Old North Church presented a different set of problems. Though also highly significant, its private owners could not manage the site's growing popularity among heritage tourists nor adequately protect it from fire hazards. Bunker Hill, under the jurisdiction of the Metropolitan District Commission, was "in deplorable condition" according to Small and, despite its iconic place in Revolutionary memory, had "no survival value" and was "of national significance for the 19th century" alone.[47] Just these three cases made clear how difficult it would be to develop a single partnership strategy suitable for so many permutations of site ownership and management.

And then, of course, there was an even more troubling question: could the commission, which had been charged by Congress to protect "colonial and revolutionary properties," reasonably act on a site like Bunker Hill, which had no tangible link to those periods outside of popular memory? It was a question intensified by the situation at Faneuil Hall. Small reported that Faneuil Hall, like the Bunker Hill Monument, possessed virtually no survival value before the nineteenth century. "The test," he explained, "is if a person who lived in that age would recognize the building as it now stands, and that Faneuil Hall would not be recognized." Tobin argued that the Historic Sites Act of 1935 protected sites, not just buildings, and that Faneuil Hall's location was itself worthy of protection. Small agreed and joined with Bortman in recognizing that "public opinion would doubtless require the commission to make some recommendations regarding improvements or changes in the condition of the market and the shops on the ground floor."[48] At this crucial moment in the development of a park concept for Boston, then, the agency's rationale for including sites such as Faneuil Hall and Bunker Hill rested not on architectural significance, nor necessarily on historical significance, but rather on the embeddedness of those places in Boston's Revolutionary memories and the insistence by "public opinion" that those memories not change.

FANEUIL HALL, URBAN RENEWAL, AND THE COST OF MEAT

The commission's preoccupation with Faneuil Hall's ground-floor shops is worth dwelling on, as it recalls a pitched battle in Boston over the appropriate ends of historic preservation, a battle into which the commission drifted almost immediately. For as long as anyone could remember, Faneuil Hall served as one entrepôt in a citywide network of outdoor market spaces. Indeed, Boston merchant Peter Faneuil, for whom the building was named, gifted it to the town in 1740 on the condition that its ground level remain a market space in perpetuity. Despite the building's transformations, and periods during which

vendors likely did not dominate its street-level arcade, meat and produce wholesale merchants had been a fixture there since at least the end of the nineteenth
century. After World War II, however, as Boston's urban renewal campaign
sought to build a new arterial highway through the center of town, the markets
became a point of contention. By 1950, for instance, Massachusetts State Senator
Charles I. Taylor sought to relocate the markets, claiming that "between four
and five million dollars are wasted each year because the Faneuil Hall market
area cannot economically handle the present volume of business."[49] Within a
year, the newly formed Massachusetts Market Authority had identified a two-
hundred-acre plot in South Bay where it aimed to build "the world's largest
market district" to relocate Faneuil Hall merchants, many of whom had already
received eviction notices. "It has become a construction race," the *Boston Globe*
reported, "between the new arterial highway and the new market district,"
and the merchants' "business depends on the new market district winning."[50]

   Certainty there were those who had been "sold" on the idea, but others
"remember[ed] Peter Faneuil and the obstacles facing him back in 1740."[51] The
obstacles they referred to regarded ensuring timely construction of the building
and also Faneuil's difficulties working with the City of Boston, but Boston meat
merchants had other reasons to draw parallels between themselves and the colonial merchants who chafed against taxation from afar. New federal standards in
1951—the very same year McCormack proposed the Boston National Historic
Sites Commission—forced Boston butchers to abandon local traditions such as
removing bone from steaks and other cuts of meat. According to "one veteran
Faneuil Hall district market man," reported the *Boston Globe*, "the only thing
I recognize there [in the new standards] is hamburg."[52] Federal regulations,
intended to standardize meat costs and availability across the United States,
received mixed reviews in Boston after their first six months. Independent
merchants complained that "there never was a shortage of anything, except
customers," and that sales had fallen with the rise of prices. Chain retailers
seemed pleased with the arrangement, as did some independent merchants
who perceived opportunities associated with postwar defense contracts, such
as with nearby Hanscom Air Force Base and the Massachusetts Institute of
Technology. "We don't like anybody meddling with our free economy," noted
one Faneuil Hall merchant, "but it certainly seems called for here."[53]

   As work continued on the Central Artery, however, the holdouts faced
increasing pressure to move on. Indeed, the artery construction aimed to
wipe out—as the *Globe* put it—"the entire market district with the exception

of Faneuil Hall."[54] The elimination of so much tax-generating commercial real estate in Boston's cramped downtown put Faneuil Hall firmly in the eyes of politicians and developers wanting to squeeze a profit out of whatever remained. At the same time, the success of the Freedom Trail had, since 1951, encouraged a whole new scale of interest in the building and its capacity to attract tourists. By 1953, for instance, Faneuil Hall's three custodians managed forty thousand visitors each year. To some, the "rich smell of raw meat which clings to the building" heightened Faneuil Hall's historicity.[55] In fact, as the years passed, something remarkable happened: Faneuil Hall's meat merchants flourished! By 1955, plans to remove and centralize its tenants in South Bay had crumbled amid a host of challenges: failed financing, ineffective city leadership, and independent wholesalers' desire to stick with a routine that worked quite well for them. The *Globe* reported that Faneuil Hall's market district, though "supposedly doomed [is] still doing business as usual and shows no signs of abandoning its centuries-old location."[56] At a time, then, when developers sought to lure white suburban housewives into sanitized downtowns, and

FIGURE 4. A meat vendor presents his wares in Faneuil Hall, 1941. Leslie Jones Collection, Boston Public Library, Boston, MA.

as supermarkets gradually displaced corner stores and merchant shops, the timeless appeal of Faneuil Hall's gritty intimacies created a real challenge for proponents of the New Boston.[57]

As we have seen, debates regarding the appropriateness of meat merchants in Faneuil Hall spilled immediately into the commission's work. At its first public hearing, for instance, G. Harris Danzberger, a public relations executive from Philadelphia, complained about "the clutter and debris" around Faneuil Hall and argued that it ought to be "restored on the pattern of Sturbridge Village or Old Williamsburg," with "cabinet-making shops, tobacco, weaving, pottery, food and herbs shops," which could turn, he supposed, just as much profit for the city.[58] Danzberger pitched the idea in a letter to the *Boston Sunday Herald*. "Is there any chance," he wondered, "of rescuing this building and restoring it as a business landmark[, a] greater source of revenue to the city and . . . a thing of beauty and a joy forever."[59] Publicly, Bortman dismissed the notion out of hand, positioning himself in a longstanding debate among preservationists over the wisdom of creating historical replicas. "Our job is limited to listing historic sites and making recommendations for their preservation," he explained to the *Globe*, "we are not authorized . . . to build colonial structures."[60]

FIGURE 5. Illustration from G. Harris Danzberger, "A Sturbridge Village in Faneuil Hall," *Boston Sunday Herald*, January 15, 1956. Clipping appears in Folder: BNHSC A 2015, 2nd Hearing 2/6/1956, Box 1, NER New England Field Office–Boston, BNHSC 1955–66, National Archives at Boston, Waltham, MA.

Behind closed doors, however, the commission sympathized with Danzberger. At a meeting that May, for instance, the commission generally agreed that the meat merchants should be relocated so that the building's first floor might be more profitably turned toward parking and meetings of the Ancient and Honorable Artillery Company, the nation's oldest military fraternal organization, whose museum, library, and meeting spaces had long occupied Faneuil Hall's top floor.[61] Later that year, the commission heard directly from the Ancients about their plans to adopt Danzberger's ideas. "The main object," they argued, "is to have the place presentable in such a manner that tourists, who come from all over the country . . . will see something consistent with our past history."[62] But what really seems to have concerned the Ancients, as Captain Thomas Carty relayed, was "the possibility of the Federal Government taking over Faneuil Hall." Carty feared that the Ancients "might lose their local identity in the vastness of the Federal Government [and thus their] local right to occupy the building."[63] Presented with these concerns, the commission suggested that the Ancients not necessarily take up Danzberger's suggestions, but rather consider the possibility of operating the building's street level as a visitor center for heritage tourists. "The important thing was effective interpretation," pointed out Regional Director Tobin. Under the right circumstances, he added, visitation could approach more than a million per year, as it had at Independence National Historical Park in Philadelphia. Appropriately managing Faneuil Hall under those conditions, Tobin emphasized, "is not only a matter of business, it is a matter of good citizenship—an investment in citizen redevelopment."[64]

In this way, the meat market debates laid bare a considerable difference of opinion within the commission over the very purpose of historic preservation and, by extension, a national historical park in Boston. On one side was Bortman, who seemed eager to turn preservation into profit. "It was a decided asset from both a historical and a business point of view," he opined, "that a number of historical places were in the proximity of a fifteen minute walk of the department stores and the business section of Boston."[65] On the other side was Tobin, whose concern for "citizen redevelopment" suggested some faith in the notion that doing good history could, alongside urban renewal, reinforce the prospects of American democracy. For a time, this difference in opinion remained just that. Tobin, while more broadly concerned than Bortman about the complexity of the meat market situation, was never convinced that the venders were themselves somehow representative of a bygone era. He agreed with Edwin Small's sentiment that "the keeping of the market men is, in effect, subsidized by the City, and hence is just as artificial as [Danzinger's] 'shoppes.'"[66]

What had begun as a polite difference of opinion, however, exploded into a full-on war during 1957. The catalyst had been the sudden death that year of Commissioner Charles Watkins. The commission acted quickly to replace Watkins and settled on Walter Muir Whitehill, renowned president of the Boston Athenaeum and voracious advocate for Boston's historic resources. During the commission's August 16, 1957, meeting, Whitehill engaged immediately with the meat market question. The issue had reemerged with the suggestion, this time by Ronald Lee, that Faneuil Hall be cast as a visitor center "for the whole Boston program."[67] Whitehill agreed to the possibility, so long as the meat stalls stayed put. "They are," he insisted, "the one living sense of the eighteenth century." Letters poured in, some no doubt at Whitehill's urging, from organizations seeking to defend the meat markets. The Society for the Preservation of New England Antiquities opposed "any changes [that would] adversely affect the appealing flavor and genuineness [sic] of this important building." The Colonial Society of Massachusetts dismissed as a "spurious masquerade" any plans to replace market vendors with "pseudo-picturesque souvenirs." The Massachusetts Historical Society "strongly opposes any step toward removing the markets in Faneuil Hall." Carty restated his concern, on behalf of the Ancients, that "housekeeping and disposal methods of the meat purveyors and wholesale vegetable and fruit dealers . . . are primitive." "It is not uncommon," he added," for visitors to have to step over or walk around decaying cabbage with its revolting odor before they can enter this historic shrine."[68]

The problem of Faneuil Hall consumed the commission's November meeting. Despite agreement that Danzberger's letter to the *Boston Sunday Herald* had created a false impression of what the commission anticipated for Faneuil Hall, tensions erupted around the issue of cleanliness. Crowninshield expressed little concern with what happened inside the building, just so long as the "exterior should be kept clean and the [vendor] canopies removed." Whitehill agreed about the canopies but noted that it was the "city's job to keep the sidewalks clean." Bortman protested, countering that the vendors made the area impossible to clean. Tobin pointed out that the city's entire historic core was "dirty and unattractive" and that Faneuil Hall was part of a larger problem that "could be controlled by leasing." Small tried to make a historical argument, suggesting that there had always been opposition to the meat markets. And, besides, in his estimation the vendors likely wouldn't remain if the canopies were removed from the building's exterior.[69] A presentation of plans for the area, sponsored by the Chamber of Commerce, further intensified disagreement. The first portrayed Faneuil Hall's first floor gutted to make room for a visitor center and museum space for the Ancients. Bortman lauded it; Whitehill chafed. The second plan, an exterior view, showed Faneuil Hall standing virtually alone, "with the unimportant old buildings removed," surrounded by highways. Whitehill railed against "the prospect of re-creating Boston from ideas without any actual detailed information to go on." We "are not dealing with another Williamsburg," he insisted, but rather with "a city that has a life of its own." [70]

The commission opted not to go on record concerning the fate of Faneuil Hall, but that didn't stop Whitehill, Bortman, and their surrogates from slugging it out in Boston's newspapers. Whitehill landed the first blows during December 1957, with editorials in the *Boston Globe* and *Boston Herald*. A summation of these appeared in the January 1958 edition of the Boston Athenaeum's newsletter, wherein Whitehill expressed his fear that "historic restoration and reconstructions," such as what had been proposed for Faneuil Hall, had become so popular in the United States as to imperil "the safety of certain historic monuments that have survived to the present day."[71] Noted Boston writer and arts promoter Francis W. Hatch bent to the cause that February, publishing a tongue-in-cheek poem on the plight of Faneuil Hall in the *Boston Globe*.[72] Ronald F. Lee reported to the regional director that Hatch's "In the Name of Peter Faneuil: Beef Before Baubles" was "widely posted in clubs, societies, and bookstores in Boston."[73] By March, pundits joked about forming a "Let-it-Alone Club . . . namely, to 'look for something which is getting along perfectly well and then,—just let it alone!" Even *the Pilot*, the official newspaper of the Archdiocese of Boston, published an editorial lambasting plans to renovate Faneuil Hall, presuming the idea must have been "brought in by gypsies."[74] The appeal to Catholic Bostonians—and thus to the predominantly Irish and Italian market vendors—drew Bortman into the fight. In a publicized telephone call with Monsignor Francis J. Lally, Bortman asked that "another side" be considered. "It is important that visitors to our city," he explained, "should be lifted by the experience of seeing our great places of history rather than filled with feelings of disappointment and revulsion."[75]

Interestingly, as both sides battled on—*the Boston Herald* generally anti-meat market, and the *Globe* generally pro—the NPS watched with careful attention, and some amusement. Small received orders to create a file of all relevant press coverage. Notes in the margins of copies that circulated among regional NPS staff suggest considerable regard for Whitehill's position, and some reflection on what the argument revealed about preservation policy going forward.[76] In the end, however, it appears that Whitehill's campaign backfired. That February, Small reported to Tobin that as a result of the media storm, Mayor Hynes had constituted a special committee to study the meat market issue. Its members included the City Art Commission chair, the mayor's industrial adviser, the president of the Boston and Maine Railroad, and none other than head Ancient, Thomas Carty. Small stated the obvious: "the composition of the committee points with little doubt to a majority in favor of getting rid of the markets." Small intimated that the mayor sought "to eliminate the markets, irrespective of the protests." In the mayor's mind, he explained, the question is: "shall we continue to operate the building mainly as a wholesale meat mart or shall we operate the building as a patriotic shrine."[77] Small suggested that the "traditionalists," if they wanted to retain any space for the markets within sight of Faneuil Hall, would be best served by imagining ways to relocate the markets into Quincy Market, where a fruit and produce exchange had vacated a few months earlier. As was so often the case, Small's sense of things would prove propitious.[78]

A WRONG TURN DOWN THE BATTLE ROAD

The story of Faneuil Hall's meat markets reveals the extent to which the BNHSC was, from its outset, deeply divided and frequently distracted from its core responsibilities. Indeed, since Small himself had already completed most of the commission's work, all that remained was to devise a way to bring Boston's various historic sites into some kind of federal stewardship umbrella. But even this seemed unmanageable, despite frequent and not-so-subtle suggestions from Wirth and Tobin to consider, and perhaps even emulate, the process that had worked so well in Philadelphia. To be fair, the BNHSC had come into existence amid radical transformations in Boston's built environment, and the temptation to respond to urban renewal—either with support, in Bortman's case, or with skepticism in Whitehill's—was difficult to resist. And yet, the impossibility of avoiding the meat market imbroglio—and, more broadly, the complexities of memory, profit, and preservation in Boston's historic core—clearly made the BNHSC eager for a problem it could realistically contend with.

Just such a problem presented itself during spring 1956. That May, Bortman concluded that since "the survey work on the City of Boston is pretty near completed, the commission should start thinking about the Concord–Lexington area."[79] The area Bortman had in mind, of course, was the celebrated Battle Road stretching between the towns of Lexington and Concord and along which Longfellow imagined Paul Revere riding to warn "every Middlesex village and farm." Bortman, incidentally, had a deep personal interest in the Paul Revere story and had even played a key role in returning Revere's so-called Liberty Bowl to the Boston Museum of Fine Arts.[80] Nearly fifteen miles northwest of Boston, however, the Battle Road presented a very different set of circumstances than Boston's core historic area. Bortman perceived it to be "the most important project the commission will have from a national point of view," and he argued that the prospect of preserving an entire road and its context was more likely to interest Congress than the possibility of protecting a few buildings in Boston.[81] What's more, the Battle Road project had already been planned for, in 1925, by landscape architect Arthur Schurcliff.[82] And, as it happened, Shurcliff sent a copy of his plans to the BNHSC that June.[83]

What made the matter of the Battle Road so pressing, in Bortman's mind, was the arrival there of the same "bulldozers and steam shovels of progress" about which McCormack had warned Congress when discussing downtown Boston. These too had been mobilized by federally funded postwar development projects, particularly the expansion of Hanscom Air Force Base. Massachusetts had set to work, just outside of Boston, on building a civil airfield with federal investment during the early days of World War II. As the war effort expanded so did the air base, where federal employees flocked to develop high-tech electronic systems, including radar, for military applications. Growth continued into the Cold War years, bringing more technicians and their families to suburban Boston. A radical expansion of State Route 128 accommodated growth along the so-called technology corridor, as did connectors including Route 2A, which transected key portions of Revere's famous ride. Road building, a proliferation of new housing, commercial development everywhere between, and profit-seeking investors complicated Shurcliff's thirty-year-old plan and signaled the likelihood that implementing it might soon be impossible. But what most startled the BNHSC were plans by the air base itself to build hundreds of new housing units right atop the Josiah Nelson homesite, where local lore recalled Nelson as the first casualty of the American Revolution.[84]

Small joined Bortman in encouraging the BNHSC toward an engagement with the Battle Road. So much had changed since 1925, he argued, that the historic landscape would soon be irretrievable.[85] Saltonstall urged the BNHSC to leave the problem of the Battle Road to the state legislature, but the committee persisted.[86] By October 1956, the BNHSC had turned full bore to the problem of the Battle Road, including by staging a conversation with various community representatives at its meeting that month. Tobin urged caution, worrying that any word of NPS interest in the area might spark a land run and make prices prohibitive even for the federal government.[87] Small threw himself entirely into the project, recalling later "that if something weren't done very soon it would be completely absorbed in a sprawling suburbia."[88] The problem, however, was proposing a boundary area inclusive of three towns—Lexington, Lincoln, and Concord—and considerable private property therein. What's more, none of the towns involved in the project had assembled property maps by the time Small arrived on the scene. He, his secretary Rita A. Farrell, Lexington town planner Samuel P. Snow, and a real estate agent named Harry Bergland worked together for a year, sifting through registries of deeds, speaking with officials, assessing property values, and drawing up maps, which avoided property severances wherever possible.[89] In conversation with Small years later, former Chief of Information Herb Evison characterized these boundary challenges as "one of the most interesting and probably one of the most complicated things that you've been involved in."[90]

Evison was right: the BNHSC's interim 1959 report on the Battle Road—a report, it's important to note, written entirely by Small and Farrell—advanced a remarkably bold and innovative plan for a new national park encompassing over seven hundred acres spread across two discrete units and at a cost of nearly five million dollars in land purchases alone (approximately $43 million today).[91] It's also worth noting that the report was a stopgap of sorts for the BNHSC, insomuch as it had to produce something for Congress after years of wheel spinning and after having received two term extensions. Small's report demonstrated that, though the BNHSC may not have yet managed the Boston problem, it had invested considerable efforts in developing a proposal for the Battle Road.

Small's was a three-part plan. First, the commission recommended that the secretary of interior, with authority granted by the Historic Sites Act of 1935, negotiate cooperative agreements with seven specific regional governments and heritage societies, and any number of others as necessary, to protect nationally significant historical properties along or adjacent to the Battle Road. A second recommendation concerned erecting a twenty-mile stretch of historical markers all the way from downtown Boston to the Barrett Farm outside of Concord, thereby marking relevant sites not otherwise eligible for protection. Finally, the commission recommended a surgical bout of land purchase intended to permanently protect a four-mile stretch of the Battle Road and Concord's famous North Bridge from "shattering changes on the historic landscape and the irrecoverable loss of historical values."[92] Small's recommendations, as put forth in the report, laid the foundation for Public Law 86–321, which on September 21, 1959, authorized establishment of Minute Man National Historical Park.[93]

With its interim report complete, the BNHSC turned once again to Boston's heritage landscape, though the Battle Road project never drifted out of focus. Indeed, Small's report seemed to suggest that Boston's problems might be untenable. He described Route 128, for instance, as "the dividing line today between the retrievable and irretrievable past," lamenting the destruction of "historical values east of Lexington."[94] Perhaps Boston, he hinted, might take cues from the mix of partnership and land purchase he proposed for the Battle Road, which could "be the mainspring by which a 'coordinated program' can work to the advantage of all groups . . . in the vicinity of Boston."[95] Chief Historian Ronald Lee encouraged the BNHSC to call "the whole business by one name and one project," rather than to conceive of the Battle Road and the Boston sites as constituting separate parks. Whitehill agreed, noting that "Lexington–Concord was merely a military excursion from Boston and is very closely tied in ordering to the proposed Boston program."[96] Whitehill's tone betrayed his concern that the BNHSC had invested far too much of its time in the Battle Road. Indeed, when the commission requested a year-long extension and additional funding from Congress in December 1957—because, as Small put it, "very little progress has been made with the major problems in Boston Proper during the past year"—Whitehill lashed out.[97] He wrote directly to Wirth that the extension was, in his opinion, "an unwarranted use of public funds" and threatened to undermine the NPS's reputation "in quarters in Boston that are now well disposed."[98] Wirth dismissed the concern, noting that the BNHSC would need the time to satisfy its legal commitment.[99]

It appears though, that Whitehill had good reason to worry that the BNHSC had lost its focus on Boston's core historic area. As late as July 1958, Small was still wrestling with problems of presenting plans for the Battle Road, and particularly how to do it on one simple map. In his report to the regional director that month, Small acknowledged that the commission was returning to the Boston problem and that it was developing an "explanatory narrative" along the lines of what it had produced for the Battle Road. The Battle Road project, it turned out, had influenced how the BNHSC had thought about its approach to Boston. But dealing with Boston, Small explained, was "more difficult" than the Battle Road "owing to the fact that the political issues and machinery for the Revolution are far less vivid and capable of reduction to simple terms than any of military nature."[100] Again, as difficulties befell the Battle Road proposal—including a "flurry of real estate activity" the NPS had evidently triggered after all—the BNHSC retreated into affairs unrelated to the fundamental task of proposing a stewardship schema for Boston.[101] Small wrote once again to Tobin suggesting that the commission seek another extension. By May, however, Wirth insisted that the commission finish its work, noting conversations with congressmen who would "look with disfavor on further extensions."[102]

A PLAN FOR BOSTON

So, what in the end did the BNHSC propose for Boston? A quick glance of its 1961 summary report suggests a straightforward plan. First, the commission recommended that the NPS coordinate management of seven national historic sites in Boston. It proposed that two of them—the Old State House and the Shirley-Eustis House—be acquired outright by the federal government. Another four—the North Square, containing the Paul Revere House; Old North Church; Faneuil Hall; and the Bunker Hill Monument—could be designated national historic sites while remaining in nonfederal ownership. That, of course, was the situation already in place at Dorchester Heights National Historic Site, which itself would constitute the seventh site in the agency's constellation of Boston historic sites. And, like Dorchester Heights, other sites remaining in nonfederal ownership would be at least partially managed by the NPS, insomuch as concerned preservation and interpretation, by way of cooperative agreements between the organizations that owned them and the secretary of interior. The creation of one or more historic districts under commonwealth law—such as had already been done at Beacon Hill and Lexington—would complete the picture. Capping it all off would be the acquisition of property in town for a visitor center, a coherent signage system for marking historic sites, and the creation of an advisory board to manage the fledgling park through establishment and negotiate the contours of its constitutive cooperative agreements for several years thereafter.[103]

Look beyond the summary, though, and the BNHSC's final report yields fascinating insights concerning the National Park Service's complex relationship with history and place making in the mid-century United States. It was a time when the NPS was still very much invested in old ideas about building parks on federally owned or donated land and then buying up whatever adjacent bits remained in private ownership. The notion that a park could be cobbled together around cooperative partnerships with nonfederal landowners—as Small had proposed at Minute Man and now in Boston—was novel in 1961. Consider that, as NPS Bureau Historian John Sprinkle explains it, the NPS had not yet even grown comfortable with the concept of a historic district.[104] Laws that built critical bridges between state and federal stewardship, such as the Land and Water Conservation Fund Act of 1965 and the National Historic Preservation Act of 1966, had yet to hit the books. There were not even standard guidelines within the NPS for purchasing land or protecting sellers' rights until the Relocation Act of 1970 created the framework for a coherent policy.[105] For decades the agency's own leaders derided so-called partnership parks as a "thinning of the blood." It wasn't until the 1980s that dramatic contractions in congressional funding forced them to endorse cooperative alternatives, such as national heritage areas.[106] But none of that existed when the BNHSC set to its work. So, what models did Small have in mind?

He may have been inspired by another innovative NPS project unfolding at exactly the same time and within just a short drive of Boston. Just as it had in Boston, the NPS became interested in the possibility of protecting portions of Cape Cod's seashore during the 1930s. Conrad Wirth, who led the agency's Civilian Conservation Corps division back then, had funded a feasibility study for protecting public seashores all along the east coast. And just as it had in Boston, World War II sidetracked the project. During the war years, however, nascent state-level conservation initiatives kept the project alive so that, by 1957 when Mission 66 monies became available, the park service—now under Wirth's directorship—swept into action. Compared to what the BNHSC had been up to in Boston, work on the Cape Cod project unfolded at lightning speed. Wirth, who personally pitched the plan to residents, clearly had a personal interest in its success. It made a difference. In 1961, Congress authorized the establishment of Cape Cod National Seashore. And, unlike any other unit previously authorized, this one would be managed

in its entirety in partnership with residents who agreed to embrace zoning
ordinances as an alternative to land condemnation. What's more, Cape Cod's
legislation established a park advisory commission—the first of its kind in
NPS history—representing all the various offices of local, state, and federal
government that might come into partnership amid the project.[107]

It's hard to imagine that the BNHSC's own suggestion that a park in Boston
also have an advisory commission wasn't in at least some way inspired by the
goings-on in Cape Cod. Meeting minutes suggest that Small and the other
commissioners were very well aware of that project. And how could they not
be? Its most visible principals—Conrad Wirth, Dan Tobin, Tip O'Neill, Ted
Kennedy, and Leverett Saltonstall—and their staffs all also had a hand in
the Boston project. It is true that, from the agency's perspective, comparing
parks in Boston and Cape Cod would have been like comparing apples and
oranges. Boston's was a national historical park and Cape Cod's a new kind
of unit, a national seashore. It was more than a semantic difference. The NPS
gathered different kinds of planners from different corners of the agency with
different priorities to work on Cape Cod. And, of course, its various private
and federal monies flowed from different sources. That everyone seemed
more eager to advance the Cape Cod project, however, speaks to the sense of
uncertainty that would linger for years in deliberations surrounding Boston's
would-be history park.

But there were also other significant changes afoot in Boston that clearly
shaped Small's thinking. It was in 1954, for instance, just a year before Congress
authorized the BNHSC, that federal redevelopment policy shifted dramatically. Whereas redevelopment had previously been pinned to "slum" clearance
and public housing, the Housing Act of 1954 moved federal policies toward
what advocates now called "urban renewal." Renewal, unlike redevelopment,
favored federal support of private developers and the building up of commercial districts. It was precisely the shift that explains why, during the 1950s in
places like Boston, chambers of commerce enjoyed powerful new alliances
with city government.[108] And, as we've seen, those new alignments triggered
other unlikely counteralignments. Consider, for instance, how Boston's meat
market debates forged new solidarities between brahmin such as Walter Muir
Whitehill and Faneuil Hall's workaday food vendors. Boston's social and
political landscape was once again in flux, and at issue were ideas about profit,
history, and the appropriate relationship of the federal government to both.

The imprint of these realignments is evident all throughout the BNHSC's deliberations, and especially so in its 1961 proposal for a national historical park in Boston. The report encourages the preservation of seven historic sites, each surrounded by a discrete historic area. An additional historical area is proposed to encompass the Old Corner Bookstore, King's Chapel, and the Old South Meeting House.[109] The use of areas as an organizing principle clearly mimicked the language of urban renewal. Consider, for instance, the Faneuil Hall area, which Small imagined as including the commercial buildings along North and South Market Streets, the Union Oyster House, the Ebenezer Hancock House, and the Boston Stone "in the block of ancient alleys and lanes circumscribed by Union, Hanover, Blackstone, and North Streets."[110] The Faneuil Hall area, according to the report, was "the only sizable part of the central core of Old Boston that is practical to consider setting apart or organizing as a perpetual area of both traditional activity and historical interest."[111] And yet, the report continued, what might become of the area was entirely subject to plans then in development for Boston's new Government Center, "a project . . . closely allied to the objectives of urban renewal." What might be done in the face of such imminent though unpredictable change? The BNHSC recommended three steps: negotiate a cooperative agreement between the Department of Interior and the City of Boston to protect Faneuil Hall; instruct the advisory board to take steps toward establishing a state historic district corresponding with the area; and, if the district did not come to fruition, instruct the board to recommend how the Department of Interior might buy up land and property toward protecting the historic area.[112]

The BNHSC's recommendations regarding the Faneuil Hall area thus also mirrored its members' conflicting attitudes concerning redevelopment and renewal. Small and Bortman, of course, were strong advocates for demolition and resident relocation. Whitehill was not. In chapter three we will see how, in the long term, Whitehill's vision in this regard came to bear considerably more on plans for a national park in Boston. Looking back on the BNHSC's final report, however, it is remarkable how fully it endorsed condemnation of private property given the ferocity of reaction among Bostonians to, for instance, the West End Development Project. "The purchase of a considerable number of properties in private ownership will be necessary," the report indicated, to eliminate "adjacent or intervening structures that are incongruous intrustions [sic] or fire hazards." Doing so, it continued, is essential for "any effective program for improvement or permanent historical renewal."[113] Areas targeted for property acquisition and demolition included the North Square Area, Paul Revere Mall within the Old North Church area, and Shirley Place. Altogether the report called for the acquisition of forty-six parcels covering more than two acres, most of it "largely occupied by outmoded and decaying tenements and commercial slums."[114] In the North Square, for instance, the report called for "removal of the privately owned structures that objectionably intrude."[115] The historical setting of the North End, around the Old North Church area, it contended, "was blotted out during the last century by intensive construction of brick tenements and a public school . . . congestion that breeds only blight and decay."[116] And only by buying up the land around Shirley Place, could the NPS restore the "magnificent setting . . . swallowed up by tenements for migrants from the central city" and consequently surrounded by "urban blight and decay."[117] Preserving historic Boston, according to the BNHSC, would require considerable destruction, and the removal of people whose lives did not affirm its ideas about the Revolution and its legacy.

* * *

Recounting the Boston National Historic Site Commission's story is vital for understanding how and why a national park got made in Boston. Although, as we will see in the following chapters, the park's 1974 authorizing legislation veered in important ways from the BNHSC's recommendations, it nonetheless perpetuated core facets of the commission's vision, which remain intact even today. The strength of the BNHSC's influence, therefore, demands that we ask a difficult question: was the BNHSC successful? Officially, at least, the BNHSC passed two critical thresholds of success. First, it satisfied a procedural audit by the Comptroller General of the United States, which found no improper conduct or use of funds.[118] Second, it spawned not just one, but two national parks. The first, of course, was Minute Man National Historical Park in 1959. The other—the one it had actually been tasked with creating—earned approval in October 1964 from the Advisory Board on National Parks, Historic Sites, Buildings and Monuments. The park's authorization a decade later certainly speaks to the BNHSC's success, delays notwithstanding.

And yet, as we've seen throughout this chapter, the BNHSC's success was not entirely unmitigated. Its membership, for instance, was temperamental and factious. In some cases, its members were so unfocused and so undisciplined that the committee's ability to deliberate succumbed to rhetorical fistfights in local and national media. Incredibly, the commission's chair disparaged "the so-called extraordinary expert" and bragged that the BNHSC's report would be "more efficient and not so controversial" because it did not "get these specialists in."[119] In other instances, he and Small conspired to remove Whitehill from the committee owing to competing viewpoints. Along the way, two members died of causes related to old age, which suggests one way in which this entirely white and privileged commission was not at all representative of the communities that, in some cases, it intended to demolish. All of them longed for Longfellow's Boston, and all of them embraced ideas about history and preservation devised during the first half of the twentieth century.

The BNHSC's dysfunction, though perhaps not unique among federal commissions, was nonetheless significant insomuch as it permitted Edwin Small to exercise an extraordinary degree of influence on its work. Without Small, it is unlikely that the BNHSC would have completed any of its work. In the end, it was Small who conducted all the important research, did all the important fieldwork, and wrote all the reports. The problem, of course, is that Small's predominance meant that his historical vision became the BNHSC's historical vision, and Small had crafted his vision during the New Deal years. In other words, although the commission's task was to devise a new plan for Boston, what it really endorsed was a refinement of a plan that had been in the works for nearly two decades. Interestingly, the most dramatic and most immediate result of the BNHSC's efforts was not a new plan for downtown Boston, but rather the establishment of Minute Man National Historical Park, a project in which Small took special interest. Recall, after all, that Small believed the past east of Route 128 had become "irretrievable." Whether or not he realized it, pushing the BNHSC toward an engagement with the Battle Road—rather than contending with downtown—promised special rewards for Small: in 1960, Wirth appointed Edwin Small superintendent of Minute Man.

Small's leadership also predisposed the BNHSC to endorse key principles of urban redevelopment and renewal, which, as we will see, threatened to undermine the NPS's standing in Boston. Small had cut his teeth on Salem's early encounters with redevelopment and thus came to the BNHSC as a proponent of public-private partnership, slum clearance, and the economics of heritage tourism. His position validated a prevailing attitude among the other members that destroying buildings and removing residents was a legitimate way to advance historic preservation. Bortman, for instance, referred to City Councilor Gabriel Piermonte as the BNHSC's "number one enemy" with regard to the commission's plans for the North End, noting that he had "already started talking about the outsiders coming and throwing people out of their homes and all of that." Watkins believed that people like Piermonte "lack imagination." "That's what I think too," agreed Small.[120] Tobin's characterization of these strategies as supporting "citizen renewal," sought to downplay the violence done by urban renewal to Boston's various communities. Whitehill, of course, spoke out loudly against demolition, which earned him the approbation of other commission members. What they failed to realize was that advocating for demolition and removal was a surefire way, by 1956, to guarantee resistance, not just from residents, but from state and federal politicians. Indeed, as we will see in chapter three, the BNHSC's failure to understand the politics of its own moment nearly derailed the park's path to authorization.

Finally, picking back through the BNHSC's story complicates the notion, common in the NPS today, that the commission set into motion NPS's first partnership park. It is certainly true that the BNHSC envisioned a national historical park organized around seven cooperative agreements with various historical associations. That said, the model imagined by the BNHSC was not new. On the contrary, the BNHSC was very much focused throughout its deliberations on the model created by Independence National Historical Park in 1948. What's more, the NPS already managed one Boston historic site—Dorchester Heights—in cooperative agreement with the City of Boston. Rather than devise an entirely new partnership template, the BNHSC rather sought to replicate the Dorchester Heights arrangement on a somewhat larger scale than what had been accomplished in Philadelphia. And the proving ground for this model was not in Boston, but rather between Concord and Lexington. Small and the BNHSC quite clearly understood Minute Man as a model for what might be done in Boston. It is worth pointing out, too, that the BNHSC's final report did not specify the scope of cooperative agreements for the park or how they should function, beyond noting that partnership ought to guarantee to the agency right of access to the public portions of the various properties and that none of them could be materially altered without written consent from the secretary of the Department of Interior. Whatever partnerships might give form to the park, then, would be the invention of its advisory board—a concept borrowed from the new Cape Cod National

Seashore—and others of the park's first-generation leaders. None of those people would be in place until 1974.

Beyond all of this, however, what is most clear is that the BNHSC understood "partnership" to mean a legal relationship between the NPS and a private organization contrived to generate profit by way of heritage tourism or economic renewal. In other words, the BNHSC deployed a partnership language borrowed from postwar urban renewal policy, language that imagined national parks as tools for changing urban landscapes. It's a different notion of partnership than what shaped deliberations at Cape Cod and that, decades later, would guide establishment of the agency's first national heritage areas. And it's very different from what we mean when we talk about cultural partnerships today, which typically involve programmatic relationships with public nonprofit organizations that, since 1969, have been legally required to serve their various publics.[121] The proposed park's would-be partners were not bound by any obligation, for instance, to require cultural diversity among board membership or to otherwise guarantee a commitment to serving all Bostonians. In that sense, then, the BNHSC definitely did not envision a modern partnership park. As we will see, however, the park's first stewards did, and their efforts would be responsible for bringing the park into conversation with people for whom Longfellow's Boston was just one part of a much more complex past.

CHAPTER 3

Losing Control of the Agenda

The Advisory Board on National Parks convened at Michigan's Isle Royale National Park for its 1960 annual meeting. Far though it was from the hubbub of city streets, the board couldn't help but ponder the agency's recent investments in urban places. Northeast Regional Director Ronald F. Lee reported on projects in Philadelphia, New York, and of course, Boston, as each related to the nation's rising tide of urban renewal. "Historical preservation," he explained, "is influencing redevelopment." In Philadelphia, he pointed out, the Society Hill renewal project dovetailed perfectly with the agency's work at Independence Hall, thanks in large part to Charles Peterson's "very prominent" role in making the Historic American Buildings Survey "a part of a [*sic*] rehabilitation of the City." Urban renewal projects in lower Manhattan, he added, created opportunities to raise matching funds for the expansion of Castle Clinton, Federal Hall, and the Statue of Liberty. "It is amazing to see how some people respond to urban historic monuments who have never seen a wilderness park." Similar possibilities awaited in Boston, he added, particularly "as a result of what happened in Philadelphia."[1]

Lee confirmed in so many words what we discovered in chapter two, that the Boston National Historic Sites Commission (BNHSC) had not so much imagined a new path for Boston as it had demonstrated how the Philadelphia example might be applied there, and how urban renewal pointed the way. What's not so clear, however, is whether—as Lee supposed—the agency's preservation ethos influenced redevelopment in Boston as it so clearly had in Philadelphia. The commission, though deeply embedded within urban renewal, conceived of its work as reactive rather than proactive with regard to setting the agency's renewal agenda in Boston. The lone dissenter, of course, was Walter Muir Whitehill, who encouraged his colleagues to take a much stronger hand in shaping Boston's new urban landscape. Although Whitehill failed to activate the commission, he did win the ear of someone with real power to advance preservation in Boston: hired-gun city planner, Ed Logue. As we will see in this chapter, Whitehill convinced Logue—in whose papers, incidentally, the

National Park Service is barely a footnote—to create his own historic sites commission with a visionary young staff of planners, including women, and a much broader sense of historical significance than what Edwin Small and others in the National Park Service (NPS) had advocated for in Boston.

The agency's aloofness from Ed Logue during the 1960s raises an important question: how exactly did NPS planners translate the commission's proposal into a full-blown national historical park if not in conversation with the man who, during those years, owned the future of Boston's heritage landscape? Stated otherwise, how exactly did the park's 1974 enabling legislation get made, and by whom? This chapter seeks answers by considering the park's formative legislative history alongside remarkable changes in Boston's political and physical landscape during the years between 1960 and 1974, as well as major shifts in NPS priorities and organization. In particular, the possibility of including the Charlestown Navy Yard within the park's boundaries, alongside significant political pressure to do it before Boston's 1975 Bicentennial celebration, put the NPS in the remarkable position of opposing legislation to authorize a park it had been planning for over two decades. Indeed, as we will see, these tumultuous "pre-park" years—a useful sobriquet that appears in the park's archival collections—created a new unit whose commitment to Revolutionary memory collided with other revolutions everywhere underway in modern Boston. It was a moment during which, as one member of the park's planning team later recalled, the NPS had "lost control of the agenda."[2]

NEW PLANS FOR NEW BOSTON

In chapter one, we explored some of the broad changes impacting the United States after World War II, and particularly those that propelled heritage tourists toward Boston in unprecedented numbers. We learned too that the postwar promise of prosperity arrived unevenly, and disastrously in some cases, especially for Americans such as those who settled in Boston's West End prior to 1953 but who were later swept away by renewal programs devised to lure whiter and wealthier people back from the suburbs. Neither the Freedom Trail nor the national parks imagined by the BNHSC had been conceived of in conversation with the people that renewal sought to remove, and thus public history making in Boston during those years itself amounted to a kind of removal wherein anything but Longfellow's Revolution constituted an obstacle. The commission, for instance, encouraged figurative removal—such as ignoring pasts outside a narrow period of significance—and actual removal of real people, such as those living in Revere Square or those who sold meat and produce in Faneuil Hall. Much of this historical vision reflected the consensus history promulgated by popular postwar American historians such as Richard Hofstadter and Daniel Boorstin, who sought to identify a collective American experience amid the fears and anxieties of the Cold War years. Their version of collective experience, however, excluded many Americans.

What is also striking about the first phase of urban renewal in Boston is how completely it seemed to have failed by 1959. Renewal projects then in progress—in the West End especially—seemed only to create more problems. Virtually no progress had been made toward developing a new Government Center, which Mayor John Hynes hoped would be a jewel in his crown. The cost of renewal had plunged Massachusetts deeper into debt, even as state legislators refused to approve a state sales tax. Work on the new Prudential Insurance building in Boston's Back Bay section had stalled, as it had on a proposed convention center downtown. Jobs were down, property taxes were up, a hundred thousand people had moved out over the course of the decade, and the city's bond rating tanked in 1959.[3] Nationally, too, the glint of postwar optimism no longer seemed so bright. The so-called Eisenhower Recession of 1958 showed that American economic growth might not be completely unfettered. Also, despite the comforts of consensus history, supposedly shared American values seemed not to be fairing so well in the war against Communism, wherein the United States suffered decided failures in Korea, Cuba, and amid the degradations of Senator Joseph McCarthy's domestic terror campaign. And, of course, civil rights activists had made major strides by 1959 on behalf of African Americans, but not without enduring tragic violence that would only intensify in the years ahead.

And then, another pivotal change for Boston. In 1959, Bostonians elected a new and new kind of mayor: John Collins. Collins believed in the big consensus vision of a mighty postwar America. He had been a Cold Warrior in the state senate before being struck down by debilitating disease. During his convalescence, Collins studied history and urban planning, and returned to politics in a surprisingly successful bid for mayor. Collins ran as a Republican against the Democrat John Powers, positioning himself as the anticorruption pick and a more devoted friend to business than Hynes had been. What's more, Collins sought to create citizens' community councils and new outdoor recreational opportunities, all toward making government more responsive to community needs.[4] Most significantly for our purposes, Collins recommitted

Boston to urban renewal, but this time with a real plan for success. Going forward, Collins announced, all city planning functions would be centralized in the office of one man: Edward J. Logue. Logue had earned a reputation for his role in reshaping New Haven, Connecticut, where he attracted substantial federal funding. Collins hoped that by making a substantial investment in Logue—including by paying him more than even Collins himself earned—Boston might finally get the federal support it needed, and the new cityscape Collins wanted.[5]

Logue's arrival in Boston in 1960, though perhaps not evident at the time, radically shifted the terms by which planners within and beyond the NPS would have to conceive of a national historic park in Boston.[6] Bostonians first glimpsed Logue's plans in September 1960, when the mayor's office debuted his $90 million development program for the city, at an event staged in Old South Meeting House. Logue envisioned an aggressive and wide-reaching program across ten renewal areas, six improvement areas, and three distinct planning areas in downtown alone. The program would be administered by a reorganized and "semiautonomous" Boston Redevelopment Authority (BRA)—now overseeing planning and renewal—with Logue at the helm. Rehabilitation, not clearance, would be a priority, although Logue warned that fighting "blight" would inevitably require the clearing of particularly challenged blocks, especially downtown.[7] Importantly, Logue's plan foregrounded community partnerships. Mayor Collins noted that "the whole emphasis on this rebuilding program is on neighborhoods [which will] have a key partnership role in the preparation and carrying out of renewal plans. I would call it planning *with* people instead of planning for people."[8]

Logue's proposal made clear too, however, that planning with business would also be a priority, particularly with regard to the Atlantic Avenue Waterfront area and in key portions of the central business district. And doing business with business in Boston meant working with the Greater Boston Chamber of Commerce. As we saw in chapter one, the chamber of commerce exercised considerable influence on matters of heritage tourism in postwar Boston, particularly through its sponsorship of the Freedom Trail. Logue's evident fondness for the chamber promised to extend that influence. "Boston is fortunate," he explained "in having a vigorous Chamber with a far deeper and more practical understanding of urban renewal than is usually the case." And it was the chamber, he noted, that "was among the first to propose redevelopment of the waterfront area . . . the city should make clear that it will cooperate in every way."[9] Logue's praise for the chamber foreshadowed a critical decision: the chamber, not Logue, would have primary responsibility for planning redevelopment around Faneuil Hall, the Old State House, and Old North Church, the critical central leg of the Freedom Trail. Together, Logue and the chamber would build "a close federation of the civic-business agencies in urban renewal . . . the Chamber, Beacon and the North Station Merchants. Sooner or later the Retail Trade Board will arrive, and there will be others." "Eventually," the chamber proposed, "it might become our local 'Old Philadelphia Development Corporation.'"[10]

Beyond demonstrating once again how formative Philadelphia's example was in shaping Boston's heritage landscape—the Old Philadelphia Development Corporation, of course, had been responsible for creating Society Hill—this exchange demonstrates that, despite the BNHSC's work to imagine a federal role in managing Boston's historic resources, heritage matters there remained a local affair, ensconced within private enterprise. Nobody associated with the NPS appears to have reached out to Logue's team until at least spring 1961. By then, however, Logue's notion of heritage tourism had already taken form. His 1960 proposal already demonstrated that influence in its homage to the Freedom Trail. Logue made the case for renewal, in part, by urging Bostonians to take walking tours. On one of his proposed tours, "you will see lovely squares, a beautiful cathedral, the city's first redevelopment project, the big department stores, Old South Meeting House and Faneuil Hall. You also will see some of the worst slums in the city plus enough shabby run-down commercial buildings to make you uncomfortable about the future of downtown." "If these walks discourage you," he added, "try the Freedom Trail. The obstacles today are far less than those which were faced and conquered long ago."[11]

The BNHSC had been aware of pending changes in Boston's landscape since the beginning. In September 1956, for instance, Small reported on a meeting with the Boston City Planning Board regarding its early plans for a new Government Center. As conceived, the project would destroy several historic properties, including the Hancock-Marshall House, the Union Oyster House, and the Boston Stone. Small promised to monitor the situation, noting that "if the commission was interested in other periods [beyond the Revolutionary era], it would be a very serious manner."[12] Within the year, it became clear to the commission that the planning board and its "parochial attitude"—as Small put it—did not share its concern with historic landscapes.[13] Whitehill urged the commission to publicize its differences with the planning board toward generating public support.[14] Lee wondered aloud whether Massachusetts' recent historic districts legislation might empower a city to establish its own historic district. Small explained that "just such a bill was killed the previous week." In Whitehill's opinion, the problem was that preservation for so long had been considered a private enterprise in Boston that the city did not perceive a mandate to intervene. "The commission," he insisted, "had power to change that." Chief of NPS Regional Planning Andrew G. Feil Jr., who attended the commission's August 1957 meeting, argued that the commission would not change anything unless it recommended a clear process. "It is not effective enough to say," he insisted, "that such and such a building should be preserved—the most important thing is to recommend how it should be done."[15]

By spring 1959, however, the commission seems to have resolved that nothing could be done about the city's planning efforts. Small wrote to NPS Regional Director Daniel Tobin that April with word that plans were in process for the new Government Center in old Scollay Square, right next to Faneuil Hall, though "any recommendations the Commission might [make] prior to adoption of a definite plan would, indeed, be premature." Small noted, too, that the commission "has been in touch continually over the last few months" with the planning firm of Adams, Howard, and Greeley, which had been retained to develop plans for the Government Center. "It goes almost without saying," Small intimated, "that any schemes that have thus far come off the draft tables will be in for hard sledding."[16] And, yet, as we saw in chapter two, Small's prediction that the Faneuil Hall meat vendors would do better to move to Quincy Market suggests that he had a broader sense of what was coming.

Interestingly, what was coming appeared to include Logue's abiding concern with Boston's historic landscapes. "Its abundance of historic sites," he wrote, "offers islands of strength around which rebuilding can confidently begin."[17] And yet, what Logue meant by "historic" was not entirely clear. He announced, for instance, that he would indeed go ahead with the city's Government Center plan, but with more planning for its "fringe areas," including Faneuil Hall and Quincy Market, which "are in daily use for their original purposes." Logue's declaration that "this is living history at its best" plunged him directly into the meat market debates that had roiled the BNHSC during the previous year. "Scornful as the purists may be of Sturbridge or Williamsburg, they help make history come alive for young and old alike. A restoration of old Boston in this area would be quite appropriate despite the shadow of the Central Artery."[18]

Would Logue's vision, as BNHSC member Mark Bortman hoped, sanitize the past toward enticing out-of-town tourists? Or would it, as Whitehill hoped, preserve the charm and traditions of Boston's historic streets and buildings?

Of course, Logue's Government Center project was just one of several that would impact portions of the city that were of immediate concern to the commission. In the North End, which "has a flavor and a way of life which should be preserved," Logue assured that clearance would be an "outrage." Rehabilitation would be key in the North End, and to achieve it Logue encouraged the city to work with "a broadly based and representative North End neighborhood improvement committee." Along the Atlantic Avenue Waterfront, including in those portions around Long Wharf just east of Faneuil Hall, Logue anticipated working with the Chamber of Commerce to once again open "Boston's window on the world." "Who would ever believe," he added," that an ancient harborfront warehouse could be converted into apartments so attractive as to enjoy a long waiting list?"[19]

Similarly, in Boston's downtown, Logue proposed "making the retail core more attractive" by working with the Retail Trade Board, but also by "separating vehicular and pedestrian traffic as much as possible." And though the commission couldn't have known it in 1960, Logue's concern with Charlestown would have considerable impact on the establishment of a national park that would ultimately span the Charles River. "Much more can and should be made of Charlestown's historic past," he argued, and the key to doing it would be working with "a representative group of Charlestown residents."[20]

Logue's 1960 proposal for urban renewal in Boston is remarkable for what it reveals about the trajectory of postwar planning. It makes clear that Logue, having learned from the examples of New York, Philadelphia, and his own work in New Haven, had in mind a distinctive set of priorities for renewal in Boston. He came with firm commitments to community-led planning. He developed, in conversation with Whitehill, a regard for heritage-consumer landscapes. And, as historian Lizabeth Cohen puts it, he intended to make private capital step up to public–private partnership building "in a wholly new way."[21] They were the very same priorities, in fact, that the National Park Service seems to have had in mind with regard to its aspirations for a national park in Boston. As we saw in chapter two, regional officers—especially Regional Director Daniel Tobin—encouraged the commission to think in these terms, as had been done in Philadelphia, rather than to simply pick and choose properties worthy of preservation. And yet, although the commission's

FIGURE 6. Cover page of a comic book printed in 1964 to promote the Freedom Trail. Record identifier 0244001-246-001-004, Mayor John F. Collins Collection, Boston City Archives, West Roxbury, MA.

final report nodded toward partnership, it stopped short of recommending a process by which the agency might build a coalition of heritage interests throughout Boston. As Whitehill suggested back in 1957, the commission had the power to change attitudes, to convince Bostonians that preservation ought not be left to private interests alone. It failed to do that, however, and in doing so, missed a vital opportunity to assert a role for the NPS in Boston at a crucial moment.

THE BRA HISTORIC CONSERVATION COMMITTEE

The BNHSC's mixed legacy is remarkable insomuch as its failures prompted a flurry of advocacy that ultimately did achieve a public role for preservation in Boston, though not at all in the way that Tobin or Small seem to have expected. Credit for bringing all of Boston's various heritage stakeholders—including the NPS—to the same table goes to Walter Muir Whitehill. During his time with the commission, Whitehill expressed a much broader vision of Boston's heritage landscape than what his cocommissioners had in mind. We've already seen in his standoff with fellow commissioner Mark Bortman over the Faneuil Hall meat markets a concern for historical continuity, and a disregard for crass profiteering. Whitehill also took issue with the NPS's periodization. Although the commission "drew up an admirable inventory of historic sites of the Colonial and Revolutionary period," he wrote, "there has been no formal or systematic policy in regard to the preservation of buildings of the late eighteenth, the nineteenth and twentieth centuries in Boston."[22] And, finally, Whitehill—unlike almost everyone else involved in the park's genesis story—did not perceive the Philadelphia model as ideal. Rather, he hoped that Boston's renewal plans "will avoid the incongruities that have occurred in the center of Philadelphia where, through too much demolition, a sense of scale has been lost." "Buildings that should not be seen together," he explained, "have been brought together unnecessarily."[23]

With these concerns in mind, Whitehill set out early on to influence Logue's preservation sensibilities. Whitehill, who like Logue belonged to Boston's swank Tavern Club, first engaged the new city planner on matters of preservation with regard to the Old Corner Bookstore.[24] The 1713 holdout at the corner of Washington and School Streets ranked among the few colonial structures that the commission reported on as having little to no likelihood of survival despite its significance. Early renewal plans targeted the site for a parking lot. Whitehill organized a grassroots campaign to save the building.

With the help of Beacon Hill Architectural Commission Chairman John Codman, he also managed to establish a nonprofit organization, Historic Boston, Inc., for the purpose of raising funds to purchase and protect the building. And he accomplished this in 1960, before the commission had even finalized its report.[25] Whitehill saw in it an opportunity to make his case for historically minded, minimally invasive renewal. That November, he shared a *New York Times* opinion piece with Logue wherein the author warned that ill-conceived renewal in Greenwich Village recalled the "piles of rubble" on view throughout postwar Berlin.[26] Logue returned thanks, congratulated Whitehill on Historic Boston's success, and promised to keep him abreast of the mayor's preservation concerns.[27]

He would more than make good on that promise within the year. Pressures quickly mounted on Logue to think about heritage concerns. In addition to the Chamber of Commerce, which by 1961 was urging Logue to create a version of the Old Philadelphia Development Corporation for Boston, and Whitehill himself, who had taken to writing Logue about rumors of demolition around Boston, other organizations also pressed Logue for insight into the future of the past.[28] The Mayor's Committee on North End Rehabilitation and Conservation, for instance, sought input from Logue, noting its concern with the future of the Freedom Trail.[29] The newly formed Council of the Freedom Trail, a coalition of organizations that managed historic properties along the trail, asked Logue to join its meetings. He demurred, though noted his interest "in the work that you are doing and [I] appreciate the invitation."[30] By the end of the year, however, Logue had devised a formal response. He'd sponsor a study of Boston's historic sites and he'd form a mayor's committee on cultural and historic matters to advise on questions of preservation and renewal. The person he'd pick to lead it all: Walter Muir Whitehill.

At Logue's prompting, Mayor Collins constituted a historic sites committee under Whitehill's direction; it met for the first time on November 29, 1961. The committee's responsibilities included surveying Boston's historic sites, compiling a citywide inventory, and guiding the BRA away from demolishing sites of particular significance amid its renewal activities.[31] Unlike the BNHSC, which shunted all of its fieldwork onto Edwin Small, the BRA's historic sites committee seems to have relished its time exploring Boston's historic landscape. A committee newsletter reported on seeing Whitehill gleefully driving his survey team around town in a Volkswagen van. Its assumptions about how and why preservation should be done were different too. Consider, for instance, the committee's call for proposals for a team to survey Charlestown. BRA Project Planning Officer John Stainton attached a cover note explaining that "it rests on the basic assumption that much of the actual process of rehabilitation will be done by the people of Charlestown who in many cases have limited means and will have to carry the work on over an extended period of time. Thus, one end product will be a guide for residents in rehabilitating their property."[32] Interestingly, the committee's Charlestown study team ultimately resolved that Charlestown should be allowed to gentrify "organically," like Society Hill in Philadelphia, though of course there was nothing at all organic about gentrification in that city or any other.[33]

Whitehill's committee then, from the beginning, conceived of preservation as a community activity. It also sought advice from leading professionals, including the NPS. Its first meeting included Edwin Small and Historic American Buildings Survey (HABS) founder Charles Peterson. It also included Mark Bortman and Ed Logue. Indeed, Whitehill set out to involve a broad coalition of public and private interests in his committee, with nearly forty members in attendance at the first meeting. At that same meeting, Whitehill showcased Peterson's work and spoke at length about involving HABS in Boston. For his part, Peterson discussed the work of the Philadelphia Historical Commission, which "has the power to defer the razing or removal of any building of historical interest."[34] Once again, Philadelphia models loomed large in Boston's nascent preservation policy.

What is so striking about Logue's approach to the problem of preservation in Boston, vis-à-vis Whitehill, is how much it resembled the BNHSC's own charge. And yet, significant differences reveal very different visions and priorities. Most immediately, Logue imposed no chronological limits on his committee. His concern was with the past, not just the Revolutionary past. What's more, primary responsibility for coordinating the committee and conducting the preliminary study of historic sites fell to Gladys Lyons, a young planner whose brief time on Logue's team made a significant impact on Boston's heritage landscape.[35] Lyons's fresh perspective contrasted with the BNHSC's membership, among whom the youngest was fifty-year-old Edwin Small. It is important to note, too, that though Louise Crowninshield's role on the commission was certainly important, men predominated throughout its deliberations. Not surprisingly, Lyons's preliminary survey of historic sites in the Government Center development area charted very different territory than had the commission. "Other than isolated landmarks of Boston's early period," she wrote, "there is precious little left of the 17th or even 18th century, but there is still valuable evidence of the past 100 years in the Downtown area."[36] Whereas the commission had sought to discover traces of Longfellow's fabled Boston, the BRA preferred a more direct encounter with the city's actual historic landscape.

And, from the outset, its approach was demonstrably more collaborative than the commission's. By February 1961, Lyons had assembled a preliminary council on historic sites and coordinated meetings with I. M. Pei's architectural team and various BRA officers.[37] Later that spring, she initiated what appears to be the first official exchange between Logue's team and the NPS, by writing to Edwin Small for insight regarding the commission's findings on the Government Center area.[38] The specific reason for her letter concerned the "frightening possibility of 15–27 Union Street being demolished . . . for a parking lot." Small explained that the commission had considered recommending that the whole block be acquired by the NPS but, after meeting with the deputy mayor in January 1960, decided that the area ought rather be designated a historic district.[39] Small noted that the 1959 Adams, Howard, and Greeley plan for the Government Center proposed a historic district encompassing the Faneuil Hall area—more or less identical to the area identified by the commission—and suggested that the BRA request the Boston City Council expand it. "Without these controls," he warned, "downtown Boston is not going to become what is hoped for under the prospects that are promised through urban redevelopment and renewal."[40]

Lyons's exchange with Small, beyond demonstrating her concern to engage an array of stakeholders, reveals how much distance had separated local and federal preservation interests prior to 1961. In another instance, BRA planners were stunned to discover so much resistance to plans to demolish a row of early-nineteenth-century commercial buildings designed by David Sears. The demolition, after all, had been proposed in the same 1959 Government Center plan that Small referred to as critical to the commission's work. As Whitehill explained in a meeting, however, Boston's "historical people did not raise a ruckus about the Adams, Howard, and Greeley plan [because it] was never widely distributed or publicized."[41] The commission had done its work largely in isolation from Boston's local preservation community, only loosely in conversation with the mayor's office, and barely at all in conversation with actual heritage tourists. Incredibly, as late as 1962, the BRA's director of administrative management sent a copy of the commission's report to his

assistant with a hasty handwritten note: "What gives on this? Has city consented to this idea?"[42] The commission and its report had already become,
by 1962, a vague and distant memory.

Historic preservation was certainly "influencing redevelopment" in Boston,
as NPS Regional Director Ronald F. Lee supposed at the Advisory Board on
National Parks'1960 meeting, but by the early 1960s, at least, that influence was
not coming from the BNHSC and it was not coming from the National Park
Service. It was coming, rather, from Walter Muir Whitehill. Indeed, during
1960–61, newspaper headlines revealed widespread fears that Ed Logue would
turn Boston into a "small Williamsburg."[43] It was Whitehill who pushed
hard against Logue to avoid fixing Boston's heritage landscape in time, but
rather to preserve its historic buildings by repurposing them for commercial
purposes. It was Whitehill, too, who encouraged Logue to adopt a much
broader model of collaborative partnership than the commission had envisioned, and to remain focused on how postwar communities might experience
the past in their neighborhoods. And it was Whitehill who pushed beyond
Revolutionary memory to encourage a much more capacious regard for the
full sweep of Boston's past. In Boston, then, as was the case in Philadelphia,
according to planning and preservation historian Stephanie Ryberg, it turns
out that it was "planners—not preservationists—who saved vast swaths of
the city's landscape," though the line between the two was not always clear.[44]
What is very clear is that, with the important exception of Gladys Lyons, all
of the decisions being made in Boston during the 1960s about what to save
and why were being made by white men with powerful interests in turning
a profit on the past.

PARK POLITICS IN BOSTON

This, then, was the setting against which, on March 20, 1962, U.S. Representative and former BNHSC member Tip O'Neill, representing what was then
Boston's Eleventh District, introduced H.R. 10836 into the second session of
the 87th Congress.[45] The bill, which O'Neill hoped would permit authorization of a new park unit as proposed in the commission's report, died almost
immediately. The busy House Committee on Interior and Insular Affairs
couldn't manage to schedule hearings and, even if it had, the secretary of the
interior had not yet reported on the bill. Nonetheless, looking back today at
the bill is instructive insomuch as it reveals how readily Bostonians would
have perceived it as akin to first-phase renewal strategies, particularly after

the arrival of Ed Logue. Beyond simply identifying properties that the government would accept by donation—the Old State House and the Shirley-Eustis House—H.R. 10836 authorized the federal government to acquire, by purchase or donation, land surrounding the Paul Revere House, Old North Church, and the Shirley-Eustis House. Once it had, and as soon as cooperative agreements could be worked out with relevant stakeholders, the secretary of the interior could establish the so-called Boston National Historic Sites, which would include the acquired properties along with Faneuil Hall, Dorchester Heights, and Bunker Hill. Each site, if not already, would be designated a national historic site. And the entire unit would be overseen by a five-member Boston National Historic Sites Advisory Board, including the president of the Massachusetts Historical Society and various appointees selected by the secretary, the governor, and the mayor, for a period of ten years.[46]

It is remarkable in retrospect that O'Neill would not have expected resistance to his bill, as proposed, given its authorization of federal land acquisition. In the North End, for instance, as we saw in chapter two, City Councilor Gabriel Piermonte had already made clear his disdain for land grabs associated with renewal. And yet, neither O'Neill nor the NPS seemed at all worried. On the contrary, when O'Neill reintroduced the bill a year later as H.R. 392, NPS Regional Director Daniel Tobin anticipated "no major conflicts . . . from the acquisition for development and renewal purposes of certain privately held commercial and residential properties."[47] Indeed, regional officers noted on a draft of the previous year's bill their interest in requesting even more authority to purchase land for office and administrative buildings.[48] However, advisors to Mayor John F. Collins saw in the bill an opportunity for the mayor to earn political capital by opposing displacement. The bill, they estimated, would disrupt over ninety families, three stores, and a "very active bakery" near Old North Church and North Square. "The interesting thing about this bill is that . . . nobody seems to be very strongly in favor of it." "One member of the commission," the report continued, "had no knowledge of the implications [that families would be dispossessed] of the bill." North Enders, it seemed, "believe that the Boston Redevelopment Authority is responsible," and even the BRA "is not in favor of this Bill." The advice to Collins was clear: here was "a splendid opportunity for the mayor to take a strong and active position as a defender of the people of the North End." Doing so "would demonstrate his concern for people's homes" and offset "some of the negative publicity which has been stirred up against them in Roxbury and Charlestown."[49]

The advice to Collins demonstrates what should have been clear from the beginning: the proposal to create a national park in Boston was, in both perception and actuality, deeply entwined with urban renewal efforts there and advanced precisely the sort of clearance agenda that Logue had worked so hard to ward against. Although the NPS's language put clearance into different terms—the regional director conceived of it as purchasing "46 parcels over 2.16 acres" rather than evicting over ninety families—it was well aware that the development of Old North Church National Historic Site, for instance, "is further tied into a proposal by the city to enlarge the Paul Revere Mall."[50] As we witnessed at the outset of this chapter, however, it was precisely this relationship between park development, preservation, and urban renewal that the NPS sought to encourage during the Mission 66 years, and which the secretary of the interior readily endorsed in the case of Boston. By the end of May 1964, the Department of Interior had reported favorably on H.R. 392, estimating that $500,000 would be required for land purchases, $5 million for a visitor center and parking facilities, and $475,000 annually for management costs.[51] When the Advisory Board on National Parks finally endorsed the proposal and voiced support for O'Neill's bill at its October 1964 meeting, it justified the plans by noting the "urgent need to preserve for the present and future generations of Americans the outstanding portions of the nation's historical heritage situated in Boston and its environs and because of the transcendent importance of the historical values represented by these seven sites."[52]

As Collins's advisors anticipated, however, not everyone was convinced. Senator Edward M. Kennedy's office, which had not yet become involved in the legislation, responded to a concerned constituent who inquired about its fate. "It seems that this bill," an assistant responded, "has stimulated a good deal of local controversy—particularly because of its rather broad and sweeping provisions."[53] O'Neill even encountered pushback from within his own district. The Mayor's Committee for North End Rehabilitation and Conservation—an organization born of Logue's insistence on community involvement in renewal planning—demanded that O'Neill oppose his own bill. "We have no choice but to fight," explained Committee Chairman Guy A. Beninati, "to protect the 96 families and 6 businesses. Certainly our cause is right and just." O'Neill ought to protect the "living present," he argued, which "in no way affects the continuation of the existence of the historic sites which mark our glorious past." What most concerned North Enders, according to Beninati, was the threat of "further inroads [from] future urban

renewal or highway activity. The whole future of the North End community
is tied into this constant nibbling at the perimeter and the heart of this vital,
viable, happy community."[54] O'Neill responded within days. "As you know, I
was a member of the Boston National Historic Sites Commission which made
the original study." "In fairness to other Members of that Committee," he
explained, "it is necessary for me to act as sponsor of the measure."[55]

Sponsoring the bill, however, did not equate to rushing it. O'Neill let
Beninati in on a bit of congressional maneuvering that would ease concerns
in the North End, at least for the short term: "I have an agreement with
Chairman Aspinall of the House Committee on Interior and Insular Affairs
that no action will be taken during the 89th Congress which will cover the
years 1965 and 1966."[56] It's hard to know what to make of O'Neill's deal with
Aspinall. Was he, indeed, concerned about the legislation, enough to stall it
pending further review? Could it have been O'Neill who was the commission
member Collins's advisors mentioned, the one who hadn't realized that the
proposed NPS unit would result in evictions? Had O'Neill shared the same
news with Bortman and Small, who gathered at his office a few months earlier
to discuss legislative strategy? If nothing else, O'Neill's deal provides some
explanation for why progress toward authorizing a new park ebbed and flowed
in following years. For instance, O'Neill did introduce new legislation in 1965:
H.R. 5607 on March 1, 1965, and H.R. 8391 on May 24, 1965.[57] This time
the bills went to committee, though Aspinall delayed hearings for an entire
year. That January, Representative John W. McCormack stepped back into
the picture to petition the chair of the subcommittee to schedule a hearing,
evidently unaware of O'Neill's deal. "Every member in the House and Senate
from Massachusetts," he wrote, "favors a Bill being reported out along the
lines of [5607 and 8391]."[58]

When the committee finally did schedule hearings in April 1966—
preliminary hearings before its Subcommittee on National Parks and Recreation—Bortman, Small, and Bunker Hill Association President and Harvard
historian Charles Elliot traveled to Washington, DC, to speak as witnesses.
O'Neill did not attend but did submit a statement. The subcommittee, chaired
by Roy A. Taylor (D–NC), included Wayne N. Aspinall (D–CO), Wendell
Wyatt (R–OR), Harold T. Johnson (D–CA), David S. King (D–UT), and
Richard C. White (D–TX). The first statement made on the bills' behalf
was the secretary of the interior's, transmitted to the house that March. In it,
the secretary summarized the work of the BNHSC, noted its findings, and

justified federal involvement by explaining that the various sites' "general state
of repair and/or interpretive potential has not been accomplished along lines
that are in keeping with their great historical value."[59]

O'Neill's statement followed suit. "The scope and expanse of" preservation,
he argued, "are beyond the reach of local groups or are too much for them to
handle." The NPS, he insisted, would "stem the tide of severe criticism" leve-
led by visitors at Boston's heritage sites. Interestingly, O'Neill—immediately
after submitting his written statement and before the hearing—requested
that Aspinall redact an entire paragraph concerning how Boston had been
criticized for being unable to manage its own historic sites. He asked, too,
that a *Boston Globe* editorial he had included be removed from the record. The
editorial, written by a tourist recently disappointed by his experience along
the Freedom Trail, described finding "nothing but a disgrace to our American
Heritage. I wonder how long it has been since your civic leaders have viewed
what visitors to your city come to see?"[60] Aspinall omitted the paragraph but
left the editorial intact.

It's not all that O'Neill withheld. An early draft of his statement suggests
that O'Neill had also considered pitching NPS involvement more directly
as an investment in urban renewal. The sentiment comes through briefly in
the conclusion to O'Neill's statement, wherein he notes that an NPS unit in
Boston would contribute "to the complete city landscape that will make up
the renewed Boston."[61] In his draft statement, however, O'Neill explored more
fully the linkages between federal preservation and urban renewal:

> Generally speaking, the same problems of neglect and blight being
> encountered today in broad programs of urban renewal are to be faced
> no less in more limited and specific endeavors to preserve and main-
> tain historic monuments, architectural survivals, and their immediate
> surroundings, which should form, to be sure, notable parts of the
> same environment . . . Among our cities, Boston is no exception in this
> respect and severe criticism of conditions has been continually voiced
> by visitors, from both far and near, who are mindful of the importance
> of the American Revolution in our history.[62]

Although the full contours of this argument did not enter into O'Neill's
statement to the subcommittee, his recognition that the bill would prompt real
estate purchase and clearance in the North End did. But unlike the Mayor's

Committee for North End Rehabilitation and Conservation, which reckoned impact in terms of families and business, O'Neill simply noted that "some 39 parcels occupied for the most part by tenements and covering slightly more than two acres will be involved."[63]

Bortman came next, delivering his statement to the subcommittee in person. Well aware of his audience, the former commission chairman pitched federal preservation of sites associated with early debates over tax policy and independence as a rare opportunity to "pay tribute to our lawmakers." He noted Congress's success in working with the NPS to establish Minute Man National Park, just years before and, "which entailed the taking over of a tremendous amount of land without one protest or without anyone complaining about dispossession or anything else." This was not true, but from Bortman's perspective it might as well have been.[64] He advanced, too, the argument made both by the secretary and O'Neill, that Boston could no longer manage on its own, though in somewhat different terms. The buildings "being presented to the nation," Bortman explained, "have been in the excellent care of people, patriotic normally but devoted to the beginnings of our country. But they are dying out."[65] Charles Elliot lodged a final statement, prepared for the occasion, on behalf of the Bunker Hill Monument Association. He too endorsed the notion that Boston could not manage its sites alone, noting specifically how neither his association nor the Metropolitan District Commission had "the authority [or] the funds to provide any 'interpretive' service to the thousands of visitors." Elliot went so far as to request that O'Neill's bill be amended to include Bunker Hill as an area to be outright acquired by the secretary. The Massachusetts General Court's Joint Resolution 2981, approved just weeks before, Elliot noted, endorsed this option in case Congress agreed to the measure.[66]

Together, then, the supporters of H.R. 8391 presented to Congress a two-prong argument in favor of a federal preservation role in Boston's heritage landscape: Bostonians either weren't able or weren't interested in doing it themselves, and preservation was an extension of urban renewal projects already endorsed by Congress. How, then, did the subcommittee respond? Though receptive to the witnesses, and especially to Bortman's heartfelt endorsement of the plan, the subcommittee raised several points of concern. The congressmen expressed real confusion, for instance, about the nature of the cooperative agreements: exactly who was getting what money to do what? Aspinall led this line of inquiry, wondering whether federal money would be invested in restoring buildings that were not fully in federal ownership. Additionally, he wondered why Boston's historic sites required federal protection when others did not. "Mt. Vernon is not a national shrine," he pointed out, adding that "these people have operated this with the same sense of zeal and patriotism in their own localities as well as many other places of the United States." Representative Johnson put an even finer point on the issue: "How are these historical sites maintained now—through admission charges?" The answer, as Bortman explained, was "no," save for the Paul Revere House and Old South Meeting House. "How," Johnson chided, "would you pay for these otherwise?"[67]

The subcommittee's second concern related to the matter hinted at in the opinion essay included by O'Neill, the problem of Bostonians' seeming indifference to their own historic sites. Aspinall asked that Elliot evaluate the author's concerns for the subcommittee. He did so by confirming that the same problems—vandalism, theft, inadequate security—were endemic at Bunker Hill, because "the Commonwealth and the City of Boston are not taking the kind of care, which the Bunker Hill Monument Association would like to see." Aspinall, who had evidently visited Dorchester Heights, confirmed the same there. "I sometimes wonder if the local people take an interest in such things as this . . . if they do not, how can we expect the Federal Government to come in and furnish the funds and the necessary guardianships of these properties." Aspinall was "puzzled" by the testimony. Why would the federal government invest in historic sites most people in Boston seemed uninterested in? Representative King agreed. There is no vandalism in Williamsburg, Virginia, he offered. "I am curious to know why there should be that great difference between the experience in Williamsburg and in Boston," especially since nearly everyone in Williamsburg is a tourist and thus "you do not have quite the local pride that you have in Boston." "It is the local people who are not appreciative," Elliot explained, along with "our present problems of the education of our youth and the so-called juvenile delinquency problem." In his opinion, too, there was a problem of leadership. "What you are saying," Aspinall quipped, "is that we do not have any modern Samuel Adams . . . in Boston." Elliot rejoined, "we have a Mark Bortman, instead."[68]

What this exchange with the subcommittee makes plainly clear is how deeply invested men like Bortman and Elliot still were in the same rhetoric of fear and deviance that William Schofield deployed a decade earlier in support of his Freedom Trail campaign. Bortman's assertion that Boston's patriotic heritage stewards were "dying out" and Elliot's preoccupation with vandalism

and juvenile delinquency still rung clear with the old tones of urban redevelopment and "slum" clearance. Specifically, it drew on a vocabulary devised
by Boston's renewal coalition, as historian Daniel Gilbert puts it, to "frame
the process [of renewal] as one of moral redemption and cleansing."[69] And it
coincided, as we will see in chapter four, with dramatic transformations in
Boston's demographic landscape. During the same years that Small and the
BNHSC weighed its proposal, affluent white Bostonians fled to the suburbs just
as Black Americans from all over came to the city seeking opportunity. What
Bortman and Elliot really feared, what they perceived as loss, was the refusal
of these new Bostonians to accept whiteness as a mark of historical authority.

Having traveled to Washington to make a case for the unparalleled significance of Boston's heritage landscape, Bortman, Elliot, and O'Neill had done
quite the opposite. On one hand, they argued that historic preservation in
Boston should be thought of as just another aspect of urban renewal, which
powerfully undersold the uniqueness of the partnership model that the NPS
had been hoping to demonstrate ever since the early days of the commission.
On the other hand, they managed to obscure whatever meaning these sites
might have had for people other than those who already valued them. Elliot's
petulant condemnation of juvenile delinquents and his fashioning of plastics
magnate Mark Bortman into a modern-day Sam Adams are particularly
noteworthy. An unconvinced public, as King put it, was "not something that
the Federal Government can do very much about, is it?" More significantly,
in hindsight, it is clear that what worried Elliot was not just vandalism, but
rather the inability of people like him and Bortman to control how the people
of Charlestown understood the past. And why would Charlestown residents
care about an old monument when what mattered far more in their daily lives
was the destructive uncertainty of urban renewal? Perhaps if Elliot had chosen
Whitehill to be his Sam Adams, or if Small were permitted to testify, the H.R.
8391 hearings might have proceeded differently. Clearly, however, the political,
class, and racial anxieties that ran through those April hearings obscured a
path to authorization. O'Neill's bill never made it out of committee.[70]

TURNING POINTS: THE BICENTENNIAL AND
THE CHARLESTOWN NAVY YARD

Efforts to create a national historical park in Boston had all but failed by
1966. As the disastrous H.R. 8391 hearings reveal, the NPS had put its chips
on the wrong advocates. O'Neill, Bortman, and Elliot might have convinced

Congress a decade prior, but by 1966, preservation sensibilities had evolved amid a shifting political landscape and increasing professionalization. Indeed, that same year, Congress—which had been prodded by the incalculable damage done to urban historic structures by urban renewal—passed the National Historic Preservation Act, which, once signed into law, radically expanded federal authority to document and protect historic sites, and to expand notions of significance beyond the long shadow of privileged white men. Whitehill had already urged Logue toward more usable pasts, and the NPS would have done well to secure his advocacy. But it did not, and Whitehill had already moved on to new projects such as advocating for the creation of a city landmarks commission.[71]

Small might have also been a more effective advocate, but he seems to have lost his appetite for the fight. Since being appointed superintendent of Minute Man National Historical Park in 1961, Small had developed a reputation as a "weak leader"—he never moved his office from Boston—and, what's more, had compromised his own credibility among colleagues by profiting from the rental of homes to Air Force personnel.[72] His path also shifted, as did the agency's broader efforts, following Mission 66 to streamline operations and centralize expertise. In 1964, Lee appointed Small acting superintendent, in addition to his responsibilities at Minute Man, of a new entity, the so-called Boston Sites Group. As Lee explained it, "grouping several areas in metropolitan Boston in one field unit for administrative purposes and assigning administration and management to one single field organization will be in the interest of efficiency and economy."[73] The Boston group was one of several administrative units of its type created under the NPS directorship of George Hartzog, who assumed leadership in 1964 and who had a particular concern for expanding urban parks. Hartzog sought to maximize efficiencies in Boston but was also concerned that urban settings with numerous units ought to have one person able to speak for the National Park Service. Small led the Boston Sites Group for a year before shifting paths once again and becoming a project coordinator, first in the Boston Sites Group and then in Region V (a predecessor to the NPS Northeast Region), where he would finish out the remainder of his career by proposing new units—including the John Fitzgerald Kennedy and Saugus Iron Works National Historic Sites—and advising others.[74]

It is worth dwelling briefly on the formation of the Boston Sites Group for what it reveals about the agency's new directions in Boston, and nationally, on the heels of Mission 66. Back in 1955, when the BNHSC was formed, the NPS still functioned more or less as it had since the New Deal, wherein groups of specialists accrued in individual parks. During Mission 66, however, NPS Director Conrad Wirth and others reimagined the agency's organizational structure in ways reflecting the corporate logic of its private-sector partners. It is noteworthy that Hartzog initiated the creation of the Boston Sites Group, given his previous experience as superintendent of Jefferson Expansion National Park in St. Louis, Missouri (now Gateway Arch National Park), which, as we learned in chapter one, also evolved with deep problematic ties to postwar urban renewal programming.[75] Indeed, just as Mayor Collins consolidated all facets of planning and development under Ed Logue, the NPS consolidated oversight for all of its National Historic Landmarks in the Boston area—including the Beacon Hill Historic District, the Paul Revere House, Lexington Green, Old North, Old South, and many others—into one office. Other historians suggest that the creation of the Boston group "foreshadowed the creation in the next decade of the Boston National Historical Park [and] set the administrative groundwork for the new regional structure created in 1973."[76] Certainly the Boston group did anticipate a redistribution of regional authority, but it did not foreshadow Boston National Historical Park so much as it responded to a management challenge created and then left unsolved by the BNHSC.

What the Boston group did foreshadow, however, was the possibility of putting organizational efficiencies on par with historical significance and profit as a justification for park building. Indeed, all three concerns came into sharp relief very quickly in Boston as a result of two remarkable failures. Bostonians learned of the first in 1968 when Secretary of Defense Clark Clifford endorsed a plan to consolidate the city's naval shipyards in South Boston.[77] The Charlestown Navy Yard, newspapers reported, would close its doors after nearly 170 years of operation.[78] Although the navy yard would not officially close down until 1974, news of its fate raised critical concerns in Charlestown, especially where residents' campaigns against urban renewal depended, in part, on the economic stability created by shipyard jobs. Others, however, sensed an opportunity at the navy yard related to news of a second failure: Boston had lost its bid to host the nation's Bicentennial. When the Bicentennial World Exposition Commission announced in 1970 that Philadelphia would host the nation's two-hundredth birthday party—which planners imagined as one part of an even larger world's fair called Expo 76—it suggested that Boston could nonetheless receive federal support for Bicentennial programming so long as "it could work in some permanent facilities of benefit to the city." BRA Director John D. Warner floated an idea almost immediately: a Bicentennial-themed "national historic park [with] a naval-marine museum on the site of the Charlestown Navy Yard." The *Boston Globe* anticipated that Warner's plan "would be an enormous fillip to Boston's Freedom Trail."[79]

The BNHSC, of course, had not considered the navy yard in its plans for a national historical park. After all, the navy yard was established in 1800, well beyond the Revolutionary period of significance identified by the commission. The BRA, however, was never so concerned with chronology. The prospects of acquiring federal land for private development, as New York City had done when the government sold off its defunct Brooklyn Navy Yard in 1968, prompted a broad view of Bicentennial programming. The USS *Constitution*, Warner suggested, could "be backed up by an historic park detailing Boston's part in the revolutionary war with special emphasis on American seapower [*sic*] through the centuries." Taking his cues from Logue's renewal strategy, Warner promised to "bring residents of Charlestown into formal discussions" and to use only half of the navy yard for a national historical park. The other half, he suggested, would attract industrial development, "which would provide jobs." Stitching it altogether would be a transportation system, such as a water ferry, since "Boston simply has not capitalized on its waterfront and water views."[80]

Within just months, Warner had refined his plan into what he termed "Prologue '75," a $56 million redevelopment plan wherein slightly more than half the funding would come from federal sources. In addition to the "national naval park" Warner imagined for the old navy yard, his plan now extended to the Freedom Trail, which would be "rejuvenated" with a network of "urban commemorative walkways" leading out "like spokes" from the Government Center to various "perception center[s]" located around town, wherein visitors might learn more about topics such as the Boston Tea Party and clipper ships.[81] Warner even imagined a perception center at Liberty Tree Park, near Essex and Washington Streets, a site that Freedom Trail boosters had long avoided, owing to its location in what they perceived to be an unsavory part of town. The weight of Warner's vision, however, still settled on the navy yard, where he now wanted to display ships "from every period in U.S. Navy history." Toward averting additional congestion, Warner promised ten acres for parking, an extension of Bunker Hill Street under the Mystic River Bridge to the navy yard, and a whole network of walking trails connecting historic sites and plazas throughout the area.[82]

Warner's proposal set off a planning frenzy, initiated by the BRA, but soon to involve the U.S. Navy and, of course, the NPS. Between 1971 and 1973, plans advanced by each organization—though sharing much in common—predictably favored particular goals. BRA plans, for instance, highlighted opportunities for private investment, including restaurants and marinas.[83] NPS planners stressed preservation priorities consistent with the navy yard's 1966 National Historic Landmark designation. And the navy, of course, sought protections for the USS *Constitution*, which it insisted must remain under the protection of the navy in perpetuity, regardless of plans elsewhere in the yard.[84] Correspondence indicates that although each of the parties remained in conversation during these years, the navy and the NPS spoke most frequently with a common voice, and often bristled against the BRA's concern for private development.[85] This dynamic may explain why the agency's final 1973 study angered NPS historians who perceived its boundary proposal—which omitted a historic dry dock and nearby Ropewalk building—as too narrowly conceived around the USS *Constitution* and the early republic, given the navy yard's significance well into the twentieth century.[86]

If the contest of plans triggered by Warner's Bicentennial aspirations hadn't produced consensus, it did rejuvenate the legislative march toward authorization.[87] On January 4, 1973, Senator Kennedy of Massachusetts introduced S. 210, legislation to establish Boston National Historical Park. That April, the navy officially declared its intent to shut down the navy yard within the year.[88] Pressure was mounting to do something with the navy yard. NPS Northeast Regional Director Chester Brooks wrote to NPS Director Ronald H. Walker regarding the navy's announcement. "Considerable pressure is being generated," he noted, "to have the property put to use for commercial and industrial purposes." Brooks reminded Walker of the agency's responsibility to the navy yard by virtue of its status as a National Historic Landmark, suggesting that it be added to the NPS system as a separate unit. Including it with legislation for the park, he warned, introduced too many contingencies.[89] Brooks noted that Senator Kennedy's bill called for a study to be made of the navy yard, to determine the feasibility of including it in the park, and that the agency "had not previously undertaken any study of the Naval Shipyard which would relate to its suitability for park use. This study of the Shipyard is now planned to determine feasibility."[90]

Political pressure mounted while planners awaited Brooks's study. That May, O'Neill and Kennedy reintroduced bills in the House and Senate.[91]

Kennedy wrote directly to Secretary of the Interior Roberts C. B. Morton, explaining that "there is a great deal of concern that additional efforts will be needed to preserve and protect [all] of these historic resources." He hoped that Morton might suggest ways to make it happen.[92] Massachusetts' Metropolitan District Commission (MDC) and BRA leadership piled on during testimony before the Senate Committee of Insular Affairs, Subcommittee on Parks and Recreation concerning Kennedy's S. 210. MDC Chairman John Sears dismissed any possibility that his organization could adequately prepare the Bunker Hill Monument for the city's Bicentennial celebration. Constant budget cuts and responsibility for numerous historic sites and thousands of acres of public land tied his hands. "I know as I stand here today," Sears testified, "that I cannot make significant improvement to Bunker Hill until the next budgetary season . . . In short, and bluntly; I have just been defeated in my last clear chance to improve Bunker Hill in time for its Bicentennial." "If the Park Service were to take over Bunker Hill," he added, "the battle would resume its rightful place, whereas today it is lost in admiration for the monument."[93]

Robert T. Kenney, head of the BRA, also strongly endorsed S. 210. "The BRA views the proposed act," he explained, "as one which shores up on-going efforts and commitments to improve the quality of the city while preserving its historic character." Kenney emphasized how the park would align Faneuil Hall, for instance, with the BRA's restoration work on the north and south market buildings that, he was keen to point out, grew out of "the first urban renewal project in this city." The problem, from Kenney's perspective, was that "urban renewal funding is being phased out and that . . . restoration projects may be coming to an end." "The private sector," he added, might not always "respond in an enlightened manner to historic preservation," owing to the whims of the economy. Kennedy's law would hedge against that tendency: "It is cognizant that tourism is a mainstay of this city's economy and that tourism is strengthened considerably by preservation of the historic sites which attract so many people to Boston." It was precisely this function of historic preservation, "as a means to augment the city's economy," Kenney explained, that animated the BRA's particular concern to repurpose the navy yard.[94]

The problem with all of this, of course, was that the research supporting the commission's 1961 proposal—the proposal S. 210 sought to implement and that encompassed surveys and lists compiled by Edwin Small beginning in the 1930s—was terribly out of date by 1973. In its testimony before the subcommittee, the Department of the Interior recounted the 1961 proposal and explained that studies of the navy yard had only just begun in June and would require until January to complete. "We will want to reflect [on] the results of that study in any recommendation we make" on S. 210. The department thus deferred on recommending action on the bill, despite agreeing "that Boston . . . will play a major role in the commemoration of the Bicentennial."[95] Secretary of Interior Rogers Morton wrote directly to Representative Henry M. Jackson, chairman of the committee, to reiterate his desire that S. 210 be deferred. "Cost estimates will have to be updated, and changes that have taken place in the area since 1961 may require revision of some recommendations." "New studies are underway," he assured, "and should be completed within fiscal year 1974."[96] But it didn't work. The Senate passed S. 210 on December 7, 1973.

House testimony concerning H.R. 7486 followed similar themes and shared concerns for the coming Bicentennial. "We do have to make the point," insisted Sears, "that for Boston the Bicentennial focusses on 1975, rather than 1976. We must get going at top speed in order to be ready." "This will," he added, "be America's last real occasion, for many years to come, to refresh its own spirit."[97] Kenney reiterated Sears's eagerness to meet the Bicentennial deadline. "It would be regrettable, indeed, if Boston marked the beginning of the bicentennial year 1975 as the 20th year of waiting for this park." Kenney had confused 1955, when President Eisenhower commissioned the BNHSC, with the year "the Boston Historic Park was first proposed to Congress," but his point still stood. Kenney's concern, however, hinged primarily on the navy yard. Failing to create a national park in Boston, he warned, might result in having to move the USS *Constitution;* "that would have the same emotional overtones as moving the Statue of Liberty to London." And, of course, the city had "already invested $56 million in an urban renewal program in Charlestown . . . we foresee further opportunities for new development."[98] O'Neill echoed previous testimony, recognizing too that the Bicentennial demanded action, though being sure to emphasize that the bill did not grant confiscatory rights to the government. He had learned a hard lesson, it seems, from earlier versions of the bill. Interestingly, O'Neill turned to a final theme that hadn't surfaced in congressional hearings since the contest over whether to create the BNHSC, two decades before. "Our historical monuments," he argued, "can provide a kind of stability and security offered by no other medium. If Americans can look to their past with dignity and pride, they are more likely to endure the travails of the future. This can best be accomplished under the auspices of the Federal Government."[99]

A CRISIS OF POSSIBILITY

The NPS found itself in a remarkable position during the spring of 1974. After having advocated for a national park in Boston for over two decades—longer, if we count Small's explorations during the 1930s—the agency suddenly got what it wanted, in spades. The BRA's urban renewal campaign, a postindustrial turn in Charlestown, and eagerness everywhere to profit from the nation's Bicentennial celebration put massive pressure on the agency to act. S. 210 and H.R. 7486 defined just one front in the political campaign to make it do so prior to the Bicentennial. Even as those bills circulated in Congress, Kennedy and O'Neill introduced additional bills, to authorize establishment of a Boston Naval Shipyard Historic Site.[100] The intent of this legislation was to protect the USS *Constitution*, permanently assigned to Boston in 1954 by Public Law 83–523, from whatever mix of private and public development might result from the other pending legislation.

The trick to all of this, of course, was that even though the NPS had finally found the political will to advance its plans in Boston, what was being proposed was not *its* plans. What the various bills proposed to create in Boston was an amalgam of the commission's 1961 report and the BRA's 1971 plan for redeveloping the navy yard. The NPS requested that Congress defer long enough for the agency to work up reasonable cost estimates, but patience was scarce amid the looming Bicentennial. Subcommittee Chairman Taylor requested a commitment from the Department of Interior by March 1, 1974, but realizing that wouldn't be possible, asked that at least a draft of the type of cooperative agreements being considered be presented to him by that date. Of course, the commission had only vaguely described what these might entail, and nobody had any sense after more than a decade of whether or not the would-be partners might agree. NPS Associate Director of Legislation Richard C. Curry wrote to the NPS deputy director that an "entire proposal cannot possibly be in place by that time."[101] He realized that if the committee acted without at least updated cost figures, it would condemn the NPS to utter failure in Boston: "we are living on borrowed time."[102]

The NPS did manage to pull together a plan in time and included within it an alternative two-year program geared only toward preparing for the Bicentennial.[103] The plan, however, only brought into focus problems that had lingered unresolved since the days of the commission. North Atlantic Regional Director Jerry D. Wagers railed against it in a memo to the associate director of legislation. "We . . . have serious reservations about the total package [the park] as it has evolved up to this point." "Sites of lesser national significance," he pointed out, "are intermingled . . . with sites of unquestioned national significance." Wagers worried too about the vagueness of the proposed partnership model. "We are concerned that the type of park proposed represents a significant departure from usual park proposals in that it depends on a somewhat loose confederation with a variety of different site owners." Wagers suggested that the plan ought rather to focus on only "the most significant sites"—Faneuil Hall, the Old State House, Old South, and a visitor center—and put the others into "a second category for further study." What's more, Wagers recommended that the agency dismiss plans for the navy yard altogether. Without a considerably larger appropriation, he wondered, what could the NPS do at the navy yard that the navy wasn't already doing? "It could be a number of years," he warned, "before the shipyard would be more than an embarrassment and a liability to the National Park Service." Wagers recognized that because "there are a number of major interests that are pushing for a National Park at the Naval Shipyard . . . it may not be possible to untrack the park proposal at this stage." Even so, "it seems questionable to us," Wagers concluded, "to accept a situation fraught with difficulties."[104]

Wagers's letter hit its mark. Later that month, when the Department of the Interior officially reported on H.R. 7486, the assistant secretary of the interior wrote to the chair of the subcommittee explaining that the department recommended against the house bill and, of course, against enacting the bill already passed in the Senate. NPS reports, he explained, estimated $14 million to get the park off the ground, whereas the proposed legislation contained just under $8.5 million. And none of the properties included, he noted, were in immediate danger of collapse or deterioration. What's more, ever since 1935, the NPS had all the legal authority it needed to support interpretation at national historic sites. It did not need new legal authority to engage those sites identified in the legislation. And besides, the proposed legislation did not clarify how partnerships would work, which would complicate any effort to coordinate interpretation, let alone create a central visitor center. "If the purpose of the legislation is to provide Federal financial assistance in time for the properties to be brought to National Park System standards by the Bicentennial," he continued, recognizing the political pressure put on the NPS in Boston, "we have great doubts as to whether, in view of the costs indicated above, this can be accomplished."[105]

A team of representatives from the Department of Interior returned to make the case when hearings resumed in May 1974.[106] Its position, of course, was not to abandon Boston's historic sites, but rather to support them with means other than traditional federal land management functions. Specifically, the sites identified in H.R. 7486 could be much better supported through the matching grant program authorized by the National Historic Preservation Act of 1966 (NHPA). Under the NHPA, the federal government could award preservation grants matching state and local contributions wherever need was demonstrated. Grant money, moreover, would not be subject to systemwide maintenance priorities, as would funds allocated to an NPS unit. And besides, Deputy Assistant Secretary Curtis Bohlen pointed out, except for the MDC at Bunker Hill, none of the other stewards wanted "to transfer ownership . . . to the Federal Government. On the contrary, all of the owners preferred to retain title." Interpretation could easily be handled under authority of the Historic Sites Act of 1935, which allowed the NPS to do the sort of interpretive work called for in H.R. 7486. And, finally, the Department of Interior saw no need to intervene at the navy yard when the U.S. Navy was already obligated by Public Law 83–523 to remain there and protect the USS *Constitution.* Authorizing a national park in Boston, Bohlen argued, would "not only [fail] to take advantage of the existing assistance programs, but by increasing the backlog it makes achieving the needed objectives highly unlikely in the near future."[107] In other words, considering the challenges facing the NPS in 1974, creating a new unit in Boston might do more harm than good. "I think perhaps what we are doing is unfairly raising expectations in the minds of the citizens of Boston that we can't fulfill."[108]

The subcommittee balked. Since last meeting in January, several members had visited Boston and toured the various sites proposed for inclusion under H.R. 7486. For them, it had no doubt been a patriotic reprieve from the daily morass of national politics, which lingered still in the aftermath of a paralyzing oil crisis, the nadir of President Richard Nixon's Watergate scandal, and an abysmal war in southeast Asia. Returning to discover that the Department of Interior opposed H.R. 7486 provoked outrage. Chairman Taylor ridiculed the notion that the navy be responsible for interpretation in the navy yard. "Well, why not return all military parks to the Department of defense," he chided, "that is where they came from."[109] He dismissed NPS cost proposals as inflated. "We attended church services [in the Old North Church, and] it appeared to me that it was in excellent condition." "Why," he

insisted, "should $325,000 be spent at that church?"[110] Representative Teno
Roncalio, of Wyoming, noted that the Department of Interior had recently
opposed the addition of several new units before asking, "does the department favor the creation of any new parks anywhere in this country and if so,
where?" Representative Paul W. Cronin, of Massachusetts, had the strongest
words. "The Department of the Interior, most particularly the Park Service,
has completely failed to plan so far as the Bicentennial is concerned." "I don't
think," referring to Bohlen's concern about fairness "that the Department has
been the least bit fair to the citizens of the United States of America in its
planning for the Bicentennial."[111] Bohlen pushed back, noting that the NPS
labored under strict spending restrictions imposed by President Nixon's own
Office of Management and Budget. "If this bill passes," he warned, the budgets
of all the other areas—including Cape Cod National Seashore, Minute Man
National Historical Park, and Arcadia National Park—would have to be cut.
"They are all going to have . . . to put some of those resources into this area."[112]

The subcommittee would not be moved. Testimony from the U.S. Navy,
including from Rear Admiral Richard E. Rumble, as well as from the BRA
and various other local and state politicians piled on. In each case, and particularly in a caustic presentation by the BRA's Bob Kenney, testimony portrayed
the NPS as a penny-pinching delinquent seeking to avoid what—amid the
time-worn symbols of Longfellow's Revolutionary Boston—amounted to
a sacred historical responsibility. A national park, they argued, necessarily
followed from the march of Bicentennial planning. It was anticipated by the
ongoing work of urban renewal and the rebranding of Boston as a heritage
destination. "Don't you see some advantage in placing it all in the hands of
the National Park Service," Taylor asked, and having "one unified type of
advertising, maybe one fee for the entire tour, bringing it up to Park Service
standards?" Creating a national park in Boston, what's more, would offset the
economic impact of a shuttered navy yard. "The city," Kenney pointed out,"
is struggling with the closing of the naval base which cost 5,000 jobs . . . We
feel that there is no question that the Charlestown Navy Yard Park should
be included."[113]

Correspondence suggests a tense mood back in Boston. In a letter to
the secretary of navy, for instance, Rumble explained that "right now the
Washington Headquarters of the National Park Service feels that they are
being overwhelmed with the U.S.S *Constitution* and Boston Navy Yard Historic
Site—more so than at any of the other proposed Sites in the Boston System.

We (the local Service representatives and myself) don't agree."[114] Nor did Congress. That July, the committee reconvened for a markup session wherein it haggled over amendments to the legislation. In the end, it made three major changes: the Charlestown Navy Yard would be included in the legislative package, though with a separate budget line; funding for Charlestown would be set at $8 million less than the NPS cost estimate; and the federal government would retain limited right to eminent domain only so far as it might be needed to acquire a suitable visitor center in downtown Boston.[115] With that, the committee reported favorably to the House on H.R. 7486 with amendments.[116] The House officially amended and passed S. 210 in lieu of H.R. 7486 on August 5 and, on September 18, the Senate approved the revised S. 210 without debate. Finally, on October 1, 1974, Public Law 93–431 authorized the establishment of Boston National Historical.[117] This legislation did not create the park as it exists today. As we will see, Dorchester Heights would not be added until 1978.[118] It did, however, lay out its broad contours and set into motion the planning that would soon establish a national park in Boston.

* * *

Recounting the rocky path to authorization between 1960 and 1974 forces us to contend with a hard truth: by most measures, Congress's addition of Boston National Historical Park to the national park system constituted a significant failure for the NPS. Most immediately, the agency failed to prevent Congress from compelling it to include a unit that it did not consider suitable for inclusion. In other words, Congress bullied the park into existence, not out of a prevailing concern for the agency's mandate, but rather to satisfy the political agendas of representatives interested in luring jobs, tourists, and federal monies to Boston amid the national Bicentennial celebration. The park was certainly not unique in this regard. On the contrary, the park's story was among only the first of many caught up in an era of so-called park-barrel politics, wherein, as Associate Director for Planning and Development Denis Galvin put it, "our formal testimony on the Hill has no credibility any more. We've lost control of the agenda."[119]

What is special about the park's story, however, is that it shows us how the NPS was in many regards complicit, even if unwittingly, in creating the circumstances that ultimately allowed for the erosion of control described by Galvin. In Boston, the problem had everything to do with the agency's posture toward urban renewal. Since as early as the BNHSC's deliberations, the NPS conceived of park building in a way that clung to old ideas about demolition and displacement. Despite Logue's new directions and Whitehill's encouragements, the agency remained steadfast in its commitment to old renewal strategies. For that, it lost considerable trust among the people of Boston. As Whitehill explained in a 1975 interview, the NPS's early endorsement of demolition and removal in Boston effectively prevented it from accomplishing anything, given the scale and intensity of resistance from Bostonians who were well aware that their own lives were at stake. "The North Enders just plain didn't like it," he noted, "and I think Charlestown was not very pleased with it either."[120] Moreover, aligning itself with urban renewal signaled the agency's willingness to advance priorities—economic stimulus, "slum clearance," downtown revival—that were neither appropriate nor advantageous to its mission. In the wake of Mission 66, which oriented the agency even more fully around profit-based private partnerships, it is no wonder that Congress considered economic stimulus on par with historical significance as reasons for authorizing a national park in Boston. The NPS had not "lost control of the agenda," as Galvin supposed, so much as its leaders had traded it in after World War II in hopes of saving a struggling park system. The park's decades-long path to authorization demonstrated just how much the NPS had lost in the bargain.

CHAPTER 4

Planning a Park for "Modern Boston and Modern America"

W alking down Congress Street," just months after Congress authorized Boston National Historical Park, Park Historian Mary
Holmes encountered an "excited Bostonian who recognized my
ranger uniform and wanted to know . . . where's the park?" Both of them,
of course, were standing in the park, but the park authorized by Public Law
93–431 barely resembled what most Americans had come to recognize as a
national park by 1974. The agency's iconic nature parks had, by the mid-1970s,
attained new heights of popularity among young white Americans distrust-
ful of modernity and activated by the new environmentalism.[1] Urban parks,
however, like Philadelphia's Independence National Historical Park and Saint
Louis's Gateway Arch National Park (formerly Jefferson National Expansion
Memorial), were still a novelty, and Boston's partnership model even more
novel besides. For Holmes, reorienting visitors to the urban partnership park
would require demonstrating how it could "help us understand our present
lives." "Let us not forget, in our enthusiasm for resources," she warned, "that
[they help] explain modern Boston and modern America."[2]

This chapter responds to two questions imbedded in Holmes's observation: what exactly did it mean in 1974 to "explain modern Boston and modern
America;" and how could Boston's fledgling park achieve it? Answering the
first question requires that we take stock of a remarkably fraught moment in
Boston history. The years immediately surrounding the park's authorization
were framed by two deeply related, though seemingly contradictory, events. On
one hand, violence triggered during 1974–76 by the desegregation of Boston's
public schools threatened to tear the city apart. On the other, the 1975–76
U.S. Bicentennial celebration sought to unite Americans in consuming the
kind of Revolutionary memory that ran all through Ed Logue's New Boston.
These events provide the crucial context for understanding the evolution in
Boston's heritage landscape during these years, which had particular bearing
on the Freedom Trail and its claim on the city's historical imagination. I

dwell on those transformations in part I of this chapter. In part II, I turn to the planning process that produced the park's first general management plan and consider, too, the basic chores of establishment that occupied the park staff during its first year.

Weighing both parts together raises critical questions about the National Park Service's capacity during the 1970s to build a partnership park in conversation with stakeholders who, in some cases, approached one another across gaping political and ideological divides. We discover that rendering the park comprehensible to visitors, and contending with the complexity of Boston's urban landscape, did—just as Holmes predicted—concern planners during the park's first years. At issue is whether it concerned them enough.

PART I: RACE, MEMORY, AND THE NPS IN BOSTON, CA. 1974

Holmes's contention that the park's success hinged on explaining "modern Boston and modern America" implied much more in 1974 than simply reflecting on the legacy of the American Revolution. Indeed, the years encompassing the park's path to authorization, presumably what Holmes meant by "modern Boston," had put Bostonians through a tumultuous period of transformation. As we learned in previous chapters, much of Boston's physical change during those years owed to the city's enormous investments in urban renewal and related programming tied to road and highway construction. Beginning during the 1950s, and spearheaded by Mayor John Hynes, urban renewal initiatives ripped Boston apart—literally in the case of the West End and construction of the Central Artery—before stitching it back together around new buildings, new people, and new ways of imagining Boston's past and future. The Freedom Trail, itself a product of urban renewal, became an emblem of Boston's transformation, a carefully crafted historical introduction to a new story of progress, written by Ed Logue and Mayor John Collins. A central finding of this study is that the National Park Service (NPS) eagerly sought in Boston to involve itself in the telling of this new progress narrative, so much so that it imagined historic preservation as a means by which to facilitate, as Regional Director Daniel Tobin put it, "citizen redevelopment."[3]

The problem, of course, was that the progress narrative endorsed by the NPS conceived of progress so narrowly as to ignore tens of thousands of Bostonians for whom urban renewal meant anything but. The West End debacle, of course, had become the stuff of nightmarish legend among working-class and nonwhite neighborhoods encircling Boston's increasingly prosperous downtown. By the late 1960s, their fears of removal and disinvestment had become a reality. The Boston Redevelopment Authority (BRA) had only ever relocated five hundred families, despite its displacement of thousands. Its South End Renewal projects, which destroyed the ethnically and racially diverse New York Streets section beginning in 1956, had only rehoused twenty-five families in new South End units by 1968. By the late 1970s, Boston had become known nationally for urban displacement and racial anxiety thanks, in part, to Richard Broadman's documentary film, *Mission Hill and the Miracle of Boston* (1978), which captured the story as it played out in the Parker Hill section of Roxbury.[4] In the end, although renewal had promised the expansion of city services—including police and fire protection and road repair—into development districts, most of it never moved beyond the downtown business and financial districts.[5] The problem was not exclusive to Boston, of course, but the pitting of ethnic white and Black Bostonians against one another and against developers raised deep wells of anxiety that had festered there among decades of corrupt politics and economic decline.

Throughout these years, the degradations of urban renewal exacerbated inequities in Boston that civil rights activists across the nation had brought into focus during the previous decade. Inspired by the national civil rights struggle and encouraged by its victories, Bostonians increasingly applied direct action to problems associated with urban renewal. Historian Thomas O'Conner notes that "Black residents used street parades, sound trucks, protest marches, and public demonstrations" to insist that the BRA recognize the needs of impoverished neighborhoods.[6] The effectiveness of postwar social movements also inspired working Bostonians to organize within their own communities. Community development corporations, advisory groups, and various other neighborhood coalitions resisted BRA plans in Roxbury, Mission Hill, Dorchester, Chinatown, and as we have seen, the North End and Charlestown. In fact, as historian Lizabeth Cohen suggests, among the great unintended legacies of Ed Logue's renewal campaign was a new era of "community vigilance and empowerment," born of resistance to Logue.[7] As a result, Boston's growing spate of community organizations managed by the late 1960s to get a seat at the city's planning table. According to historian Lawrence Kennedy, "no longer could planning be done exclusively in corporate board rooms and government offices . . . It now had to take into account the wishes of ordinary citizens."[8] The NPS and the Boston National Historic Sites Commission (BNHSC) had nodded casually toward community engagement, of course, but the "ordinary citizens" they engaged prior to 1974 primarily consisted of businesspeople and heritage boosters, all of whom were white and embedded in deep webs of privilege. The weight of Kennedy's observation, as we will see, would factor significantly in the park's path to establishment.

The NPS's fortunes in Boston would also hinge on recognizing the deepening racial contours of inequity and dissent across the city. Boston's population had transformed significantly during the years leading to authorization. Between 1950 and 1960, for instance, the decade during which the BNHSC devised a plan for what would become the park, Boston's African American population grew by sixty percent. The growth owed in large part to a wave of southerners looking for opportunity in the North's postwar industries. The new arrivals also included middle-class Americans eager to study in Boston's universities or seek work in its burgeoning military and high-tech economies. The confluence of these groups amid a high tide of social activism reactivated Boston's Black civil rights community in a way unseen since the early decades of the twentieth century. By 1963, new civil rights organizations—the Emergency Public Integration Committee and the Boston Action Group, for instance—appeared in Boston alongside older reenergized organizations such as the National Association for the Advancement of Colored People (NAACP) and the Congress of Racial Equality (CORE), in collective direct action such as against companies like Wonder Bread; Sears, Roebuck and Company; and Trailways Bus Company, which refused to hire Black workers. Elsewhere, Black parents organized to demand better access to education and to fight de facto segregation in schools. By 1969, grassroots community organizers had managed to distribute over a thousand students of color among better-funded, primarily white, Boston schools by taking advantage of open enrollment policies.[9]

The problem of school segregation, which persisted in Boston despite the U.S. Supreme Court having ruled it unconstitutional in 1954, reflected—and, in fact, compounded—the same kinds of systemic inequality that ran though all facets of urban renewal.[10] By the time that the park began down its path to authorization, these and other nested problems had grown worse amid a calamity of U.S. foreign and domestic policy. The Vietnam War, which disproportionately impacted poor and nonwhite Americans, drove up inflation and forced cuts in precisely the kind of social programs that sought to ameliorate poverty. The resulting anxiety that seemed everywhere present in the United States by the late 1960s appeared in Boston too, and often at historic sites associated with the nascent national historical park. The NAACP staged

Freedom Sunday rallies at Faneuil Hall in 1964, while the Old State House proposed a "Freedom Trail of Negro History." Activists rallied at Old South Meeting House in 1969 in support of Puerto Rican Independence. Vietnam Veterans Against War staged an antiwar rally at Bunker Hill in 1971, despite the Metropolitan District Commission's refusal to grant it permission. A year later, 1,500 antiwar protesters converged at the Charlestown Navy Yard, where one heckler yelled "go back to Cambridge, why don't youse? Charlestown takes care of itself." Even at the height of the 1973 legislative campaign to authorize the park, pro- and anti-abortion rights advocates clashed at Old North Church.[11] Just these few examples illustrate the extent to which Bostonians, even by the late twentieth century, lived with their past. In this light, Holmes's urging that the park explain "modern Boston and modern America" reflected a concern that the NPS not simply engage the present, but that it do so in a way that sustained its partners' long-term investments in a usable past.

In 1974, however, the year of the park's authorization, the NPS's most widely visible entanglement with "modern Boston and modern America" was just beginning to unfold at Dorchester Heights. The NPS added Dorchester Heights to the National Register of Historic Places in 1966, but it had not been included in Boston National Historical Park by Public Law 93–431. The law did, however, list the site among one of five areas that could be included under appropriate circumstances without additional congressional action. As we will see, with considerable encouragement from U.S. Representative John Joseph "Joe" Moakley, representing Massachusetts' Ninth Congressional District, the park did expand to include Dorchester Heights. But what put a national spotlight on Dorchester Heights beginning in 1974 was neither the NPS nor the war monument located there, but rather its location adjacent to South Boston High School. Occupying about a third of Thomas Park, South Boston High became a focal point of a citywide school busing crisis triggered by court-mandated desegregation of the Boston school system beginning in 1974. Orders to exchange one-half of South Boston's predominantly white sophomores with one-half of Roxbury High School's predominantly Black students inspired months of protest, counterprotest, and numerous incidents of racial violence at the school—including a stabbing—all with the Dorchester Heights Monument as a backdrop. The park's first superintendent, Hugh Gurney, visited South Boston High in 1975 to discuss its interface with Dorchester Heights. It was the first time he had been required to pass through a metal detector. "That was my introduction," Gurney recalls, "to inner-city schools."[12]

Dorchester Heights was not the only park affiliate to appear in the national spotlight cast by Boston's school busing crisis. Indeed, busing protests and related violence continued for years across Boston. Photojournalist Stanley Forman captured one particular incident in a 1976 Pulitzer-winning photograph that shocked Americans with its portrayal of "a young, White man [Joseph Rakes] lung[ing] at a Black man [Ted Landsmark] with the sharp point of a flagpole, with the American flag attached."[13] Seen in the center background of Forman's photograph is the Old State House. Gurney recalls the image "going viral" in and beyond Boston. *Ebony* magazine recalled the incident, wherein "White demonstrators within sight and sound of Faneuil Hall [yelled] 'we got ourselves a nigger!'" "Do the people of Boston," it wondered, "understand what Bostonians were fighting for 200 years ago?"[14]

It was precisely the question that the park promised to answer, though by 1976, as we will see, how and whether it could was still a matter of debate

FIGURE 7. Joseph Rakes attacks Ted Landsmark with the Old State House in background, as portrayed in Stanley Forman's "The Soiling of Old Glory" (1976). "The Soiling of Old Glory," Pulitzer Prize 1977. Stanleyformanphotos.com.

among a planning team flown in two thousand miles from the NPS Denver Service Center to set the park's path. One way or the other, it was very clear by 1976 that no matter how it proceeded, the park would be a product of the place and politics that produced it, a fact—as Mary Holmes's insight suggests—that was not lost on the park's first managers.

The Freedom Trail and Boston's Gas Lamp Renaissance

The years leading to and encompassing the park's authorization had plunged Boston into a tumult of racial, political, and social discord. And yet, for some Bostonians, the dream of urban renewal—clean streets, lively commerce, evidence of progress—had indeed begun to materialize. By 1965, the coexistence of these parallel worlds was evident in the *Boston Globe*, for instance, wherein reports of antiwar protests and escalation in Vietnam might be interspersed with articles like Joe Harrington's survey of gas lighting in Boston. Boston was experiencing a "gas lamp renaissance," Harrington explained, spearheaded in Beacon Hill, Newton, and other tony neighborhoods in and around Boston. Some Bostonians, it seems, preferred the late nineteenth-century gas lighting technology to electricity for its gentle light, even going so far as to install stylized colonial fixtures near sites including Paul Revere's house, which appeared in a photograph accompanying Harrington's article. "Some residents of the North End . . . claim [the gas lamps] do not shed sufficient light for the area," he noted, "though they have proved very popular with tourists taking photographs" (see figure 3, page 47).[15]

What Harrington described, of course, were early ripples in a rising tide of gentrification that would wash over Boston during the next decade and then well beyond. Urban renewal had indeed begun to attract new, and new kinds of, people to Boston. In the South End, for instance, white middle-class "urban pioneers" began buying up and restoring century-old townhouses as early as 1962. These new arrivals discovered in the old immigrant South End the possibility of living affordably, close to downtown, and in neighborhoods that eschewed the racial homogeneity and cultural sameness of postwar suburbs. In many cases, the urban pioneers found common cause with their immigrant and working-class neighbors of color in resisting the BRA's renewal plans, which sought to divide the South End and displace thousands of low-income residents.[16] Indeed, coalition politics in the South End held the BRA at bay for well over a decade, and sometimes captured widespread attention, as in 1968 when residents erected a plywood tent city to raise awareness of the need for affordable housing in Boston. In the end, though, and despite these successes, statistics reveal the true impact of gentrification on the South End. From 1960 to 1980, twenty-five thousand poor and working-class South Enders—half of them Black—lost their homes to renewal, replaced in part by nineteen thousand new white middle-class residents. The South End's historic nineteenth-century architecture had been preserved. But, as author Jim Vrabel puts it, "if people make a neighborhood, an argument can be made that [the South End] was replaced."[17]

If anyone was in a position to benefit from Boston's gaslight renaissance, it was the progenitors of the Freedom Trail. As we learned in chapter one, the Freedom Trail concept championed by Old North Church Rector Robert M. Winn and newspaper man William Schofield in 1951 evolved rapidly, though informally, in subsequent years. In 1957, the Boston Advertising Club made promotion of the trail a pet project, placing it under the supervision of its Public Service Committee, which then consisted of Club President Phil Nutting, Past President Richard Berenson, and Robert Friedman, whom the committee appointed project manager. The Advertising Club formalized a stand-alone Freedom Trail Committee in 1958 and then, in 1960, established a joint public service committee with the Greater Boston Chamber of Commerce to manage the trail. Recall from chapter three that these were heady days for the chamber, buoyed as it was by Ed Logue's probusiness renewal aspirations and his fondness for the Freedom Trail. Investing in the trail meant investing in a future for Boston tied to urban renewal.[18]

The committee had achieved a great deal by 1965. Cochair Robert Friedmann noted how frequently the trail appeared in tourist guides. The "increase in visitors," he observed, "speaks for itself." And yet, problems—which Friedmann considered "the results of this tourist influx"—remained.[19] Tourists still complained, for instance, about untoward sights along the trail. We cannot know exactly what Donald A. Armistead and his family witnessed in Copp's Hill Burying Ground, because Armistead would "not go into further detail" about the "gross, callous and flagrant disrespect" perpetrated "almost daily by children, teenagers, and some adults, weather permitting." Mrs. Jack Gold reported the same, noting a "half dozen boys . . . making themselves at home in the historic spot smoking and setting small fires." D. K. Benson, a missile avionics engineer from California, complained to Mayor Collins about the "difficulty in following the trail due to the very poorly marked route." Benson proposed a novel solution: "may I suggest a painted stripe on the sidewalks to follow and thus ease the problem for others who will be coming later?"[20] Whether or not Benson deserves credit for imagining what is now the Freedom Trail's iconic red line is unclear. The concept has typically been attributed to the trail's own Richard Berenson.[21] That a missile designer from California proposed it, however, captures precisely the Cold War moment that defined heritage tourism in postwar Boston.

Visitor comments like these encouraged Berenson and Friedmann to advance the Freedom Trail's fortunes. In 1964, under their leadership, the joint committee incorporated to form the nonprofit organization that still operates today as the Freedom Trail Foundation. Friedmann was the foundation's first president, with Berenson as its treasurer and the mayor as honorary chairman. Just a year later, the mayor constituted a Freedom Trail Commission, lodged within the parks department, with Berenson as the chairman.[22] The act that established the commission charged it with "designat[ing] a route . . . not over three miles in length, along which persons may walk and pass not less than twelve historic places."[23] Berenson and Friedmann, it seems, had devised a business strategy à la Ed Logue's New Boston: their Freedom Trail Foundation would harvest private capital through fundraising and charitable programming, while the Freedom Trail Commission would manage what facets of public policy—such as relating to sidewalk repair, signage, and street cleaning, for instance—related to goings-on along the trail.

The genesis of these organizations, almost simultaneously, resulted from a deal—likely brokered by Berenson—to create a Freedom Trail Information Center on Boston Common, attached to the subway entrance at Park and Tremont Streets. The Massachusetts Bay Transportation Authority and the Boston Parks Department pledged to pay for the building, while the Chamber of Commerce promised to staff it and keep it equipped with maps and other items provided by the Freedom Trail Foundation. A press release explained that "young women in blue and gold colors" would meet there with 700,000 visitors annually and distribute "Freedom Trail Booklets donated by John Hancock Mutual Life Insurance Co. and information on the New Boston." In 1966, after a year of operation, the *Boston Globe* reported considerable activity at the new center. "The girls often enjoy just chatting with tourists, many of whom return later for more talk or to ask for a date." "I fell in love this summer because of my job," one attendant confided.[24]

And yet, incorporation wasn't a cure-all. Visitors still grumbled about conditions. In 1967, for instance, Wilma Little from Richmond, Indiana, complained to the governor that the courtyard of Old North Church "was filled with dirty old men that looked like New York's bowery. We had to step over human body waste in order to read some of the plaques."[25] Visitors complained too about erratic and inconsistent hours of operation at the various sites they encountered along the trail.[26] Berenson responded to many of them himself, insisting that their inconveniences resulted from the Freedom Trail being a "living trail," which is precisely—as he explained—what made it unique, unlike "cold, austere monumental places, such as Independence Hall." Indeed, insisting on keeping the Freedom Trail open and accessible—to tourists, as well as investors—proved a successful strategy. By 1966, the foundation began running full-page ads in the *Boston Globe* advertising "subscriptions" to the Freedom Trail at a five-dollar junior share, a ten-dollar senior share, or a twenty-five-dollar corporate share.[27] Increasingly, in the run-up to the Bicentennial, the foundation sponsored speaking events, charitable dinners, film premiers, concerts, and anything else that might raise money for the trail while also boosting interest in it. Locally, at least, the impact was real. Bostonians came to appreciate the trail as a community asset. Not only did kids fall in love at its information center, but "young mothers . . . change diapers, tourists bring their lunches in and young couples agree to meet there."[28]

A Walkway to the Sea and Boston's Festival Marketplace

Despite evident success along the Freedom Trail, a deep irony within Harrington's so-called gaslight renaissance bore profound significance for the new national park: the industrial largess recalled by turn-of-the-century gaslights had all but vanished. Despite brief periods of growth during the World Wars—and a long devastating decline between them—Boston's traditional goods-producing mill economy was moribund by the 1950s. Of course, unlike more wholly industrial cities like nearby Lowell, Boston's fortunes had been more deeply rooted in serving the financial needs of the region's broader industrial economy. That trend continued with new kinds of industries: health care, computers, third-party service providers, and durable goods manufacturing. These new sectors favored professional and technical specialists over blue-collar laborers. They also created considerable demand for labor characterized as unskilled, such as custodial work, thereby exacerbating class disparity throughout Boston. Other problems lurked too. Though federal defense spending poured into these new industries during the immediate postwar decades, de-escalation in Vietnam and contractions in the nation's space program triggered precipitous job losses during the early 1970s. And it was the sudden reversal in federal spending that triggered President Richard Nixon's 1973 decision to close the Charlestown Navy Yard. The navy yard had sustained nearly fourteen thousand employees just a decade before; by 1970 five thousand people still worked there.[29] A quarter of them had accrued enough seniority to retire. Younger employees had opportunities to transfer to the nation's other navy yards or find new work in private industry. But middle-aged workers like fifty-six-year-old John I. Beach readily understood that "no private company is going to hire me . . . and there aren't enough government jobs to go around."[30] Like Boston itself, navy yard employees found themselves caught up in an era of economic transition that left few options for people in the middle.

The nagging dichotomies that typified Boston's transformations during the late twentieth century reshaped the city's political landscape too. John Hynes, and John Collins before him, had dominated mayoral politics for nearly two decades by reinvesting in Boston's downtown. Urban renewal made sense then because it promised to reverse decades of downtown disinvestment by the four-term James Curley administration, which favored Boston's ethnic white neighborhoods. By the late 1960s, as we've seen, the tides had reversed again. Urban renewal's excesses in downtown—such as the wholesale replacement of Scollay Square with the new modernist Government Center—and especially the BRA's insistence on profiting from displacement in the West and South Ends, focused the 1967 Boston mayoral campaign on the concerns of residents determined to resist renewal everywhere else. Kevin White, who won the election, did so in part by assuring voters a greater role in city politics for Boston's neighborhoods. Sure enough, once elected, White opened new city offices throughout Boston, invested in infrastructure and capital improvements beyond downtown, and made himself and the police more present in Boston's Black communities.[31]

And yet, despite all of this, White remained powerfully committed to urban renewal and downtown's business set. In fact, it was White who oversaw the final transformation of Boston's downtown renewal district into the heritage consumer landscape that frames how virtually all visitors experience the park to this day. The Government Center had been completed, of course, but the portions of downtown circling it remained unplanned for, including historic Faneuil Hall and, to its east, the three neoclassical granite buildings of Quincy Market, built during 1824–26. As we saw in chapter three, Walter Muir Whitehill had convinced Ed Logue to protect portions of Boston's historic landscape,

FIGURE 8. Richard S. Robie (left), president of the Chamber of Commerce, presents Richard Berensen (right) with a check for the Freedom Trail at the Paul Revere House in 1968, with Mayor Kevin White (center). Brearley Collection, Boston Public Library, Boston, MA.

but by 1969, when the BRA received a federal preservation grant for Quincy Market, it still had no plan for these buildings.

Architect Roger S. Webb and his newly formed Architectural Heritage Foundation had set to work on a preservation plan in 1966. So had competing architect and restaurateur Benjamin Thompson, whose vision included folding all of the buildings into a distinctive retail experience. Thompson engaged James Rouse, who had gained notoriety for his pioneering designs of shopping malls and planned communities. Together with Thompson, Rouse reimagined the Faneuil Hall and Quincy Market areas as what they termed a "walkway to the sea," borrowing a phrase from Ed Logue, a transitional area between the waterfront and the Government Center wherein locals and visitors alike would shop, dine, and imagine themselves as part of historic Boston.[32] Between 1972 and 1973, just as the political fight over the park heated up, so did the competition between Webb and Rouse to win Mayor White's favor. The BRA initially sided with Thompson, but the city council sided with Rouse, who bundled his proposal with $500,000 for Bicentennial programming. In the end, White opted for Rouse, whom he claimed had "won my heart and mind." With that, and considerable efforts by White to convince investors, Rouse set to developing the nation's first festival marketplace, portions of which opened to great fanfare during August 1976.[33]

The Bicentennial in Boston

Rouse's offer of Bicentennial funding reminds us just how deeply concerns over planning the nation's two-hundredth birthday celebration seeped into the economic, cultural, and political landscape. Indeed, in a letter to one of the architects managing the Faneuil Hall project, White complained about slow progress on "one of the most important restoration projects in America." "What you may not be aware of," he grumbled, "is the importance this project plays in Boston's Bicentennial celebration, and the interest and time that I have

FIGURE 9. The festival marketplace concept as it appeared in 1980 along the Freedom Trail, with Quincy Market to the right and Faneuil Hall in the background. The assault on Ted Landsmark occurred just blocks away. Boston Landmarks Commission image collection, Collection 5210.004, Boston City Archives, West Roxbury, MA.

devoted to guarantee its successful completion before the summer of 1975."[34] White's missive reminds us that if urban renewal created the overarching framework for gentrification in Boston, then it was the national Bicentennial celebration that activated it. We've already seen in chapter three how Congress bullied the park into existence, not out of a prevailing concern for the agency's mandate, but rather to satisfy the political agendas of representatives concerned with luring jobs, tourists, and federal monies to Boston amid the national Bicentennial celebration. Rouse's development campaign demonstrates how Bicentennial concerns literally reshaped, up until the very last minute, the historic landscape that Congress authorized the park to manage.

In other ways, too, Bicentennial build-up had already set the stage for park planning, even in ways not immediately evident to the NPS. Bicentennial planning in Boston had, after all, been orchestrated by the same people who set out after World War II to create a profitable heritage landscape. The Chamber of Commerce initiated Bicentennial planning in 1962, having been inspired that year by a visit to the World's Fair in Seattle, Washington. The chamber applied to the Bureau of International Expositions that November and, in 1963, organized the World Freedom Fair, Inc. nonprofit organization to coordinate—in partnership with the BRA—all planning activities associated with the Bicentennial and a World's Fair for Boston. By 1966, World Freedom Fair, Inc. operated its own office with six employees. Importantly, the organization's staff included two BRA planners appointed especially for the job, showing once again how thoroughly the Logue model of private–public partnership had infiltrated Boston's civic landscape during the 1960s. The Freedom 75 group, as it had become known, even reached out to Walter Muir Whitehill for support. Whitehill dismissed the project as "hucksterism" and sent a copy of his grumpy "Cerebration versus Celebration" essay instead.[35]

Boston's World's Fair aspirations, as we learned in chapter three, succumbed in 1970 to the whims of federal Bicentennial planning. It was a great disappointment to BRA planners who had been planning diligently for Expo 76, in part owing to Mayor White's strong support for it. They had conceived of a massive floating city-of-tomorrow connecting Columbia Point in Dorchester to Thompson Island. Modular communities, floating gardens, and a massive glass dome all pointed to a futuristic next chapter for urban renewal. The project's potential environmental impact on Boston Harbor, however, drew staunch opposition including from Massachusetts State Senator Joe Moakley, who opposed it even before learning of the World Exposition Commission's

decision against a World's Fair in Boston. It was precisely this showdown over
the harbor and the future of its islands that would lead to establishment in
1996 of the Boston Harbor National Recreation Area.[36]

The BRA's planning did pay off, however, insomuch as it laid the groundwork—in its Prologue 75 proposal—for a whole host of local Bicentennial
programming, including a navy yard heritage experience and an expanded
Freedom Trail. White assigned responsibility for coordinating these activities to the Mayor's Office of the Boston Bicentennial, which he established
in 1972. True to form, the city's new Bicentennial office then immediately
created Boston 200, a nonprofit corporation charged with operating Boston's
Bicentennial programs. Its director, Katharine D. Kane, played a pivotal role
in shaping Boston's Bicentennial experience and, as we will see, figured significantly in early conversations with NPS planners about the shape of the
park. Under Kane, Boston 200 advanced two major interpretive initiatives that
largely defined visitor experience of Boston's Bicentennial heritage landscape.
The first, "Citygame," encompassed three exhibits arrayed across the city that
sought to focus Bicentennial tourists on "the city itself . . . Boston's cultural
and educational institutions, its fascinating ethnic neighborhoods, its historic
areas, and its citizens themselves become the basis for celebration." The first of
Citygame's exhibits, "The Revolution: Where It All Began," moored visitors in
a Revolutionary past. The second two—"The Grand Exposition of Progress
and Invention" and "Where's Boston: Visions of the City"—explored the
nineteenth and twentieth centuries.[37]

Tying it all together was Boston 200's second interpretive initiative, a series
of eight neighborhood discovery trails and a Black Heritage Trail. Six of
these—Charlestown, Waterfront, Beacon Hill, South End, Cambridge, and
Back Bay—expanded the Freedom Trail concept into adjacent neighborhoods
by equipping tourists with maps highlighting important historic sites along
the way. The pioneering Black Heritage Trail, which ranked among the first
publicly funded walking tours of African American history in the United
States, primarily chronicled Boston's nineteenth-century Black community
and mostly followed the path still marked today.[38] And finally, Boston 200, in
partnership with the Freedom Trail Foundation, radically expanded Boston's
favorite historical footpath. The *Boston Globe* reported that "now there are 2
Freedom Trails to follow." Former U.S. Senator Leverett Saltonstall, who
had since replaced Friedmann as president of the Freedom Trail Foundation,
explained that the trail had been expanded into a North End loop and a

Downtown loop. "City workers have erased the old Freedom Trail," the *Globe* reported, "and have painted new red lines along downtown sidewalks marking the two loops." Saltonstall explained that the change was intended to ease tourist congestion during the busy Bicentennial season. What's more, for the first time in history, all of the Freedom Trail sites had begun to coordinate their hours "for tourist convenience."[39]

The Bicentennial years—which formally began in Boston during 1973, in connection with the centennial of the Boston Tea Party—thus nourished the park's partner sites like never before and significantly strengthened the Freedom Trail's hold on the city's popular historical imagination. It also produced, in many cases, thoughtful and innovative programming. Historian M. J. Rymsza-Pawlowska recounts how Citygame's "The Revolution: Where It All Began," staged by Boston 200 in the Old Quincy Market, deployed all manner of innovative interpretive strategies to confront modern visitors with the emotional weight of choices made by the Revolutionary generation.[40] Boston 200 also sponsored performances of "We've Come Back for a Little Look Around," a joint project of the NPS and Temple University, wherein student actors imagined on stage, and in conversation with Bicentennial audiences, what would happen if Benjamin Franklin returned to experience 1970s America. Audience engagement seems to have been a key facet of Boston 200 programming. Its walking trails, for instance, had been developed in conjunction with a National Endowment for the Arts-funded Bicentennial discovery network project to study Boston's neighborhoods and the reactions of people who might tour them. The Boston City Archives contains folders of handwritten feedback from school children who were taken on prototype tours around the city. One such tour occurred in Charlestown, where one student just couldn't fathom how she could "acquire an understanding of the significant (if any) role that Charlestown played in the formation of America today by just finding out the difference between a federalist building and a victorian building."[41] Her misgivings notwithstanding, Bicentennial-era programming cemented the Freedom Trail's grasp on Boston's historical imagination, so much so that in 1976 the NPS included it on its new and growing list of National Recreation Trails.[42]

Elsewhere, Bicentennial programming channeled the anxieties of late twentieth-century America. Activists representing the entire spectrum of American political concerns gathered in Boston for a 1973 Boston Tea Party reenactment, where members of the People's Bicentennial Commission stole the show by rowing around the harbor wearing a giant Richard Nixon mask and royal robes emblazoned with oil company logos.[43] Historian Tammy Gordon argues that the Bicentennial celebration expressed a shifting American zeitgeist, one wherein distrust of government spawned a new sense of individualism, alongside renewed faith in the market to bolster democracy. Prize-winning journalist Ellen Goodman captured that sensibility in Boston, observing at the time that though "the buycentennial [*sic*] burgers and red, white and blue ice cream bars had come and gone . . . we have more trees, an expanded Afro-American museum, a renovated nineteenth-century marketplace, a water fountain here, and a historical marker there." "In Boston," she concluded, "we have seen a Bicentennial that enriched rather than ripped off our heritage."[44]

Goodman's conflation of heritage, profit, and urban progress recalled a long tradition in Boston, detailed in chapter one, of linking Revolutionary memory to economic growth. Certainly Goodman, a stalwart advocate for social justice, perceived real democratic value within the Bicentennial's impact. Boston 200's innovative history programming suggests that, to some extent, she was right. And yet, the consumer impulse coursing through all of it recalled the same economics of white prosperity underlying renewal efforts during the 1820s, colonial revivalism during the 1870s, and "slum clearance" during the 1950s. It is this facet of Revolutionary memory, in fact, that explains why it has prevailed in Boston since the 1820s. Traditional icons of Revolutionary memory, such as Paul Revere, fit easily into modern notions of entrepreneurial citizenship. Bicentennial programming, as Gordon shows us, made the connection even more overt, reinforcing at every turn the idea that wealth (or the quest for it) and consumerism are predictors of virtuous citizenship. Consider, for instance, the Bicentennial Birthday Book campaign wherein the city of Boston issued a catalog of gifts, ranging from bike racks to playgrounds, that ordinary citizens might purchase by way of expressing their patriotism.[45] Against this backdrop, it is hardly any surprise at all that legislators dismissed NPS concerns that, as proposed, the park was neither historically cogent nor practically feasible. Amid the consumerist rhetoric of Bicentennial fervor, and given the NPS's eager embrace of urban renewal, Congress readily conflated the pursuit of profit with the work of history. Indeed, by the time NPS planners arrived in Boston to imagine a new national park, much of the imagining had already been done for them by the Bicentennial and its boosters. History in Boston meant a robust Freedom Trail that, though occasionally capable of confronting difficult pasts, equated old stories about Revolutionary memory with modern notions of progress, profit, and privilege.

The New History and a New NPS

The conflation of history, profit, and progress in Boston during these years showcases a remarkable irony at play in the park's intellectual genesis. At exactly the same time that planners and politicians butted heads over the park's authorizing legislation, and with it the park's historical contours, American historians had ignited a firestorm of revisionist Revolutionary historiography. The spark, it turns out, was a probing debate about the causes of the Revolution: Was it really about power, or were ideas at its core? If it was about power, then was it economic or political power? If it was about ideas like liberty and virtue, then how did Americans end up so beholden to market forces by the middle of the next century? What about people with no consumer or political power? How did women, the poor, and the enslaved experience the Revolution? How did they make claims to citizenship? All of these questions had been presaged by the same twentieth-century concerns—civil rights, war, class strife, Watergate, the Bicentennial itself—that had set the United States on edge after World War II. Volumes of top-shelf scholarship poured out of American universities beginning in the 1960s, all of which dismantled the consensus history that had very much lodged itself in the BNHSC's vision of Longfellow's Boston. And yet, remarkably, none of this new scholarship seems to have found its way into official conversations surrounding the park's authorization, even though many of its leading figures, most notably Alfred Young, staked their claim in Boston within spitting distance of the Freedom Trail.[46] It is doubly ironic perhaps that Young, who had already established himself by 1974 as an authority on radicalism among working people in Revolutionary Boston, was ideally suited to counter the Bicentennial's rhetorical admixture of citizenship and consumerism.

A third irony, then, is that at exactly the same time, young historians—weaned on precisely the work Young and his colleagues advanced during those years—were seeking out NPS jobs in surprising numbers. They did so because, by the 1970s, the number of baby boomers seeking university jobs vastly outnumbered the number of undergraduate students studying history in American universities. As anthropologist Cathy Stanton and others have pointed out, this first-wave job crisis in university history departments not only prompted a significant investment in public history training within the academy, it also propelled a generation of progressive historians into public-sector history professions. Many young historians who did sign on with the NPS, however, found themselves caught up in mountains of compliance work

created by preservation legislation such as Section 106 of the 1966 National
Historic Preservation Act. In these cases, though the NPS employed historians, newly hired historians did not necessarily have the opportunity to shape
interpretation or contribute to arguments about significance. Others, however,
did have a profound impact on NPS history programming, as evidenced in
Stanton's study of Lowell. And, as we will see, they would have a significant impact in Boston too, but not at the outset. On the contrary, planning
for the park remained very much within a consensus framework during the
Bicentennial years despite the presence in Boston and beyond of a growing
corps of young innovative historians with a particular talent for challenging
old ideas about the Revolution in American memory.[47]

The fact that trained historians did not figure more prominently in the park's
planning saga, despite their availability, also reflected agencywide realignments
during the turbulent 1970s. The Bicentennial era was a difficult one for the
NPS. The spring 1974 park hearings before the Subcommittee on National
Parks and Recreation, detailed in chapter three, reveal just how hard they were.
Why was it that the agency had such an adversarial relationship with Congress
over Boston at a time that, from all outward appearances, the NPS seemed more
popular than ever? As we have seen, one reason concerned the legacy of Mission
66. Under Director Conrad Wirth, the NPS had embraced profit-based private
partnership as a strategy to cope with crumbling infrastructure and dated
programming. The BNHSC endorsed this model by linking the park to urban
renewal. By putting economic stimulus on par with historical significance as a
rationale for authorizing new units, however, the NPS effectively devalued historical arguments—and, consequently, historical expertise—in its deliberations.
Thus, Denis Galvin's lament that "we've lost control of the agenda."[48] It was
the NPS, after all, that had surrendered the agenda by elevating the expertise
of pundits, politicians, and developers as it had in staffing the BNHSC. How
could Galvin and others suddenly resist a course correction that agency leaders
had themselves introduced? Congressional ire over NPS insistence that the park
not be authorized reflected this collision of expectations and foreshadowed a
new era of what would come to be known as "park-barrel politics."

But on the ground too, late twentieth-century trends in federal policy
making—toward smaller government, fiscal austerity, deregulation, and private
sector investment—created immediate challenges for an agency that had come
of age amid the big-government largesse of the New Deal. We saw several of
these problems aired during the spring 1974 hearings. How, for instance, could

the NPS pay for the park amid strict spending restrictions and hiring ceilings imposed by the Office of Management and Budget (OMB), an office created by President Richard Nixon in 1970 precisely for this purpose? Remarkably, the subcommittee seemed not to understand that no matter how much money Congress appropriated, OMB restrictions limited what could be spent. The impossibility of reconciling congressional expectations with the agency's mandate in these circumstances deeply complicated the park's path to authorization. Similar battles played out elsewhere in the system. During the same period, for instance, the NPS opposed authorization of two other large urban units— Cuyahoga Valley National Recreation Area between Akron and Cleveland, Ohio, and Santa Monica Mountains National Recreation Area outside Los Angeles, California—to no avail. So, while the Bicentennial put a spotlight on the NPS during the 1970s, and brought considerable attention to Boston, it also saddled the agency with a crippling unfunded mandate for growth.[49]

Part of the problem owed to the agency's own inconsistencies. George Hartzog, who encouraged growth during his 1964–73 stint as director, altered NPS organizational structure an astounding seven times. The tumult of presidential politics after Watergate introduced more directors with mixed agendas. Ronald H. Walker replaced Hartzog in 1973; Gary Everhardt replaced Walker in 1975; William J. Whalen replaced Everhardt in 1977; and Russell Dickenson replaced Whalen in 1980.[50] The NPS's position in its showdown with Congress during these years was clearly weakened by its inability to articulate a clear and consistent vision. So too was it impacted by the shift under these directors toward what author Russ Olsen refers to as a "philosophy of decentralizing decision making to regional cities."[51] Decentralization figured significantly in the park's planning saga. It did so most immediately by way of changes in the system's regional structure. Almost immediately on taking charge in 1973, for instance, Director Walker eliminated the Boston Sites Group and divided the Northeast Region—which had been headquartered in Philadelphia—into a North Atlantic Region, headquartered in Boston, and a Mid-Atlantic Region, headquartered in Philadelphia. What is more, even before Walker's transitions, the NPS had moved, under Hartzog, toward a system of decentralized planning and interpretive services. Although deliberations over the park prior to the 1973 legislative drive had remained predominately in local hands, responsibility for planning after authorization would shift to the Denver Service Center, through which the NPS routed all planning activities beginning in 1971.[52] Amid these changes, then, the agency's presence in Boston had grown simultaneously stronger and weaker, a seeming contradiction that, in many ways, characterized the complex negotiations surrounding the park's authorization and that—alongside decentralization and the allure of private partnerships—created critical challenges for those within the agency who were concerned with doing good history in Boston.

PART II: PLANNING A MODERN PARTNERSHIP PARK, CA. 1974

My purpose so far in this chapter has been to demonstrate just how complex and confusing Mary Holmes's "modern Boston" really was at the time of the park's authorization. It was home, on one hand, to scores of Bostonians for whom the promises of urban renewal—indeed, the promises of American democracy as enshrined along the Freedom Trail—had turned out to be lies. On the other hand, it was home also to scores of Bostonians whose prosperity seemed to align perfectly with the trail's fortunes. People whose fate hung somewhere in the middle worried about factory closings, agonized over their children's education, rallied against political opponents, and confronted violence in the streets. Boston was privileged during those years with a corps of young historians who understood the origins of these problems. And yet, their quiet insight could hardly break through the din of patriotic nationalism promulgated by a federal government concerned to boost consumer spending. At the same time, the one federal agency capable of shining a critical light on the nation's two-hundredth birthday found itself embroiled in its own legitimacy crisis. A radical redistribution of expertise, sharp spending limitations, and the politicization of unit authorization called into question the agency's mandate. What, under these circumstances, could the NPS bring to a city like Boston where the heritage landscape—indeed, the very meaning of history itself—had been forged more than a century before, and powerfully reinscribed by the BNHSC, the Freedom Trail Foundation, Boston 200, and the park's very own authorizing legislation?

An awful lot, according to the park's Denver Service Center (DSC) planning team. Because the park represented, from its view, "an entirely new character of park, as well as an entirely new character of park management," the planning team had approached its challenge "in a spirit of cooperation and venture." It set as its goal the "structuring of a park and park organization that will reflect the unique character of the culture that produced the sites." And, of course, it sought to imagine a park "with the thought of sharing responsibilities, costs, and operations . . . with all concerned organizations and interested citizens." Ultimately, the planning team set out to create a park that would be "sensitive, in all instances, to the needs and requirements of the community, its people, and the organizations" responsible for preserving its constituent sites in the first place.[53]

But could the planning team achieve such lofty goals given the particularities of the park's path to authorization? The park had been authorized, after all, against the wishes of the NPS, without adequate area studies, and in a rush to capitalize on the Bicentennial. Expectations were high that the NPS would play a key role in welcoming hundreds of thousands of celebrants to Boston. And then, of course, was the matter of the Charlestown Navy Yard, a last-minute legislative addition that largely confounded the agency's intent to tell the story of the American Revolution in Boston, and that created immediate management concerns by merit of its sheer size and complexity. The park welcomed its first superintendent, Hugh Gurney, in June 1975.[54] But it needed so much more: a visitor center, more staff, an advisory commission, interpretive programs, and on top of it all, it would need to negotiate complex cooperative agreements with five different historic sites, and all from scratch. This is to say nothing of the even more oblique challenges associated with community engagement and stakeholder relations. The NPS would now have a hand in managing properties in portions of Boston where residents had been struggling for years against the whims of urban renewal and the ravages of social and racial inequality. The NPS Washington Service Office urged that "cooperative agreements should be the first order of business at this time," but clearly at stake in the park's first days would be the possibility of creating a park that would be meaningful to neighbors as well as to tourists.[55]

Considering Alternatives

Minutes from the park's first formal meeting after authorization indicate that finding common ground—and making sense of what Public Law 93–431 actually stipulated—was a challenge from the outset. Forty-one NPS officials, park planners, and park constituents gathered on the morning of November 21, 1974, in Room 927 of the aptly named John W. McCormack Post Office and Courthouse to discuss next steps and respond to draft management objectives circulated in advance by the NPS.[56] NPS State Liaison Jack Benjamin introduced the meeting, noting that the campaign to authorize the park had "been a long, hard process," so long, in fact, that he "wasn't sure exactly when the idea was born." NPS Deputy Director David A. Richie spoke next, thanking everyone for their efforts, but then immediately turned to a concern that lingered throughout the meeting. "The NPS is worried," he explained, "about the expectations of many people that money would come with passage of the legislation." Richie noted that the normal appropriations process would not play out until July, well after the beginning of Bicentennial festivities. "We had hoped to be able to divert some of this year's funds to begin significant Bicentennial projects this year," he added, but "we have been advised recently that no longer can this be expected." Although the NPS, in Richie's words, was "optimistic for the future," by late 1974, it was "restrained in what we can offer and what we can hope to accomplish."[57]

Despite having been warned of this likely predicament by the NPS throughout the 1973–74 legislation drive, the park's partners lashed out. BRA Director Robert T. Kenney suggested that the NPS join in organizing an effort to convince Senator Edward M. Kennedy to advance a supplemental appropriations bill. Richie reminded Kenney that, regarding budget matters, the NPS reported to the OMB and, since the OMB was lodged within the executive branch, the NPS could not encourage the Senate or anyone else to act against it. Gail Rotegard, second in charge at Boston 200, shared her understanding that cooperative agreements would have to be signed before Congress would consider supplemental appropriations. Richie explained that agreements would be needed to fund rehabilitation work at the various sites, but that they were not necessary to fund other projects, including interpretation. Jack Benjamin urged that "it is critical to get staff on board . . . to get the necessary technical and professional support at the sites." One after another, however, representatives of the park's constituent sites insisted that what they wanted, and expected, was money. The Bostonian Society needed money to preserve the Old State House; the city needed money to repair Faneuil Hall. William B. Osgood, representing the Paul Revere House, suggested that perhaps the NPS could "help in identifying the problems," even if it was not in a position to pay for solutions. But First Naval District Commander Thomas Coyne and Lewis Whittemore, representing the Ancient and Honorable Artillery Company, brought the discussion back to money, insisting that the sites needed money to manage buildings and collections.[58]

Beyond money, the park's constituent sites worried too over the nature of cooperative agreements. Old North's vicar, Robert W. Golledge, was solely concerned, as he put it, with "developing a relationship with the National Park Service." Old South's Robert C. Dean argued with Benjamin about the

legislation's requirements regarding cooperative agreements, and the BRA wondered what had become of verbal agreements made with the NPS prior to
authorization. "Those agreements," Benjamin responded, could be used "as
options." Rotegard suggested that Boston 200 should represent the various sites
going forward, though the NPS insisted on dealing individually with its partner
sites. Richie noted too that the planning process should be "available to any of
the interested public in Boston." Benjamin reminded everyone that this "is a new
process and maybe the first time that PLANNERS in preparing management
objectives have attempted to get everyone involved." Richie noted that, beyond
the challenge of attempting a new kind of planning process, the park faced
another problem: "no new area study was done for the park as a whole [before
authorization]—this is unfortunate but true. Because of this, we do not have
a basic planning take-off point that we normally have." As the meeting wound
down, it became increasingly clear that each of the sites had its own unique
concerns, that almost everyone had different ideas about what Public Law 93–431
promised, and that some among the site representatives perceived—correctly
or not—that the NPS had not been entirely forthright, prior to authorization,
about the meanings and possibilities of federal partnership in Boston.[59]

Disagreements and misunderstandings notwithstanding, the meeting constituted a critical first step—specifically, the preparation of a Statement for
Management—toward developing a general management plan (GMP) for the
new park. The planning team invited site owners and other stakeholders back
for meetings during February 1975 to discuss a revised thirteen-page draft
statement of objectives for planning and management.[60] The revised draft
clearly responded to the concerns voiced by site owners at the previous meeting.
Portions concerning cooperative agreements with constituent sites carefully
emphasized that the NPS sought to "achieve a common set of standards while
at the same time maintaining the diversity and variety of the individual sites."
They expressed a concern to protect the sites' ability "to contribute funds,"
and the NPS's intent to compile a "management inventory" of tasks the agency
could assist with immediately "within the limits of the legislative authorities
and congressional appropriations." All of these provisions responded directly
to concerns expressed at the park's start-up meeting, just months before.[61]

More broadly, the draft objectives reveal emergent concerns that would, in
following years, consume administrative energies. The navy yard, of course,
figured prominently. Completing land transfers in and around the yard was a
priority, as was determining how to manage parking and traffic flow, including

a "bicycle trail connecting all sites." Concern for managing Section 106 procedures and developing a reuse plan for the navy yard also show the extent to which park planners understood early on the magnitude of their work in Charlestown. More broadly, the draft management objectives restated Public Law 93–431's interpretive focus on the "American Revolution and the founding and growth of the United States." Indeed, it is within this document that we see the first official NPS expression of interest in cooperating with sites on the Freedom Trail, and specifically, the Freedom Trail Foundation. That said, the draft management objectives also identify a parallel interpretive path for the navy yard, which would be "interpreted in line with the significance of the site and its contribution to the development of the United States Navy and Naval technologies, its environmental relationship to Charlestown and Boston and the U.S.S. Constitution." From the outset, then, it was clear that the NPS conceived of the navy yard and its downtown sites as separate entities, physically and intellectually.[62]

Throughout spring 1975, the park's planning team mulled over responses to its proposed management objectives, toward completing the next step in the GMP process, environmental assessment, wherein various ways to configure a park—"alternatives" in planning parlance—are imagined and circulated for comment. In early February, NPS Regional Director Jerry Wagers announced two public meetings, one at Faneuil Hall and another at the Kent School in Charlestown. The purpose of these meetings, according to Wagers's announcement, was to "insure [sic] that a broad segment of the public has an opportunity to become aware of the proposed park and to express any concerns . . . which might otherwise be overlooked by our planners."[63]

Devising alternatives for the park required the added work of assessing base-level operational requirements, a task bypassed during the rush to authorization and thus still remaining to be done. A statement of minimum requirements for operation issued by the planning team in May reveals just how much work needed to be done to get a park up and running in Boston, regardless of the alternatives, which were then still in development. It also reveals the disproportionate costs associated with the navy yard. The planning team estimated that minimum operations would require a total of $1,267,000. Of that, nearly half would be required for structural maintenance and other maintenance contracts associated with the navy yard. Key contract work included installation of heating, ventilation, and air-conditioning systems, the addition of boundary fences and safety rails, cleanup throughout, landscaping around the USS *Constitution*, and installation of exhibits. The remaining funding, as apportioned by the planning team, would pay for a full battery of professional support personnel assigned to assist partner sites with maintenance, security, and interpretive planning throughout the park. Bunker Hill needed paint and roof repairs, as did Faneuil Hall. The Old State House needed paint too, inside and outside, as well as plaster repair. Beyond all of this, Old South's brick steeple and roof needed extensive repairs. All of this work, planners realized, would need to be completed by May 1976 in order to accommodate Bicentennial visitors. The planning team worried about interpretation too, but clearly recognized that first-year activities would revolve around maintenance and cleanup.[64]

During July 1975, the planning team circulated its draft environmental assessment.[65] Boston National Historical Park, they asserted, was a brand-new type of park and, as such, had required an entirely new approach to planning. In this case, it meant planning "in a spirit of cooperation and venture, with the goal of structuring a park and park organization that will reflect the unique character of the culture that produced the sites." It meant also "sharing responsibilities, costs, and operations . . . with all concerned organizations and interested citizens." The proposed alternatives, therefore, sought to be "sensitive . . . to the needs and requirements of the community, its people, and the organizations," which had preserved the park's constituent sites in the first place.[66] In every instance, "maximum participation by site owners and the public in the planning and decision-making process is earnestly solicited." It was this facet of the planning process, according to the report's authors, that constituted "new planning procedures," so new in fact that the report included a visualization of its engagement strategies. In other words, it was the extent to which planners engaged various non-NPS stakeholders in the development of the park's draft alternatives that distinguished this process from any others that had preceded it.[67]

What, then, had this process of radical public engagement revealed about the significance of the park's constituent sites and their meanings? The draft assessment proposed three levels of significance, intended as frameworks for interpretive programming: global, overarching superthemes; central themes derived more specifically from the "American experience;" and site themes concerning the particularities of each historic structure and its associated characters. Interpretation, the planners indicated, should link together multiple themes, but should always be "bound together by the idea of revolution." Super themes and central themes, the planners suggested, should focus on the significance of the Revolution, philosophical radicalism (including "today's philosophic radicalism"), and a consideration of the "dynamics of change." Site themes should showcase familiar stories from Boston's Revolutionary past. The Old State House "will emphasize Boston's role in independence," and "free speech during the revolutionary period, as well as in today's world." Faneuil Hall, too, would foreground free speech and "local citizen participation in government." Old North, because it "supported the lanterns," would focus on the Revolution and "the idea of ongoing growth and change." Bunker Hill "represents the armed expression of revolution," and offered opportunities to examine "American's tradition of honoring." And, finally, the navy yard, because it "was the landing area for the first attack on Bunker Hill," would "reflect the growth of the nation it served," and also prompt a consideration of navy technology, and the history of Charlestown. The draft assessment entirely omitted mention of the USS *Constitution*.[68]

Of primary concern to reviewers of the draft environmental assessment were its four alternative proposals for what the new park might actually look like. The first alterative proposed limiting NPS involvement to an advisory capacity, abandoning the concept of a central visitor center altogether and leaving the seven affiliate sites to manage on their own, though with some coordinated marketing and interpretation. Alternative two proposed a central visitor center and transportation hub in the navy yard and required that each site have an equal role alongside the NPS in sustaining management, operations, and interpretation. A third alternative, described as "a park that interacts with the larger community and is an active part of that community," imagined a visitor hub in downtown Boston. The NPS, in this case, would liaison with the city to provide information, transportation, and "support in achieving other community goals." The NPS would also assume most interpretive and financial responsibilities, while sharing management and operations with the sites. Finally, alternative four imagined the same configuration as alternative three, but proposed centralizing sales of items from all the various sites' gift shops in the NPS visitor center.[69]

The team shared its alternatives with the North Atlantic Regional Office, which then distributed it to site owners for review during October 1975. Reactions, insomuch as they are retrievable in NPS records, were mixed. William B. Osgood, who had attended the park's start-up meeting, so surprised the NPS with his "direct and unfavorable response," that Regional Chief of Interpretation James Corson raised it in his response to the preliminary alternatives.[70] Corson had attended most of the planning meetings along with the site managers and, although he perceived much that was good about the alternatives, he noted too that "on the negative side there is also a lot to be said." Most significantly, from Corson's vantage point, the planners had simply not fully grappled with the scale and depth of local interests. Encouragements, for instance, to relocate the Bostonian Society from the Old State House—evidently what angered Osgood—demonstrated "so little apparent comprehension of the facts both psychological and actual." The alternatives, he continued, were "based upon an assumption that it is o.k. for us to be egocentric and defensive about our interests . . . because all the others will be glad to have us take their burdens over." But functions that the planners perceived as burdens to the sites, such as distributing tourist information or managing gift shop sales, were precisely what sustained Boston's downtown heritage landscape. What message would the NPS be sending if it centralized those functions in a visitor center located way across the river in Charlestown? "If we will ever have a park," Corson noted, "we must reassure and serve."[71]

The planners might have avoided these missteps had they consulted with the Boston National Historical Park Advisory Commission. The commission's first meeting, however, was not even scheduled until December 8, 1975, for the purpose, as it turns out, of considering the draft alternatives. Recall that Public Law 93–431 stipulated that the park be managed in conversation with an advisory commission for its first decade. As we learned in chapter two, the park had been born of the work of another advisory commission, the Boston National Historic Sites Commission. Much had changed, however, with regard to the conduct of federal advisory commissions since those days. In fact, the Federal Advisory Committee Act of 1972 laid out clear guidelines intended to guarantee that independent advisory commissions were just that, independent, and that they include a variety of perspectives. The new guidelines produced an advisory commission very different from the one that first imagined the park. As of the first meeting, six of its members had been appointed, three by the governor and three by the mayor. They included Byron Rushing, an African American civil rights activist and president of Boston's Museum of Afro-American History; Massachusetts Secretary of Environmental Affairs Evelyn F. Murphy; Katherine Kane, former director of Boston 200 and then deputy mayor; urban planner and Charlestown community advocate Maurice O'Shea; and Guy A. Beninati, a history teacher at Boston Latin and president of the North End Union.[72] The commission's chair, installed by the governor, was none other than Richard A. Berenson. The park advisory commission, then, unlike its predecessor, did include members who actually represented the communities the park stood to impact most. Berenson's leadership, however, recalled Mark Bortman's leadership of the old BNHSC, and by extension, the significant influence wielded by the Boston Chamber of Commerce ever since the Logue days.

For its part, the advisory commission did not know how to respond to the agency's preliminary alternatives at its first meeting. Most members still could not quite grasp the process. Several wondered how they could evaluate alternatives without having site representatives present. Indeed, how could alternatives be evaluated at all without first firming up cooperative agreements? Berenson explained as much, though added that everyone agreed "that a strong city-oriented Visitor Center is very desirable."[73] That seems to be the extent of the advisory commission's input on the draft alternatives since, by its next meeting, park planners had already issued a final revised set of alternatives reflecting feedback from site owners and various city and state agencies.[74] They included one major difference: the insertion of a new first alternative that allowed for the possibility of no action at all.

Responses to alternatives one and two were primarily negative, though most people recommended specifically that the Bostonian Society retain its active involvement in operations at the Old State House. Most respondents also indicated that they expected a more extensive role for the National Park Service at all of the partner sites. A minority of voices endorsed the third alternative, but most stakeholders disliked the possibility of situating the park's primary interpretive center at the navy yard, removed as they perceived it to be from the "more significant Revolutionary War shrines." For his part, Superintendent Gurney suggested that a satellite visitor center be considered for Charlestown, since many park visitors started at the USS *Constitution*. Alternative five generally lacked support, as it tended to exclude existing site owners from participation in programs and local citizens from use of the sites. It would also lead to development of an entirely new transportation systems instead of modifying existing systems. Eagerness to leverage Boston's public transit explained why almost everyone, it seemed, supported having a large central visitor center downtown, wherein park information, interpretive content, and city guides might be shared broadly. In Gurney's estimation, support for alterative four was practically unanimous.[75]

The advisory commission endorsed alternative four as well, though with significant reservations and with important recommendations. Indeed, the advisory commission took its review function seriously, charging a subcommittee with devising a position statement. The statement is a critical park document insomuch as it demonstrates an early and clear statement of what neighbors believed to be the real value of an NPS partnership park. Alternative four, in the advisory commission's judgement, "appropriately highlights the unique urban character of the park, and can best draw on the rich resources of local pride and traditions of use and involvement." The advisory commission worried, however, "that the assessment seriously neglects transportation" and insisted that the NPS study transportation and mobility issues in a comprehensive way. Additionally, the commission sought to complicate NPS ideas of what constituted the park's community. Boston, it argued, was composed of many kinds of communities, and thus more care was needed to define how the park might serve all of them. At issue, for instance, was access to open space. The commission called for open public spaces to be made available proximate to all of the park's sites, and especially at Bunker Hill. What's more, the commission proposed that "an informal group of community advisors" be called upon to ensure that NPS programming remain meaningful to all park neighbors. Priority should be given to the young and the elderly, considering their preponderance in all areas touched by the park.[76]

In its endorsement of alternative four, the advisory commission made very specific recommendations about the park's interpretive direction that bring us full circle to Mary Holmes's concern that the park "explain modern Boston and modern America." "The Supertheme Revolution is seen as appropriate only," the advisory commission concluded, "if the Boston story is fully and clearly told." It worried that the planning team's focus on living history, Bicentennial America's interpretive mode *du jour*, threatened to obscure a "much more important" focus on social and political issues. The commission preferred that the park build capacity "to make these issues, which dominated town life before and during the Revolution, come alive for the visitor." And it recommended that it do so by ensuring that "scholars from Boston area universities be involved in the further development of interpretive themes and exhibitions."[77]

In its final assessment, then, the advisory commission warned that the NPS ought to stop putting the cart in front of the horse. Just as actual historians needed to be involved in interpretation from the start, so did the commission need to be consulted before the NPS advance such major decisions as where to put its visitor center. "The Commission members felt strongly that many decisions already made, such as the Visitor Center choice, will have a shaping influence on the Park, and they are concerned that Park Service commitments may have precluded certain options." Because alternative four placed so much emphasis on integrating park functions with an urban community center, the report concluded, it must involve commission members "who are both representative of a broad spectrum of local groups and residents of communities affected by the park. They can play a key role in realizing a goal of a park that is truly involved with the community and reflective of its richness."[78]

A Year in Review

In hindsight, the advisory commission's statement is remarkably prescient, insomuch as it grasped key challenges—the decentralization of NPS expertise, the absence of scholars in interpretive planning, reductive bureaucratic notions of "urban" and "community"—that, as we saw in Part I, would increasingly plague the NPS system-wide during the late 1970s. Its awareness of these problems, in fact, is so remarkable that it raises even more questions about the agency's effectiveness during 1974–75 in making sense of the Boston we explored in Part I, and for which the NPS was tasked with designing a national park. Were planners concerned with Boston's racial turmoil? Were they sensitive to its history of urban renewal? Did they know how many people had been forcefully removed from portions of the city that the NPS would now be responsible for interpreting? Answering these questions is difficult, but we are fortunate to have some insight, owing to the presence of Dennis Frenchman at the park's first meeting. Frenchman, representing MIT's Department of Urban Studies and Planning, had set out that year with his research partner, Charles Davies, to make a case study of the park planning process. Over the following year, Frenchman and Davies interviewed project principals, including park neighbors, about the challenges of planning an urban park. Their interviews are invaluable for what they reveal about the circumstances under which the park was conceived.[79]

Most immediately evident in their findings is the commitment of agency planners to build an effective park, even despite the agency's efforts to derail authorizing legislation just a year earlier. Denis Galvin, for instance, was now eager to "make a more coherent experience for the visitor" among "a series of isolated structures." "What we've got to do," he cautioned "is to make certain that our decisions do not have adverse impact on the community." Regional Park Planner Charles Clapper agreed that "the feds can't move in and just take over." "The level of cooperation that we've got to deal with here makes it different [than other parks]," he added, "I think there's an opportunity here for a new kind of relationships between the federal government and the state government and the local governments, and private landowners."[80]

Building those relationships, however, would require overcoming decades of entrenched concern and, in some cases, animosity. In Charlestown, for instance, where the NPS would now have responsibilities at the navy yard and the Bunker Hill Monument, many residents agreed with their neighbor Helen Myers that "we're an afterthought on [sic] the city." "We're like a passageway between suburbia and Boston," she explained, "they circle us with the expressway . . . and the Mystic River Bridge . . . only because it was the most convenient way." Another neighbor, Patricia Ward, worried that the NPS might limit neighborhood access to Bunker Hill, which was "the only green area in the town." "A lot of things that are done in Charlestown aren't done for Charlestown people; they're done for outsiders." Vincent Strout, president of the Bunker Hill Monument Association, dismissed Ward's notion that Charlestown's children should be able to play at Bunker Hill. "We did not envision it as a playground for young children, or as a walking place for dogs, or as a football field, or as an after-hours trysting place for lovers; and this is what is has become." Douglas P. Adams, however, pushed back: "Strout doesn't live here, hasn't for fifteen years, did you know that? These people can come in and say that they represent such-and-such and so-and-so, and the Park Department can believe it if it wishes, but it will be fooling itself if it does."[81]

The NPS recognized, as Galvin explained, that building relationships with community stakeholders would be key to the park's success. Its encounters in Charlestown, however, revealed that identifying who actually represented those voices might be just as difficult. It was a problem that, by 1975, had been exacerbated by the agency's own internal realignments. As Deputy Regional Director David Richie explained, the centralization of planning function in Denver, over two thousand miles away, had created real barriers to actual community-based problem solving. Planners "come in for bits and pieces," he explained, "but they're not really well-oriented and connected and integrated into the whole scene." Cam Hugie, the Denver Service Center (DSC) planning team captain assigned to the park, seemed to confirm that impression. "We haven't had the people of Boston really get involved that much," she observed, "they haven't seemed to want to." Hugie explained that "we're kind of dealing with the people of Boston along with the owners of the sites, because in many cases they are the same." Her impression, of course, was completely inconsistent with how residents of Charlestown, as Frenchman and Davies showed, related to the Bunker Hill Monument Association. Nan Rickey, another member of the DSC planning team assigned to interpretation at the park, expressed her concern to "respond to community needs as the community expresses them. And by community I mean not only the average person, but also the people who have cared for these buildings all these years and people who occupy them now." That these groups were, in many regards, mutually exclusive, was not immediately evident, it seems, to the NPS planners from Denver.[82]

Challenges also appear to have grown up early on around the park's interpretive direction. The park's authorizing legislation had largely committed the park an engagement with Boston's Revolutionary past. Vincent Strout, of the Bunker Hill Memorial Association, agreed and imagined "the various sites as an object lesson in American history." But planners found stringing together the seven sites to be a challenge. Rickey was "interested in not being limited in the interpretation." "It's difficult," she noted," to do an overall interpretive job." She worried that, other than Old North Church, the sites "don't speak to the larger issues that I would like to see communicated." Robert Golledge, the vicar of Old North, worried that the NPS might focus too narrowly on the site's history at the expense of modern uses. "I don't want any Smokey Bears giving the interpretation here," he quipped, evidently not realizing Smokey Bear's affiliation with the U.S. Forest Service. Golledge worried too that his customary funders might withdraw, assuming—wrongly, of course—that NPS funding would replace their contribution. "It's not always the way things are, it's the way people think they are that really affects you." The Paul Revere House's William Osgood appeared too in Frenchman and Davies's interviews and expressed his hope "that the Park Service will not so emphasize the eighteenth century. I am very much against . . . trying to freeze history." Osgood hoped that the NPS would expand interpretation beyond the seven sites to include the entire city. "I want [visitors] to take away a feeling of [the city's] past, but also of its present, and of its future." Walter Muir Whitehill resurfaced yet again to warn that sites like Old South had "been the scene, for nearly a century, of various activities that the Park Service could not readily carry on." "If there is any attempt to tell hundreds of thousands of lunkheads what they're about," he added, "that's got to be done in a separate information center, somewhere else."[83]

Frenchman and Davies's study, then, largely confirms what the park advisory commission had intimated in its assessment of the park's planning alternatives. Agency planners, flown in from across the country, had very little sense of what really concerned the park's actual stakeholders. Indeed, they barely seem to have understood who the stakeholders were. What's more, as late as winter 1975, it was very clear that the park's planners, its historic site partners, and its immediate neighbors all had different ideas about what the park should be about. Galvin summarized the concern in a simple question: "What are the central themes?" By the summer of 1975, nobody seemed to know. Galvin and others in the planning team had begun to discuss freedom of speech and the expression of rights as a unifying theme. There was also an interest in how park resources communicated the physicality of Boston's evolution over the long eighteenth century. The navy yard, of course, complicated the situation, and Galvin suggested that the park might tell the story of how one city transitioned from a preoccupation with intellectual ferment during the late eighteenth century toward a broader sense of national enterprise embodied by the navy yard's nineteenth-century saga. For her part, Rickey had begun to conceive of the park as "a series of beads on a very strong cord, the beads being the sites and the cord, maybe, being the federal involvement—rather invisible, as cords very often are when pearls are strung in a necklace." Not unlike the BNHSC before it, the park's planning team had come up against a central tension: Would the park organize itself around a coherent story about the past? Or would its network of relationships itself be the message? By 1975, the park's planners concluded, almost entirely on their own it seems, that these options were mutually exclusive.[84]

Finally, complicating every facet of the 1974–75 planning conversation were protracted delays in congressional appropriations for Boston's new national park. As agency officials warned during hearings over H.R. 7486, authorizing a new park in no way guaranteed timely or adequate funding for the work that needed to be done in Boston, especially in time for the Bicentennial. It should have come as no surprise, then, when the Department of Interior's appropriation bill, H.R. 8773, stalled that year amid complex negotiations over mining rights in the parks, concessions, wildlife conservation, and American Indian tribal rights.[85] Few of these issues, of course, directly concerned the park, which did not figure at all in House debate. And yet, in Boston, anxiety mounted over funding delays. Letters poured into Representative Tip O'Neill's office from constituents pleading with him to intervene. *Boston Globe* publisher Davis Taylor wondered if "without ruffling anyone, you could tell me whom . . . I might see who could expedite" work around the USS *Constitution.* Mayor White complained that forcing the appropriation had "been a low priority matter for the Park Service" and that its negligence "will effectively stop the efforts underway in Boston to plan for the park." BRA director Robert T. Kenney had clearly learned from the park's start-up meeting and now understood that the "administration," and not the NPS, was responsible for the delay. He was, nonetheless, "very concerned" that if long-range planning didn't start, "the park will languish." Even the Massachusetts Bay Transit Authority petitioned O'Neill, hoping that he might move things along in time for its debut of an Orange Line extension to Sullivan Square.[86]

None, however, worried more than Katharine D. Kane, director of Boston 200. Kane wrote to O'Neill about her understanding that HR 7486's $27 million authorization would "assure that the expertise and assistance of the National Park Service would be devoted to these key sites during the high bicentennial vision period." Its "promise," she continued, has "made it difficult to privately raise even small amounts of money for these projects—leaving them essentially without financial and technical assistance for the upcoming period of great visitor attention and use."[87] Kane's letter is significant in that it demonstrates the extent to which the legislative process leading to the park's authorization, and its politicization by Bicentennial boosters, had miscast the agency's mission and responsibilities, and implied a promise—as Kane put it—that was neither realistic nor responsible. O'Neill, however, had been instrumental in making the promise, and so he set to finding a way to realize it. He wrote, for instance, to Sidney R. Yates, who chaired the Subcommittee on the Interior House Committee on Appropriations, warning that "the National Park Service will attempt to tell your Committee that the funds, even if appropriated, cannot be reasonably expended. This is not the case." O'Neill conveyed Kane's concerns about fundraising and suggested that the NPS could actually get the job done for as little as $4 million. "I am very hopeful that you . . . will be able to make these funds available as soon as possible," he added, "in light of the large number of people who are planning to visit these sights during the summer of 1975."[88] Despite his efforts, H.R. 8773 only passed in the House on July 23. It lingered in the Senate until November and then only advanced to conference in December, becoming law later that month.[89] In the end, after the NPS divvied up its cut, the park received $2,267,000, with an extra $159,000 for a transitional period during July to September 1976.[90] The park, then, would have to get its legs on a budget.

A National Park with Local Roots
Completion of the planning team's environmental assessment, flawed though it was, satisfied a final step toward drafting the park's first general management

plan. What's not evident in the environmental assessment, however—or Frenchman and Davies's interviews with its principles—is the significance of the work already being done on the ground in Boston and behind the scenes by NPS staff and committed partners to build durable community partnerships that paved the way for establishment. Most significantly, whereas the park's DSC planners were largely detached from the realities of heritage concerns in Boston, its first superintendent—Hugh Gurney—already had his ear to the ground. Gurney was the perfect pick for a Revolutionary War park, which confirms that the park's meanings had in some ways already been settled. He had first worked for the NPS during college as a seasonal park ranger historian at Colonial National Historical Park in Yorktown, Virginia. After earning an MA in history at the University of North Carolina, Gurney returned to work with the NPS at Morristown National Historical Park, in Morristown, New Jersey. A succession of appointments followed: Harpers Ferry National Historical Park; Saint-Gaudens National Historic Site; Perry's Victory National Monument, where Gurney first served as a superintendent; and finally, a super-intendency at Saratoga National Historical Park, with responsibility for five different units. Altogether, Gurney had spent about twelve years with the agency prior to arriving in Boston, learning to manage historical sites associated with military history, its memory, and especially colonial and Revolutionary pasts.[91]

But beyond being committed to the interpretation of Revolutionary pasts, Gurney was also mindful of Boston's complex community structure and its recent history. He grew up near Boston and, as a child, cherished riding the elevated railway to and from his grandparents' house in Medford. Later, while studying history at Tufts, Gurney worked part time for an Italian American import/export business for which he ran bills of lading all throughout Boston's North End. The experience gave Gurney an insider's knowledge of the North End's ethnic fabric and confronted him with urban renewal all the while. What's more, Gurney was fully aware from the outset that managing the park would be difficult. He had visited the site for a superintendent's conference before hiring on and had toured the navy yard with Jack Benjamin, who by then had been appointed to oversee the transition.[92] It was Benjamin, in fact, whom Gurney credits with helping him get established. Benjamin took Gurney around the city, introducing him to the park's principal stakeholders—historic site managers, the BRA, city hall, and the navy—and sat in on meetings until Gurney got his legs. Benjamin's help typified just one of many instances wherein the park's early success relied on the commitment of a few passionate staffers.

According to Gurney, the most pressing issue facing him upon arrival was the disposition of the navy yard. The park's authorizing legislation set January 1 as the date by which the NPS would be responsible for management of the facility, though many questions about the transfer remained unanswered. As we have seen, for instance, the park planning team had yet to determine exactly how to make sense of the navy yard within the park's broader interpretive mandate. The NPS, as Gurney puts it, "had not thought it through," and most people involved did not have an opinion. Gurney recalls that the decision to preserve the navy yard as an industrial site, rather than as a stylized nineteenth-century mixed-use leisure space—as the BRA proposed—owed to NPS Regional Assistant Director for Planning Ross Holland's insistence that the facility's twentieth-century history be showcased. The BRA's proposal had been tied to plans to construct the John F. Kennedy Presidential Library in the navy yard. Holland and Gurney traveled to Washington, DC, by request of the Department of Interior to meet with representatives of the Kennedy Library project. Holland spoke bluntly: "If you put this in the Navy Yard, it's just like dropping a bomb!" The Kennedy Library representatives, who hadn't expected any opposition to their plans, were startled and quickly withdrew the proposal. When Gurney and Holland returned to Boston and reported on the meeting, Regional Director Jerry Wagers was astounded: "You really said that, Ross!?" He wasn't alone. Nan Rickey, for instance, recalls pushing back against preservationists who wanted to restore the old Ropewalk building "back to some time." By that point there was no machinery remaining in the building, "but you could see the pattern of the machinery by the hemp streaks on the ceiling . . . that was the most evocative thing about the whole place." It was, in Rickey's estimation, "all you needed."[93] It was the intensity of their vision, Gurney explains, and an insistence that the navy yard be appreciated for its twentieth-century significance, that formatively shaped the navy yard's first GMP and its interpretation ever since.

But of the scores of meetings Gurney recalls from his first days at the park, most of those concerning the navy yard, had to do with practicalities. All of the yard's buildings, for instance, were heated by steam generated at a central power plant. What would happen to the buildings if the navy shut down the power plant on January 1? Gurney and others, fearful that resources might deteriorate quickly, managed to convince the navy to run the plant through spring. This type of frequent though informal negotiation was typical of the navy yard transition and reveals ground-level concern both within the navy and the NPS to ensure the integrity of historical resources throughout the facility. It was the navy, for instance, that inadvertently designated Building 125 as collections storage by choosing it as a staging space for anything its team discovered during the transition process that might be of historical significance. Gurney appreciated the navy's efforts in this regard, and in fact, relied on them during the park's lean early years.[94]

Importantly, Gurney's reliance on former navy staff continued beyond transition too. He hired long-time navy yard Chief of Maintenance Maynard Spekin, for instance, to serve as the park's chief of maintenance after transition. Bringing Spekin aboard was a managerial masterstroke. Most obviously, Spekin brought to the park an intimate knowledge of the navy yard and its operations. Beyond that, however, Spekin's deep familiarity with Boston made him an essential problem solver. When the Queen of England arrived in the navy yard for a Bicentennial visit, it was Spekin who magically turned up yards of red carpet for her disembarkation. It was Spekin, too, who assembled the park's crack maintenance crew, largely from the ranks of laid-off navy yard workers. They included Dave Rose, whose knowledge of the yard would prove essential in dealing with years of deferred maintenance as well as with navy yard workers who remained as part of the maintenance staff for the USS *Constitution* and who did not necessarily grasp the park's mission in Boston. When diversity quotas figured in hiring priorities—if the park "needed more Black faces," as Gurney puts it—it was Spekin who would find a "fantastic Black carpenter." Spekin's ability to liaison between the park and its constituent communities, especially in Charlestown, and specifically by helping local laborers transition into NPS jobs, contrasted considerably with outreach done by the planning team which, as we saw above, "haven't had the people of Boston really get involved that much." The navy yard's transition into NPS ownership was a very visible metaphor during the 1970s for Boston's broader transition into a postindustrial economy. People like Spekin eased the transition and demonstrated to locals how the NPS could be part of the solution, even if it may have also been part of the problem.[95]

Locally, Gurney relied too on the remarkable influence of Richard Berenson who, as he puts it, "would go to bat for the park, and had the ability to do it."[96] The governor had appointed Berenson to chair of the park's advisory commission pursuant to Public Law 93–431. Gurney perceived immediately that Berenson had more than a casual audience with Mayor Kevin White and various city hall staffers. "For a lot of people," according to Gurney, "a word from Richard Berenson was all it took." Gurney recalls that if the sidewalks needed repair or the Freedom Trail's painted red stripe had faded, Berenson would invite Gurney and the head of Boston public works to have lunch at the Harvard Club, where it was "yes, Dick, we'll get right on it." Gurney met frequently with Berenson, up to twice a month, about all matter of issues related to the park, and especially its reliance on city services. Berenson's status, Gurney explains, made challenging problems manageable. "He was one of the reasons that we were as successful as we were."[97]

The case of the park's downtown visitor center demonstrates how local connections—including Berenson's—eased the park's path to establishment. Tom Coleman, a property acquisition specialist with the NPS regional office, visited Gurney in Boston shortly after he arrived there for duty. Coleman explained that he was shopping around for a suitable visitor center building but was unsure of where to locate it and so requested guidance from Gurney. Gurney dismissed one option, an empty second floor in a BRA-owned building adjacent to the Union Oyster House. It was too far from the Freedom Trail, he argued. Coleman returned a month later having identified the Easton Building at 15 State Street. Gurney liked it. The location was right, situated as it was adjacent to the Old State House, where Gurney knew that the city had plans to close State Street to foot traffic.

What made the building even more attractive, however, was its owner. Ned Johnson, a partner in Fidelity Investments, was an old Bostonian who wanted the building protected from demolition. Denis Galvin caught wind of the situation and worked with Coleman to cut a deal with Johnson: if Johnson was willing to pay for extensive renovations before the NPS purchased the building, then the NPS would be able to cover those costs in the purchase price and also move the newly formed North Atlantic Regional Office into the building, further protecting it from inappropriate development. Johnson agreed. As we've seen, this was precisely the kind of backroom dealing that the advisory commission worried about, and it is worth wondering how Berenson addressed the issue privately with people on either side of the issue. It was a boon, however, for Johnson, a problem solved for Gurney, and for the regional office it was an opportunity to get situated without having to wait years for another appropriation to pay for remodeling. It also turned out to be a good opportunity for Berenson: in the end, 15 State Street included offices alongside the NPS visitor center for use by the Boston Convention and Visitors Bureau. "I'm sure that was because of Berenson," Gurney recalls, "making sure we were tied in."[98]

Finally, though Gurney found himself instantly caught up in navy yard concerns, real estate deals, staffing, and the business of forging local relationships, there was the matter too of articulating cooperative agreements with the park's five nonfederal contributing sites. How to do it, however, was anyone's guess. Public Law 93–431 mandated that cooperative agreements be negotiated between the park and its partners, but neither it nor the BNHSC before it had provided any specific guidance regarding process or content. Gurney called on his own experience and found models in agreements that had been in operation at sites he had previously supervised. They included, for instance, an agreement between the Saratoga National Historical Park and a nearby historic house museum, and one that he had discovered in use at Hampton National Historic Site in Maryland. For the most part, however, Gurney recalls cutting the agreements more or less from whole cloth. His partner in doing so was a Boston attorney named Jason A. Aisner, who had become involved in the campaign to fund the USS *Constitution* Museum, and who took a personal interest in helping Gurney get the park up and running. Aisner, according to Gurney, played a pivotal role in imagining the contours of the park's cooperative agreements, and was specifically involved in drafting agreements with the *Constitution* Museum and Old South.[99] These early documents, whose genesis we will trace in chapter five, provided the structure for a partnership model that would prove influential beyond even the park. They became the templates, as Gurney recalls it, for cooperative partnerships at Lowell and other units besides.

* * *

The Boston National Historical Park was gradually conceived of over nearly a half century by a mixed cast of politicians, heritage boosters, federal advisory commissioners, and numerous well-known and not-so-well-known NPS personalities. It was designed, however, in just a few short months by a handful of NPS planners in Denver, Colorado. I have sought in this chapter to capture the strange suddenness of that moment, and the impossibility of the task demanded by Congress and put upon the planning team. It was, in critical ways, the park's formative moment. It was a moment in which new ways of imagining park partnerships were put into place without clear guidance for making them work. It was a moment in which mischaracterizations of key stakeholders and vague notions of community ignored the reality of lives lived for generations in adjacent neighborhoods. It was a moment wherein misconceptions about federal funding and the government's responsibilities to partner sites were left to linger on. And, finally, it was a moment wherein old ideas about the Revolution and its meanings—ideas underlying the very race and class anxieties that ripped Boston apart during the 1970s—were left intact. As sociologist Meghan V. Doran demonstrates, Boston's school desegregation debates recapitulated those old ideas into new ways of reckoning the history of race and power in Boston that still complicate educational reform efforts there today.[100] This is to say that, in hindsight, we can see how high the stakes were for history in the park's founding moment, and how unable its planners were to grasp the opportunity.

The planning team, of course, should not bear all the blame for these missteps. Its inability to manage an impossible task was symptomatic of a difficult turn in the agency's own institutional history, one from which it is not clear the NPS ever fully recovered. As we will see in subsequent chapters, though, that formative moment echoes throughout the park's administrative history and presumably will continue to do so until reckoned with. And yet, as we have also seen, solutions to problems imbedded in the park's hasty planning process appeared almost immediately in the work of a mixed cast of agency staff, private citizens, public servants, and concerned neighbors, who took it upon themselves to build a park that could work. It was Gurney, for instance, who calmed William Osgood after that contentious first meeting.[101] It was Berenson who turned the gears at city hall. It was Spekin who ensured goodwill for the agency in Charlestown. And, as we will learn in chapter five, it was advisory commission members like Byron Rushing who insisted that the park be accountable, not just to the park's stakeholder communities, but to history as well. The park's early success, then, seems to have pivoted on the hard efforts and sincere commitments of a dedicated corps of Bostonians. But why then did Boston need a national park, if Bostonians were adequately situated to "explain modern Boston and modern America" on their own? Was it, as site managers expected from the start, all about money? Though it had taken a half century to create a national park in Boston, its purpose was hardly more settled after the Bicentennial than it had been at the outset.

CHAPTER 5

The Problem with History, the Problem with Race

The nation's Bicentennial celebration officially ended on July 4, 1976. The wave of patriotic tourism it set in motion, however, surged for years, bringing scores of new heritage tourists to Boston. They included Charles Battles, a twenty-six-year-old history teacher from Pennsylvania who, along with his wife, chaperoned a dozen high school students on a four-day tour of historic sites in and around Boston during November 1977. Battles and his group visited the Bunker Hill Monument one Monday afternoon before walking to the intersection of Bunker Hill and Lexington Streets to await the bus to downtown Boston. Just before the bus arrived, however, five men sprung from a parked car and set upon Battles and his students with golf clubs, axe handles, and hockey sticks. Several of the children ran, but four others and Battles himself suffered beatings severe enough to put them all in the hospital. The attack lasted an excruciating five minutes and continued even after the bus arrived. One bystander reported that it "was the worst thing I ever saw. It was vicious."[1]

What had triggered the attack? By all accounts it was unprovoked. Police explained that "there was only one apparent motive . . . race prejudice."[2] Battles and his school group were Black; the attackers white. It was the latest incident in a long history of racial violence in Charlestown. The attack recalled, for instance, a gruesome riot in 1919 spurred by five white sailors who went on a murderous rampage through Charlestown, randomly attacking Black people in revenge for a perceived slight.[3] More recently, school desegregation had triggered a rash of "virulent" racial violence, nearly igniting a "second Battle of Bunker Hill."[4] Charlestown wasn't alone. White and Black girls had come to blows at a South Boston school just weeks before, setting off mobs of white protesters. In Dorchester, "gangs of White youths" attacked Hispanic and Haitian neighbors.[5] But what set the Bunker Hill incident apart was its raw savagery and its patriotic backdrop. Reflecting on the event, Mayor Kevin White worried that "we still have a virus here, and that virus is ugly.

And that virus keeps acting up, and this time it was worse than Landsmark." White, of course, was referring to the attack on Theodore Landsmark—by a Charlestowner no less—immortalized by Stanley Forman's famous 1977 photograph showing the incident unfold within eyeshot of the Old State House.[6] Jane Edmonds, of the Massachusetts Commission Against Discrimination, explained that we "feel the Freedom Trail belongs to all of us." She agreed with one of Battles's students who "believes that if Black people can't go to the Bunker Hill Monument, then maybe all the historical monuments should be moved to a neutral site."[7]

FIGURE 10. Charles Battles appears on the front page of the *Boston Globe* alongside a photograph celebrating white children enjoying autumn. From the *Boston Globe*. © 1977 Boston Globe Media Partners. All rights reserved. Used under license.

The events of November 1977 make powerfully clear that, three years after Congress authorized Boston National Historical Park, issues of race and memory remained deeply entwined within its boundaries. And the knot only seemed to tighten. Police arrested three men in conjunction with the Bunker Hill attack, each of them identified by Battles's students. In December, however, an all-white jury acquitted them, and the investigation closed despite demands that Boston police, or perhaps even federal investigators, continue the search. "It's impossible," Battles lamented, "for Blacks to achieve any type of legal success in Boston."[8] Park Superintendent Hugh Gurney raised the matter of "racial incidents" at a meeting of the park's advisory commission in May 1978. Overall, however, conversations about the park's path to establishment clung more closely to operational concerns and to the difficulties of imagining a future for the Charlestown Navy Yard than they did to bridging the deep divide between patriotic memory and structural inequality for which the park was ground zero.[9]

Whereas in the previous chapter my purpose was to shed light on the park's formative first years, my intent here is to explore the subsequent evolution of managerial strategies that ultimately set the stage for how and why the park functions as it does today. Getting those strategies into place, it turns out, was complicated significantly by several fundamental changes to the park's core structure, including the addition of the Dorchester Heights Monument in 1978 and authorization of the Boston African American National Historic Site in 1980. Additionally, complex and sometimes contentious conversations concerning a general management plan (GMP) for the navy yard—not to mention the practical challenges of making the navy yard safe and accessible for visitors—continued to create administrative and intellectual hurdles for the young park. A key question, then, concerns how well the park's public–private partnership model prepared it for a future wherein Bicentennial-era sensibilities no longer defined Americans' experience of the past. How well was such a model prepared to do history in a park where the historical stakes were not yet entirely evident? And how well was it prepared, we must ask, to contend with history in a place where a dozen young Americans could still be beaten publicly at a national historic site because of the color of their skin?

THE PATH TO ESTABLISHMENT

As we saw in chapter four, the Bicentennial years revealed all the many possibilities and challenges awaiting the park's management team. The National

Park Service (NPS) and the Boston Redevelopment Authority (BRA) planners, park staff, the advisory commission, and a whole host of neighbors and advocates worked with one another, sometimes productively and sometimes not, to make sense of the agency's role in Boston. Several significant developments ushered the park toward establishment. In November 1976, for instance, the Metropolitan District Commission (MDC) transferred ownership of the Bunker Hill Monument to the National Park Service. The MDC, of course, had been trying to unload the monument for years, stymied as it was by budget shortfalls and public discord. The park, however, framed the transfer as a victory for its partnership model. It was, according to the park's newsletter, "the culmination of cooperative efforts between federal, state, and local organizations whose common interest lies in the continued preservation and interpretation of this important part of our national heritage."[10]

Critical too was the addition of Dorchester Heights to the park's slate of sites. On November 10, 1978, Congress added Dorchester Heights National Historic Site to Boston National Historical Park by way of Public Law 95–625, the National Parks and Recreation Act of 1978. It was a remarkable moment for the entire park system. The Omnibus Act of 1978 emerged from the largest parks bill in history and was responsible for the creation and expansion of dozens of NPS units across the nation. It was also notable for catalyzing concerns about congressional "park barrel politics."[11] In Boston, however, PL 95–625 primarily made legal changes that had already been agreed to. It granted authority to the NPS, for instance, to receive Building 107 in the navy yard from the BRA. It authorized the NPS to acquire the land it needed to create a new entrance into the yard from Charlestown. And, most significantly, it included Dorchester Heights within the park's management dossier. It was an especially remarkable moment for those few people who recalled that the political campaign to authorize a national park in Boston had begun at Dorchester Heights. Indeed, eighty-nine-year-old retired congressman John McCormack—the man who started that campaign—personally attended the ceremonies on March 8, 1980, during which the city formally transferred the monument to the National Park Service.[12]

It was not McCormack, however, who got Dorchester Heights into the omnibus bill. The person responsible for introducing that legislation was Congressman John Joseph (Joe) Moakley, who joined McCormack on the stage that day. Moakley, who like McCormack was a native of South Boston, had worked his way through the ranks of state and local government. During

1953–61, he served in the Massachusetts House of Representatives for the Seventh Suffolk District. He won a bid for state senate in 1965 and represented the Fourth Suffolk District until 1971. That year, Moakley ran against School Commission Chair Louise Day Hicks, Boston's leading school segregationist, to represent the Massachusetts Ninth District in the U.S. House of Representatives. Hicks won in 1971 but lost to Moakley in a rematch the following year. Joe Moakley thus began in 1973 what would be a nearly thirty-year career in Congress. Prior to Hicks, Moakley's seat had belonged to McCormack. Moakley biographer Mark Robert Schneider notes that McCormack had "rounded up the votes" to pass the New Deal legislation that, in many ways, defined Moakley's boyhood years in Boston. It was only fitting then that Moakley carry on the tradition of supporting Bostonians, and their national park, began by his predecessor.[13]

It wasn't the first time that Moakley had involved himself in the conversation about a national park in Boston. He had jumped immediately into the heritage fray in 1973 when the navy announced its plans to shutter the navy yard. Two issues struck Moakley as particularly worrisome: the threat of lost jobs and the possibility of the USS *Constitution* being relocated. As we saw in chapter three, worries about the *Constitution* faded when the navy reaffirmed its commitment to Public Law 83–523 (1954)—the product of another legislative drive by McCormack—which eventually mandated perpetual preservation of the ship in Boston. In 1973, Moakley joined with Representatives James A. Burke and Tip O'Neill to introduce H.R. 7486 alongside Senator Edward M. Kennedy's S. 210, thus cementing McCormack's legacy and initiating what would be the final push toward authorizing a sprawling park in 1974, one that had been previously imagined as being solely situated in downtown Boston. Like the others, Moakley advocated for authorizing the park in time for the Bicentennial; he was also instrumental in getting Boston designated as an official American Revolution Bicentennial City in January 1974.[14] As we will see, especially in chapter six, it would not be the last time Joe Moakley proved critical to the park's success.

What finally poised the park for establishment, however, was the completion of its two-volume general management plan in 1979. All the planning and wrangling and deliberation had finally come to an end, almost. There still was the matter of a GMP for Dorchester Heights. That would be volume three. And, as we will see, volume two—the navy yard's plan—required revision almost immediately, a process that would take another seven years to complete. Completing the core plan, however, was the critical last step toward establishment, and as we saw in chapter four, not at all an easy step. In his 1979 annual report, Superintendent Gurney recalled, as if to exhale, that it had been "an enterprising year for Boston National Historical Park."[15]

A WORKING PARK

All the while, key facets of park operations had begun to emerge from the vagaries of planning. Most significant, perhaps, was the building up of core park staff. Hugh Gurney, of course, had reported for duty in June 1975, and had settled into a home with his wife in Ipswich. By January 1976, Gurney had hired eight other people. By December, the park employed sixty-four people.[16] Their profiles reveal how the park's various divisions developed distinct personas early on. The Division of Protection, for instance, drew heavily from local communities. Frank Montford transferred from the regional office to be protection chief. He supervised Dan Lynch and Bill Fitzgibbons, both residents of Charlestown, and Elmer Chapman, who had worked at the navy yard prior to its closure.[17] Protection's lone outsider, Judy Myzel, came to the park from Penn State University. The Division of Interpretation, however, skewed toward Philadelphia. Chief of Interpretation Dave Dutcher transferred from Independence National Historical Park, as did Frank Hadden. Bob Londorf, who was originally from Philadelphia, came to the park after graduating from Kenyon College. Interpretation's one local hire was John Cook, from nearby Watertown, who came to the park from Minute Man National Historical Park and who was then president of the Military Collectors of New England.[18] Though certainly not unique in this regard, it is clear that the park conceived of different aspects of its operations as having different relationships to locality.

Interestingly, given the complexity of historical issues at play in the park's planning saga, hiring staff with history training does not appear to have been a priority. Gurney, of course, had earned an MA in history, but by 1974 his professional competencies lay primarily in park management. Victor Jorrin, who had already been working on navy yard projects for the regional office, signed on as the park's historical architect, but as a preservationist, he was more concerned with advocating for significance rather than interrogating it. And the park's first historian, Mary Holmes, whom we met in chapter four, had trained in Johns Hopkins University's MA program for teachers. She came to Massachusetts in 1971 to develop educational programming for the Essex Institute, in Salem, and then worked with Boston 200's Division of Visitor Services during the Bicentennial years. Others at the park tasked early on with confronting complicated pasts—especially curators Arsen Charles and, later, Peter Steele—brought to their work training in exhibit development and museum practice, but again had not prepared specifically to wade through the intertwined histories of race, class, gender, memory, and urban change, which contextualized every aspect of the park's story.[19] As we learned in chapter four, top-shelf historians with precisely those qualifications were everywhere seeking jobs during the 1970s. None, however, found their way to the park until, as we will see below, Paul Weinbaum arrived in 1981.

Throughout the 1980s, the park's employee ceiling allowed the superintendent to keep between sixty and seventy employees on staff at any given time. It was a big workforce, but still hardly large enough to manage the scale of labor necessitated by a sprawling park and, of course, an impossibly demanding navy yard. As Administrative Officer Bob Pribula put it during one squad meeting, "the park has a problem in being able to do all of the [maintenance] projects listed because we do not have staff to supervise them properly."[20] From the beginning, then, the park struggled to align the size of its staff with the scale of its responsibilities. Gurney at least found in this challenge an opportunity to diversify his workforce. He made "much effort" to recruit seasonal applicants "of diverse backgrounds" from local schools and organizations. By 1978, Gurney reported that "our summer staff proved very effective . . . and we were pleased with the outcome of our efforts."[21] Gurney clearly imagined possibilities in NPS employment to provide all matter of life training. "We [try] to give our laborers," he explained, "a lot of experience in general maintenance which should help them in the future, whether it be working in our park or civilian employment." He thought it important also to "help them develop good work habits such as getting to work on time, staying on the job, [and] being dependable."[22]

Whereas a growing staff revealed signs of life within the park, its new visitor center signaled outwardly that the NPS had come to Boston. The proposed visitor center in the Easton Building at 15 State Street had begun to take shape by spring 1977. Its "purpose and objectives," according to the park, were "to provide an information and orientation center for visitors to the Freedom Trail and the Historic Sites," where visitors might encounter fuller interpretation. The visitor center would not serve food, but it would be designed intentionally to accommodate as many kinds of visitors as possible, including people with disabilities. David Sasanelli had been put in charge of designing exhibits for the building, with input from the then only seven-year-old Harper's Ferry Design Center.[23] At a meeting of the advisory commission, commission member Guy Beninati noted that it would be critical to plan landscaping at the visitor center "in keeping with the new image of the area." Beninati was referring to the city's plans to create a pedestrian-only mall on State Street surrounding the Old State House, plans that had been made possible by two public works bills totaling $6 million that President Jimmy Carter had just signed into law.[24] Later, the advisory commission debated who ought to narrate the visitor center's orientation film, variously suggesting "a young boy, a cab driver, the mayor, [or] someone with a distinct 'Boston' flavor to his speech."[25] It was a debate that presaged concerns among the advisory commission that "somewhere along the way," as Interpretive Specialist Francis Kolb put it during a 1981 advisory committee meeting, the park "seems to have lost its identity." The visitor center, as Kolb and others saw it, was the place where the park's focus might be brought more squarely back to the city.[26]

The park celebrated the grand opening of its new visitor center on April 19, 1978, the anniversary of the Battles of Lexington and Concord.[27] During its first year, as Gurney put it, "the Visitor Center took on the character of a regional and national source of information as well as being there to serve Boston." A decision had been made to concentrate all visitor services on the first level, which improved the agency's visibility in Boston and also freed up the second level for educational programming and other activities. Beginning in 1978, for instance, the Department of Environmental Management equipped the visitor center with an exhibit concerning the Harbor Islands, including a slide show that Gurney reported running "instead of the 'Freedom Trail.'"[28] A local school program called "Boston Voices" turned the second level into a theater briefly during 1979. Over time, the visitor center came to be seen as a community resource. In 1981, for instance, park management briefly allowed the Guardian Angels—a volunteer organization committed to crime prevention—to use the visitor center's restrooms at night.[29] It did, at least, until later that year, when the Eastern National Park and Monument Association paid for a major renovation of the visitor center and opened a sales desk on the first floor. Gurney reported that the desk, staffed by park interpreters and volunteers, generated a "lively and profitable interest" among visitors.[30]

Getting the visitor center right was crucial for a park that still struggled with explaining to its public what—and where—exactly it was. In the first years after authorization, the park sought to increase public awareness by running radio spots and plastering city buses with signs and fliers. Uniformed rangers distributed park literature at busy points along the subway system and answered whatever questions passersby might have.[31] At a meeting of the advisory commission in 1977, Gail Rotegard, of Boston 200, suggested that the park consider how city organizations and friends groups—like those that Independence National Historical Park had cultivated in Philadelphia—could "aid a park such as Boston NHP." Might it be possible, she wondered, to leverage the "widespread enthusiastic support" that Boston 200 had amassed during the Bicentennial? Gurney thought so, and he agreed that friends organizations could be especially useful for providing funding that the city might not be willing to make available.[32]

Finding community partners beyond the park's contributing sites thus became a priority. By late 1977, for instance, the park debuted its Historic and Urban Environmental Studies (HUES) program, developed in partnership with the Boston University Urban Environmental Studies Program. The partnership had been put in place by a cooperative agreement between the park and the Human Environment Institute of Boston University, signed in January 1977.[33] HUES sought to educate children in grades five through twelve about Boston's urban environment by involving them directly in hands-on learning exercises. The program, directed by Ellen Fineburg and Peter Holloran and housed in the Navy Yard Marine Barracks, specifically engaged students in the greater Boston school system with an eye toward balancing participation across inner city and suburban schools. In 1979, for instance, HUES staged a career education program for all District Three middle schools, and a magnet program for Dorchester and Arlington students.[34]

Similarly, by 1981, the park had begun exploring ideas—including essay and drawing contests for local kids—for facilitating engagement between the park and its neighbors. The park's advisory commission communicated, for instance, with the Boston School Commission, through which it requested support to develop curriculum that would make the "Freedom Trail sites more meaningful to the children who visit." That year, NPS interpretive specialist Cynthia Kryston began assembling an educational program for the park, with input from all the various sites along the Freedom Trail, and hoped to find a partner within the public school system to help her. The theme was "community" and reflected Kryston's hope that more Boston schoolkids might visit the site at a time when ninety percent of school visits came from outside Boston.[35]

In 1982, the advisory commission constituted its own education subcommission, which debuted a plan that December to engage Boston students with an art poster, essay, and oratory contest. The NPS refused to assist with the printing costs associated with the project, so the commission sought solutions with the superintendent of Boston's public schools.[36] By May 1983, the John Hancock Life Insurance Company had contributed $16,000 in support of the contest. At the same time, however, advisory commission member Maurice O'Shea, who spearheaded the effort, had become acting president of Bunker Hill Community College, leaving planning for the contest at a standstill.[37] Soon, though, the commission was back on track and had field-tested five site-based educational curricula designed for fourth graders. "We have almost a tiger by the tail here," Commission Chair Richard Berenson declared, noting the possibility of five thousand student visits during the 1984–85 school year.[38] Indeed, by summer 1985, the education program appeared wildly successful, so much so that the Boston school department agreed to fund all transportation costs for the coming school year.[39] And for the first time, it had a name: People and Places.[40]

PARTNERSHIP ALONG THE FREEDOM TRAIL

Firming up relationships with contributing sites remained a top priority as well. Gurney recalls the park's early relationship with its partnership sites as overwhelmingly positive. "People were favorably disposed toward us," he recalls. In planning conversations during fall 1975, Regional Chief of Interpretation James Corson had worried that the NPS might be perceived by its community stakeholders—especially sites along the Freedom Trail—as a competitor. From Gurney's perspective, at least, there was no sense of competition between the NPS sites and others along the trail, in part because the park was careful to include all of the sites in its visitor pamphlets. More significantly, Gurney recalls that the park got along well with its neighbors because Richard Berenson worked hard to encourage cooperation. At advisory commission meetings, for instance, Berenson ensured that representatives from all of the sites and other contributing organizations—including the convention bureau, public works, and the MDC—involved themselves. "We had probably more people sitting around the room to assist," according to Gurney, who recalls that "Dick could turn to whoever and get a response."[41] In this light, it is not surprising that the park's partner sites were much less frequently mentioned by name in monthly meeting minutes during these years than were the navy yard, Dorchester Heights, and no end of personnel and compliance issues.

What is more, by spring 1976, the NPS had just about completed drafting its first cooperative agreement between the park and a partner site, in this case the Old South Meeting House. It was an agreement, Gurney noted, that the park intended to use as a model for other sites.[42] And so it did. By late 1978, draft agreements had been worked out with Old North Church, the Paul Revere Memorial Association, the Bostonian Society (Old State House), Faneuil Hall, and the Boston Convention and Visitors Bureau (CVB). The agreements with the CVB, the Paul Revere Memorial Association, and the Bostonian Society went into effect by the end of the year. The NPS signed its agreement with the city regarding Faneuil Hall in 1981.[43] In some cases, the agreements produced immediate outcomes. The Bostonian Society, for instance, received a new library "in accordance with their Cooperative Agreement."[44] In other ways, too, the park had an immediate impact on its partner sites. By the end of 1978, for instance, historic structure reports had been completed for Faneuil Hall, Old South, and Bunker Hill. The Historic American Buildings Survey (HABS) program came to the Paul Revere House in 1979, bringing with it a team of architects, historians, and of course, new prospects for preservation funding.[45] That same year, even before it had signed a cooperative agreement with the city, the NPS inspected electrical and plumbing systems in the Old State House, aided with minor repairs, and repainted the Bostonian Society's third-floor office in preparation for its grand reopening. At Old South, all matter of work was in progress by 1979: new wiring for exhibits, extensive electrical repair throughout the building, repair of broken glass, and certainly many other items beyond.[46] The park's Section 106 files confirm that, although compliance actions focused primarily on projects within the navy yard during the park's first years, by 1979 all manner of NPS projects were in motion at the Old State House, Old South, the Paul Revere House, and at the Bunker Hill Monument.[47] All of it made an impact. By the end of 1981, Gurney reported that "since the Park Service presence has been downtown . . . the sites themselves have expanded their hours and their programs noticeably."[48]

This is not to say that there were not problems to contend with. The anxieties concerning the agency's role in Charlestown, detailed in chapter four and documented by MIT's Dennis Frenchman, appear to have continued through the Bicentennial. Gurney still wondered about how to best handle the Bunker Hill Monument. There was "some feeling," he explained to the advisory commission, that as a monument, its grounds should not be treated as

a public space "as it is now for the people of Charlestown." O'Shea fired back
that Charlestown needed public space, that it would be "a mistake to take it
away," and that "the NPS also feels the community is important."[49] Concerns
about conditions elsewhere along the Freedom Trail also worried the advisory
commission. Some members noted in 1981 the presence of sleeping "vagrants"
in parks and the prevalence of vandalism and litter in cemeteries along the trail.
Berenson sought to encourage a city-sponsored program wherein Freedom Trail
storefront owners might be convinced "to take care of their own 'front yards.'"
What was clear, though, was that the Freedom Trail required a substantial
financial investment, though the "possibility [for funding] is dim."[50] The situation only worsened during the following year. At its April 1982 meeting, the
commission agreed that cleanliness and maintenance had worsened alongside
an overall "deterioration of city services." Charlestown neighbor Pamela Brusic
apologized for admitting that locals "refer to the grounds [of the Bunker Hill
Monument] as the 'Bunker Hill dog bathroom.'" Gurney pledged the park's
support for the city's trash pickup campaign but admitted that he'd need
funding for tools and other supplies in order to help out.[51]

The advisory commission's concerns regarding the Freedom Trail reflected
a shifting dynamic in Boston's heritage landscape, which became increasingly
evident during the 1980s. Up to and throughout the Bicentennial years, Richard
Berenson had exerted a quiet though powerful influence over goings-on along
the trail. As Gurney indicates, a word from Berenson in city hall went a long
way toward fixing everyday problems along the trail. Increasingly during the
1980s, though, Berenson's backroom influence was not enough to ease all of
the park's bureaucratic complexities. In March 1981, for instance, the Freedom
Trail Commission worked around Berenson and called directly upon Chief of
Interpretation Frank Hadden at the last minute to work up a laundry list of
projects needing to be done along the trail. The commission reviewed the list
at a meeting and pledged to fund all maintenance along the trail that year.[52]
This scenario concerned Gurney, who clearly perceived a need to better prepare
park staff to manage its relationship with the Freedom Trail and its various
authorities. Within the year, Gurney announced his desire for a "top level
management person to visit each site on a regular basis." "The assignment
would be of considerable importance," he pointed out, "and would require
that the person be available as the park's contact/liaison with site managers."[53]

In other regards, too, the park sought to bring collaboration with its constituent sites into the open, rather than continue to manage challenges along the

Freedom Trail in case-by-case negotiations. During spring 1983, for instance, the advisory commission discussed for the first time the possibility of selling a unified ticket for all of the park sites. Although the NPS had no model for such an arrangement, the commission hoped to launch a one-year pilot toward encouraging unity among the sites.[54] At first, the NPS expressed support for the idea. Later that year, however, the agency confronted a "congressional moratorium on charging fees," wherein parks could only charge entry fees for special services. What's more, regulations prohibited federal employees from collecting money on behalf of private groups, thereby making it impossible for NPS staff to sell tickets for several of the park's contributing sites.[55] A series of meetings over the following year seem not to have provided any alternatives, and during spring 1984 the commission discussed the possibility of a four-site ticket.[56] In this way, and as would become increasingly clear over time, the park's ability to intervene along the Freedom Trail hung—sometimes precariously so—in the balance between agency policies and partner needs.

INTERPRETATION AFTER THE BICENTENNIAL

Nowhere was this balancing act more evident during the park's first decade than in the work of its interpretive staff. NPS interpretation got off to a late start in Boston. The park had been authorized, after all, amid the Bicentennial celebration, which produced possibly the nation's largest-ever coordinated interpretive event. Planners could put off interpretive decisions, in other words, because the park wouldn't be immediately expected to generate its own interpretive momentum. But even without the Bicentennial, it was evident from the beginning that the contours of heritage interpretation in Boston would be bound by the partnership model to follow the Freedom Trail. As NPS Planner Nan Rickey explained it in a 1974 interpretive proposal, the park had been conceived of as a "confederation" and, therefore, interpretation would necessarily depend upon, and evolve along with, the outcome of cooperative agreements. The plan that Rickey and her team envisioned in 1974, therefore, was "not intended for accomplishment in time for the Bicentennial." "There is greater interest," they determined, "in the federal presence after the Bicentennial."[57]

Unable to anticipate the precise nature of that post-Bicentennial federal presence, however, Rickey proposed a schematic approach to interpretation, predominated by printed park guides and audiovisual programs concerning "the significance of the Revolution," and "the men of the Revolution." Because Dorchester Heights and Bunker Hill were already slated for federal ownership,

Ricky proposed exhibits for those sites: "Siege of Boston" at the former and "British and Americans who Fought Here" at the latter. More specifically, Rickey recommended that a coordinating curatorial position be established at the park in order to facilitate object conservation and cataloging across the various sites. Once that work was complete, she suggested, collections management could be easily sustained through contract labor readily available in Boston.[58]

Despite its interpretive holding pattern, the park was at least perceived as making a positive impact on interpretive goings-on in and around Boston. The advisory commission noted, for instance, that interpretation at the Paul Revere House had been "below standard . . . but now with Park Service technical assistance, is much improved."[59] The advisory commission also involved itself in reviewing a new route for the Freedom Trail, which was planned to begin at Boston Common and end at the navy yard. In a rare commitment of city resources, the Boston Traffic Commission pledged to install new signs along the trail, reflecting, no doubt, Berenson's influence, but also some faith in the agency's stewardship. The Council of Historic Sites, at least, "declared [through Berenson] their appreciation for what the NPS is doing."[60]

Meeting minutes reveal that by the end of 1977, however, some among the interpretive division worried that "operations seem to be moving slowly." Others explained away the lull as owing to a drop off in visitation since the Labor Day holiday.[61] By spring 1977, park management noticed a precipitous decline in visitation at all sites except for Faneuil Hall, which benefited from its proximity to the new festival marketplace. Among the major reasons given by the advisory commission for the drop off was "post-centennial backlash." O'Shea suggested that it was time to move beyond the "monumental stage" at the park's various sites, and into a "living history" stage. He indicated that the Museum of Science and the Aquarium had been "extremely successful" in their use of first-person interpretation. Gurney suggested that the park ought to bring back visitors "who hadn't been in the city for years as a tourist" by emphasizing community involvement. Seminars and other interactive activities at the sites, Gurney explained, might just bring back people who had not visited since the days of the Bicentennial. Berenson shared that the Tourist Development Council thought it was time to "reverse the way Boston has always been advertised, with the emphasis on History," and instead emphasize the "new Boston" and its opportunities for entertainment.[62]

What O'Shea and the others had in mind was a deeper investment in precisely the kind of experiential history that Boston 200 had pioneered in

Boston and that had become popular across the nation during the 1970s.[63] During the following year, as visitation rates stabilized, the park deployed two groups of roving interpreters along the Freedom Trail, while increasing tours at Bunker Hill, the navy yard, Faneuil Hall, and Sam Adams Park.[64] It appeared to pay off. By the end of the year, Chief of Interpretation Dutcher reported that summer 1978 visitation figures "had broken all records." Bunker Hill, he added, experienced a sixty-two percent increase over the previous year.[65] At the same time, visitation spikes raised concerns about whether or not costumed interpretation adequately communicated the agency's presence along the Freedom Trail. James Corson, regional director of interpretation, raised the issue during a fall 1978 advisory commission meeting. Corson recommended that the park develop a film and bookstore for its new visitor center along with musical performances and programming for children.[66]

By 1979, however, costumed NPS interpreters had become a fixture along the Freedom Trail. The park's newsletter, for instance, profiled Sarah, "A proud Bostonian" from 1811, played by Park Ranger Sue Gochenour. "Sarah speaks from another era," it explained, "she speaks of her city and its romance with the sea," as well as the threat of British impressment, rumors of a second war with England, and her memories of "her father's vivid tales of the Revolution."[67] That summer, visitors might have also encountered a one-act play, titled "Boston Voices," concerning the days leading to the Revolution, created by the Boston Arts Group, and performed daily on the mall in front of the visitor center. At Old South, local actors portrayed Cotton Mather, Susan B. Anthony, Henry David Thoreau, and others. An evening performance of sea shanties debuted in the navy yard in August.[68] In the navy yard, too, summer 1979 was the first time that interpreters experimented with dividing their program into three themes, concerning shipbuilding and repair, varieties of labor, and the lives of the people who lived and worked in the navy yard.[69] Most immediately, however, costumed interpretation had come to be seen as a tool for boosting visibility. When it seemed that the NPS wasn't grasping visitor attention, such as in 1983 when Berenson noted poor visibility at the Boston Massacre site, Gurney and his staff deployed costumed rangers.[70]

A PLAN FOR THE NAVY YARD

That interpretation got off to a slow start in Boston reflected the persistent demands put on the superintendent and his staff by the navy yard. Gurney realized early on that the navy yard would consume as much time as he would give it. Anticipating this problem, and despite having situated most of the park's staff in navy yard offices, Gurney chose 15 State Street for his own office, because he "didn't want to get so wrapped up in the navy yard that I wasn't paying any attention to the other places."[71] And yet, the navy yard constantly clamored. There was, for instance, the problem of access.[72] Because the long reach of the Mystic River Bridge (officially known as the Maurice J. Tobin Memorial Bridge) into Charlestown limited potential entry points into the yard, some people worried that "the Park [not be] used as a highway into the area."[73] There were concerns, too, about visitor services, especially the perennial problem of transportation back and forth across the river, and how the NPS might work with the BRA to provide parking and concessions.[74] And then, of course, there was the constant haggling over how to manage the daily labors necessary to sustain the yard's physical integrity; park staff could not do it alone. During the fall of 1977, for instance, Gurney looked to a young adult employment training program to provide seventy-six eighteen-to-twenty-four-year-old short-term laborers to work on rehabilitating structures. It was something, he noted, that "the Carter administration is anxious" to accomplish.[75]

All of these concerns were intensified by a lingering question: what was the navy yard about? It was a question, as we've seen, left unanswered by Congress amid the rush to authorization in 1974. The BRA had initially sought to create there a stylized nineteenth-century residential and commercial district. As we saw in chapter three, however, NPS Regional Assistant Director for Planning Ross Holland argued forcefully that the facility's twentieth-century history be showcased. After authorization, these camps shifted and evolved. On one hand, there were those like USS *Constitution* Commander Tyrone Martin who favored the "historical setting" rather than the "industrial character" of the navy yard. In hindsight, of course, it is clear that the navy yard's industrial character ranked among its key historical assets. But at the time and amid the waves of deindustrialization then washing across the nation, Martin clearly sought to imagine a past more dignified than what he perceived amid the navy yard's shuttered buildings and abandoned machinery. He proposed that many of the yard's buildings—including Hoosac Stores—be removed and that its pavement be replaced with grass and cobblestones "in keeping with the period," by which Martin presumably referred to the early republic. Others, including Gurney, proposed alternatives to demolition, such as using the navy yard's large industrial buildings for parking from which shuttles might distribute visitors among the park's various sites.[76]

For its part, the BRA had come to appreciate the navy yard's industrial character. Marsha Myers, a BRA preservation planner, attended the December 1976 meeting of the advisory commission and explained that the "entire ship-yard is an historical landmark and the problem is how to use it and also pre-serve its history." "The industrial character of the yard," she insisted, "must be preserved." Myers explained that the BRA was particularly concerned to maintain the Ropewalk and Chain Forge, which had not been originally included within NPS boundaries. The BRA hoped, however, that the NPS would shoulder most of the costs associated with preserving the Ropewalk, seeing as the city could not afford it.[77] And yet, within months, it became clear to the BRA that restrictions associated with the buildings' National Historic Landmark status would make them "difficult to market," raising considerable questions about who, ultimately, should be in control.[78]

During following years, the NPS and its partners explored a range of planning alternatives for the navy yard. In 1978, for instance, the advisory commission staged an open meeting wherein it hosted the planning team from the NPS Denver Service Center (DSC), various park staff, and numer-ous Charlestown residents for the purpose of gathering public comment on the agency's plans for the navy yard.[79] Gurney introduced the session with an overview of the navy yard, its history, and its key management challenges, including the problem of transportation. David Weiner, of the BRA, presented its plan for the navy yard, which included one hundred acres of new develop-ment, a sixteen-acre public park, a historical monument, and thirty buildings slated for conversion into mixed-use housing, offices, and commercial space. The remaining fifty-eight acres, according to Weiner, would be developed into twelve hundred units of housing. The whole project would require up to ten years to complete and would cost private developers about one hundred million dollars.[80]

Seventeen attendees—a mix of local residents and representatives of stake-holder organizations—filled out survey forms devised by the planning team to gauge public response to their plans. Responses reveal a sophisticated concern for the intersections between history, memory, and the likely impacts of navy yard development on Charlestown and its people. Most respondents worried that commercial development be done "properly." One person insisted that there was "NO room for a McDonald's," and yet respondents vaguely supported controlled shipbuilding and repair operations in the yard. Similarly, survey respondents were concerned that the site appear as an industrial and educational space, though they also expected that the navy yard would provide recreational activities and public events such as concerts. Most respondents worried about increased traffic in Charlestown and widely supported public transit options. Many hoped to keep the park free of vehicles entirely and to locate parking under the Mystic River Bridge. Nearly everyone believed that the NPS should be responsible for managing the entire area, though the group was divided over how much of the navy yard should be owned by the federal government.[81]

What is most interesting about the surveys is what they reveal about how the navy yard figured in the historical imagination of its neighbors. Though some people thought about the navy yard's significance as an ongoing process that deserved interpretive attention in all periods, most of the surveys indicated an emphasis on the long nineteenth century, which ended with the close of World War I. Many of the suggestions for the park's continued significance emphasized the role that interpretation played in crafting patriotism and portraying national development. However, by connecting locations such as the Ropewalk, Chain Forge, and the Commandant's House with pivotal events such as the world wars, respondents also conveyed their understandings of the navy yard as an essential part of the global warfare of the twentieth century. And yet, when asked more specifically about building restoration, respondents overwhelmingly expressed interest in adhering to a turn-of-the-century aesthetic. Included in this ideal was the function of the Commandant's House. Many believed it best for this space to be filled with period furnishings and opened for tours and possibly social events. The surveys also showed a desire to bring in other vessels than the USS *Constitution* and an almost unanimous rejection of moving the *Constitution* from its location, toward portraying the site as an authentic and "functional" navy yard.[82]

With regard to the look and feel of the site, respondents concerned themselves with authenticity and cohesiveness at the navy yard, both as a historical site and as a piece of the Greater Boston area. While there was little agreement as to which historical period would shape the look of the site, many argued for the inclusion of green spaces and general cleanliness in a space that showed elements of all periods of the site's use. In addition to the inclusion of an interpretive center within the yard, the responses also showed support for a walking trail between Bunker Hill and the navy yard and the beginnings of an oral history project about the influence of the yard during its active years. Support for these plans show the degree to which the respondents felt that the navy yard fit into the larger historical milieu of Boston.[83]

The public meeting had been a success. At least it had been from Gurney's perspective. He reported to the advisory commission that reaction to the plan "was fairly positive." The BRA's David Weiner agreed and appreciated how well the event had gone over. Not everyone, though, was so sure. O'Shea thought otherwise: "from the point of view of the citizens of Charlestown that may not be the case." "There was a real feeling," he said, "that the meeting was run in a somewhat patronizing way." People worried navy yard plans might not come back "to the people of the communities" for additional input before finalization. O'Shea added that their "concern was not noted in the minutes of the meeting." Beninati sounded a note of concern too, suggesting that changes to the navy yard might have impacts on the North End, though there were no plans to consult its residents. Dutcher suggested that the problem might be alleviated by distributing the *Broadside,* the park's internal newsletter, to all of its various neighbor communities. Rotegard and Gurney noted that the park had just hired a permanent community liaison whose job it would be to facilitate ongoing exchange.[84]

And yet, tensions between the NPS—specifically the DSC—and the BRA had grown acute by spring 1978. Amid efforts by the NPS to accommodate public feedback, Weiner "plead[ed] for some sanity in the planning process." Constant tweaking not only demonstrated a lack of faith in BRA planning efforts, he insisted, but it also undermined the city's ability to secure committed redevelopment dollars. Some of the DSC team's proposals, Weiner went on, were "ridiculous and disrespectful to [BRA] planning process." Beninati demanded that the park be thought of as a living thing, not a museum, which should be open to all of Charlestown. Commander Martin warned against creating what he perceived to be a "macadam desert." Overall, the commission expressed frustration with a set of planning alternatives that failed to recognize the "history of community planning and agreement." It believed that the DSC had been too heavy-handed and that, going forward, final decisions should be made between the BRA and the park alone.[85]

The DSC returned a year later with a fresh round of alternatives for the advisory commission. All of them imagined expansive boundaries for the NPS, none of which had been previously negotiated with the BRA. Alternative one proposed a "monument restoration approach," wherein demolition and reconstruction would be used to return the yard to how it might have appeared in about 1910, including with a trolley system. A second alternative proposed three "time zones": a historical monument zone, a residential zone approximating the yard during the 1940s, and an "industrial character zone" keyed to 1973. Alternative three sought to create a "community oriented urban park," with historic buildings adapted for mixed-commercial use befitting the needs of neighbors and, ultimately, a new generation of residents. Both alternatives two and three included a bus system.[86]

Responses to the new alternatives were decidedly mixed. O'Shea expressed the advisory commission's preference for a combination of alternatives two and three and supposed that in this case the commission's voice approximated the public's. The BRA's Paul Kelly was clearly nonplussed. The BRA, he insisted, would demand a fourth alterative, one with a considerably smaller boundary expansion. From Kelly's perspective, the BRA could not "go along with" any of the alternatives as proposed. O'Shea agreed that, in public meetings concerning the navy yard, participants hoped that as many buildings as possible would be made available for development "and to the tax rolls." Victor Jorrin, for the NPS regional office, wondered whether it would appease the BRA if the DSC proposed a fourth alterative allowing cooperative use of Building 123 and Dry Dock 2. Kelly wouldn't commit, noting that it "would depend" on the uses.[87]

The navy yard tug of war evidently proved too much for the NPS. At the next meeting, in November 1979, a decision was announced without any further discussion: the navy yard would be preserved overall as it appeared in 1973, though the NPS would acquire several buildings from the BRA that it would then restore to their 1910 appearance. What's more, the planning process would thereafter remain in Denver, where Gurney and Dutcher would travel that winter to help write the final draft.[88] Clearly, the DSC did not share the advisory commission's belief that decisions about the navy yard ought to be settled by the park and the BRA alone. So far as concerned collaboration on volume two of the park's general management plan, the conversation was over.

But even after the agency approved the park's plan, conversation continued about planning problems in the navy yard. When the commission regathered in April 1980—at a meeting attended by the new regional director, Richard Stanton—a DSC representative reiterated what had been decided with regard to the navy yard plan. Berenson inquired about the Ropewalk and Chain Forge buildings. Gurney explained that negotiations with the BRA had gone on for years and that the BRA seemed willing to transfer the Ropewalk to the NPS, but only with a promise of quick rehabilitation.[89] The BRA's Marcia Myers asked for an interpretive plan that provided a "lively experience" for visitors, including in areas surrounding the yard. Gurney noted that, with regard to all of these matters, appropriations would be an issue, and that the BRA should share whatever ideas it had immediately, so that the NPS could work out a plan and avoid another "stalemate."[90]

Negotiations between the NPS and the BRA concerning the Ropewalk continued for years in fits and starts. Uncertainty about the disposition of the property sometimes led to mishaps, such as in 1981when a BRA contractor began demolishing the building, unaware of its significance.[91] When the NPS and the BRA did meet about the Ropewalk, old disagreements persisted about whether the navy yard should be an industrial site or a historic one. At the advisory commission's April 1982 meeting, for instance, yet another conversation about the Ropewalk segued into conversations about razing Hoosac Stores.[92] That building—which was then without plumbing, heat, and other utilities—had been the subject of a legal inquiry by the U.S. Attorney's Office during 1981 concerning the right of a tenant to remain there. The Departments of Interior and Justice decided that they did have that right and issued a special use permit to that effect. It was owing to the building's usability, demonstrated by these circumstances, Curator Peter Steele countered, that Hoosac Stores was precisely the kind of building that should be rehabilitated.[93]

Amid all of these concerns, it had become clear that the navy yard's general management plan was already inadequate to its purpose. Under the leadership of a new superintendent, John Burchill, the park proposed a revised plan for the navy yard in 1986. The advisory commission reviewed it that spring. Burchill had added to park staff an assistant superintendent for planning and development, John Debo, and his revised plan called for improvements in three areas "compatible with the historic scene" to provide visitors with food, water, shade, seating, and other services. The plan also committed the NPS to allowing development of the Ropewalk and Chain Forge with private funding, though it also required that developers provide exhibit space and interpretive facilities, while sustaining the "historic character and fabric" of the buildings.[94] The park's encouragement of private investment in historic structures, which will return as an important theme in chapter six, signaled an important turn that recalled Boston's mid-century urban renewal campaigns. Most immediately, however, it pointed to an anxious awareness that "the Navy Yard suffers from a lack of appropriate development [and that] key historic resources are deteriorating."[95]

THE PROBLEM WITH HISTORY

As the navy yard story makes clear, park managers found themselves confronted time and time again with complex historical questions. Some of these questions, of course, concerned the Revolutionary past, but the majority by far related to matters of race, class, memory, and urban change during the last century. It is truly remarkable, in this light, that a national historical park of this scope and complexity did not seek early on to more fully engage trained historians in these discussions. It certainly benefited from the insights of people with expertise in historic preservation, architecture, material culture, archeology, and other history-adjacent fields. But, if archival records are any indication, it does not appear that professional historians with historiographical sophistication and an ability to understand the park in broad geographic and chronological context had any significant role in shaping the park during its first years. It's a remarkable situation, though not at all surprising. Others have documented how the agency's investments in historic preservation, dating all the way back to the New Deal and intensified since 1966 by the National Historic Preservation Act, have increasingly focused NPS historical expertise on matters such as compliance research and nominations to the National Register of Historic Places. Conceptualizing a unit's historical meanings, and communicating with visitors about those meanings, has consequently become the work of interpretive staff and resource managers who may or may not have expertise in historical methods and content.[96] As of 1980, the park employed staff members with a great depth of knowledge concerning immediate concerns, such as how to sustain colonial architecture and even how to preserve a battleship, but none, it seems, had the breadth of knowledge to craft a convincing historical narrative encompassing all of it.

This is not to say that the park was not interested in doing history. On the contrary, the park briefly employed oral historian Judy Dunning during 1977 to design an oral history project for the navy yard. Dunning, who would later earn notoriety for a similar program supporting Rosie the Riveter World War II Home Front National Historical Park in Richmond, California, trained ten interpreters to conduct interviews with people who had worked at the navy yard prior to its closure.[97] Only a few months later, Curator Peter Steele began planning a special exhibit for summer 1978 featuring artifacts and photos gathered from informants.[98] The project that Dunning designed not only legitimized the arguments of those who had long supported embracing the navy yard's industrial past, it generated content that continues to buoy navy yard interpretation today.

Doing oral history, however, is not the same as thinking historically about problems of park management. There is very little evidence of any historical thinking as regards park management during its first decade. Historical matters, for instance, rarely figured in advisory commission meetings, perhaps because park historians rarely participated in the meetings. Squad meeting minutes too are silent on matters of history until 1981, when Frank Montford announced that Paul Weinbaum had been hired from Statue of Liberty National Monument to fill the park's historian position.[99] Weinbaum gradually contributed more and more during subsequent meetings, usually in connection with the various National Register nominations, including a particularly complex project related to Hoosac Stores, that he had been tasked with.[100] He became even more present in monthly meetings following a reorganization of meeting protocol during 1982, after which routine reports concerning historical tasks reveal greater detail about the range of activities requiring historical insight.[101]

Weinbaum's case is an important one and worth dwelling on for the insight it provides toward understanding how history did and did not figure during the formative years of one of the agency's foremost history units. At the time of his hire, the historian's position was managed by Frank Montford, division chief for planning and historic preservation. Montford had previously been chief of protection and was not trained in any particular way to oversee or implement history projects. "He knew he needed a historian because it was on his organization chart," as Weinbaum explains it, but "he didn't know what a historian did."[102] Weinbaum, who had earned a PhD in history from the University of Rochester, worried that his specialty in antebellum U.S. social history might not have prepared him adequately to work at a park concerned primarily with histories of the navy and the American Revolution. Colleagues Weinbaum had met while working for the NPS at the Statue of Liberty assured him that it wouldn't matter, and as it turned out, they were right. As Weinbaum explains it, though the park was prompted by the National Historic Preservation Act (NHPA) to include a historian in its organizational chart—an innovation at that time—nobody at the park had any sense of what a historian's job should be. At least, nobody in Weinbaum's division did. It's a remarkable scenario given that, of course, this was a park conceived of, presumably, to do history. The work of giving tours and speaking to the public about the past had been relegated to the Division of Interpretation, as was typical in the agency. Weinbaum thus lingered quietly in meetings with maintenance crew and resource specialists until Montford charged him one day with a task that was, in hindsight, remarkably consistent with the park's *raison d'etre:* figure out how to make its historic buildings turn a profit.[103]

The buildings in question belonged to the historic Hoosac Stores warehouse complex.[104] Because the NPS had acquired the property with its authorizing legislation but did not consider it directly relevant to the navy yard, it sought to profit from it under circumstances amenable to the agency's preservation mission. The NHPA provides to the NPS a leasing authority wherein publicly owned historic buildings can be let to private tenants who agree to perform approved maintenance and, in some cases, rehabilitation.[105] To be eligible, however, properties must be included on the National Register of Historic Places. The park had a tenant already picked out for Hoosac Stores, but it had not yet been able to make a convincing argument for adding the building to the register. Weinbaum conferred with NPS Regional Historian Dwight Pitcaithley, who explained how cultural resource managers conceive of significance with regard to register nominations. With that, and having dug through the archival record, it occurred to Weinbaum that the building's significance had much less to do with architecture than it did with trade. This was an epicenter of Boston's global trade network, after all, and by researching the railroad and steamship companies that moved freight through the stores, Weinbaum demonstrated how powerfully the building figured in the story of American economic growth.[106] It was a historical argument, and a good one at that, precisely because it demonstrated how the park could reimagine its significance far beyond what planners had done originally, by thinking hard about Boston's place in broad geographic and chronological contexts. By 1981, context was precisely what the park needed.

Weinbaum had achieved his goal, so well in fact that Pitcaithley encouraged him to seek designation for two more buildings—an entire district—contributing to the Hoosac Stores story. He did, and in 1985 the Secretary of Interior added all three buildings to the National Register.[107] In the meantime, however, the park had lost its tenant for Hoosac Stores, and Weinbaum suddenly perceived that his accomplishment had cost him goodwill within the park. Hoosac Stores had become "an albatross," in part because the NPS was now responsible for costly NHPA Section 106 compliance.[108] From the perspective of his division, which was oriented solely around preservation and planning, Weinbaum had created more work for staff who were already spread too thin. And yet, Weinbaum had uncovered important content for park interpreters. Owing to the park's internal organization, however—an organizational structure introduced by Mission 66 era reforms—the historian and interpretation staff had no functional relationship with one another. Weinbaum thus found himself in the peculiar position of being criticized for doing good history.

Weinbaum's experience makes clear that, from the beginning, the park had a history problem. Not only did its managers misunderstand history and, therefore, fail to value it, its organizational structure prevented good history from reaching the public. The obstruction occurred in at least two ways during Weinbaum's tenure. First, project collaborators disinclined toward social history might simply erase Weinbaum's contributions. Weinbaum had been tasked, for instance, with developing a historic structure report for Building 28. His research uncovered remarkable insights. It turned out that would-be Supreme Court Justice Felix Frankfurter once intervened in a labor dispute at Building 28. Even more significantly, Weinbaum discovered that during World War I the navy had to physically alter Building 28 to prevent men on the first floor from harassing women on the second floor through loosely fitted floor boards. The building's architecture, Weinbaum showed, was an index of early twentieth-century gender discord. These were revelatory discoveries. Weinbaum's collaborators, however, considered his history irrelevant to the purpose of the report and summarily dismissed it.[109]

A second and perhaps even more problematic obstruction concerned engagement with historical content within the Division of Interpretation. Although the park's historian had no formal relationship with interpreters, Weinbaum nonetheless took it upon himself to share research with the division that he thought might advance the park's interpretive agenda. In one case, Weinbaum shared the results of a pioneering project concerning Faneuil Hall and public memory. Even before historian Alfred Young's important work on Revolutionary memory in Boston had reached wide circulation, Weinbaum posed a critical question: when did the phrase "Cradle of Liberty" become associated with Faneuil Hall? Weinbaum could not answer the question definitively, but what he learned was just as important. It appeared that the phrase had not entered into common use until the 1820s, long after the Revolutionary era during which most people—including the park's interpreters—presumed it had. In hindsight, the significance of Weinbaum's discovery is clear. As we learned in chapter one, Boston's Revolutionary memory was largely contrived, beginning during the 1820s, by Whigs and, later, abolitionists who variously struggled to set a political and moral agenda for the nation. This is to say that the Freedom Trail's prevailing historical narrative is loosely based on ideas about the Revolution that came into being long after the Revolution ended. Weinbaum shared his discovery with the park's interpreters, but as he recalls, "they didn't want to hear it!" According to Weinbaum, "I was not popular with the interpreters. I told the truth."[110]

Weinbaum's revelation concerning the "Cradle of Liberty" confirmed a problem that careful observers would have seen too in the agency's tense negotiations in Charlestown over plans for the navy yard and, to a lesser extent, at the Bunker Hill Monument. All of these sites, though historically significant, had accrued considerably more meaning among Bostonians for their mnemonic value. In the same way that Faneuil Hall—as Weinbaum demonstrated—had become significant for how it was remembered by ante-bellum Americans, so had Bunker Hill become significant during the same period as a way of remembering the Revolution. The navy yard too had become a nexus of memory among Bostonians struggling to understand a shifting economy. Considering why these sites had been remembered, how, and by whom, as Weinbaum demonstrated, had the power to reveal deep currents of cultural politics in Boston. Was it just a coincidence that Faneuil Hall's abolitionist history had, over the decades, been obscured by its Revolutionary history? Might it not have been important to confront that history in a city and at a time when, just years before, Black children had been beaten publicly for visiting Bunker Hill? Was this not the job of the national historical park in which they were beaten?

RACE, MEMORY, AND DORCHESTER HEIGHTS

It is clear that, from early on, the park's inability to foreground history, and its unwillingness to plumb memory, enabled a remarkable indifference to the long and complicated history of race in Boston. A critical finding of this study is that, with one important exception, neither matters of race nor regard for African American history figured significantly in any of the official conversations associated with the creation and management of a national park in Boston prior to the Bicentennial. This is to say that, for twenty-five years, nobody within the NPS or any of its partner organizations in Boston thought to insist that the experience of Black Americans be considered essential in our national retelling of the Revolutionary saga. During exactly the same years, as we've seen in previous chapters, developers removed Black families from Boston's historic neighborhoods, forcing them to the periphery, while white Bostonians terrorized Black Americans with public intimidation and violence. The NPS, alongside Boston's public and private power brokers, thus participated in a systematic citywide program of racial erasure for much of the twentieth century. Decades of scholarship show us that this is neither a surprising nor unique story. But Boston's complicity in nationwide efforts to marginalize Black people cannot be allowed to obscure the fact that the park was born of, and not just amid, a scorching cauldron of race hatred and violence.

The painful confluence of race and memory, illustrated so powerfully by the stories of Ted Landsmark and Charles Battles, was everywhere on display in Boston during the 1970s. Ignoring it required intent and, by May 1978, it appears that Superintendent Hugh Gurney was no longer willing to choose ignorance. It was that May that he raised before the advisory commission the specter of Charles Battles, whose attackers had been acquitted earlier that year. Since then, both NPS and navy personnel had suffered sporadic instances of abusive racially charged language and threats. Gurney pledged to protect "minority visitors" and employees from subsequent attacks and announced that he had initiated conversations with Charlestown community organizations about ways to move forward. He also announced his intent to increase police protection in and around the navy yard during summer months.[111] Problems persisted, however, and the advisory commission lamented that the "security of and access by minorities" had been a real problem since the park's inception. That problem extended to park workspaces too. Frank Montford reported, for instance, that equal opportunity posters in Building 109 had been defaced. Montford admonished staff that "under no circumstances should items posted on bulletin boards be tampered with," but there seems to have been no mention of the circumstances surrounding these specific posters.[112] Reports suggested that Deputy Mayor Clarence "Jeep" Jones—Boston's first Black deputy mayor—might involve himself in addressing the problem, and both Gurney and Berenson stressed education and business outreach as salves, but clearly decades of removal, mistrust, and violence had lodged themselves deep within the park's genesis story and were not going to vanish anytime soon.[113]

Indeed, contending with race violence was a fact of life for park staff. During July 1981, for instance, NPS interpreters leading a Freedom Trail walk intervened in "a potentially serious racial incident" at Paul Revere Mall, when they protected "blacks . . . who were being heavily harassed by local youths." Gurney noted Revere Mall as a frequent problem area with "heavy drug traffic" and deferred to Berenson who, as usual, pledged to take up the problem with the city.[114] The park considered stationing a racially mixed team of interpreters at the mall, which "has been a serious trouble spot for both minority groups and employees," but the inclination to let Berenson handle the problem typified the park's typically laissez-faire approach to problems of racial violence.[115] It was an approach that clearly did not work. By 1982, despite working with the Boston Committee, Gurney reported continued difficulties, including constant efforts to remove graffiti from Augustus Saint-Gaudens's famous 1897 *Memorial to Robert Gould Shaw and the Massachusetts Fifty-Fourth Regiment* at 24 Beacon Street. Just a few years later, New York Theological Seminary Registrar Leslie McEwen recounted how, right in front of the Paul Revere House, "a young White male . . . took the opportunity to tell me, 'there are no coloreds in this neighborhood—no niggers allowed here.'" McEwen lamented that even "in the South I received more respect than I received on the streets of Boston." Gurney understood the problem. The "poor reputation the City has in the area of race relations," he said, "is still deserved."[116]

It is worth noting that, back in 1978, the park had inherited an incredible opportunity to confront problems of race and violence head on in South Boston. The Omnibus Act of 1978, as we have seen, had only just brought Dorchester Heights into Gurney's management dossier. And Dorchester Heights, given its location adjacent to South Boston High, had been at the center of Boston's school busing crisis just four years earlier. Busing, of course, was not the only cause of racial tension in South Boston. As we learned in chapter one, it was rather a symptom of longstanding frictions between the neighborhood's white ethnic Irish majority and relative newcomers, including African Americans, who arrived in increasing numbers throughout the twentieth century and especially after World War II. Their presence meant that South Boston was a place where local memories had as much to do with battles for civil rights as they had to do with battles with the British. It explains why Representative McCormack's campaign beginning in 1938 to secure federal recognition for the monument and for South Boston's Evacuation Day parade—the campaign, in fact, that paved the way for the national park—sought so aggressively to cast South Boston's history as white Irish history. The monument and the holiday, which conveniently coincided with St. Patrick's Day, had after all been contrived together amid a wave of early twentieth-century patriotic white nationalism. The message then, as well as in 1938, and possibly again in 1978, was clear: South Boston's history is white history.

The NPS thus had a remarkable opportunity in 1978 to change course, to reimagine Dorchester Heights as inclusive of all Americans. Certainly, it had the tools to do it. The park's nascent oral history program could have documented how and why different kinds of people had experienced the monument since its dedication, less than a century before. The DSC could have repeated in South Boston the community engagement model it experimented with in Charlestown. Gurney could have appointed a Black site manager toward signaling a new era. It seems, though, that bereft of historical context and without concern for the politics of memory, the park took a very different approach to Dorchester Heights. In April 1979, when the park assumed responsibility for Dorchester Heights, Gurney put Vincent Lombardi, a white protection ranger, in charge of the unit along with a crew of six maintenance staff.[117] Lombardi immediately set his crew to cleaning up "years of litter and broken glass [and the] hazards of dead trees and stumps."[118] South Boston Councilman Ray Flynn and Senate President William Bulger applauded the effort, hoping that the increased NPS presence at Dorchester Heights would "help develop civic pride [and] further help in combatting vandalism at the Monument."[119]

Having cleaned the site, and after establishing a security protocol there, Lombardi prepared to develop a general management plan for the new unit. To get ready, he enrolled in a course on urban parks management, wherein participants visited South Boston to meet with community leaders concerning the challenges of managing Dorchester Heights. He and his team were "able to see first hand the difficulties minorities might encounter as they attempt to visit a National Historic Site which has been set aside for the enjoyment of all citizens."[120] Squad meeting minutes from this period shed light on Lombardi's evolving approach to planning. He hoped, for instance, to directly engage neighbors in planning rather than utilize the DSC, suggesting, perhaps, the extent to which park management had grown weary of decentralization during its previous planning forays.[121] He worried too that "perhaps too much emphasis is being placed on racial problems when writing the GMP—it may exacerbate the problem as it focuses on it."[122] Getting Dorchester Heights into shape, in Lombardi's view, was primarily a matter of reducing crime and encouraging positivity. Picking up trash from the monument grounds, after all, "takes up a good deal of staff time." There too was the constant problem of dogs running loose. And then there was the constant threat of violence.

"An employee was unhurt," according to squad meeting minutes, "when a homemade explosive device that was thrown at him did not explode."[123]

For its part, the advisory commission suggested that Lombardi call a public meeting to discuss "appropriate use" of the park and possibly even stage there a farmers' market, "as it once was." Lombardi did stage a community meeting during the summer of 1981, at which he reported "lively" conversation among eighty attendees. "The main issue," it seemed, "was night security—neighbors object to kids drinking, being nuisances at the Monument in the evenings." Lombardi suggested that everyone petition Congressman Moakley for support. Councilman Flynn, who attended the meeting, wondered why the NPS did not provide security all night at the monument, as it did at Bunker Hill. Lombardi argued that the best way to combat misuse of Dorchester Heights was to promote appropriate use, suggesting that concerts and farmers' markets were excellent tools for dissuading loitering. It turned out, too, that neighbors felt let down by the Boston Police Department, which they claimed was not responsive to their calls. Lombardi insisted that the park seek possibilities to amend its legislation to establish concurrent jurisdiction with the police at Dorchester Heights.[124]

Contending with Dorchester Heights brought park staff increasingly into conversation with South Boston's white political leadership. During 1981, for instance, Lombardi and Gurney met with Flynn—and Berenson, of course—to discuss ways to improve access among Black Bostonians to South Boston. Flynn recommended forming a Thomas Park resident group to help with the problem.[125] Overall, however, Lombardi reported that "the whole tone of the site changed dramatically in that people living around the heights enjoy coming there in the evenings," whereas before transfer to the NPS, "site neighbors were afraid to be there at night."[126] And yet, one stubborn problem persisted. Despite all of his efforts to make the unit safer, Lombardi remained "unable to attract minorities to work at the site."[127] According to him, the problem owed to people having "heard so much about the scarcity of jobs that they may feel there is no use in applying."[128]

But clearly other challenges complicated the possibility of diversifying staff at Dorchester Heights. Key among them, no doubt, was the fact that white supremacy and racial violence were endemic throughout South Boston. During the same year Lombardi wondered why Black Bostonians wouldn't work at Dorchester Heights, three Black families who lived just down the street from the monument surrendered their public housing after enduring constant assault—including a fire bombing—and threat of violence from their white neighbors. Indeed, the NAACP scheduled its annual meeting that year to take place in Boston so it could raise awareness of the problem.[129] Gurney blamed the "news media [for being] very negative during the NAACP Convention," but lauded his staff for offering support at "potential trouble spots," including Paul Revere Mall, Bunker Hill, and the Charlestown Bridge.[130] But even constant vigilance couldn't prevent incidents at Dorchester Heights such as one "including a 'molotov cocktail' and another involving the uprooting of a new tree.[131]

The park's inability to hire Black staff at Dorchester Heights surely owed as well to the longstanding expectation—dating back to the NPS's loose affiliation with the South Boston Citizens' Association (SBCA) in 1938—that the agency's role in South Boston was to police Black people. Consider how, in 1984, a change in security detail at the monument triggered sudden backlash among the South Boston Residents' Group, a descendent organization of the SBCA. Its vice president, James Diperri, worried about how the "planning and the maintenance of Dorchester Heights has been dramatically changed from the condition it was in when it was opened by the federal authorities back a few years." "All that has been gained may be lost," he warned, adding that "the community is very disturbed." That the new plan had been implemented without community input also worried DiPerri. "If there are any problems at the site," he explained, "it becomes a problem for the neighborhood." What's worse, nobody in charge at the monument was easily accessible to its neighbors. DiPerri requested on behalf of the residents' group that the advisory commission help convince the park to resume previous staffing levels. Berenson and Gurney explained the changes, and Gurney provided a phone number to call in the case that DiPerri could not locate the site manager.[132] Nearly fifty years after McCormack and Small haggled over Dorchester Heights' historical significance, white people in South Boston could still rely on a direct line to the NPS.

THE BOSTON AFRICAN AMERICAN NATIONAL HISTORIC SITE

Clearly, by the mid-1980s, the park struggled to find a way to contend with issues of race and violence at Dorchester Heights. But what is perhaps most remarkable about the park's errand in South Boston is that it was just one of two simultaneous forays into complicated histories of race and power in Boston. The other, in which the NPS intentionally focused on Black history, was considerably more successful. Its success had everything to do with Byron Rushing. Rushing, like so many African Americans during the 1960s, came to Boston for an education. While studying at Harvard, he became involved in Boston's burgeoning civil rights movement, including pushing back against Ed Logue's redevelopment plans, which cultivated his interest in Black history. Around 1970, Rushing learned that a building on the north slope of Boston's Beacon Hill—originally built in 1806 as an African church and known as the African Meeting House—was up for sale and that a fledgling African American historical association sought to purchase it. Rushing helped the organization raise money to buy the building and, once it had, agreed to become its first executive director. So was born Boston's Museum of Afro-American History, where Rushing worked from 1972 until 1984.[133]

Rushing was the only person to formally insist, prior to the Bicentennial, that a national historical park in Boston must contend with histories of race and enslavement. As Rushing recalls it, his involvement began when he was invited by Senator Edward Kennedy to testify in public hearings concerning the proposed park. Rushing testified that "the definition of revolution was too narrow for the park. And that they had to understand that the period that they're talking about was really for all intents and purposes revolution for White people. Because for the period they're talking about, Black people, most Black people, were enslaved."[134] Rushing's testimony hit its mark. A few weeks later, one of Kennedy's staff called Rushing and asked if he'd want the African Meeting House included in the proposed park. Rushing demurred but indicated his interest in considering the possibility after the park was established. With that, Kennedy's office recommended that Rushing be included on the Boston National Historical Park Advisory Commission.[135]

Rushing's appointment to the advisory commission, in hindsight, was among the most important turns in the park's story. Rushing, alongside Beninati and O'Shea, advocated for a much more capacious approach to community engagement than the park's progenitors had ever imagined. And it was Rushing, of course, who insisted that the NPS confront African American history in Boston. It was at the same meeting, in fact, where Gurney first raised the issue of racial violence that Rushing introduced his work on Boston's Black Heritage Trail.[136] The possibility of creating a Black Heritage Trail, Rushing explained, had emerged from a research project concerning the history of African Americans in Boston and in New England.[137] Rushing and his team at the museum had identified sixteen individual buildings, including the

African Meeting Hosue that, together, constituted "the largest concentration of pre-Civil War Black history sites anywhere in the United States."[138] When Rushing returned to join the April 1980 meeting, he reported that authorizing legislation to create Boston African American National Historic Site was already before Congress. NPS Regional Director Stanton added that he was very optimistic that the bill would pass. He was right, Congress authorized the Boston African American National Historic Site in PL 96–430 (1980).[139]

Importantly, though PL 96–430 created an entirely new unit that was organizationally discrete from Boston National Historical Park, its rough outlines mirrored the older park's partnership model. Gurney recalls having encouraged Rushing to think of Boston National Historical Park's authorizing legislation, and its reliance on cooperative agreements with site owners, as a model for the new unit. A key difference, however, is that Boston African American National Historic Site would have to wait years before receiving its budget allocation from the NPS. Rushing was stunned to discover that authorization had not delivered funding. He contacted Congressman Moakley, whom he had known for many years, and asked for help. Rushing recalls that Moakley went to the "chairman of the budget committee and was able to get us bumped up. The park service was not happy about that."[140] Gurney recalls the same incident quite differently. One day in January 1980, the park received a call from the office of U.S Representative Dan Rostencowski of Illinois, the then-powerful Democratic chair of the House Ways and Means Committee. An aid from Rostencowski's office, it turned out, was coming to town and hoped to tour sites associated with Boston's African American history. Gurney, who couldn't reach Rushing in time, met with the aid and led him on a tour of the Chain Forge, Ropewalk, and the African Meeting House. What's more, Gurney shared a million-dollar list of preservation needs Rushing had compiled for the meeting house. Gurney thought nothing of it until that November, when he discovered that, tucked into Congress's 1981 Interior appropriation bill, was one million dollars earmarked for restoration of the African Meeting House. The bill even included a familiar list of needed work. The NPS Washington Service Office was furious with Gurney, given that the Department of Interior had not itself included this money in its annual budget. Gurney, however, was grateful for it.[141]

Preliminary management of the new unit fell to Gurney.[142] And, as he had done at Dorchester Heights, Gurney appointed a site manager. In this case, however, he appointed a Black woman named Dorthea Powell, whom he hired from the regional office.[143] Powell set to work with Rushing and others on assembling a brochure, while Gurney helped carve out office space in the Smith School, hired several interpreters, and initiated work on a historic structure report. Unlike Dorchester Heights, which the park conceived of primarily as a custodial project, plans for Boston African American National Historic Site grew almost entirely out of a singular focus on historical research. And its key leaders—Powell and Rushing—were both African American and both shared a commitment to exploring African American history. The unit had emerged, after all, from Rushing's research project concerning Boston's Black history. That precedent continued into the fall of 1981, when the site hosted a historiography planning conference wherein staff from the NPS office in Washington, from the regional office, and from the park gathered along with Byron Rushing to create the framework for a "bank of research on Beacon Hill's Black community."[144] The NPS had thus launched two new initiatives during the late 1970s to assert itself in matters of race and memory in Boston: one born of a critical interest in the past, the other concerned primarily with law enforcement. The imprint of those founding moments remains evident today.

* * *

We began this chapter with a question: how well was the Boston National Historical Park prepared to contend with history in a place where history had rendered people like Charles Battles and Ted Landsmark vulnerable to America's worst instincts? The answer, this chapter suggests quite clearly, is that the park was not at all prepared. In every regard, it lacked the expertise, the resources, and the focus necessary to understand, let alone contend with, the complexity of Boston's historical milieu. Of course, the park's authorizing legislation did not overtly commit its staff to thinking about issues such as race and power during the last century. And yet its partnership mandate necessitated cooperation with organizations—including schools, cultural nonprofits, and even briefly the Guardian Angels—for which race and power were the prevailing concerns of the day. Without clear guidance, then, the choice of whether or not to engage these issues, and at what length, fell time after time to the park's superintendent. We see in this chapter how significantly his choices depended on matters of funding, human resources, agency prerogatives, and the perpetual problem of making the navy yard accessible and meaningful. We see too that, had it not been for the park's advisory commission, the superintendent's choices could have been very different. How would the story change, we might wonder, were there a different superintendent, with different values, and unfettered by an advisory commission? Chapter six will answer precisely that question.

In the meantime, however, it is worth noting that none of these problems were unique to Boston National Historical Park during the late twentieth century. By those years, for instance, it was rare for any national park to have a staff historian, let alone one as thoughtful and exacting as Paul Weinbaum. It is nonetheless important to document the park's challenges, common though they may have been, toward illustrating how administrative problems—no matter how seemingly inconsequential—so frequently equate to front line problems. In Boston, as we have seen, an early and persistent problem with publicity translated readily into an interpretive problem. A poorly managed planning process in Charlestown translated into a difficult community engagement problem. And, in so many respects, the park's history problem was always a race problem. It is evident from the park's archival records that, during its first decade, the superintendent and division officers perceived all of these challenges as management problems that, to a greater or lesser degree, could be dealt with by adjusting the number and format of monthly meetings or by taking any number of leadership courses offered by the NPS. Going forward, we will see that looking inward for solutions could not, by definition, solve critical challenges facing the agency's first partnership park.

CHAPTER 6

Managing Memory in the New Economy

It appeared atop the editorial section of *the Boston Globe* on Monday morning, August 13, 1984: "USS *Constitution* Disgraced." In just a handful of paragraphs, the newspaper's editorial staff excoriated the National Park Service (NPS). "The National Historical Park," it inveighed, "is a national embarrassment, while its surroundings are a disgrace." At issue was the impossibility of accessing the USS *Constitution* without "a 20-minute endurance hike . . . along heavily congested streets." And for what? Even if you could reach the ship, it would mean "standing and baking in line along the edge of its pier for perhaps a half-hour [because] there are no benches." the *Constitution*, the *Cassin Young*, the USS *Constitution* Museum, and the Boston Marine Society Museum were all worth visiting, for sure, as was the adjacent city park. "Getting around," however, meant "a hot and dirty trudge across acres of asphalt . . . not unlike a trip to the parking lot of a suburban shopping mall." Worse yet, the NPS meant it to stay that way, "the official explanation [is] that they want the navy yard to look as it did . . . in 1973." The *Globe* was incredulous. What the park needed was a water-taxi, a shuttle bus, benches, some shade, and perhaps, some imagination. Otherwise, the *Globe* concluded, "the park is an insult, to the great ship that is berthed there and to the great maritime traditions of the city."[1]

The next morning, Superintendent Hugh Gurney opened his monthly squad meeting by asking if any of the division heads would like to begin with a "start-off question." Donna Robertson did. "What will be the repercussions," she wondered, "of the article written in the *Boston Globe* about the disgrace of Boston National Historical Park?"[2] According to her, "they really 'socked it' to us; made us look entirely at fault." Dorthea Powell noted that, ironically, new benches were already on their way to the park. Victor Jorrin "feels there is no justice." According to Frank Montford, the *Globe* had sent someone to talk with "the people at the Museum," presumably meaning the USS *Constitution* Museum, as well as the Boston Redevelopment Authority (BRA) and Chief of Interpretation Lou Venuto, but clearly neither he nor the rest of the division chiefs felt that the park had been treated well. Only Gurney suggested that "we are not entirely without blame." The park was, after all, "accountable for not having ordered the benches long ago."[3]

Just about a month later, Hugh Gurney announced his retirement.[4] Whether or not the *Globe's* criticism had any bearing on Gurney's decision to leave, it did signal several problems that had remained devilishly persistent throughout his tenure.[5] There was, for instance, the difficulty of getting around a park that spanned over forty acres of busy downtown Boston. Then too was the problem of the massive navy yard and its tendency to confound visitors and exhaust staff. Evident also in the *Globe's* critique was confusion regarding what the national park actually was and who was responsible for what. What was the navy's role in all of this? Who was really in charge of the visitor experience aboard the *Constitution?* And why should the *Constitution,* just one among several partner sites, be the locus around which to evaluate the NPS's work in Boston? The park's staff was right to be outraged. And yet, Gurney's response revealed his understanding that, fair or not, the *Globe's* critique signaled a critical problem of perception: if its public perceived the park to be a disgrace, then how could it be anything else?

My purpose in this chapter is to understand how and why public perception of the park changed so dramatically in the years following Gurney's departure. Indeed, by the late 1990s, the park had tapped into millions of dollars of congressional funding, staged blockbuster preservation projects, and appeared as cosponsor of all manner of civic programming. All of this raised the park's public stock and points to Gurney's successor, Superintendent John Burchill, as being responsible for the park's renaissance during these years. But here too are problems of perception. As we will see, Burchill's arrival coincided exactly with important changes in Boston's political and economic landscapes, changes that fundamentally reoriented the city's economy around a burgeoning white upper class. Entertaining this new demographic, and reinforcing its ideas about nation and progress, became a cornerstone of Boston's new economy during the 1990s. Burchill met the demand by investing more than ever in the Freedom Trail. If this was success, however, it was only partial. As historian Alfred Young observed in another *Globe* feature, the Freedom Trail had become by 2004 "a victim of its greatest successes."[6] Renewed enthusiasm for the old familiar icons of Longfellow's historical imagination, he argued, had once again obscured actual history. In other words, though the park had certainly expanded its capacity to serve heritage tourists, it was still unclear—even

two decades past authorization—whether the park was able or willing to do
history for all Americans.

RISE OF THE NEW OLD BOSTON

The fate of Boston National Historical Park has always hung in the balance
of city politics. Some observers might conclude that because the city has rarely
contributed direct funding to matters of historic preservation and interpretation—a tendency, in fact, that has defined Boston's heritage landscape since
the nineteenth century—that there is somehow a disconnect between the
park and city hall, cooperative agreements notwithstanding. As we have seen,
however, city politics have exerted considerable influence on the park's fate
ever since it was first imagined by John McCormack and Edwin Small during
the 1930s. And because Boston city politics have vacillated so wildly since the
collapse of Mayor James Michael Curley's political machine in 1950, so has
the story of the park. Whether the politics of urban renewal, the politics of
school desegregation, the politics of deindustrialization, or Boston's ubiquitous politics of class, ethnicity, and religion, city hall's political orientation
has largely set the tone for the park's planners and its managers. We know
from dozens of park histories that local politics bear influence on all NPS
units. Urban parks, however, may be distinctive in this regard, and Boston a
special case therein.

The transition from Gurney to Burchill in 1984 suggests that what has
made the park special is the suddenness of shifts in managerial strategies
necessitated by Boston's mercurial political milieu. Gurney, for instance, had
assumed leadership amid Mayor Kevin White's campaign for reelection in
1975. Although White had come into office as a champion of civil rights and
an advocate for community engagement—themes that clearly shaped expectations for the park and its advisory commission—his mayoral victory in 1975
marked a turning point wherein White shuttered the "little town halls" he
had established throughout Boston's neighborhoods and instead turned his
attention almost exclusively to downtown economic redevelopment. White's
turn inward, and his return to the sort of machine politics that characterized
his predecessors, triggered other changes that shifted the ground beneath
Gurney's feet. A citywide tax referendum, for instance, drastically reduced
city tax revenue just as the United States plummeted into the 1979 energy
crisis, and then a prolonged global economic recession that triggered austerity
measures throughout Gurney's remaining time in Boston.[7] Gurney had worked

diligently, if not always successfully, to embrace community engagement—
including around matters of racial violence—and to leverage the Bicentennial
era's financial and patriotic largesse. Neither of those resources were in ready
supply in Boston by 1984.

What's more, it was unclear what Boston's decades-long investments in
urban renewal had achieved for the city by the early 1980s. Real estate developer James Rouse's Faneuil Hall festival marketplace concept was clearly a
success for well-healed heritage tourists, and cities across the United States
had already begun to mimic its example. But statistically, Boston had not yet
rounded whatever corner planner Ed Logue and the Chamber of Commerce
had aimed for. The city's population, for instance, was still declining. And
tangles of traffic still mired motorists and pedestrians all across town, so
much so that plans for a new development project, this time aimed toward
routing traffic beneath Boston, began circulating in 1982. Incredibly, the city
that had invested so much effort in reinventing itself after World War II, and
which had displaced so many people to make it possible, appeared by 1982 in
a prominent study of threatened American cities. The report's authors ranked
Boston in graver danger even than Detroit, Michigan, which by then had
become a disastrous symbol of America's postindustrial collapse. It comes as
no surprise, then, that also in 1982, attendance at the park dropped six percent despite a concurrent nine percent increase across all NPS urban parks.
The park had always been subject to the whims of Boston's political and
economic directions, a fact that surely weighed on Superintendent Gurney as
he approached a decade of service in Boston.[8]

And yet, remarkably, as soon as Gurney left, the park's fortunes appear to
have changed again. Certainly, his replacement, Superintendent John Burchill,
had something to do with the shift. But it's worth noting that, once again,
statistics tell a compelling story that, in this case, began even before Burchill
arrived. For instance, whereas city growth was down 1.29 percent in 1980, it
rebounded over the decade, climbing to 0.2 percent in 1990.[9] What caused
the change? Urban economists Barry Bluestone and Mary Huff Stevenson
identify a "triple revolution," wherein during a short period of time, Boston
welcomed a sudden influx of immigrants, its economy pivoted sharply to a
"mind-based" economy, and growth in surrounding regions leveraged Boston's
access to a powerful northeastern metropolis. These changes benefited the
park significantly, insomuch as they increased its access to private and public
investment, while also attracting throngs of affluent visitors and residents to

downtown. But not everyone benefited equally from Boston's transformation. On the contrary, the particularities of its triple revolution sent downtown real estate costs skyrocketing, triggering new depths of ethnic poverty and reactivating the kind of residential segregation that activists struggled against all throughout the twentieth century.[10] In other words, Boston's urban crisis did not disappear so much as it transformed.

And it transformed in a way that, by all appearances, seemed to have achieved the goals of urban renewal. The sudden influx of wealthy young white residents, for instance, triggered a wave of gentrification.[11] New stores, cafes, restaurants, and housing, often featuring adaptive reuse of old buildings, suggested new life for the old city. Though less visibly, even Boston's Black residents participated in the economic upturn, so much so that it seemed old battle lines between Black and white residents might be fading. Boston's new mayor, former City Councilor Raymond Flynn, certainly confirmed that impression when he won office in 1984. Reacting against White's turn away from Boston's neighborhoods, Flynn positioned himself as a populist mayor concerned about working people and willing to talk critically about race. Doing so, of course, was much easier amid Boston's newfound economic prosperity. And, too, the new immigrants partly responsible for Boston's turnaround, especially low-wage workers from Asia and Latin America, lacked the political capital to make visible how unevenly distributed the new prosperity really was. In fact, the shift to a federal block grant system beginning in the late 1970s removed much of the community engagement that had been a feature of late-phase urban renewal, making it harder for otherwise disenfranchised populations to have any say in city politics. Taken together, as historian Jim Vrabel puts it, these changes created a passive political climate in Boston that was largely opposed to earlier renewal strategies—such as demolition and displacement—though primarily oriented around the needs of prosperous young white newcomers. It was a prime opportunity for the NPS, whose rustic charms appealed powerfully to this demographic, to generate popular support among people for whom history and consumerism seemed natural partners.[12]

THE NPS IN AN AGE OF AUSTERITY

This is not to say that all was well for the national parks in 1984. On the contrary, the agency was still finding its way amid a significant political shift in Washington, DC. The election of President Ronald Reagan in 1981 finally extinguished what remained of the New Deal Era progressivism that had buoyed the NPS for much of the twentieth century, which even during the Carter administration manifested in Gurney's wholehearted embrace of worker training programs. Most significantly for the NPS, Reagan's choice of James G. Watt to direct the Department of Interior reversed a generation of funded growth throughout the system. Watt insisted that parks ought to pay for themselves and that, until they could, the agency's priority ought to be nourishing recreation in the so-called crown jewels—large iconic nature parks like Yosemite and Grand Canyon—while encouraging private partnership and a customer-service model everywhere else. Watt's mandate, of course, conflicted with the Organic Act of 1916, which committed the system to ensure that all of its resources remain safe and accessible to everyone. Employee morale suffered all throughout the system during these years, especially as threats to the power of the agency's director resulted in politicization of its leadership and an expectation that the agency should do considerably more with substantially less funding.[13]

At first it seemed that Watt's appointment might not be entirely disadvantageous for the park. At a May 1981 meeting of the advisory commission, members discussed the new Secretary of Interior and how his policies might impact their work. Steven Lewis, from the NPS regional office, summarized the state of affairs and explained that the park's partnership configuration made it "very sympathetic to the policy direction of this administration."[14] At the same time, the impact of Watt's austerity regime became almost immediately evident. Funding for operations in 1981, for instance, could barely cover pay raises. Staff considered ways to minimize costs such as by reducing evening hours at the visitor center and at Bunker Hill, and by closing the navy yard at night.[15] Even beyond Watt's resignation in 1983, federal cost-cutting strategies during the Reagan years created considerable system-wide stress. Burchill worried, for instance, that the introduction of federal budget limitations by way of the Gramm–Rudman–Hollings Balanced Budget Act would "be a real challenge to the Park."[16] He was right. During fiscal year 1986, the new law cost the park $360,000 in funding.[17] But funding shortfalls weren't the only problem. Austerity measures triggered a wave of complications throughout the agency. Staff meeting minutes from these years show evidence of considerable turmoil within the regional office. In April 1987, for instance, it announced that "due to numerous employee transfers and resignations, this office is experiencing an extreme back-up in processing" routine paperwork. The NPS detailed staff from Gateway National Recreation Area and Statue of Liberty National Monument just to help clear the backlog.[18]

In hindsight, the Watt years triggered what might be termed a "managerial turn" in NPS history. This is to say that, after 1980, approaches to solving the agency's most dogged challenges—underfunding, understaffing, and overuse—increasingly foregrounded cost-sharing, fiscal efficiencies, work-flow routinization, and beginning in 1987, computerization and data centralization. As we will see, all of these strategies had impacts in Boston. In some ways, the managerial turn shifted power away from parks and into regional offices. The consolidation of all agency financial services beginning in 1987, for instance, had precisely this effect.[19] In other ways, the managerial turn's concern with self-study generated considerable insight into the problems that the NPS would have to contend with if it were to survive into the new century. A series of reports, including the 1992 *Vail Agenda*, laid bare just how dire the agency's situation was at the end of the twentieth century.[20] It was the 1992 report, in fact, that prompted a significant agencywide reorganization in 1994, the first time NPS organizational structures had been comprehensively reworked since the New Deal Era.[21] As the park understood it, the reorganization implemented changes that had emerged amid the managerial turn. An article in the park's newsletter, the *Broadside*, explained that the change sought primarily to reduce full-time equivalencies (FTEs), to reduce management levels and personnel overhead, and to fix up a failing system infrastructure.[22] This, at least, is how the park experienced the 1994 reorganization. In many ways the park, by merit of its partnership model, had become willy-nilly a seedbed for just this kind of managerial experimentation. For that reason, and owing to expanded concern for urban parks during the 1990s, Boston National Historical Park would—by the turn of the century—become an incubator for NPS professionals throughout the system.[23]

MANAGING THE MANAGERIAL TURN

Back in 1982, however, if we are to take the *Globe*'s word for it, the agency's work in Boston was anything but a model. How then do we explain the park's reversal of fortunes by the end of the following decade? Before answering that question, it is important to take stock of just how much the park had actually accomplished, newspaper editorials notwithstanding. We learned in chapter five how dynamic the park had grown during those years, but it's worth restating that—despite its difficult legislative genesis and the Bicentennial's long shadow—the park had fully come into its own by 1982. That year, the park welcomed 1.7 million visitors: about 870,000 in the so-called south district, which referred to the downtown sites; 800,000 in the navy yard; 101,000 at Bunker Hill; and 19,000 at Dorchester Heights.[24] And it did this while developing new management plans, creating innovative interpretation, and managing sites that had been added to the park's dossier since authorization. That it achieved all of this amid the degradations of Watt's leadership is remarkable and speaks powerfully to the importance of Gurney's early vision.

Even more remarkable, perhaps, is how effectively the park developed navy yard programming, despite how awkwardly the site fit into the park's broader concern with Revolutionary pasts. A case in point is the popularity of the USS *Cassin Young*.[25] In June 1978, the NPS acquired the *Cassin Young* for repair and indefinite exhibit at the navy yard. The ship, built in 1943 and deployed during World War II and the Korean War, had been repaired at Charlestown during the 1950s. Since then, the navy had put it into reserve at the Philadelphia navy yard in the so-called mothball fleet. This time around, the ship was put in at Dry Dock 1 in October 1979 for sandblasting and repainting. Dry Dock 1 itself had only just been designated a National Historical Engineering Landmark by the American Society of Civil Engineers. Park Ranger Linda Canzanelli observed that, together with the navy yard and the *Constitution*, the *Cassin Young* would "tell the story of naval shipbuilding and the development of the United States Navy."[26]

The ship's path to Boston was not entirely certain. Indeed, the question of whether or not to bring the *Cassin Young* to the navy yard hit right at the heart of the complex debates that had developed in connection with the general management plan (GMP) process. Gurney, along with Peter Steele and Ross Holland, supported acquisition of the *Cassin Young*. Denis Galvin, however, who by then served as regional assistant director of operations, vehemently opposed it.[27] Gurney recalls that Holland, a regional assistant director for planning, was the strongest advocate for the navy yard's historical value and was adamant that it be preserved as an industrial site.[28] Maintaining the ship in real time for visitors in Dry Dock 1 certainly showcased the site's industrial character.[29] The *Cassin Young* ended up being a popular addition, although it was difficult to manage. Vandalism became a problem almost immediately. Despite the presence of interpreters, the number of visitors and the size of the ship meant that plexiglass shields, ropes, and other barriers were required to curtail inappropriate behavior. Again, however, numbers tell the story. In 1982, 180,000 of the navy yard's 800,000 visitors toured the *Cassin Young*.[30] It and the visiting ships program, inspired in part by the Queen of England's visit aboard the *Britannia* in 1976, remain among the most popular facets of navy yard programming.[31] It was aboard the *Cassin Young*, as well, that the park developed a powerful Volunteers in Parks (VIP) program that maintained the ship to navy standards and, over time, expanded to support the downtown visitor center.[32]

Other aspects of the park's success during the 1990s also originated during Gurney's superintendence. The possibility of revitalizing the area surrounding Hoosac Pier, for instance, first came before the advisory commission during its April 1982 meeting, when news arrived that Massport, the Massachusetts port authority, was considering the area for its purposes.[33] Massport Planner Anne Meyers assured the commission that Massport would provide parking for the resulting commercial development so as not to "throw a lot of cars into a community that already has a problem."[34] A year later, Park Planner Deborah Szarka reported that preliminary plans for the area had been completed and that work would begin during summer 1983. The plans called for two new red-brick buildings including surface parking, a restaurant, and office space. What's more, Park Historian Paul Weinbaum's nomination project for the National Register of Historic Places still had the potential at that point to provide "curatorial functions for the park." Szarka noted that "many groups" had expressed a desire for large public spaces on the pier, which the NPS considered "commendable."[35]

It was also during spring 1982 that the park and the advisory commission first took up the problem of the Commandant's House at the navy yard and whether to treat it as a house museum or as a working building. The house had functioned as both for the previous six years, and concerns arose about the evident wear it had suffered as a result. Curator Peter Steele argued that the building should be treated as a historic house museum, wherein all social functions would be prohibited. Gurney noted that, despite inevitable pressure from local organizations, the time might be perfect for Steele's proposed change. Just that year, newspapers reported outrage over accusations that Interior Secretary Watt had misspent public funds on expensive social functions at the historic Arlington House atop Arlington Cemetery in Washington, DC. "After debacles such as at Arlington House, with Secretary Watt, the public may better understand why the Park Service would take such a stand."[36] At the same time, the Charlestown Historical Society had previously hosted events in the house and wished to again. Following considerable debate, Advisory Commission Chair Richard Berenson constituted a subcommittee to examine the problem.[37] At the following meeting, it was announced that a comprehensive plan for use of the Commandant's House would be scheduled.[38]

But even though the park had achieved considerably more in the navy yard than the *Globe* had credited it for in 1982, there were still signs of problems already emerging within the park's managerial structure. Even before Watt's appointment, Gurney dwelled at length on how best to manage his staff. On April 21, 1980, the day the park's reorganization went into effect, Gurney announced that he would hold "squad meetings" each week with the four staff members directly under his supervision: the chief of visitor services, the administrative officer, the chief of planning and historic preservation, and the Dorchester Heights site manager. Gurney then distributed meeting minutes among the division chiefs and instructed them to share with other employees "for the efficient dissemination of information to all employees."[39] That Gurney preferred staff meetings be called "squad meetings" speaks to a military ethos that runs all through early minutes.[40]

After a few years, it seems that park staff sought more and different kinds of ways to engage one another. In late 1981, for instance, nonsupervisory staff requested an opportunity to meet at least once without supervisors present. Their request came in conjunction with planning for a park-wide general staff meeting slated for January 1982. Meetings wherein all employees had an opportunity to encounter one another all at once were rare at the park. Vince Lombardi, site manager at Dorchester Heights, suggested that the 1982 meeting might be used to orient staff to the park's various preservation functions, given that "many employees do not understand how the preservation center really operates."[41] That they did not reveals a considerable day-to-day distance between divisions, and also illustrates the priority placed by management on preservation among other functions such as history and interpretation.

There are other signs, too, that, by 1982, staff meetings might not have been functioning as well as possible. During these years, the park engaged a management consultant to recommend ways to boost efficiency and morale. Recommendations included creating "a pervasive climate of acknowledgment [that] can make monetary rewards and official awards seem less important than is usually supposed. There are entire voluntary systems where acknowledgement and the experience of personal growth are the only rewards—and people work long and hard to get them." Staff might also, he suggested, pay out of their own pockets to participate in Werner Erhard's controversial Erhard Seminars Training, to help them more fully appreciate their own potential.[42]

What's more, a curious entry in one set of squad meeting minutes indicates that, in light of the consultant's recommendations, there should be "no more zingers." "If someone should slip and zing someone else," the minutes continue, "the zinger must pay the zingee two compliments."[43] At the same meeting, the superintendent's secretary explained that "she felt somewhat at a disadvantage being asked to join the discussion of the new squad format, which is an outgrowth of the participatory training session, since she did not attend the session and had no idea what the others were talking about."[44] Perhaps unsurprisingly, she announced at the same meeting that she intended to leave the park at the end of the month.

Minutes from subsequent meetings reveal an almost obsessive preoccupation with making meetings more efficient, including by designating a timekeeper to limit how long staff might discuss any one issue. The source of the time pressure, according to the minutes: new financial and compliance regimes, wherein the necessity of updating performance standards and conducting appraisals seemed to eclipse all other responsibilities. The proliferation of assessment responsibilities and the constant threat of budget shortfalls created real anxieties. During a November 17, 1983, meeting, for instance, the deputy superintendent reported that "morale is a problem especially in light of A-76," which referred to a revision of federal guidelines for achieving cost efficiencies through competitive contracting. "Some bad rumors are going around," he noted, adding that the "problem is that the accurate information is no better than the rumors."[45] Gurney sought to improve the situation by adjusting meeting formats, but his efforts proved largely ineffective and, over time, revealed an even more significant underlying problem. During a March 1, 1983, meeting, discussion turned to the problem of cooperation and a need "to work more closely together as one park, not as individual divisions."[46] It was the segregation of park staff into discrete units—the Dorchester Heights crew, the navy yard staff, Bunker Hill rangers, and the downtown cohort—that seemed to be creating the problem. In other words, those features that made the urban partnership park so unique had, in this case, nurtured discord among its staff.

No matter how Gurney addressed it, the problem continued to intensify. At a January 1984 meeting, the superintendent and division leaders brainstormed what might be causing it. Suggestions included that bad morale "may be a reaction against maintenance," though in what way exactly is not clear. "Unequal treatment on training [and] leave charges," emerged as a possibility too. Numerous suggestions concerned problems associated with inconsistent response from superiors to staff who arrived late to work or stayed longer than necessary. A culture of surveillance and "note taking" had emerged. But also, and perhaps more importantly for this study, it seems that "people do not feel they work for [the park, but] just their unit, such as Bunker Hill."[47] By spring 1984, the superintendent's weekly meeting was collapsing. Gurney asked his division heads why the meetings were no longer productive and wondered that perhaps the management consultant had not been effective after all.[48]

This episode, and Gurney's responses to it, reveal the extent to which rising professionalization within cultural work throughout the United States during the 1980s subjected workers to new regimes of surveillance, uncertainty, and—in this case—painfully awkward moments of professional encounter.[49] And, in hindsight, it was a moment that revealed just how deep the divides had grown in Boston. In a last-ditch effort, Gurney asked that division chiefs come to squad meetings with a question that might encourage convivial discussion among the group. It was precisely this impulse that encouraged Donna Robertson to ask about the *Globe* article in 1982. And though it is uncertain whether Gurney perceived it, the questions and answers revealed a deep sense of divide among his staff over some of the most important issues concerning the park. At the conclusion of a May 1984 meeting, for instance, Chief of Planning and Historic Preservation Frank Montford asked, "What do you feel is the most abused historical object in the Park?" Most everyone present answered in turn: Bob Pribula worried about Bunker Hill, Jerry Swofford named the Old State House, Montford picked the navy yard, and Gurney chose Faneuil Hall. Neither Deputy Superintendent Wendell Simpson, Simpson's secretary Donna Robertson, nor Dorthea Powell registered a response.[50] A couple months later, Simpson asked, "What is the main resource in the Park that should be the primary interest as far as historic preservation?" Once again, a round of answers: Pribula identified the "Red Line," Swofford picked the USS *Constitution*, Paul Weinbaum named Faneuil Hall as did Powell, and Gurney and Simpson named the Old State House.[51] Remarkably, by 1984, the park's staff did not appear to share a common vision, a common sense of purpose, or even a fundamental knowledge of what one another did. Just a few months later, Gurney retired, leaving the park and the NPS for good.

A NEW SUPERINTENDENT FOR A NEW ERA

The NPS appointed Gurney's replacement, Superintendent John Burchill, on October 1, 1984. Unlike Gurney, who had grown up on Boston's periphery,

Burchill was born in Boston and had grown up in West Roxbury. Also, unlike Gurney, Burchill had no history training. In 1961, he earned a BA in business administration from the University of Massachusetts at Amherst and then graduated from Suffolk University Law School with a JD in 1967. He began his career as an attorney for the Army Corps of Engineers, and then transitioned into a series of positions in the NPS, including at Cape Cod National Seashore, Big Cypress National Preserve, Yosemite National Park, Yellowstone National Park, and Lowell National Historical Park.[52] Whereas Gurney's experience had prepared him to lead a Revolutionary War history park, Burchill's experience had clearly prepared him to run an urban partnership park. It's precisely what he had done as superintendent of Lowell National Historical Park where, beginning in 1981, Burchill worked with U.S. Senator Paul Tsongas to secure $12.5 million for the restoration of the Boott Cotton Mill.

Just as Edwin Small's work in Salem anticipated his urban renewal vision for a national park in Boston, so did Burchill's experience of urban renewal in Lowell lay the groundwork for his management strategy in Boston. Lowell National Historical Park had emerged, shortly after its authorization in 1978, as a jewel in the agency's small crown of urban parks. It was the vanguard, as anthropologist Cathy Stanton explains it, of Lowell's culture-led redevelopment program and modeled there a decentralized park that, not unlike Boston, anticipated the heritage areas that are common today.[53] As the park's public relations officer explained it, Burchill "formed coalitions and partnerships with business and civic leaders and with the Lowell Plan . . . which spurred further development and attracted new business to the City of Lowell."[54] The Lowell Plan, an organization formed at Tsongas's urging in 1979, functioned as "a kind of business-sponsored think tank for [Lowell's] redevelopment project."[55] Working closely with private interests had, of course, become a priority during Secretary Watt's administration, and Burchill appears to have embraced it wholeheartedly during his time in Lowell. This was not, however, the sort of public–private partnership that Ed Logue championed, wherein community organizations could count on a seat at the planning table. In Lowell, rather, the notion was that public partners, such as the NPS, would guarantee a public voice simply by merit of their presence. But would the NPS really guarantee a public voice during the Reagan era? Stanton shows us that it aimed to in Lowell, owing in part to the presence there of a handful of progressive staff, but primarily to the insistence of local community advocates that it should. Boston's staff shared neither Lowell's progressive bent nor its corps of historians, however, and so it remained to be seen just how vigorously Burchill's management style would accommodate, say, the voices of Boston's new immigrants.[56]

Unsurprisingly, Burchill's appointment introduced a shift in leadership style in Boston that reflected changes in the city, changes in the agency, and new priorities in the superintendent's office. The shift is immediately evident in the superintendent's annual reports, which beginning in 1984, demonstrate considerably more concern with performance assessment, accountability, and human resources than had been the case in previous years. Staff meeting minutes during the same period are more detailed and reveal an expanded slate of meetings. That year, for instance, the park staged evaluations of personnel management and property management procedures. It implemented new guidelines for merit promotion and reported for the first time on the management of Official Personnel Folders (OPFs) and Employee Performance Folders (EPFs).[57] Burchill's agenda followed closely the agency's prevailing concern with financial efficiencies. He reversed, for instance, Gurney's decision to locate the superintendent's office at 15 State Street, where the navy yard's distractions wouldn't be all consuming. Burchill instead consolidated his leadership team in the Marine Barracks, toward "sav[ing] the government significant time and money."[58] And it was during these years, too, that he set out to contend with the morale problem that harried Gurney. Almost as soon as he arrived, for instance, the new superintendent began planning the first of what would become a new tradition: annual Christmas parties. It was just one of many ways Burchill sought to encourage *esprit de corps* where, it seemed, there had been none.

Key to his strategy was restructuring the park's leadership team. Throughout 1984 and into 1985, the superintendent worked with the NPS regional office to develop a new plan for staffing the park.[59] It included keeping on Deputy Superintendent Wendell Simpson, who enforced Burchill's vision on the ground. It also included an assistant superintendent, John Debo, who "became part of the management team," with particular responsibilities for planning and historic preservation.[60] Debo, incidentally, had served as Burchill's assistant superintendent for planning and development at Lowell National Historical Park.[61] He introduced an urban affairs specialist, Carter Lowe, and in time a public relations officer.[62] Burchill also had plans for interpretation, including a new supervisory park ranger, but these plans were not included in the first round of changes. It's worth noting, too, that Burchill's reorganization took place against the backdrop of a march toward computerization, which began in earnest during the late 1980s amid system-wide changes in accounting functions.[63] In other words, Burchill was an early and vigorous champion of the managerial turn in NPS history, which during those years transformed the agency.

This is not to say that Burchill's approach to park management was impersonal. On the contrary, if staff meeting minutes are any indication, the new superintendent reveled in throwing retirement parties, giving awards, hosting the annual Christmas party, and otherwise being at the center of an organizational community he sought to encourage from early on. Indeed, Burchill relied on his officers to extend the superintendent's gaze into all aspects of park operations. "No communication leaves the park," ordered Deputy Superintendent Wendell Simpson, "without the Superintendent's signature or his seeing it. John wants to know everything that is happening in the park."[64] Burchill sought also to make routine inspections of cooperative sites by himself or by one of his two assistants, although the practice seems to have ebbed and flowed over the years.[65] The change in managerial style was immediately perceptible to park staff. Within a month of Burchill's arrival, Deputy Superintendent Simpson observed "a noticeable change in pace," adding that "it is to our best interest to observe and adjust to the new style of management that we are experiencing, in a spirit of cooperation, as quickly as possible."[66]

Managing park staff with a combination of morale-building techniques, strict oversight, and delegated authority allowed Burchill to focus his own attentions on park stakeholders, and especially would-be funders. Unlike Gurney, whose schedule was almost entirely consumed by the navy yard and personnel issues, Burchill's schedule reveals a primarily outward-facing superintendent. Luncheon meetings, press events, meetings of historical associations, book readings, and civic events consumed his time, as did meetings at the regional office. On a very rare occasion, Burchill met with someone to discuss the park in terms of its broader historical purpose.[67] He spent the lion's share of his time building and maintaining public relations. In some cases, he mixed the personal and professional. Burchill was a member of the Irish Charitable Society, for instance, and served on the board of A Christian Ministry in the National Parks. This may explain his encouragement of staff to participate in multidenominational Sunday services aboard the USS *Constitution*."[68] In other instances, too, Burchill's outward-looking superintendence blurred the delicate line between public and private. Most significantly for our story, Burchill joined and eventually led the board of the Greater Boston Convention and Visitors Bureau.[69] For Burchill, it was a capacity-building strategy hearkening back to his days in Lowell.

FROM PARTNERSHIP PARK TO MANAGERIAL PARK

On the face of it, Burchill's mingling of public and private appeared very much like a fulfillment of the park's partnership mandate. If we look more closely, however, records reveal how Burchill's public-facing leadership served just as often, if not more frequently, to consolidate the park's position within Boston and within the agency. This is to say that, though the park had been authorized for the purpose of serving its partner sites, by the late 1980s the park's *raison d'être* seemed rather more frequently oriented around selective, large-capital blockbuster preservation projects. The shift likely owed in part to the disbanding of the park's advisory commission, which by 1986 had completed the decade of service required by the park's authorizing legislation. And it most certainly owed to a proliferation of compliance mandates, performance assessments, and other facets of an increasingly bureaucratized agency. Managing the park, in other words, increasingly became the purpose of managing the park. Regardless of its causes, the park's shift from a pre-occupation with managing partnerships to a concern with managing itself is powerfully evident in meeting minutes. During Gurney's time, grappling with questions about the navy yard's historical value or Dorchester Height's significance frequently filtered into management discussions, owing to planning demands and the constant tug-of-war between the NPS and the BRA. By the mid-1980s, however, staff meetings revolved almost entirely around event planning, employee awards, navy yard maintenance, interactions with city services and government, personnel and finance concerns, and compliance with constantly shifting regional and agencywide mandates.

The turn inward had considerable impact on the park's evolving relationship with its partner sites. Gurney had a direct relationship with each site, owing to his personal negotiation of first-generation cooperative agreements. Since the agreements were already in place when Burchill arrived, however, he related to the sites quite differently. Consider, for instance, the park's relationship with the Paul Revere Memorial Association. As Executive Director Nina Zannieri explains it, by the mid-1980s, it was clear that the association was not receiving as much financial support from the NPS as had others among the partner sites. Among the reasons, she discovered, was that the association had looked

and asserting its presence had become a priority for Burchill soon after his arrival. In 1985, for instance, he hired a public relations director whose sole job it was to raise awareness of the NPS's presence in Boston.[73] Later on, when Burchill's officers met collectively with site managers—"cooperator meetings," convened infrequently beginning in 1989—they spent as much if not mor time reporting on park projects as listening to partner needs.[74] Important and all the while, the park's partner sites had matured significantly since Bicentennial years. Indeed, many of them had hired their first paid execu directors during the Bicentennial, which triggered a wave of professionaliza thereafter. Zannieri, for instance, had arrived in 1986, an experienced her professional and in charge of public relations. In other words, wheth not Burchill perceived it, the park's partner sites were becoming increa better equipped to manage their own affairs and, in some cases, had be cultivate better-trained and more forward-looking staff than had the It was a crucial development, though one the park's leadership did n to fully appreciate in the moment.

Another important indicator of the park's managerial turn dur years was Burchill's preference for consolidation. It too appeared, o face, to serve public needs. Consolidating functions within the par some cases, enhance services beyond the park. For example, by 198 had managed to shift security services within the navy yard, whi partly managed by contractors in the past, entirely to the park's pro Doing so saved upwards of thirty thousand dollars a year.[76] It als a sense of comradery, which Burchill leveraged toward expandi footprint. Within the year, for instance, Burchill encouraged Division to build on its successes by becoming involved in co reach, especially because "we have the resources available to st in the area."[77] The suggestion took hold. By 1988, the Prot was in conversation with residents near Bunker Hill abou neighborhood watch program, and it was considering the sar Heights and Smith Court.[78] Their progress around Bunker significant, insomuch as it reveals how reliant Burchill's succ throughout Boston. Charlestown experienced rampant ge this period owing to a concentration of capital associate "mind" economy. Consequently, establishing a neighborl near Bunker Hill in 1988 was an entirely different prop have been in, say, 1978.

It was one reason why, at the close of his second year in Boston, Burchill resolved "to become more involved with the city and state functions."[79] Doing so promised to turn real profits amid Boston's economic turnaround. For example, Burchill put the idea of providing food service before the advisory commission during its June 1985 meeting. It was part of a broader initiative to include a visitor center at the navy yard, for which several buildings had been already proposed.[80] Including a food concession, however, required additional steps, such as coordinating with city inspectors and negotiating with service providers. Preservation Specialist Steve Carlson managed much of it, including the renovation of Building 10 to accommodate a restaurant and serving areas. The park awarded its food service contract to Boston Concessions Group in 1988, and the so-called Shipyard Galley opened for business a year later.[81] Similarly, Burchill's willingness to cooperate with city services revived otherwise moribund conversations about public transit in and around the park. In 1988, at his encouragement, the Massachusetts Bay Transit Authority considered several options—including a water ferry between Pier 4 and Long Wharf—before settling on a new shuttle bus service from the parking garage (Building 199) to Building 5, paid for with mitigation funds from the Central Artery north area project.[82] These were not revolutionary changes, but they reveal the extent to which the park was becoming a more integral part of Boston's commercial tourism infrastructure.

As a result of changes like these, the park's daily operations appeared considerably more corporate than they had under Gurney. Some of the change really was a matter of appearance. Whereas photos suggest that Gurney always wore his uniform in public, Burchill was just as likely to show up in a business suit. But much of the change had to do with Burchill's consolidation campaign, which touched every facet of park operations.[83] To be fair, it was Gurney who had initially considered consolidating all navy yard staff into a single building and even including a park library there. It was Burchill, however, who actually sought to consolidate all park staff in the navy yard. The acquisition of Building 107 from the BRA, by way of Public Law 95–625 (1978), got the ball rolling. Staff consolidated artifact and records storage in Building 107, with help from a service-wide historic accountability project.[84] The Maintenance Division also moved into Building 107 in 1987, "resulting in increased efficiency and better communication with the Maintenance personnel," and also freeing Building 10 for the food concession.[85] The Administrative Division moved to the Marine Barracks from Building 109 in 1989.[86]

Finally, Burchill's years as superintendent coincided with a dramatic change in staffing. Indeed, almost as soon as he arrived, key members of the park's first-generation management team left Boston for other opportunities within and beyond the NPS. Vince Lombardi, who had figured so prominently at Dorchester Heights, left in 1984 to become operations manager at Strawbery Banke Museum in Portsmouth, New Hampshire.[87] Victor Jorrin, longtime historic architect for the park and for the region, departed in 1985 for Women's Rights National Historical Park in Seneca Falls, New York. Chief of Interpretation Lou Venuto left in 1985 too, transferring to Edison National Historic Site. Administrative Officer Bob Pribula and Deputy Superintendent Wendell Simpson rounded out a key batch of important first-generation departures in 1986, as did Frank Montford in 1991.[88] Debby Szarka, who had coordinated planning at the park for years, left also in 1990.[89] Simpson would return briefly but only before going on to become Superintendent of Canaveral National Seashore in Florida. His departure prompted the hire of John C. Benjamin from Grand Canyon National Park and also resulted in the promotion of Curator Peter Steele to assistant superintendent for planning and development.[90] Navy Yard Supervisory Park Ranger Bill Foley signed on in March 1986 and, in just a few years, would become chief of interpretation for the navy yard. In December 1986, Tony Tommell became supervisory park ranger for interpretation at Faneuil Hall and Dorchester Heights, hired on from the U.S. Marine Corps Museum in Quantico, Virginia.[91] And, significantly, Curator Arsen Charles retired in 1995, after having served at the park nearly twenty years and having invested mightily in building the navy yard's artifactual collections.[92]

Burchill's leadership thus created opportunities for new voices to join the park and also for a select few familiar voices to speak even louder.[93] Importantly, in coming years, many of those new voices would—like Burchill himself—come to the park from Lowell. Celeste Bernardo in interpretation, Peter A. Promutico in administration, and Martin Blatt in cultural resource management all arrived at the park during the 1990s from Lowell. Though Boston's authorization had preceded Lowell's, and presumably inspired it, it appears that the flow of influence had reversed itself under John Burchill.[94]

PRESERVING ICONS OF THE FREEDOM TRAIL

Richard Berenson introduced Burchill to the advisory commission in December 1984. Just as soon as he did, Regional Director Steven H. Lewis warned the commission that funding for park projects had grown thin and that "we must all look for new ways of doing things that do not require appropriated funds."[95] In hindsight, it seems that Burchill took up Lewis's warning as a singular focus for his superintendence. That he had to reflects, in part, agencywide funding limitations set against a precarious national economy. Recruiting seasonal staff, for instance, had become increasingly difficult with the rise of housing costs in gentrifying Boston. Gurney had tried to fix the problem in 1983 by renovating the second floor of the Marine Barracks into dormitory housing.[96] The problem intensified, however, and by 1988, Burchill was reporting major staff shortages. The park simply couldn't fill lapsed positions, due to budget constraints that prevented the recruitment of qualified staff. It was a problem that grew particularly acute as government salaries failed to keep pace with Boston's skyrocketing cost of living.[97] What's more, a long lapse in the Budget Division created major difficulties with implementing the agency's new Centralized Accounting Operations Division, resulting in late payments to park vendors. Turnover had become especially frequent among poorly paid protection rangers, for whom living in Boston had become a practical impossibility. Additional lapses in cultural resource management "have severely taxed the ability of staff to simultaneously keep many major projects on schedule and of quality." Inadequate review and long waits for consultation and preparation assistance "have compromised performance . . . and relief is needed."[98]

Finding new streams of income had become a matter of survival. Beyond the challenge of paying for operating costs and the inadequacy of salaries, there remained unresolved questions about how to support the constituent sites and, specifically, what should and should not be funded by the NPS. The agency's mandate, of course, required that it support preservation and interpretation at all of the sites. But what about incidentals? This question had already become pressing under Gurney as first-generation partnership agreements came up for renewal. When the Old South agreement approached expiration in January 1982, for instance, Bob Pribula suggested at a staff meeting that "site expenses such as telephones and electricity should not be paid by the Park Service."[99] In Lowell, Burchill had dealt with similar problems by partnering with Senator Tsongas and focusing on a single blockbuster preservation campaign at the Boott Mills complex. Could the same strategy work in Boston? Certainly, the park had its share of potential blockbuster preservation projects, considering that none of its most iconic Revolutionary-era structures had received significant attention since the Bicentennial. But who in Boston could provide the kind of support Burchill had found in Tsongas? Who in Boston had the right mix of local pride and political clout to help Burchill land a big preservation victory?

At the advisory commission's November 1985 meeting, Burchill announced—after being superintendent for only a year—that proposals to fund restoration of Faneuil Hall and the Old Statehouse, as well as select properties in the navy yard, were already before the House Senate Conference Committee. Senator Ted Kennedy was responsible for the navy yard project, but the much larger proposals—projects that could fundamentally alter the park's trajectory—owed to the efforts of U.S. Representative Joe Moakley.[100] The suddenness and scale of the announcement must have been a surprise. Moakley's interest in the park was well established, but there had been no mention of meetings between him and Burchill in staff meeting minutes. Indeed, the first mention occurred in 1987 when "the Superintendent and Assistant Superintendent met with Congressman Moakley . . . to discuss budget and projects at Faneuil Hall and the Old State House."[101] Clearly, Burchill had been working this angle from early on, perhaps as early as that first meeting with the advisory commission. His efforts were about to pay off.

How was it, though, that Burchill found such a ready and willing partner in Congressman Moakley? We saw in chapter five that Moakley, a devoted native of South Boston, was willing to go to bat for the park, in part owing to its presence at Dorchester Heights, where his predecessor, John McCormack, had first proposed the idea of a national park. Moakley had also played an integral role in securing authorization for Boston African American National Historical Site (NHS). Not only was Beacon Hill within Moakley's congressional district, but he had developed a close and supportive working relationship with Byron Rushing, a key advocate in the establishment of that site, dating back to their encounters during 1970s congressional campaigns. And, as Rushing explains it, Moakley had a real concern to advocate on behalf of Black Bostonians. It just so happened, too, that Paul Tsongas had been a key supporter of the legislation that authorized Boston African American NHS.[102] Burchill had arrived in Boston, therefore, amid a ready-made coalition of powerful park advocates with whom he shared particularly deep working-class roots in South Boston. Burchill even had a cousin, Molly Hurley, who worked at Moakley's Boston office. So, even though, as Public Affairs Officer Sean Hennessey put it, Burchill and Moakley were "cut from the same cloth," it's clear, too, that Burchill had multiple points of contact with a deep network of political operatives already activated against the conservative turn in federal policy making.[103] Insisting on federal support for popular preservation projects of national significance was a great way to join that fight during the 1980s.

It is important to note, too, that, amid Boston's economic turnaround, the park's success aligned with Moakley's determination to create economic opportunity within the city's heritage industry. Recall from chapter five that what first sparked Moakley's interest in the proposed park was not preservation or history, but jobs. The threat of lost jobs in 1973 was what activated Moakley's preservation impulse. The possibility of monetizing gentrification is what sustained it. Back in September 1980, just as Moakley had become involved with Boston African American NHS, House Ways and Means Committee Chair Dan Rostenkowski—who, as we discovered in chapter five, also played a critical, albeit anonymous, role in the site's genesis—wrote to Moakley encouraging him to participate in hearings concerning extension of the Tax Reform Act of 1976. Rostenkowski hoped to use Boston as a case study in demonstrating how effective tax incentives had been since the Bicentennial in encouraging the kind of heritage-themed gentrification that was quickly transforming neighborhoods adjacent to the park. Moakley did and, eventually, became so involved that he later introduced legislation to expand the tax break to multifamily rental properties. In this way, Moakley demonstrated a concern that gentrification not price working-class residents out of downtown Boston. It was a strategy that did not work in the long term. And it is a reminder of how deeply the park's fortunes during these years were imbedded within a new economy that consistently privileged wealthy white Americans. Moakley tried to change that but was not able to. As far as the NPS was concerned, though, Moakley's support for preservation tax credits and other tools of gentrification was good business. And it explains in hindsight why Burchill was so readily able to apply the lessons of Lowell's culture-led development in Boston's burgeoning new heritage economy.[104]

What Burchill discovered in Moakley, then, was a champion for the park who was willing and able to bypass entirely the agency's budget process, just as he had done to speed up appropriations for Boston African American NHS. Indeed, Moakley was even willing to bypass federal process by taking his demands directly to the Interior Subcommittee on Appropriations and its chair, Sid Yates. And so he did. Beginning in 1985, Moakley began a campaign to convince the Committee on Appropriations that the NPS had been negligent in Boston for not making good on its commitment to sustain its partner properties. He argued that Faneuil Hall and the Old State House—both, incidentally, within Moakley's district—required special attention in order to make them safely accessible to visitors. For two years, Moakley submitted reports and testimony insisting on the need for federal preservation funding, despite counterarguments by the Department of Interior that the scale of required work was not so great. By early 1986, the park had enough confidence in Moakley's advocacy to initiate start-up conversations concerning preservation projects at both buildings.[105] And, sure enough, by June 1987, the subcommittee approved full construction funding for Faneuil Hall and adequate design funds to move the Old South project forward. A year later, House and Senate committees approved full construction funds: $5,556,000 for Faneuil Hall; $5,280,000 for the Old State House.[106]

Moakley's victory at Faneuil Hall and the Old State House triggered what must have seemed like a tsunami of funding victories. $1.6 million materialized in 1990 for planning projects at Old South, Dorchester Heights, and Boston African American NHS.[107] In 1994, Moakley secured another $500,000 to support rehabilitation of Dorchester Heights. Later that year, he announced a $3.7 million appropriation for restoration of the Old South Meeting House.[108] This is not to mention significant appropriations secured by Senator Kennedy for conversion of Building 28 for use by the USS *Constitution* Museum. There was something going on in every corner of the park, it seemed. Burchill described the "scope and level of activity" like "a ball that seems to roll on and getting bigger each day." There's "a lot of activity," he added, "with a lot of opportunity for the Park."[109] And so there was. In 1992, the park celebrated the reopening of Faneuil Hall and the Old State House with considerable fanfare and lots of media attention.[110] Five years later, Dorchester Heights and the Old South Meeting House debuted new facilities with festivities of their own. And, in time for the 1997 USS *Constitution* bicentennial, the USS *Constitution* Museum debuted a new theater and new exhibit spaces, all tied together by innovative design and construction.[111] There was so much activity, in fact, that Secretary of Interior Manuel Lujan made a special visit, the first time in the park's history that it had received such a visit. The park's success, Secretary Lujan observed, "tells me that a strong unified cooperative effort has been established between the Freedom Trail cooperatives, private business, city and state officials in a joint effort to continually maintain and preserve the historical structures that has [*sic*] made Boston a great visitor attraction."[112]

It certainly appeared that way and, in many regards, it was. Burchill, by way of directing Moakley's interests, but also by tapping into agency resources and encouraging private giving to the charitable donations that grew up around all of the park's various preservation campaigns, managed a remarkable record of accomplishment at the park in just over a decade: $1 million for Boston African American NHS; $13 million for Faneuil Hall; $6.5 million for the Old State House; $7 million for the USS *Constitution* Museum; $6 million for Dorchester Heights; and $7.2 million for Old South Meeting House.[113] And, importantly, each preservation project, beyond expanding access to visitors and making Boston's historic icons safe, created new opportunities for interpretation. Faneuil Hall would include new contact areas as well as exhibit space, and a slate of new exhibits would be planned for the Old State House.[114]

What exactly might fill these new interpretation spaces, however, was not entirely clear. Content and layout planning sessions began in 1988 and produced several alternatives, through a process that included the park, the Denver Service Center, the regional office, the city, and Goody, Clancy and Associates—the firm responsible for coordinating the project.[115] The final vision, presented at a May 1990 special hearing of the Boston Landmarks Commission in Faneuil Hall, proposed sustaining the building's historic function as a meeting hall, but also "resum[ing] its historic role as marketplace."[116] Faneuil Hall, it turned out, would return as a commercial space. Sure enough, over the 1994 July fourth weekend, the new Grasshopper Shops—stylized nods to the building's colonial past—opened at Faneuil Hall.[117] Burchill, who incidentally had only just been reelected director of the Greater Boston Convention and Visitors Bureau, had really spurred remarkable growth at several of the park's Freedom Trail sites. It was the kind of growth, in fact, that hearkened directly back to Boston's postwar years, and the heady meat market debates that roiled Boston's heritage boosters a half century before.[118]

REIMAGINING THE FREEDOM TRAIL

Burchill's various development projects garnered considerable excitement among preservation enthusiasts and heritage tourists during the 1990s. They reminded onlookers that the NPS had a role downtown, a fact easily missed after years of concerted focus at the navy yard. They also reflected and, in some ways, advanced the park's evolving relationship with the Freedom Trail and the Freedom Trail Foundation. Under Superintendent Gurney, the park had largely followed the guidance of Richard Berenson on matters concerning the Freedom Trail. Conversely, Burchill took a considerably more aggressive position regarding the trail, seeking to mingle the park more directly with it. Staff meeting minutes reveal a conscious effort beginning during 1987 to "develop an association between the National Park Service and the well-established Freedom Trail."[119] Interestingly, the park appears to have begun its late-1980s Freedom Trail campaign in Charlestown and moved gradually toward downtown, in conjunction with Burchill's preservation projects. In 1987, for instance, the park involved itself by lobbying the Charlestown Neighborhood Council to allow the NPS to take the lead in painting a new red line connecting Bunker Hill and the navy yard.[120] Charlestown District Chief of Interpretation Bill Foley had taken over the project by 1988, working with Commissioners Joseph F. Canavan and Richard A. Dimino on the line, while also taking the opportunity to encourage Revolutionary-era arms demonstrations by costumed interpreters at Bunker Hill and in the navy yard.[121] In this way, the park's increased engagement with the Freedom Trail crossed over into its interpretive strategies.

Burchill's ability to involve the park more directly in goings-on along the trail reflected an important transformation then underway within the Freedom Trail Foundation. The foundation had always been, as Richard W. Berenson puts it, a "map publisher." It had been conceived by his father as a promotional organization, a way to encourage visitation toward generating revenue at the sites that might then be invested in preservation.[122] The Department of Interior recognized Berenson's vision in 1988 by awarding him its highest civilian honor, the Conservation Service Award.[123] But, when he passed away just two years later, a new generation of leadership sought new possibilities for the Freedom Trail Foundation.[124] Richard W. Berenson undertook a pro bono consultant project on behalf of the foundation. As he describes it, it was the first time anyone had taken an analytical approach to determining the foundation's vision. And the results suggested that what the foundation needed to do was to refocus its energies on getting people onto the trail and engaging them while there. In other words, whereas the foundation had previously limited its activities to marketing and promotion, its board resolved by the late 1980s to move more broadly into programming and interpretation.[125] Its president, Warren Berg, who had experience with museums by way of his leadership of the Museum of Science Board of Trustees, understood the new direction and, in just a few years, would hire on the foundation's first executive director to supervise the transition.[126]

In the meantime, evidence of the foundation's new directions and its impact on the park appeared throughout meeting minutes. By early 1988, for instance, the park had become involved in "a Freedom Trail Public Relations group . . . formed to assist in the marketing of the Freedom Trail."[127] Toward encouraging precisely this type of engagement, Burchill had hired a public relations officer, Chris Stein, who immediately involved himself in Freedom Trail activities. Stein served as a project manager, for instance, for a partnership with the Boston Convention and Visitors Bureau to create a promotional video concerning the Freedom Trail.[128] Just a few months later, Burchill made a remarkable announcement: the city had agreed to invest $350,000 in a comprehensive design study of the trail, including interpretation, signage, maintenance, marketing, and transportation.[129] It was an important commitment from the city, and a boon to a park for which funding shortfalls constantly loomed. NPS activity along the trail expanded almost immediately. Group reservations for Freedom Trail interpretive tours increased. The park introduced additional ninety-minute Freedom Trail tours on the weekends, and expanded operations even further by adding two weekday tours to the schedule.[130] The park and the foundation had become so intertwined, in fact, that in 1992 when the foundation hired its first executive director, Fred Davis, he moved its offices into the basement of the Commandant's House, smack dab in the middle of the navy yard.[131]

Davis's hire marked another important shift in an organization that once was primarily focused on fundraising and promotion. It, like so many other heritage organizations in Boston during the 1980s, had taken a decided step toward professionalization. Indeed, the shift had already been initiated under Warren Berg. In 1990, for instance, the foundation secured funding to hire a part-time coordinator to manage the People and Places school program.[132] Candace Lee Heald, who it hired for the position, arrived with degrees from Brown University and the University of Delaware.[133] Nancy Grey Osterud, who replaced Heald three years later, earned a PhD in American Civilization from Brown.[134] This was a far cry from the foundation's early days amid the swank men's clubs of mid-century Boston. Instead, by this time the foundation had concentrated on becoming a modern cultural organization with real investments in highly trained staff specialists. In Osterud, it had even hired a prominent feminist and historian. By the 1990s, then, the foundation had embraced an operational model wherein the qualifications of its staff approximated and, in some cases, surpassed those of their colleagues in the NPS.

The confluence of all these factors—the city's draft Freedom Trail study, reorganization within the foundation, Berenson Jr.'s analytic approach, not to mention Boston's economic transformations and the completion in 1992 of Burchill's preservation projects at the Old State House and Faneuil Hall— prompted the NPS to intervene in the Freedom Trail in a way that it had never done before. By summer 1995, park staff had begun working with a private consultant team to develop a comprehensive Freedom Trail planning study. The study proposed to develop "a vision of what the Freedom Trail stands for, its educational and economic values, and the role it should play in the life of Boston and the nation." It would be developed, moreover, "through an interactive process with involvement from the public, local government agencies, private organizations and business interests as well as the cooperating agencies along the Freedom Trail."[135] The NPS unveiled the result at a public debut in May 1996: a forty-page report titled "The Freedom Trail: A Framework for the Future." Mayor Thomas Menino attended the event and announced a $500,000 challenge grant to re-mark the trail in red brick, to add bronze medallions in front of all of its historic sites, and to install a new batch of Freedom Trail signs. Moakley threw his hat in too and along with Congressman Chester Atkins, secured $500,000 in appropriation for Freedom Trail planning.[136] What's more, Menino pledged an additional $15 million over five years for street improvements and the renovation of facilities along the trail. All of it would be done in 1997, just in time to celebrate the USS *Constitution*'s bicentennial.[137] It was a stunning gesture, and the biggest single investment in the Freedom Trail by the city since its commitment of support for the Boston Common visitor center two decades before.

What was it about the report that so persuaded Mayor Menino to make this remarkable investment? Most clearly the report laid out a broad concern with the health of Boston's heritage economy. Although overall visitation to Boston had been up in recent years, historic sites along the Freedom Trail had not seen a proportional uptick. In other words, tourist dollars were not penetrating Charlestown or downtown as fully as they might. The report's authors noted a wide range of reasons that they might not be. Boston was a different town than it once had been, with a considerably more diverse population. Its residents and a new generation of visitors had a greater appetite for complex histories that refused the consensus claims of postwar historians, claims the report indicated that were still readily evident along the trail. There was also the problem of inhospitable stretches of trail, especially between the North

End and Charlestown, on which pedestrians felt unmoored or even unwelcome. And then there was the problem of preservation. Congress had, through the NPS, invested considerable preservation monies, but that funding would not last, and it was evident that some source of revenue would be necessary to maintain the trail's iconic sites.[138]

But what made the report even more compelling was its suggestion that the trail, so long thought of as just a line, might rather be thought of as a story. Telling that story and making it available to visitors made powerful sense. Doing it would require, according to the report, a new dedicated visitor center, living history programs, an audio tour, expansion of the already successful People and Places program, and maybe even a sound and light show on Constitution Avenue. It would also require the establishment of a Freedom Trail Task Force including representatives from the constituent sites, the tourism industry, the city, the NPS, and other private and public organizations. This is to say that, for the first time since Ed Logue, a plan to coordinate public and private investment along the Freedom Trail seemed to be in place. And, within months, it appeared to be working. A partnership program produced the "Hit the Trail! Passport" in 1996 to coordinate visitor experience across the various sites.[139] By 1997, the city had begun replacing faded old portions of the Freedom Trail's iconic red trail with brick.[140] And the Freedom Trail Foundation had hired a new executive director, Linda C. McConchie, to make good on the trail's new plan. Like its other recent hires, McConchie brought to her job a wealth of specialized experience as an independent consultant, a special events coordinator for the governor's office, and as executive director for the Salem witch trial tercentenary. Having hired her, the foundation announced its plans to relocate its offices to the Old Corner Bookstore, long ago preserved by Walter Muir Whitehill's grassroots campaign, thus signaling a new era for the organization, a nod back to its beginnings amid postwar renewal, and perhaps a turn toward independence from the National Park Service.[141]

TOWARD A NEW HISTORY IN AN OLD PARK

What makes "The Freedom Trail: A Framework for the Future" so fascinating for our purposes is how much it resembled previous arguments—made by William Scofield, the Chamber of Commerce, Small and Bortman, and the BRA—for investing in Boston's heritage infrastructure. All of them, to varying degrees, made the case primarily in economic terms. In that regard, the Freedom Trail report is no different. Unlike its predecessors, however, the Freedom Trail report does include a notably more sophisticated historical argument. "The Freedom Trail," it argued, "is a unique seam between historic and modern Boston."[142] It was not a path into some authentic past, as previous boosters liked to claim, but rather a lens through which to glimpse the full span of change over time in Boston's urban landscape. And though nods to Revolutionary memory and Longfellow's Boston certainly appear throughout the report, it is much more clearly focused on exploring the "legacy of the struggle for Freedom" and taking stock of how historical knowledge has changed over time. This was a considerable shift for all parties involved along the Freedom Trail, one wherein reflexivity and nuance seemed finally to have pushed back against the histrionics of postwar nationalism. Had public history along the Freedom Trail taken a critical turn by the 1990s? Or was this just another instance, as Richard Handler and Eric Gable famously observed at Colonial Williamsburg during the same years, of progressive history awkwardly mapped onto old ideas about memory and profit. Was this, in their words, just "the new history in an old museum?"[143]

The answer would have varied considerably depending on where and how visitors experienced history programming. History interpretation along the Freedom Trail, for instance, remained largely invested in guided tours of Boston's Revolutionary past and occasional bouts of living history. For instance, a popular summer interpretive program during these years featured a reenactment of one of the last town meetings convened in the Old South Meeting House prior to the Boston Tea Party. The program began in 1981 and resulted from a collaboration between the park and the Old South Association. Costumed interpreters dramatized the event while inviting audience members to participate. Its goal was to prompt participants to wonder how "Samuel Adams [would] handle the types of characters who show up at our town meetings, especially the ardent Tories?"[144] Following national trends, costumed interpretation and other facets of so-called living history thrived at the park during the 1980s. At Bunker Hill especially, the NPS promoted first-person costumed interpretation of military history and frequently showcased reenactors dressed as Revolutionary-era soldiers. Though notable for its encouragement of audience engagement, none of this programming appears to have moved far beyond content developed during the Bicentennial years.

Conversely, at Boston African American NHS, visitors encountered considerably more forward-looking interpretation concerned specifically with fathoming the shifting meaning of freedom in Boston since the Revolution. The Black Heritage Trail encompassed a hive of activity during those years, thanks to investments in preservation by the NPS, Moakley, and others. These had made possible completion of preservation work at the African Meeting House in 1987. What's more, the site's manager showcased new research, and frequent exhibits, including Smithsonian traveling exhibits, that situated the unit's interpretive themes within a broad historical context, often using art and performance to connect with visitors. Indeed, as early as 1982, programming associated with the unit had grown so robust, that park staff wondered, "should BOAF [Boston African American NHS] interpreters compete with Byron's [Museum of Afro-American History] guides?"[145] Rushing would, within the year, win election to the Massachusetts House of Representatives, where he would go on to represent the Ninth Suffolk District for over three decades. His organization remained, however, and continued to guide goings-on at the Boston African American NHS.[146]

Glimpses of progressive critical history could be seen elsewhere around Boston as well. A coterie of public school educators, for instance, devised the Boston Women's Heritage Trail in 1990, to reverse the tendency at all of Boston's historic sites to valorize only the Revolution's famous men. In 1996, the History Project organization mounted a major exhibit at the Boston Library concerning gay and lesbian history since the seventeenth century. Indeed, Boston's heritage landscape featured prominently in the Gay Pride movement, including a landmark speech delivered by activist Larry Kramer at Faneuil Hall in 1987. Even the Paul Revere House, one of the park's constituent sites, had embraced critical social history early on and even published research concerning immigration in the North End.[147] Perhaps most relevant to this study, the Bostonian Society mounted a stunning exhibit at the Old State House during 1992–94, with funding from the National Endowment for the Humanities (NEH). The exhibit and an accompanying book, both titled *The Last Tenement: Confronting Community and Urban Renewal in Boston's West End*, for the first time grappled with the fact and legacy of urban renewal in Boston. The timing of this exhibit, coinciding as it did with a moment of considerable growth and change in Boston's urban landscape, was remarkably provocative at the time. And it reflected a longstanding effort by the Bostonian Society to reunite and empower people who had been displaced by postwar renewal campaigns. This was the best of critical history in Boston during those years, though it was not work that the park involved itself in. Indeed, no staff from the park or the regional office appear in the project's lengthy acknowledgments.[148]

But why was that? Why did the NPS appear only to encourage critical public history at Boston African American NHS, and not elsewhere? It is worth noting that Park Historian Paul Weinbaum and several assistants were, during 1984, deeply involved with the Beacon Hill unit. As we might suspect, though, owing to the agency's bifurcation of history and interpretation, their involvement appears to have been almost entirely limited to the preparation of National Register nominations for its various sites—an incredible fifteen nominations that year alone.[149] As we learned in chapter five, much of the historical momentum atop Beacon Hill owed to the research agenda that Rushing and the Afro-American museum had built into its agenda at the outset. Weinbaum recalls Rushing's powerful imprint on the new unit, noting that it was his "interpretive turf."[150] And because Boston African American NHS had its own authorizing legislation, separate from, though administered by, Boston National Historical Park, it mostly stayed that way, firewalled, as it were, from Boston's other units.[151] Louis Hutchins, who replaced Weinbaum as park historian in 1991, recalls a fraught relationship between the two units, owing to their awkward administrative relationship. But what made the problem considerably worse was Burchill's evident disregard for the unit and its staff. Hutchins recalls Burchill treating the site superintendent poorly in meetings. "Burchill was essentially a racist," he recalls, "he dismissed [Boston African American NHS]."[152] As we will see, Burchill's evident racial anxieties were not limited to Beacon Hill. It was, rather, just one facet of a larger problem undergirding the park's reinvestment in Revolutionary memory during the 1990s.

Another problem, as Weinbaum explains it, owed to the narrow period of significance allowed for interpretation by the park's authorizing legislation and those charged with translating it into practice. In 1985, for instance, Weinbaum worked under Curator Peter Steele and with several consulting historians from nearby universities on a new NEH-funded exhibit for the Old South Meeting House. Weinbaum wanted very much to explore "the 20th-century history of free speech in Boston . . . and the role that Old South plays in that." The Old South Meeting House has, since 1916, hosted a public forum series on current events. Its topics—which, over time, have included censorship, Nazism, and abortion rights, to name just a few—chronicle the concerns of Americans across the twentieth century. Placing Old South's forum series at the center of

its new exhibit would have opened up considerable opportunities for investigating what the park's authorizing legislation terms the "growth of the United
States." Weinbaum's NPS colleagues, however, "did not feel it could tell that
story extensively." That type of history, Weinbaum recalls, wasn't considered
"part of the mission of the Park, as it's legislated."[153] What the exhibit team
settled on instead was a careful detailing of the public meetings that occurred
in Old South during the years leading to the American Revolution. Critics
panned the final exhibit. Weinbaum notes a litany of problems stemming
from the team's laser-like focus on the building's Revolutionary history. "We
missed the . . . triangle trade totally," he notes, thus missing a key opportunity
to engage with histories of race and power. "We documented every meeting[,
but the] exhibit failed to get at the meaning of the Revolution."[154]

Except for perhaps at the Boston African American NHS, then, history
programming in the park during these years appears to have followed rather
then led trends in Boston's heritage landscape.[155] Meeting minutes reveal
Weinbaum's attempts to speak with interpretative staff throughout the 1980s
about aspects of the park's history that might encourage more innovative
perspectives on the past.[156] Overall, however, these efforts appear to have had
little impact. Interpretation remained largely focused on finding new ways to
deliver old ideas about Revolutionary pasts. This is not to say that the park did
not value interpretive method. On the contrary, during these years, interpreters
explored all matter of ways to engage visitors. In the navy yard, an innovative
costumed interpretive program featuring Rosie the Riveter explored labor and
women's history. Along the Freedom Trail, Ranger Matt Grief used puppetry
to reach new audiences. And the park's tradition of accommodating visually
impaired visitors expanded during these years to include other vectors of disability.[157] Despite all of this, however, the content of interpretation remained
squarely focused on narrow periods of significance that largely excluded any
possibility of complicating the recent past; thinking broadly across chronology,
as Weinbaum had hoped to do at Old South and at Building 28; or reaching
audiences such as those among Boston's newest immigrants whose stories were
not at all reflected in the park's historical narrative.

Weinbaum had at least managed to influence what the superintendent
believed to be the role of the park's historian. When he left to permanently
join the regional office, the park sought to replace Weinbaum with someone
who, beyond managing National Register nominations, could also contribute to the development of permanent exhibits, as Weinbaum had done at

Old South and elsewhere. The park's preservation program had created a need for new exhibits, especially in the navy yard, Faneuil Hall, and the Old State House. With that in mind, the park hired Louis Hutchins in 1991 to replace Weinbaum. Hutchins had earned an MA in American History from the University of California at Berkeley and came to the park after serving as a historian for the Historic American Engineering Record and at the Smithsonian Institution's National Museum of American History. Publicly, Burchill noted Hutchins's "skills in developing exhibits [as the park] goes forward with major new permanent exhibits."[158] Behind the scenes, however, Burchill seemed more excited about the fact that Hutchins had once interned with Joe Moakley. He was eager, too, that Hutchins not lead the park into histories that exceeded what Burchill considered to be the park's mandate. His advice for Hutchins: "I don't want you to be another Paul Weinbaum."[159]

Hutchins, who was entirely new to the NPS, immediately recognized the hard row he'd have to till at Boston National Historical Park. He found himself pressured to publish incomplete research on unfamiliar topics. He discovered deep rifts between his office, the Division of Cultural Resources, and the navy yard's chief of interpretation. He witnessed entrenched racism "very explicitly" in the park's highest office. On one occasion, for instance, Burchill drove Hutchins and Steele through his childhood neighborhood in South Boston, telling stories about people he lived near and worked with during stints as a bartender. "The way he talked about Black people," Hutchins recalls, "was highly offensive." Hutchins learned gradually that "history was viewed by the [park] leaders as the icing on the cake," something done after preservation, primarily to fill exhibit spaces or signal outwardly a concern for public engagement. He felt, however, that the historian's role should be "to work closely with interpretation; to make sure the stories they were telling were accurate, and engaging, and pushing the understanding of history beyond the old narrative." To achieve it, he worked as Paul Weinbaum had tried, to provide direction for tour leaders in the park's downtown interpretation office. This time it worked. With support from a division head that did value history, Hutchins organized seminars with interpretive staff to read and discuss recent scholarship concerning the social history of the Revolution. Hutchins's supervisor didn't consider the work important. And Burchill "didn't care." Hutchins, however, persisted, given what seemed to him the enormity of the park's history problem.[160]

Did Hutchins's history activism shift the balance at Boston National Historical Park? It's hard to know. Certainly, it inspired the downtown interpreters, and no doubt expanded their capacity to move some visitors toward a more nuanced engagement with the Freedom Trail. Hutchins also advised the committee that produced "The Freedom Trail: A Framework for the Future." Perhaps his role explains the report's remarkable awareness of the limitations of history making along the Freedom Trail during those years. In the navy yard, however, Hutchins encountered insurmountable barriers. In one case, he worked with a young interpreter who developed a walking tour of Charlestown, focusing on the homes of people who worked in the navy yard during the early twentieth century. His goal was to end the tour at Bunker Hill with a discussion of the struggle to desegregate Charlestown High School. According to Hutchins, Navy Yard Chief of Interpretation Bill Foley "cut the whole thing down fast" when he found out. Foley had cultivated deep ties in Charlestown with the Bunker Hill Monument Association, led then by the bombastic James Conway, whose family owned the Charlestown *Patriot* newspaper. All of it was too much for Hutchins who, after five years, left the park "very unhappy" amid a government shutdown and the prospect of being continually undermined.[161]

In his place, the park hired Martin Blatt, who had served as chief of professional services and supervisory historian at Lowell. Blatt signed on in Boston during 1996 as chief of cultural resources and supervisory historian.[162] Blatt's arrival marked an important turn in history making at the park. Unlike his predecessors, Blatt came to the park a seasoned NPS historian with particular interests in the histories of labor and political radicalism, including in Boston. He had earned his PhD at Boston University, under the direction of the Pulitzer Prize-winning historian Robert Bruce and Howard Zinn, whose *People's History of the United States* was one of the most influential American history books of the twentieth century. Blatt had published books with scholarly presses, sat on the board of directors of the Massachusetts Foundation for the Humanities, and had spent several years working for Governor Michael Dukakis, including on his failed 1988 presidential election campaign, all before coming to Boston. At Lowell, where he had worked during 1990–96, Blatt made important contributions to the Boott Cotton Mill Museum, which had become noteworthy for modeling critical public history.[163]

Blatt's commitment to doing progressive history became evident almost immediately after arriving in Boston. He learned that a committee had been formed under the direction of Ken Heidelberg, site manager at Boston African American NHS, to commemorate the centennial of Augustus Saint-Gaudens's

monument to Robert Gould Shaw and the Fifty-fourth Massachusetts Regiment. As Blatt explains it, the committee was in disarray, and so he asserted
control over its planning, in partnership with the Massachusetts Historical
Society's then-senior associate editor, Donald Yacovone.[164] Together, the
two historians devised an entirely new kind of event for the park. Theirs was
purposefully reflexive and situated in a broad historical context reflecting
the scholarship of that moment. It is a difference that is evident in Blatt's
description of the event:

> In 1897 the Monument was dedicated to Shaw. In 1997 the "rededica-
> tion" transformed the Monument. In this centennial the entire frame of
> reference was the Monument to Robert Gould Shaw *and* the Fifty-fourth
> Massachusetts Regiment. We demonstrated clearly that blacks were not
> passive creatures freed by President Lincoln but rather a vital force in
> the Union victory. The sculpture evokes the reality and possibilities of
> racial cooperation. Our centennial involved rededication to the ideals
> that the Monument represents—a struggle for social justice and unity
> between blacks and whites to advance common ideals.[165]

It was a remarkable turn for history making at Boston National Historical
Park. Simultaneously backward-looking and forward-looking, Blatt's vision—
and his willingness to assert it across divisions—promised to bring the park's
resources and its partnerships into a productive conversation about historical
complexity and nagging problems of social injustice.

Blatt and Yacovone did not stop there. They staged, alongside the monument's formal rededication, a two-day symposium at Suffolk University
showcasing important scholars who contributed essays to a book published
by the University of Massachusetts Press.[166] They also hosted the largest-ever
gathering of Black Civil War reenactors in an encampment on the Charles
River, with nearly three thousand visitors. Various speakers, including Byron
Rushing, addressed the crowds. Blatt and Yacovone even convinced retired
General Colin Powell to deliver the event's keynote speech.[167] By way of comparison, the park hosted another commemorative event that summer, the
rededication of Dorchester Heights on June 21, that Blatt did not plan. That
one-day event included remarks by Congressman Moakley and participation
by a handful of white battle reenactors who created "a sense of authenticity
[alongside] two teams of oxen."[168] Whereas the Dorchester Heights event

repeated familiar tropes from the usual playbook of Boston's Revolutionary memory, Blatt's event broke entirely new ground, engaged new audiences, and earned for the park considerable media attention. It signaled an important turn toward precisely the kind of critical public history that the park had needed all along in order to make sense of its own genesis story, to grapple with the history of racial violence that had shaped it, and to signal that the NPS was committed to serving all Americans.

It was not the kind of programming, however, that Superintendent Burchill wanted for his park. For his part, Burchill ignored the Shaw commemoration until word spread that Colin Powell and Byron Rushing were scheduled to appear. Uninterested in Shaw, and incensed that Blatt had not reserved space for the superintendent to speak at a public event, Burchill called him into his office, closed the door, and let fly: "Who the fuck do you work for . . . Do you work for Rushing, or do you work for me!?" In the end, Blatt and Yacovone agreed that Burchill could have a few minutes to introduce the event. What the confrontation with Burchill revealed, however, was a deep-seated hostility among park leadership to programming that shifted focus away from blockbuster preservation projects and that otherwise complicated patriotic narratives of American progress. It is one of many accounts that point to a climate of unease at Boston National Historical Park during those years, as well as a workplace run through with anxiety about race and power.[169]

Blatt struggled against that tendency, in part, by advancing many successful progressive public history projects beyond the scope of his regular duties.[170] Some of these, particularly a public art project by Krzysztof Wodiczko concerning street violence, cosponsored with Boston's Institute for Contemporary Art and staged at the Bunker Hill Monument during 1998, earned national attention for the park and put it briefly at the center of important conversations about memory and citizenship.[171] Behind the scenes, however, the Wodiczko program intensified anxieties within the park concerning the meaning and uses of history. As Blatt tells it, Burchill and his chief of interpretation, Bill Foley, favored the soothing and uncomplicated reaffirmations of patriotic nationalism typified by battle reenactments and oxen teams. They agreed with James Conway, head of the Bunker Hill Association, who publicly clashed with the Institute of Contemporary Art's director over the event, telling her that it "tarred" Charlestown's character.[172] Theirs was a vision of the park that had underwritten Burchill's preservation successes for over a decade and that, as we've seen, had been promulgated by Boston's Whig elite centuries before.

* * *

John Burchill left the park in 2000 to become a special assistant to the regional director. "It is astonishing to me," he wrote upon announcing his departure, "that in my years as Superintendent I never had an untoward incident or encounter. There has never been any animosity, personally or institutionally."[173] This is hardly true. As we've seen, Burchill had a temper that surely caused more than a few hard feelings over the years. His choice to ignore those moments, though, is revealing, insomuch as it underscores a similar attitude about the historical past. From what we can gather from his speeches and management priorities, it is clear that Burchill perceived in Boston's history a succession of selfless heroic white men who prevailed against great odds to make our nation, slowly but surely, a better place for everyone. It is a wrongheaded notion, of course, a fact that should have been made clear to him by his own staff and by the important public history being done all around Boston during the 1990s. It is a notion, however, that undergirded Burchill's political alliances, that wooed donors, that animated remarkably successful preservation campaigns, and that in many ways fed Burchill's hopes for his own legacy. In other words, it was a way of thinking about the past that got results at a time and within an organization that largely eschewed history. Owing to its success during the 1990s, and perhaps also to the sudden deaths of Moakley in 2001—and Burchill himself just a year later—this era in the park's history holds a special place among many staff who remain at the park today.[174]

In hindsight, however, Burchill's success and the park's consequent growth, created significant challenges. As I've suggested, Burchill's attitude toward history, his tacit endorsement of white supremacy, and the resistance to critical interpretation his superintendence encouraged was deeply problematic. Even more hazardous than his own attitude toward history was his support for staff, such as the navy yard's chief of interpretation, whose understandings of the past had no grounding in historical scholarship. More concerning yet was Burchill's simultaneous commitment to building up and expanding the Freedom Trail Foundation's capacity to do its own interpretation. Unlike the park, which at least kept historians like Weinbaum and Blatt on staff, the foundation had no structural requirement to include historical expertise among its staff or on its board. To make matters worse, Burchill's Freedom Trail study put the foundation on equal terms with the park's other cooperating

organizations, which had in fact began operating as serious history organizations during this period. If the park did not value history and it did not
value critical interpretation, then what would the NPS have to offer the sites
once Moakley's fundraising magic vanished? Joint educational programming
like the People and Places program was certainly important. But what reason
beyond it would there be to cooperate? It was this question, above all, that
poised the park and its partners for a difficult road ahead.

Lost and Found on the Freedom Trail

"The Freedom Trail Park," everyone called it that.

—Byron Rushing (2005)

This is a book about loss. Nearly seventy years ago, William Schofield proposed that Boston create the Freedom Trail so that tourists looking for Paul Revere's House, the site of the Boston Massacre, or any number of other schoolbook icons, not get lost along the way. I have sought to demonstrate throughout these chapters that what really got lost in that moment was any possibility of challenging a story about the Revolutionary past that, for well over a century, had equated American prosperity with white privilege. The Freedom Trail literally inscribed that story onto Boston's streets with the blunt logic of a simple red line. Its logic was the logic of economic recovery, urban renewal, the festival marketplace, heritage tourism, and blockbuster historic preservation. It was the same logic, in fact, that seduced the National Park Service (NPS) after World War II and that compelled the agency to establish a national historical park in Boston that was barely sustainable and hardly historic. It was the kind of logic that excused the park from having to contend with histories of racial violence, even when the park itself was at the center of national dialogues about racial violence. It is the way that millions of people have and still do learn about history in Boston. When Byron Rushing recalled that "everyone called" Boston National Historical Park the "the Freedom Trail Park," he captured in just a few words the realization that so startled me at this project's outset, and what must have been obvious to Bostonians from the beginning: the park and the trail are, in essence, the same idea.[1]

At the core of that idea is the notion that history should turn a profit. Although the NPS has always relied on private interests for its survival, I have sought to show how at one park this public agency rationalized its dependency on private capital after World War II. The result for federal history making in Boston—including the denigration of historical expertise, chronological myopia, and the privileging of white American exceptionalism—was devastating. For a period of time, during the park's first decade, progressive advisory commission members, including Rushing, resisted these tendencies. Their impact, however, was mitigated by the advisory commission's powerful chair, whose commitments to postwar economic redevelopment kept the park bound to a vision articulated for it during the 1950s by a federal commission whose members' ideas about history and citizenship had matured during the 1930s. Almost as soon as the advisory commission's authority expired, a new superintendent arrived whose uncritical devotion to the patriotic icons of American nationalism—and an overt hostility toward those who would question them—reconceived the park as a mechanism for delivering big-ticket congressional funding to the historic sites that most vividly recalled Longfellow's mythic Boston. It would be the last time the park received a major infusion of congressional funding, thus cementing in place a sense of mission that lingers there today.

Conversely, the NPS has also accomplished incredibly valuable work in Boston. From the beginning, its emphasis on community-engaged educational programming has demonstrated just how powerfully the urban park concept can benefit young people, especially those who are disadvantaged by structural inequality in American schools. The park has also been an agency leader in accommodating visitors and staff who contend with all manner of disability. Its historians and cultural resource specialists, too, have done remarkable work, especially given the impossibility of their task. Visitors who seek it out can find nuance, for instance, in the Charlestown Navy Yard's exhibits or while exploring the Bunker Hill Monument Museum. That these facets of the park experience have moved beyond the hypernationalism of decades past is a tribute to many diligent staff who work tirelessly behind the scenes to inch the agency's glacial bureaucracy toward something resembling a critical engagement with the past. And let us not forget the park's constituent sites and their own staffs that, as we have seen, have for decades sought to do good history in Boston, with or without NPS support.

And yet, despite all of this, something is still lost in Boston's public historical landscape. It is hard to get at in the agency's records. Deciphering the history of any national park after the 1990s, in fact, is impossibly complicated by a documentary record that, since the digital turn, amounts to stacks upon stacks of dense compliance reports and sterile memoranda. Neither federal archivists nor historians have yet to contend with email records in any meaningful way, thereby foreclosing opportunities to retrieve the myriad exchanges preserved in daily correspondence. Oral history helps, of course, but it is capricious, dangerously so when not balanced against other forms of evidence. Beyond all of that, decades of funding shortfalls and inattention have put the agency's meager corps of record-keepers into a fundamentally untenable situation. Federal guidelines require that archival researchers be accompanied at all times by qualified staff. Every moment I spent picking through records in Building #107, I did so accompanied by one of just two people tasked with managing all of the park's vast collections. It occurred to me more than once that if I slowed my pace, or followed too many investigatory dead ends, I would cost some other researcher critical access to the park's institutional memory.

So where then do we pick up the trail? As I noted at the outset, tragedy consumed the park's attentions during the years following Superintendent John Burchill's departure. The attacks of September 11, 2001, sent a shock wave through all federal facilities, requiring years of expensive and time-intensive security protocols. Just two years later, in a remarkably prescient essay for the *Public Historian*, Park Historian Martin Blatt noted that two of the planes "turned into suicide flights" on 9/11 had originated at Logan Airport, just minutes from the park.[2] Blatt's essay, in fact, introduced an entire special issue of public history's premier journal on work being done in Boston, and the possibility there of finally moving beyond those in "the Boston Tourism industry who choose to celebrate uncritically the realization of liberty in eighteenth-century Boston."[3] Tragedy notwithstanding, it appeared to Blatt and numerous contributors—including historian Alfred Young and Paul Revere House Executive Director Nina Zannieri—that the 1996 Freedom Trail report really had pointed toward a new era of critical public history in Boston. Key to making it happen, they suggested, would be developing a coherent story along the Freedom Trail that embraced fluidity, change, and reinvention. It would take a story, as Blatt put it, that might "counter the approach that sells history as yet another commodity." Blatt worried, however, that all of it might come to naught amid collapsing budgets, and the likelihood that "the national and international political framework" would erode trust among visitors wary of more violence.[4] He was right to be worried. In 2013, as the nation slowly recovered from 9/11, two men terrorized Boston anew. The so-called Boston Marathon Bombing that year thrust the park immediately

back into a defensive posture, scattering possibilities once again for making
the new history stick.

I first became involved with the park in 2011, in the space between those
awful moments, at the invitation of staff charged with organizing a scholars'
visit in preparation for revising the park's general master plan. I was impressed
then with the capabilities and vision of the folks I encountered. A new chief
of interpretation was asking all the right questions. A new superintendent, the
park's first Black superintendent, seemed to be doing all the right things, and
had breathed new life into the park's relationships with its partner sites.[5] The
project team even managed to pull former park historian Paul Weinbaum out
of retirement to join in a smart conversation about what the park had been
and what it could be. But when I returned in 2015, the picture had changed
yet again. A grim mood lingered in the wake of the marathon bombing. In
quiet conversations, staff shared with me a sense of hopelessness. They worried
about funding, the efficacy of agency leadership, the inane bureaucratization
of history making. They worried, most of all, about the impossibility of
making change in Boston. Old habits, old ways of thinking, and old systems
of power and capital seemed everywhere entrenched. Sure enough, within the
year, those new forward-looking staff—including the superintendent—had
set out in search of new prospects.

My sense is that the tumult I encountered in Boston during those years was
evidence of a park left drifting by the collapse of a preservation mission that,
largely defunded, left little but uncertainty in its wake. I've not attempted a
close analysis of the park's recent past owing to imbalances in the documentary
record, and my own inability in today's pandemic landscape to do the kind
of ethnographic research necessary to fill the void. While we wait for that
important work to be done, there are other ways to begin pondering the fate of
public history in the park since the turn of the twenty-first century. One way to
do it is by listening to precisely those people who neither the Boston National
Historic Sites Commission nor the park's planning team ever quite managed
to contend with: the park's neighbors. Fortunately for us, Bostonians—like
people living all across the Unites States these days—are speaking clearly
and loudly about the place of history in their lives. What they are saying in
Boston has remarkable resonance in light of the histories that bind together
the National Park Service and the Freedom Trail. Consider, for instance, the
tour guides employed by the Freedom Trail Foundation who, after years of
mistreatment, are now demanding basic labor rights, including pay raises and

protections against workplace injury.[6] Their struggle makes quite clear that the historical significance of economic self-determination and equal opportunity—key themes in the Freedom Trail's Revolutionary mythology—has meant less to the trail's stewards than does the possibility of profiting from the labors of a contingent workforce. The ranking of revenue above equity is itself a tacit interpretive theme bound up long ago with Revolutionary memory in Boston, and later fixed into the Freedom Trail's DNA by the Chamber of Commerce. That these workers' demands are perceived as radical today in a city whose past is distinguished by a tradition of radicalism suggests that, on this topic at least, history hasn't yet won the day.

Nor has it provided the reckoning with race and power that Bostonians still demand. Opportunities to confront histories of enslavement, racial discrimination, and violence in the park and beyond have been ample from the outset. Not only are these themes central to the park's enabling legislation, they inhere in every single facet of the park's genesis story and in the stories of each site that it is bound by law to support. And yet, with a few important exceptions, the park has limited its most rigorous and consistent engagement with histories of race to the properties included within the Boston African American National Historical Site and that dot Boston's Black Heritage Trail, which winds through Beacon Hill's tony North Slope. The addition of this unit to the park's management dossier was certainly a major windfall. But rather than being inspired to contend with its lessons elsewhere, the park has remained largely content with the intervention atop Beacon Hill, far from where debates over renewal, school desegregation, and racial violence created the very circumstances of this park's birth.

The consequences of the agency's milquetoast positions on race and power are perhaps most evident today at Faneuil Hall. Beginning in 2018, newspapers reported on demands by the New Democracy Coalition that Faneuil Hall be renamed so that it no longer commemorate a slave trader. The problem of Faneuil Hall's ties to enslavement had, in fact, been flagged as a concern for the park by Blatt during renovations funded by Burchill's preservation campaign. Blatt proposed then that the park mount a major reinterpretation of Peter Faneuil as an enslaver. Others balked, insisting that the topic was not appropriate for an NPS visitor center.[7] Because the park once again favored the work of white heritage tourism over the work of history, it fell to others in Boston to insist on historical accountability at Faneuil Hall. The New Democracy Coalition's founder, Kevin Peterson, did just that by organizing protests and boycotts in 2018. Boston Mayor Marty Walsh opposed renaming efforts but supported public discussion around the possibility of installing a monument, designed by artist Steve Locke, that would pull back the curtain on Faneuil's complicity in the slave trade. Peterson, in turn, opposed the monument, suggesting that it excused Walsh from having to contend directly with Faneuil Hall. The NAACP pushed back even harder, claiming that the process of selecting Locke to lead the recommemoration was not adequately transparent.[8] Conversations about race, power, and memory thus devolved into a contest of wills. The NPS, of course, is perfectly positioned to mediate these disagreements and point a light forward. So far, however, it has not.

This is not to say that the NPS has ignored histories of race and enslavement in Faneuil Hall. Even Blatt admits that the recent kerfuffle has prompted important new exhibits and a video that help visitors understand the history of slavery. What's more, the park hosted a "day of healing" in Faneuil Hall, complete with costumed interpreters, to commemorate slavery's four-hundredth anniversary.[9] The problem, however, is that all of these events take place in Faneuil Hall's staid Great Hall, a second-floor space that, though deeply historic, is safely sequestered from the building's bustling first floor, where the vast majority of visitors limit their encounter to a stop at the park's contact station and a turn through the building's stylized "colonial" market stalls. This strict separation of spaces is not an accident. The building's current consumer space was conceived of and installed back in 1994 with preservation funding raised by Superintendent Burchill and Congressman Moakley. It's the same space, in fact, where local venders once sold meat and produce to actual Bostonians. They did, at least, until the NPS, the Boston National Historic Sites Commission, and other agents of urban renewal conspired to replace the vendors with souvenir shops like what they had seen in Colonial Williamsburg. History on the second floor, profit on the first. The park's current inability to take control of the agenda, as it regards the problem of race, power, and memory at Faneuil Hall, is thus an artifact of decisions made long ago by NPS leaders eager to profit from Boston's postwar investments in urban renewal.

That too is a story that Bostonians are demanding to hear. Consider, for instance, the "Redlined" project, a potent mix of art, advocacy, and public history sponsored in 2015 by the City Life/Vida Urbana organization in Boston's Jamaica Plains neighborhood. Community volunteers, working with artists and social justice advocates, used historic maps and a rolling athletic field chalker to represent on Boston's streets the red lines once drawn on real estate maps by white mortgage lenders bent on divvying up neighborhoods by race and wealth.[10] "Redlining," as it has come to be known, was a legal practice encouraged by the federal government as early as 1936 in its Federal Housing Administration underwriting manual. The decades of discriminatory lending practices that followed segregated American cities and undermined efforts by all but white Americans to accumulate generational wealth.[11] These, of course, were the very same discriminatory housing policies that buttressed mid-century urban renewal and that, in Boston, blazed the path for another red line: the Freedom Trail. The messy pile of red chalk heaped upon Jamaica Plains' sidewalks is a provocative foil to the tidy red line maintained by city workers five miles away in downtown Boston. That they are two sides of the same story is obvious to people who did not benefit from urban renewal, and apparently imperceptible to those who did.

Histories of all of Boston's red lines, then, must figure prominently in interpretation along the Freedom Trail and in the Charlestown Navy Yard if the NPS is to finally make good on its obligation to serve all Americans. And yet, after decades of plan making and engagement initiatives, the park seems still unable to make itself meaningful to neighbors. As recently as 2019, a senior planner for the National Parks of Boston, the latest incarnation of the old Boston Sites Group, opined that "people don't know about [urban national parks]. Our population is becoming diverse and urban-centered, so how do we make our parks more relevant to the communities in which they're located?" It's a question that echoes themes advanced by the agency's 2016 Urban Agenda, an initiative designed to make urban parks more accessible and more meaningful to the people who live near them. It's a question, too, that could have been asked verbatim, and probably was, by the Denver-based planning team back in 1974, when they were flown in to decide what Boston National Historical Park would be about. In fact, the rhetoric and goals of the latest NPS "place making" projects in Charlestown seem lifted directly from a half century ago, when a previous generation of well-intentioned young planners scratched their heads and wondered why neighbors felt "unwelcome" in the park.[12]

Might the problem rather be that people know all too well about urban national parks and have rejected them? If nothing else, this study demonstrates that, in Boston, people have understood quite well since the 1930s what the National Park Service was about in Boston. Black newcomers to the city certainly understood during the 1930s that the NPS was about lifting up Irish Americans. Resistance to its plans in the North End during the 1950s very clearly demonstrated that people understood that the NPS was about demolition and removal. Rooms full of irate neighbors are good evidence, too, that during the 1970s, people were quite aware of the agency's place in Charlestown. So, who exactly is the NPS worried about? Who does it think is not adequately aware of urban parks? Is it worried, like William Scofield was seventy years ago, only about affluent white tourists, people like me and my family, who may not live in Boston but who readily pay into its economy? What is for certain is that decades of insisting that neighbors be educated about a park that they already understand full well, while simultaneously ignoring histories of renewal and racial violence, is disingenuous. It is a woeful strategy for doing public history anywhere, let alone in Boston. That, at least, is the message that we might expect the NPS to gather from the artists, protesters, and activists today who are asserting control over the agenda. Will the agency hear their message? Is it even able to?

I, for one, am not convinced that it is. The National Park Service, like the nation itself, was born full of democratic potential, and yet it has frequently sacrificed its possibilities to the shabby chauvinisms of patriotic memory. I have dwelt on problems of inequity associated specifically with urban renewal, and especially the persistence of racial violence and erasure in Boston's public historical landscape. Volumes too could be written about ethnocentrism, homophobia, and gender discrimination in an agency that Denver Service Center Planner Nan Rickey recalled as being defined by "masculinity . . . and the rigidity of what was left of the old Army system."[13] The point to be made is that if the NPS is ever to serve Americans equally, and without prejudice, it will have to do much more than add an interpretive theme here or consult more historians there. It will, rather, have to undertake a deep foundational restructuring that compels each of its units to take their administrative histories seriously. In recent years, commentators have rightly decried the assault on federal agencies put into motion by President Donald Trump. It is true that the NPS suffered during his administration. This study shows, however, that its problems long predate Trump. In Boston, it was the choice by agency leaders to bind up park planning with urban renewal that, ever since, has made it virtually impossible for the park to discern what its problems really are.

The impossibility of self-awareness, a problem that is endemic throughout the NPS, is itself a symptom of the agency's deep misunderstanding of history and its uses. That the NPS has a history problem is well known, a fact deeply documented by the *Imperiled Promise* report, jointly published in 2011 by the Organization of American Historians and the National Park Service. Among the report's key findings is that trained historians, where employed by the NPS, are mired in the endless compliance work mandated by the National Historic Preservation Act (NHPA) of 1966.[14] At the same time, and perhaps consequently, the agency's organizational schema lumps historians in with cultural resource specialists—the people who steward artifacts, buildings, and historical documents—rather than the interpreters who are in charge of communicating the significance of those resources to the visiting public. The administrative history of Boston National Historical Park perfectly illustrates this dynamic. Park leaders have always expected the work of history to be, first and foremost, the work of gathering data to support preservation priorities. And though NPS historians play important roles in developing museum content and exhibits at partner sites, the far more immediate challenge of talking with people about the Revolution and its legacies belongs entirely to interpretive staff. For the NPS in Boston, then, history is neither a process for inquiry, nor a tool for self-assessment. It is, rather, a mixed bag of data and narrative, two components manufactured on opposite ends of the shop and then distributed for assembly to whomever can afford a stroll along the Freedom Trail.

Grappling with the origins of the agency's history problem is critically important if the NPS is ever to change course. The case of Boston National Historical Park shows us that its roots run far deeper than the NHPA or, as the authors of *Imperiled Promise* recount, NPS Director George Hartzog's decision during the 1960s to insulate the public from "introverted, inarticulate" historians.[15] Indeed, in Boston, the agency's history problem was already fully formed by 1938, when NPS historian Edwin Small argued with Congressman John W. McCormack over Dorchester Heights' significance. This was not an argument about what stories to tell about the past or how to tell them. That Small quibbled over the monument's relevance to Boston's Revolutionary story shows us that the rough outlines of that story and its terms had, in fact, already been set. This was, rather, an argument over real estate, a disagreement about which places the federal government should invest its money in, toward turning the greatest mnemonic returns. It was, in other words, an argument about preservation.

The agency's history problem has always been its commitment to historic preservation. This is a jarring claim, perhaps, and hard medicine, no doubt, for the brilliant corps of preservation professionals who make up much of the agency's history trade. And yet, despite recent arguments that historic preservation is nearing a critical turn, the history of Boston National Historical Park makes quite clear why organizing a park around buildings and profit rather than, say, people, has a deeply deleterious effect on how Americans learn about the past.[16] We've seen, for instance, how the group of buildings selected for this park were effectively preselected for it by a lone white man, Edwin Small, whose ideas about the past had been formatively shaped by a previous generation of privileged colonial revivalists and the economic logic of urban renewal. Small's belief in saving the "significant" bits of history, and demolishing whatever else might better serve as a parking lot, repeated within the agency's preservation ethos retrograde ideas about gender, race, ethnicity, and class. The Boston National Historic Sites Commission, whose members had real financial stakes in expanding Boston's tourism economy, rubber-stamped Small's list, thereby legitimizing his vision, naturalizing the Freedom Trail's claims to historical authority, and once again binding history to profit. Congress made it law in the park's authorizing legislation. In Boston, therefore, the NHPA ends up requiring that staff continually protect, manage, and defend the rationale underlying a set of architectural resources that are fundamentally bound up with white privilege. Their work legitimizes the trail, the trail legitimizes their work, and so it goes in an endless cycle of self-referentiality. Smart interpretation and creative programming can draw attention to this unfortunate fact, but can it ever change it? Can it really break the cycle? Can it ever, as Blatt hoped, "counter the approach that sells history as yet another commodity."

Congress's insistence that the NPS also preserve buildings associated with the Charlestown Navy Yard created such a burden for this predictably underfunded park, that the day-to-day rhythms of the site—building maintenance, compliance routines, personnel management, and keeping visitors safe and content—stifle virtually all incentive to interrogate the historical legitimacy of the park's core narratives. Despite the best efforts of an impressive series of committed park historians, we've seen how one superintendent kept the entire park afloat during the 1990s precisely by exploiting the fundraising potential of Revolutionary memory. His was the same strategy used by the South Boston Neighbors Association, back in 1938, to keep Black people out of South Boston. It was the same strategy William Schofield's Freedom Trail relied on to keep white suburban tourists away from Revere Beach and the

North End's "salami counters." And it was the same strategy that allowed the NPS to excise from its historical vision the atrocious acts of violence perpetrated by white people on Black people along the Freedom Trail during the 1970s and since. The case of Boston National Historical Park shows us that preservation, even when couched in progressive commitments to community engagement, deploys ideas about memory and profit that necessarily privilege whiteness. When preservation thus becomes the goal of preservation, ideology is the inevitable result, and in Boston that ideology has always been tinged with white supremacy.

Boston is only one park, of course, but it is one of many that the NPS is fond of calling "America's greatest classroom." How, then, can we move the lessons taught in these classrooms beyond the ideologies bound up in preservation and profit? As I write this, Americans are pulling down monuments all over the country because they understand that the statues and obelisks and other contrivances of patriotic memory long funded by this nation's monied elite have for too long done the remembering for us. And that legacy is often evident in national parks. Here in Philadelphia's Center City and adjacent neighborhoods, for instance, where the demolition of historic buildings by private developers runs amok, and even despite its designation in 2016 as the nation's first World Heritage City, preservation only seems to count in wealthy white neighborhoods like Society Hill that abut Independence National Historical Park.[17] The good news is that people everywhere are insisting on new directions. Back in Boston, even as I pen this conclusion, the Boston Art Commission has voted to remove from Park Square a replica of Thomas Ball's 1876 "The Emancipation Group," a sculptural portrayal of a freedman kneeling before Abraham Lincoln.[18] These people have rejected an old vein of monumental memory that obscures the efforts by Black people to secure freedom. They have rejected memory, and now seek an encounter with history. But can the NPS deliver it? What will the agency have left when the monuments are gone? Are we really lost without the Freedom Trail?

I don't think so. In fact, I contend that only by stepping away from the trail can we begin to do good public history in Boston. This book is a starting point for those who are willing. Boston National Historical Park is an ideal setting in which to explore the histories of Cold War America, urban renewal, race and power, capitalism, and the politics of memory. It is a park wherein the resources are infinitely better suited to exploring the nation's last hundred years then its first. And it is a park for which the enabling legislation was so loosely phrased as to encompass all of these topics and more. Some will contend that a park's mission is not simply defined by its authorizing legislation, but also by Congress's intent. As Paul Weinbaum puts it, you "can't create wholesale."[19] As the park's administrative history shows us, however, Congress's intent in Boston had little to do with the Revolution and everything to do with creating jobs, fighting Communism, promoting patriotic nationalism, and intervening in a failed postindustrial economy. All of those themes are ripe for interpretive treatment. Others will contend that, congressional intent notwithstanding, the park is nonetheless bound to serve a public fascinated by Revolutionary memory. Public service, however, does not equate to choosing one public over another. Americans who topple monuments or who demand that Faneuil Hall's name be changed or who insist on a living wage for tour guides, or who have been deprived of any voice at all in the nation's heritage debates, are equal stakeholders with those who buy souvenirs along the Freedom Trail. It has become easy to forget, since the days of Secretary James Watt's tryst with private capital a generation ago, that customer service need not be the prevailing logic of history making in the national parks. It's a realization that will only take hold in Boston once the Freedom Trail becomes the subject of interpretation rather than its rationale.

The NPS will not make that change, however, on its own. As we've seen, the park's preservation ethos and its embeddedness in the flow of heritage capital keeps Revolutionary memory perpetually intact. Rerouting the Freedom Trail, as it were, will take considerable encouragement from beyond the agency. Activists have begun the campaign in Boston. They need support, however, from historians elsewhere. Certainly, more than a few professional historians, including myself, have served on advisory committees and review panels for the NPS. Our tendency, however, encouraged by the networks of capital and privilege that inhere in our own professional world, is to perform expertise, to narrate knowledge with the expectation that agency staff will somehow implement it in toto. But if we are to have any impact at all—if we are, that is, to regain control of the agenda—we must work together with our federal colleagues outside the structures of privilege that, within both of our organizations, exist primarily to aggregate wealth. We must stop thinking that there is a meaningful difference between history done within and beyond academia. And we must find ways to work outside the myriad funding mechanisms that continually pull history making back into a bottomless pit of whiteness.[20] We must, in short, reconceptualize the work of professional history. Choosing not to will leave us, no matter who or where we are, lost on the Freedom Trail.

NOTES

ABBREVIATIONS

BNHP   Boston National Historical Park
BNHSC   Boston National Historic Sites Commission
BRA   Boston Redevelopment Authority
CRM   Cultural Resources Management
MDA   Metropolitan District Commission
MIMA   Minute Man National Historical Park
NARA   National Archives and Records Administration
NHP   National Historical Park
NRIS   National Register Information System

PREFACE

1   See Seth C. Bruggeman, *Here, George Washington Was Born: Memory, Material Culture, and the Public History of a National Monument* (Athens: University of Georgia Press, 2008).
2   Anne Mitchell Whisnant, Marla R. Miller, Gary B. Nash, and David Paul Thelen, *Imperiled Promise: The State of History in the National Park Service* (Bloomington, IN: Organization of American Historians, 2011).
3   Chatelain was the agency's first chief historian. For a discussion of his vision, see the prologue to Denise Meringolo, *Museums, Monuments, and National Parks: Toward a New Genealogy of Public History* (Amherst and Boston: University of Massachusetts Press, 2012).

INTRODUCTION: LOST ON THE FREEDOM TRAIL

1   The many others who've repeated this ritual include other academics, like myself, who rely on first-person accounts of the trail to introduce book chapters. See, for instance, Augusto Ferraiuolo, *Religious Festive Practices in Boston's North End: Ephemeral Identities in an Italian American Community* (Albany: State University of New York Press, 2009), 1–2.
2   Freedom Trail Foundation, "The Freedom Trail 2017 Official Brochure" (2017), author's personal collection.
3   Annette Miae Kim, *Sidewalk City: Remapping Public Space in Ho Chi Minh City* (Chicago: University of Chicago Press, 2015), 199. Kim provides a lengthy analysis of the Freedom Trail and its appeals on 199–220. Thanks to Gary Scales for this reference.
4   My account of this episode appears in Seth C. Bruggeman, *Here, George Washington Was Born: Memory, Material Culture, and the Public History of a National Monument* (Athens: University of Georgia Press, 2008), 5.
5   On the agency's internal funding woes, see Laura B. Comay, "National Park Service Appropriations: Ten-Year Trends" (Congressional Research Service, R42757, July 2, 2019). On its maintenance backlog, see, for instance, Josh Hicks, "National Park Service Delayed $11 Billion in Maintenance Last Year Because of Budget Challenges," *Washington Post* (March 25, 2015). Long-term declines in public funding for cultural organizations are well documented by numerous reporting agencies. See, for instance, Ryan Stubbs and Patricia Mullaney-Loss, "Public Funding for the Arts, 2019," *GIA Reader* 31, no. 1 (Winter 2020).
6   Regarding the agency's contradictory mandate, see Robin W. Winks, "The National Park Service Act of 1916: 'A Contradictory Mandate'?" *Denver University Law Review* 74 (1997): 575–624. Writing on the fraught relationship between public and private interests in national parks dates back to foundational treatises by John Muir and Frederick Law Olmstead. Scholarly treatments have expanded the analysis to show how the NPS has always been embedded in profiteering, genocide, imperialism, and other facets of American failure. Representative

examples include Alfred Runte, *National Parks: The American Experience* (Lincoln: University of Nebraska Press, 1987); Richard West Sellers, *Preserving Nature in the National Parks: A History* (New Haven: Yale University Press, 1997); Thomas Patin, "Exhibitions and Empire: National Parks and the Performance of Manifest Destiny," *Journal of American Culture* 22, no. 1 (Spring 1999): 41–60; Mark David Spence, *Dispossessing the Wilderness: Indian Removal and the Making of National Parks* (New York: Oxford University Press, 1999); and Ari Kelman, *A Misplaced Massacre: Struggling over the Memory of Sand Creek* (Cambridge: Harvard University Press, 2013). For an overview of nationalism and its problematic expressions in the agency's history program, see John Bodnar, *Remaking America: Public Memory, Commemoration, and Patriotism in the Twentieth Century* (Princeton: Princeton University Press, 1992), 169–205.

7   See Charlene Mires, *Independence Hall in American Memory* (Philadelphia: University of Pennsylvania Press, 2002); Hal Rothman, *The New Urban Park: Golden Gate National Recreation Area and Civic Environmentalism* (Lawrence: University Press of Kansas, 2004); and Cathy Stanton, *The Lowell Experiment: Public History in a Postindustrial City* (Amherst: University of Massachusetts Press, 2006).

8   Denis Galvin, then NPS deputy director, quoted in David Foster, "'Park Barrel' Politics Seen as Redefining 75-Year-Old National System," *Los Angeles Times* (October 13, 1991).

9   For an overview of the national heritage area concept and its history, see Alan W. Barton, "From Parks to Partnerships: National Heritage Areas and the Path to Collaborative Participation in the National Park Service's First 100 Years," *Natural Resources Journal* 56 (Winter 2016): 23–54; and Brenda Barrett and Eleanor Mahoney, "National Heritage Areas: Learning from 30 Years of Working to Scale," *George Wright Forum* 33, no. 2 (2016): 163–74.

10   Amy Tyson, *The Wages of History: Emotional Labor on Public History's Front Lines* (Amherst: University of Massachusetts Press, 2013); and Stanton, *The Lowell Experiment.*

11   For an account of labor organizing in public history trades over time, see Allana Shaffer, "From the Frontline to the Picket Line: Public History and the Cultural Labor Revolution" (MA thesis, Temple University, 2020).

12   For visitor statistics, see the variety of reports available at National Park Service. "Boston NHP (BOST) Reports." NPS Stats: National Park Service Visitor Use Statistics, https:// irma.nps.gov/STATS/Reports/Park/BOST. For a superb overview of the park's structure, its significance, and the history of its contributing resources, see BNHP, National Register of Historic Places Nomination, NRIS 15000195 (2014).

13   Consider, for instance, Kelman, *A Misplaced Massacre.*

14   See, for instance, Joan M. Zenzen, "Why Administrative Histories Matter," *Public Historian* 38, no. 4 (November 2016): 236–63.

15   Some key points of access into this conversation include John C. Teaford, *The Rough Road to Renaissance: Urban Revitalization in America, 1940–1985* (Baltimore: Johns Hopkins University Press, 1990); Eric Avila and Mark H. Rose, "Race, Culture, Politics, and Urban Renewal: An Introduction," *Journal of Urban History* 35 (2009): 335–47; and Alexander von Hoffman, "The Lost History of Urban Renewal," *Journal of Urbanism* 1 (2008): 281–301. For a broad overview, see Ann Pfaul, David Hochfelder, and Stacy Sewell, "Urban Renewal," in *The Inclusive Historian's Handbook,* https://inclusivehistorian.com/urban-renewal/. For a useful discussion of inter-sections between heritage tourism and urban renewal in cities with important parallels to Boston, see Aaron Cowan, *A Nice Place to Visit: Tourism and Urban Revitalization in the Postwar Rustbelt* (Philadelphia: Temple University Press, 2016), especially the introduction and ch. 1.

16   Erica C. Avrami, "Preservation's Reckoning," in Avrami, ed., *Preservation and Social Inclusion* (New York: Columbia University Press, 2020), Online eReader edition, https://www.arch.columbia. edu/books/reader/503-preservation-and-social-inclusion#reader-anchor-23. For examples of histories of preservation in other American cities, see Randall F. Mason, *The Once and Future New York: Historic Preservation and the Modern City* (Minneapolis: University of Minnesota Press, 2009); Stephanie R. Ryberg, "Historic Preservation's Urban Renewal Roots: Preservation

and Planning in Midcentury Philadelphia," *Journal of Urban History* 39, no. 2 (2012): 193–213; and Stephanie E. Yuhl, *A Golden Haze of Memory: The Making of Historic Charleston* (Chapel Hill: University of North Carolina Press, 2005). For additional context on preservation in American cities, as well as insight concerning the interplay of preservation and economic development, see Randall F. Mason and Max Page, *Giving Preservation a History: Histories of Historic Preservation in the United States* (New York: Routledge, 2003). Preservation's reckoning, as it were, has already prompted several rejoinders, including Marla Miller and Max Page, *Bending the Future: Fifty Ideas for the Next Fifty Years of Historic Preservation in the United States* (Amherst: University of Massachusetts Press, 2016); Stephanie Meeks, *The Past and Future City: How Historic Preservation is Reviving America's Communities* (Washington, DC: Island Press, 2016); and Max Page, *Why Preservation Matters* (New Haven: Yale University Press, 2016).

17 In this way, my understanding of whiteness aligns with the Smithsonian Institution's National Museum of African American History's position, which is explained at *Talking About Race,* https://nmaahc.si.edu/learn/talking-about-race/topics/whiteness. Other works that have shaped my understanding of whiteness include Ta-Nehisi Coates, *Between the World and Me: Notes on the First 150 Years in America* (New York: Spiegel & Grau, 2015); George Lipsitz, *The Possessive Investment in Whiteness: How White People Profit from Identity Politics* (Philadelphia: Temple University Press, 1998); and David R. Roediger, *The Wages of Whiteness: Race and the Making of the American Working Class* (New York: Verso, 2007).

18 Joan Zenzen, for instance, considers the administrative history of Wolf Trap National Park toward showing how the NPS has sought over time to prevent researchers from exploring histories that might embarrass the agency. See Zenzen, "Why Administrative Histories Matter," 248–52. In recent years, the agency has visibly struggled with its willingness to publicly contend with chronic gender discrimination and sexual harassment within its own ranks. See Lyndsey Gilpin, "The National Park Service Has a Big Sexual Harassment Problem," *Atlantic* (December 15, 2016), https://www.theatlantic.com/science/archive/2016/12/park-service-harassment/510680/.

19 Examples include Karilyn Crockett, *People before Highways: Boston Activists, Urban Planners, and a New Movement for City Making* (Amherst: University of Massachusetts Press, 2018); Nick Estes, *Our History Is the Future: Standing Rock versus the Dakota Access Pipeline, and the Long Tradition of Indigenous Resistance* (New York: Verso, 2019); Michael Liu, *Forever Struggle: Activism, Identity, and Survival in Boston's Chinatown, 1880–2018* (Amherst: University of Massachusetts Press, 2020); Brandi Thompson Summers, *Black in Place: The Spatial Aesthetics of Race in a Post-Chocolate City* (Chapel Hill: University of North Carolina Press, 2019); and Coll Thrush, *Native Seattle: Histories from the Crossing-Over Place* (Seattle: University of Washington Press, 2008).

20 Lizabeth Cohen describes media portrayals of Logue in *Saving America's Cities: Ed Logue and the Struggle to Renew Urban America in the Suburban Age* (New York: Farrar, Straus, and Giroux, 2019), 149.

CHAPTER 1: REMEMBERING THE REVOLUTION IN OLD AND NEW BOSTON

1   Boston National Historical Park Act of 1974, Pub. Law 93–431, Oct. 1, 1974, 88 Stat. 1184.

2   For another treatment of the park's early commemorative history, with particular attention to its monuments, see BNHP, National Register of Historic Places Nomination, NRIS 15000195 (2014), 108–33.

3   Scholarly accounts of these instances are prevalent. See, for instance, Bob Gross, "Commemorating Concord," *Common-Place* 4, no. 1 (October 2003), http://www.common-place-archives.org /vol-04/no-01/gross/index.shtml; David Waldstreicher, *In the Midst of Perpetual Fetes: The Making of American Nationalism, 1776–1820* (Chapel Hill: University of North Carolina Press, 1997), especially ch. 1; Simon P. Newman, *Parades and the Politics of the Streets: Festive Culture in the Early American Republic* (Philadelphia: University of Pennsylvania Press, 1997); and Joseph Ellis, *His Excellency: George Washington* (New York: Vintage, 2004), 150.

4   Michael A. McDonnell, "War and Nationhood: Founding Myths and Historical Realities," in *Remembering the Revolution: Memory, History, and Nation Making from Independence to the Civil War,* ed.

Michael McDonnell, Clare Corbould, Frances M. Clarke, and W. Fitzhugh Brundage (Amherst: University of Massachusetts Press, 2013), 21, 34.

5   Karsten Fitz, "Commemorating Crispus Attucks: Visual Memory and the Representations of the Boston Massacre, 1770–1857," *Amerikastudien / American Studies* 50, no. 3 (2005): 468. See also, Mitch Kachun, "From Forgotten Founder to Indispensable Icon: Crispus Attucks, Black Citizenship, and Collective Memory, 1770–1865," *Journal of the Early Republic* 29, no. 2 (2009): 249–86; and Stephen Kantrowitz, "A Place for 'Colored Patriots': Crispus Attucks among the Abolitionists, 1842–1863," *Massachusetts Historical Review* 11 (2009): 96–117.

6   Jason Shaffer, "Making 'An Excellent Die': Death, Mourning, and Patriotism in the Propaganda Plays of the American Revolution," *Early American Literature* 41, no. 1 (2006): 7.

7   Alfred F. Young, *The Shoemaker and the Tea Party: Memory and the American Revolution* (Boston: Beacon Press, 2000), 113–16.

8   Recent years have witnessed an outpouring of scholarship concerning memory and nationalism during and shortly after the American Revolution. Representative works, from which much of this section draws, include Michael G. Kammen, *A Season of Youth: The American Revolution and the Historical Imaginative* (Cornell: Cornell University Press, 1988); Sarah J. Purcell, *Sealed with Blood: War, Sacrifice, and Memory in Revolutionary America* (Philadelphia: University of Pennsylvania Press, 2002); Waldstreicher, *In the Midst of Perpetual Fetes;* Lee Travers, *Celebrating the Fourth: Independence Day and the Rites of Nationalism in the Early Republic* (Amherst: University of Massachusetts Press, 1997); G. Kurt Piehler, *Remembering War the American Way* (Washington: Smithsonian Institution, 1995), especially ch. 1; H. G. Jones, ed., *Historical Consciousness in the Early Republic: The Origins of State Historical Societies, Museums, and Collections, 1791–1861* (Chapel Hill: North Caroliniana Society and North Carolina Collection, 1995); and McDonnell, et al., *Remembering the Revolution.* On the purposes Revolutionary memory is put to today, see Andrew M. Schocket, *Fighting over the Founders: How We Remember the American Revolution* (New York: New York University Press, 2015).

9   Construction on Washington's monument in Baltimore began in 1815.

10 On early commemorative architecture associated with George Washington, see Seth C. Bruggeman, *"Here, George Washington Was Born": Memory, Material Culture, and the Public History of a National Monument* (Athens: University of Georgia Press, 2008), ch. 1. Custis is profiled in Bruggeman, "More than Ordinary Patriotism: Living History in the Memory Work of George Washington Parke Custis," in McDonnell, et al., *Remembering the Revolution,* 127–43.

11 Whitney A. Martinko, "Progress and Preservation: Representing History in Boston's Landscape of Urban Reform, 1820–1860," *New England Quarterly* 82, no. 2 (June 2009): 310–11.

12 Mishaps and missteps delayed its completion until 1842. See Young, *The Shoemaker and the Tea Party,* 113–16.

13 Fay Campbell Kaynor, "The Province House and the Preservation Movement," *Old-Time New England* 74, no. 262 (Fall 1996), 5–31; and Abbott Lowell Cummings, "The Old Feather Store in Boston," *Old-Time New England* 48, no. 4 (1958): 85–104.

14 See, for instance, John Seelye, *Memory's Nation: The Place of Plymouth Rock* (Chapel Hill: University of North Carolina Press, 1998). On Mather specifically, see William Van Arragon, "Cotton Mather in American Cultural Memory, 1728–1892" (PhD diss., Indiana University, 2006). Van Arragon shows, for instance, on 184–85, how the site of Mather's home in North Square figured for some as a kind of commemorative space.

15 Edward Tang, "Writing the American Revolution: War Veterans in the Nineteenth-Century Cultural Memory," *Journal of American Studies* 32, no. 1 (1998): 63–80.

16 See, for instance, Keith Beutler, "Emma Willard's 'True Mnemonic of History': America's First Textbooks, Proto-Feminism, and the Memory of the Revolution," in McDonnell et al., *Remembering the Revolution,* 169. A great deal has been written about Lafayette and nineteenth-century reliquary sensibilities. See, for instance, Thomas A. Chambers, *Memories of War: Visiting Battlegrounds and Bonefields in the Early American Republic* (Ithaca: Cornell University Press, 2012), ch. 3.

17 On these counts, see William Hunting Howell, "'Starving Memory': Antinarrating the American Revolution," 93–109; and Caroline Cox, "The First Greatest Generation Remembers the Revolutionary War," 110–26; both in McDonnell, et al., *Remembering the Revolution.*

18 Michael McDonnell, Clare Corbould, Frances M. Clarke, and W. Fitzhugh Brundage, "The Revolution in American Life from 1776 to the Civil War," in McDonnell, et al., *Remembering the Revolution,* 2.

19 Richard S. Newman, *The Transformation of American Abolitionism: Fighting Slavery in the Early Republic* (Chapel Hill: University of North Carolina Press, 2002).

20 Martinko, "Progress and Preservation," 308–10.

21 For this argument, specifically, see Whitney A. Martinko, "Byles versus Boston: Historic Houses, Urban Development, and the Public Good in an Improving City," *Massachusetts Historical Review* 18 (2016): 119–52.

22 See Young, *The Shoemaker and the Tea Party.* The quote is from Young, "Revolution in Boston? Eight Propositions for Public History on the Freedom Trail," *Public Historian* 25, no. 2 (Spring 2003): 30.

23 It is worth noting, though, that how white abolitionists and Black abolitionists preferred to remember race and the Revolution differed significantly. See Margot Minardi, *Making Slavery History: Abolitionism and the Politics of Memory in Massachusetts* (New York: Oxford University Press, 2012), ch. 4 and 5.

24 Donald M. Jacobs, *Courage and Conscience: Black and White Abolitionists in Boston* (Bloomington: Indiana University Press, 1993), 120.

25 Robert Pinsky observed that Senator Edward Kennedy had memorized portions of the poem. See Robert Pinsky, "Poetry and American Memory," *Atlantic* (October 1999): 60.

26 Revere had earned some notoriety in Boston by the middle of the nineteenth century. In 1851, for instance, May Street was renamed Revere Street. Outside of New England, however, Revere barely figured at all in Americans' memory of the Revolution. David Hacket Fischer, *Paul Revere's Ride* (New York: Oxford University Press, 1994), 331.

27 Several scholars have explored the poem's long-unrecognized abolitionist intent, including Jill Lepore, "How Longfellow Woke the Dead," *American Scholar* 80, no. 2 (Spring 2011): 33–46. Lepore further considers the role of Revolutionary memory in recent politics in *The Whites of Their Eyes: The Tea Party's Revolution and the Battle over American History* (Princeton: Princeton University Press, 2010). See also, Kammen, *A Season of Youth,* ch. 4; and Evert Jan van Leeuwen, "The Graveyard Aesthetics of Revolutionary Elegiac Verse: Remembering the Revolution as a Sacred Cause," in McDonnell, et al., *Remembering the Revolution,* 75–76.

28 This brief account draws on much more extensive engagements with the Bunker Hill story, including Minardi, *Making Slavery History,* ch. 3; and Purcell, *Sealed with Blood,* ch. 5. For a detailed recounting of the monument's construction, see BNHP, National Register of Historic Places Nomination, NRIS 15000195, 112–27.

29 Hale's involvement resulted in a massive public subscription movement that leveraged the unique fundraising power of women's organizations. It also included a women's fair at Faneuil Hall, which anticipated the sanitary fairs that, decades later, would raise support for the Union Army, often in ways tied to historical themes. On the Faneuil Hall women's fair, see Polly Kienle, "The Bunker Hill Monument Fair of September 1840," https://www.nps.gov /articles/bunker-hill-monument-fair.htm; and Abby Goodnough, "Bunker Hill Monument, Championing an Unsung Hero," *New York Times* (July 4, 2010).

30 "Revolutionary Battle Monument Movement, 1823–1890," extracted on June 29, 2011, from Saratoga National Historical Park Historic District National Register Documentation draft, prepared by Public Archeology Laboratory, Inc. for the National Park Service, Northeast Region, n.p.

31 Minardi, *Making Slavery History,* ch. 3.

32 On the historiography of the Revolution, see Michael A. McDonnell and David Waldstreicher, "Revolution in the Quarterly? A Historiographical Analysis," *William and Mary Quarterly* 74, no. 4

(October 2017): 633–66. On Bancroft and plagiarism, see Eileen Ka-May Cheng, "Plagiarism in Pursuit of Historical Truth: George Chalmers and the Patriotic Legacy of Loyalist History," in McDonald, et al., *Remembering the Revolution, 144–61.*

33   Colonial revival scholarship is voluminous. The most recent overview appears in Richard Guy Wilson and Shaun Eyring, eds., *Re-creating the American Past: Essays on the Colonial Revival* (Charlottesville: University of Virginia Press, 2006). For an overview of colonial revivalism and historic preservation in Boston at the turn of the twentieth century, see BNHP, National Register of Historic Places Nomination, NRIS 15000195, 133–37.

34   On Wallace Nutting's aggressive promotion of the colonial revival sensibility, see William L. Dulaney, "Wallace Nutting: Collector and Entrepreneur," *Winterthur Portfolio* 13 (1979): 47–60.

35   For a broad overview, see Karal Ann Marling, *George Washington Slept Here: Colonial Revivals and American Culture, 1876–1986* (Cambridge: Harvard University Press, 1988). On the transformation of colonial revival sensibilities into a twentieth-century antique consumer industry, see Briann G. Greenfield, *Out of the Attic: Inventing Antiques in Twentieth-Century New England* (Amherst: University of Massachusetts Press, 2009).

36   Craig Bruce Smith, "Claiming the Centennial: The American Revolution's Blood and Spirit in Boston, 1870–1876," *Massachusetts Historical Review* 15 (2013): 7–53.

37   See Martinko, "Byles versus Boston." Martinko develops this argument more fully across the early national American experience, and in view of its embeddedness in capitalism, in *Historic Real Estate: Market Morality and the Politics of Preservation in the Early United States* (Philadelphia: University of Pennsylvania Press, 2021).

38   Michael Holleran, "Roots in Boston, Branches in Planning and Parks," in *Giving Preservation a History: Histories of Historic Preservation in the United States, ed.* Max Page and Randall Mason (New York: Routledge, 2004), 83.

39   The history of historic preservation in Boston has been recounted frequently, including by Michael Holleran, *Boston's "Changeful Times": Origins of Preservation and Planning in America* (Baltimore: Johns Hopkins University Press, 1998), especially ch. 9; Charles B. Hosmer Jr., *Preservation Comes of Age: From Williamsburg to the National Trust, 1926–1949* (Charlottesville: University Press of Virginia, 1981), wherein Appleton and his activities are showcased in chapter three; and throughout James M. Lindgren, *Preserving Historic New England: Preservation, Progressivism, and the Remaking of Memory* (New York: Oxford University Press, 1995). Walter Muir Whitehill worked diligently to make postwar preservationists, including the NPS, aware of Boston's preservation past. See, for instance, Whitehill, "Neglected Assets," a talk delivered at the fourth Citizens Seminar on the Fiscal, Economic, and Political Problems of Boston and the Metropolitan Community, Boston College, February 26, 1963, Folder: Historic Sites Committee, Box 148, Mayor John F. Collins Papers, Boston City Archives, West Roxbury, MA. This story also appears throughout BNHP, National Register of Historic Places Nomination, NRIS 15000195; Revere's story appears specifically 103–8.

40   Lodge's remarks are reprinted in *A Record of the Dedication of the Monument on Dorchester Heights, South Boston, Built by the Commonwealth as a Memorial of the Evacuation of Boston, March 17, 1776, by the British Troops* (Boston: Wright and Potter Printing Company, 1903).

41   Holleran, *Boston's Changeful Times,* 165.

42   Quoted in Holleran, *Boston's Changeful Times,* 264.

43   For an overview of Beacon Hill and zoning, see Holleran, *Boston's Changeful Times,* 262–67. On the proliferation more broadly of downtown land-use zoning policy during these years, see Alison Isenberg, *Downtown America: A History of the Place and the People Who Made It* (Chicago: University of Chicago Press, 2004), 101–7.

44   See, for instance, Seth C. Bruggeman, "'A Most Complete Whaling Museum': Profiting from the Past on Nantucket Island," *Museum History Journal* 8, no. 2 (2015): 188–208. On Shurcliff, especially, and the commodification of authenticity generally, see Stuart Hobbes, "Exhibiting Antimodernism: History, Memory, and the Aestheticized Past in Mid-Twentieth-Century America," *Public Historian* 23, no. 3 (2001): 39–61.

45   See, for instance, Laurence F. Gross, *The Course of Industrial Decline: The Boott Cotton Mills of Lowell, Massachusetts, 1835–1955* (Baltimore: Johns Hopkins University Press, 1993).

46   *Boston Sunday Globe*, September 22, 1985, quoted in Thomas H. O'Connor, *Building a New Boston: Politics and Urban Renewal, 1950 to 1970* (Boston: Northeastern University Press, 1995), 72.

47   O'Connor, *Building a New Boston*, 18–19. Boston's struggles during the 1920s and 1930s are detailed on pages 3–19.

48   Edwin Small quoted in "Dorchester Heights," NPS Cultural Resources Management Bibliography (CRBIB) #015856, September 29, 1938, 3–5.

49   For an overview of these transformations, see Harlan D. Unrau and G. Rank Williss, "Expansion of the National Park Service in the 1930s: Administrative History," https://www.nps.gov/parkhistory/online_books/unrau-williss/adhi.htm, ch. 2; and Denise D. Meringolo, *Museums, Monuments, and National Parks: Toward a New Genealogy of Public History* (Amherst: University of Massachusetts Press, 2012), 110–15.

50   Tracy Campbell, *The Gateway Arch: A Biography* (New Haven: Yale University Press, 2013), 40. Campbell details this episode throughout chapter two. The agency's partnership in St. Louis is also discussed in Eric Sandweiss, *St. Louis: The Evolution of an American Landscape* (Philadelphia: Temple University Press, 2001), 233.

51   Pondering the scale of damage done by demolition in and around Independence Mall is a preoccupation among people concerned with Philadelphia pasts. Consider, for instance, Tommy Rowan, "How Independence Park Brought Drama from the Start," *Philadelphia Inquirer* (April 19, 2021); and Dennis Carlisle, "An Architectural Graveyard at Independence Mall," *Hidden City* (December 12, 2016), https://hiddencityphila.org/2016/12/an-architectural-graveyard-at-independence-mall/.

52   See Charlene Mires, *Independence Hall in American Memory* (Philadelphia: University of Pennsylvania Press, 2013), ch. 7; Pauline Chase-Harrell, Carol Ely, and Stanley Moss, *Administrative History of the Salem Maritime National Historic Site* (Boston: NPS North Atlantic Regional Office, 1993); and, for more on Salem, Hosmer, *Preservation Comes of Age*, ch. 8.

53   Bruggeman, *Here, George Washington Was Born*, 10–11.

54   On Chatelain's vision and his relationship with Peterson, see Meringolo, *Museums, Monuments, and National Parks*, 99–108. Regarding the history program's aggressive expansion during these years and its commitment to patriotic nationalism, see John Bodnar, *Remaking America: Public Memory, Commemoration, and Patriotism in the Twentieth Century* (Princeton: Princeton University Press, 1992), 175–79.

55   Small was born in 1907 in Goshen, Connecticut, and took his BA (1930) and MA (1934) in history from Yale University, where he wrote a thesis concerning the development of the Adirondack Forest Preserve.

56   S. Herbert Evison, Oral History Interview of Edwin W. Small, October 19, 1971, Transcript 388, Subseries B: Interview Transcripts, 1938–1978, Series II: S. Herbert Evison's National Park Service Oral History Project, 1952–1999, NPS Oral History Collection, 1937–2017, NPS History Collection, Harpers Ferry Center for Media Development, Harpers Ferry, WV, 3–4. See also, Joan Zenzen, *Bridging the Past: An Administrative History of Minute Man National Historical Park* (Boston: NPS Northeast Region History Program, 2010), 35. Meringolo discusses Lee and others among Chatelain's nascent history corps in *Museums, Monuments, and National Parks*, 112–15.

57   Chase-Harrell, et al., *Administrative History of the Salem Maritime National Historic Site*, 4. Hosmer discusses the very first NPS historic site—the Old Courthouse associated with the Jefferson National Expansion Memorial—and generally the implementation of the Historic Sites Act in *Preservation Comes of Age*, ch. 8.

58   Hosmer quoted in Chase-Harrell, et al., *Administrative History of the Salem Maritime National Historic Site*, 7.

59   This is summarized in Chase-Harrell, et al., *Administrative History of the Salem Maritime National Historic Site*, 7–11.

60   Hosmer, *Preservation Comes of Age*, 175.

61 On Crowninshield's role at George Washington's Birthplace National Monument, see Bruggeman, *Here, George Washington Was Born*, especially ch. 4.

62 Small cited in Chase-Harrell, et al., *Administrative History of the Salem Maritime National Historic Site*, 10.

63 Small cited in Chase-Harrell, et al., *Administrative History of the Salem Maritime National Historic Site*, 97. Barnette's role is described throughout, including on page 17.

64 McCormack biographer, Garrison Nelson, suggests that McCormack's nephew and his chief of staff "sanitized" the files. See Nelson, *John William McCormack: A Political Biography* (New York: Bloomsbury Academic, 2017), 5–6.

65 Consider that, at the same time he was working to win federal protection for Dorchester Heights, McCormack was also preparing to sponsor the Alien Registration Act of 1940, also known as the Smith Act, which permitted surreptitious arrests by the FBI of suspected subversives in several American cities. My reading of McCormack's politics follows Lester Ira Gordon, "John McCormack and the Roosevelt Era" (PhD diss., Boston University Graduate School, 1976); and Nelson, *John William McCormack*, ch. 6–9.

66 Nelson, *John William McCormack*, 59.

67 Anthony Bak Buccitelli, "Remembering Our Town: Social Memory, Folklore, and (Trans) Locality in Three Ethnic Neighborhoods in Boston" (PhD diss., Boston University, 2012). Buccitelli covers the history of the parade on pages 227–31.

68 Secretary of the Commonwealth, *Acts and Resolves Passed by the General Court of Massachusetts in the Year 1938 Together with Tables Showing Changes in the Statues, Etc.* (Boston: Wright and Potter Printing Company, 1938), ch. 80, 54–55. The law remains today as Section 12K, Ch. 6, Title II, Part I of the Commonwealth of Massachusetts General Laws.

69 Thomas H. O'Connor, *South Boston, My Home Town: The History of an Ethnic Neighborhood* (Boston: Northeastern University Press, 1994), 124.

70 According to the South Boston Citizens' Association, the group coalesced in 1880 to "further the interests of the locality in which they resided." See the association's Facebook page, which serves as its primary website, https://www.facebook.com/pg/South-Boston -Citizens-Association-417334460199/about/?ref=page_internal.

71 "Plan for Memorial at Site of Evacuation Being Pushed," *Boston Globe* (July 23, 1937). Reports of McCormack's meetings with the SBCA and mayor's office appear in "Bishop Winner in South Boston," *Boston Globe* (November 13, 1937); and "South Boston," *Boston Globe* (January 20, 1938).

72 Federal Writers' Project of the Works Progress Administration of Massachusetts, *Massachusetts: A Guide to its Places and People* (Boston: Houghton Mifflin Company, 1937), 136.

73 Rheable M. Edwards and Laura B. Morris, "The Negro in Boston," report commissioned by the Action for Boston Community Development (1961), 11, 13.

74 "An Act Authorizing the City of Boston to Convey the Dorchester Heights Monument and Adjoining Land in the City of Boston to the United States of America for Preservation and Maintenance as a National Historic Monument," *1939 Massachusetts Acts*, v. 148 (April 21, 1939), 121–22.

75 See advisory board catalog cards scanned and shared by NPS Bureau Historian John Sprinkle. Relevant minutes include VIII, 2 (2), August 15–18, 1938; XI, 9 (21), November 7–9, 1939; XII, 10 (2), March 25–31, 1940; and XXIV, p. 14, April 26–27, 1951.

76 Shirley Place, the Longfellow House, the Old State House, King's Chapel, the Bunker Hill Monument, Concord Bridge and Lexington Green, Dorchester Heights, Old North Church, Faneuil Hall, and the Harrison Gray Otis House all made the list by 1947. National Park Service, "Proposed Areas Resumes" (1947), I-28, Park History Program, Washington, DC. Thanks to Bureau Historian John Sprinkle for providing digital copies of these materials. For a discussion of this process under the Historic Sites Act of 1935 and beyond, see Sprinkle, *Crafting Preservation Criteria: The National Register of Historic Places and American Historic Preservation* (New York: Routledge, 2014).

77 Jim Vrabel, *A People's History of the New Boston* (Amherst: University of Massachusetts Press, 2014), 9.

78 Although in many regards these initiatives did revitalize urban centers during the second half of the twentieth century, they also did irreparable harm—especially to those communities most vulnerable to the problems urban renewal sought to eliminate. Starting points for this conversation include Christopher Klemek, *The Transatlantic Collapse of Urban Renewal: Postwar Urbanism from New York to Berlin* (Chicago: University of Chicago Press, 2012); Thomas J. Sugrue, *The Origins of the Urban Crisis: Race and Inequality in Postwar Detroit* (Princeton: Princeton University Press, 1996); Jon C. Teaford, *The Rough Road to Renaissance: Urban Revitalization in America, 1940–1985* (Baltimore: Johns Hopkins University Press, 1990); and the essential Jane Jacobs, *The Death and Life of Great American Cities* (New York: Vintage, 1992, orig. 1961).

79 Lizabeth Cohen, *Saving America's Cities: Ed Logue and the Struggle to Renew Urban America in the Suburban Age* (New York: Farrar, Straus, and Giroux, 2019), 153–55.

80 O'Connor, *Building a New Boston*, ch. 3. For a visual survey of the project's impact on Boston, see Yanni K. Tsipis, *Boston's Central Artery* (Charleston, SC: Arcadia Publishing, 2001).

81 For overviews, see O'Connor, *Building a New Boston*, ch. 5; Herbert J. Gans, *The Urban Villagers: Group and Class in the Life of Italian-Americans* (New York: Free Press, 1962); and Cohen, *Saving America's Cities*, 150–60. On the South End specifically, see Langley Carleton Keyes Jr., *The Rehabilitation Planning Game: A Study in the Diversity of Neighborhood* (Cambridge, MA: MIT Press, 1969), ch. 3. Urban renewal displacement statistics are available at Digital Scholarship Lab, "Renewing Inequality," *American Panorama*, ed. Robert K. Nelson and Edward L. Ayers, https:// dsl.richmond.edu/panorama/renewal/#view=-4750.95/-816.65/6.87&viz=cartogram&cityview =holc&city=bostonMA&loc=16/42.3612/-71.0603.

82 The primacy of the Chamber of Commerce in Boston's renewal schemes supports Alison Isenbergs's observation that postwar downtown renewal pivoted on retail, though appeals specifically to women appear less frequently in Boston's renewal rhetoric than appeals to historicity. Isenberg, *Downtown America*, especially ch. 5.

83 A published version of Quincy's 1837 account appears as "Old Houses," *Southern Literary Messenger* 5, no. 12 (December 1839): 793–98, quotation 793. Martinko explores Quincy's account in "Byles versus Boston," 137–38.

84 "Ad Club Boosts 'Freedom Trail,'" *Boston Globe*, March 30, 1958.

85 Henry Moore, "Trudging over Hub's Historic Loop Makes Leisure Profitable," *Boston Herald*, December 9, 1934. Interestingly, although walking tours had been a fixture of that decade's popular WPA city guides series, Boston—unlike, say, Philadelphia—did not get its own guide. Instead, it was included as part of the Massachusetts state guide and lacked a map.

86 Winn "narrated" this tour in a pamphlet titled "A Guide at a Glance of Historic Boston," printed by Old Christ Church in 1947, https://archive.org/details/guideatglanceofhoowinn /mode/2up.

87 Moore, "Trudging over Hub's Historic Loop Makes Leisure Profitable."

88 There are no comprehensive histories of the Freedom Trail. What accounts do exist include Matthew Grief, "Freedom Trail Commission Report," BNHP (1995); Freedom Trail Foundation, "Freedom Trail Establishment," https://www.thefreedomtrail.org/about/freedom -trail-establishment; and Susan Wilson, "History Notebook: Inventing the Freedom Trail" (March 1996), https://www.thefreedomtrail.org/sites/default/files/content/PDFs/invent-ing_the_freedom_trail.pdf. Importantly, Schofield's newspaper was a leading advocate for urban renewal in Boston. It championed, for example, demolition of the South End's New York Streets neighborhood during 1952–1957, and then built its new headquarters in the "renewed" area. Vrabel, *A People's History of the New Boston*, 12, 47–49. Cohen mentions this also in *Saving America's Cities*, 158.

89 Bill Schofield, "Have You Heard: Hub Needs 'Liberty Loop,'" *Boston Evening Traveler*, March 8, 1951. This and others of Schofield's essays from the *Evening Traveler* are available in photocopy in Folder: Fr.Tr. Foundation, Box: Am Hist to Freedom Trail, Historian's Files, Division of

Cultural Resources, BNHP Archives, Charlestown, MA. The quotation "Swamp Yankee descendant" is from an interview with Schofield in Wilson, "History Notebook: Inventing the Freedom Trail."

90 Bill Schofield, "Have You Heard: Historian Seeks Giant North End Park," *Boston Evening Traveler*, March 13, 1951.

91 Bill Schofield, "Have You Heard: 'Freedom Way' Sign Idea Big Hit," *Boston Evening Traveler*, March 19, 1951.

92 Bill Schofield, "Have You Heard: 'Freedom Way' Sign Idea Big Hit."

93 On the challenges of commemorating Sacco and Vanzetti, see Stephanie E. Yuhl, "Sculpted Radicals: The Problem of Sacco and Vanzetti in Boston's Public Memory," *Public Historian* 32, no. 2 (2010): 9–30. See also, Richard Kreitner, "Anarchy in the BPL: A Little-Known Legacy of Mayor Menino," *Boston Globe*, November 23, 2014.

94 Robert F. Friedman to Governor John A. Volpe, October 13, 1966, Folder: Office Files: Department of Public Works, Freedom Trail Foundation, 1962–64, Box 80, John F. Collins Papers, Boston City Archives, West Roxbury, MA. BNHP revisited the possibility of interpreting the Liberty Tree during a symposium it hosted in 2007.

95 Daniel A. Gilbert, "'Why Dwell on a Lurid Memory?': Deviance and Redevelopment in Boston's Scollay Square," *Massachusetts Historical Review* 9 (2007): 103–33.

96 Bill Schofield, "Have You Heard: 'Freedom Way' Sign Idea Big Hit."

97 For more on Revere Beach, see Mark Allan Herlihy, "Leisure, Space, and Collective Memory in the 'Athens of America': A History of Boston's Revere Beach" (PhD diss., Brown University, 2000).

98 Bill Schofield, "Have You Heard: 'Freedom Way' Sign Idea Big Hit."

99 William G. Schofield, *Freedom by the Bay: The Boston Freedom Trail* (Chicago, New York, and San Francisco: Rand McNally & Company, 1974), 11.

100 Bill Schofield, "Have You Heard: Hub Will Go Along the Freedom Way," *Boston Evening Traveler*, March 31, 1951.

101 "Mayor Hynes Establishes 'Freedom Trail' to Aid in Guiding Visitors to Historic Spots," *City Record*, June 9, 1951, 607, https://www.thefreedomtrail.org/about/freedom-trail-establishment.

102 Bill Schofield, "Have You Heard: Streets Clean; Dotty Loves Richie," *Boston Evening Traveler*, June 25, 1951.

103 Joan McPartlin, "Along Boston's Freedom Trail: 40,000 People Take This Path Each Year," *Boston Globe*, October 6, 1953, 16.

104 Devin Manzullo-Thomas, "Exhibiting Evangelicalism: Commemoration, Conservative Christianity, and Religion's Presence of the Past," (PhD diss., Temple University, 2020), 106–28. Other reflections on religion along the Freedom Trail include Heather D. Curtis, "Massachusetts: A Teacher Strolls Along the Freedom Trail," *Religion and Politics*, July 30, 2012, https://religionandpolitics.org/2012/07/30/massachusetts-a-teacher-strolls-along-the-free-dom-trail/; and Chris Cantwell, "Exhibiting Faith: Religion and Public History," *Religion in American Studies*, March 8, 2013, http://usreligion.blogspot.com/2013/03/exhibiting-faith-religion-public.html.

CHAPTER 2: IMAGINING A NATIONAL HISTORICAL PARK FOR BOSTON

1 McCormack is described by Edwin Small in S. Herbert Evison, Oral History Interview of Edwin W. Small, October 19, 1971, Transcript 388, Subseries B: Interview Transcripts, 1938–1978, Series II: S. Herbert Evison's National Park Service Oral History Project, 1952–1999, NPS Oral History Collection, 1937–2017, NPS History Collection, Harpers Ferry Center for Media Development, Harpers Ferry, WV.

2 See Charlene Mires, *Independence Hall in American Memory* (Philadelphia: University of Pennsylvania Press, 2013).

3 On the history of Philadelphia's heritage infrastructure, see Gary B. Nash, *First City: Philadelphia and the Forging of Historical Memory* (Philadelphia: University of Pennsylvania Press, 2006).

4   For an overview of the history and operation of Boston's local historic districts, see Massachusetts
     Historical Commission, "Establishing Local Historic Districts," June 2003, reprinted March
     2007, https://www.sec.state.ma.us/mhc/mhcpdf/establishinglocalhistoricdistricts.pdf.

5   Evison, Oral History Interview of Edwin W. Small, 1–5, 59–60, 63; and Joan Zenzen, *Bridging
     the Past: An Administrative History of Minute Man National Historical Park* (Boston: NPS Northeast
     Region History Program, 2010), 34.

6   The quote is from Freeman Tilden, *Interpreting Our Heritage* (Chapel Hill: University of North
     Carolina Press, 2007, orig. 1957), 103. Note that Tilden's seminal *Interpreting Our Heritage* was
     itself funded with Mission 66 dollars. As crucial as it is to NPS history, Mission 66 remains
     understudied. Conrad Wirth's own account of it appears in his book *Parks, Politics, and the
     People* (Norman: University of Oklahoma Press, 1980). Assessments of its impact with regard
     to design and landscape appear in Sarah Allaback, *Mission 66 Visitor Centers: The History of a
     Building Type* (Washington, DC: National Park Service, 2000); and Ethan Carr, *Mission 66:
     Modernism and the National Park Dilemma* (Amherst: University of Massachusetts Press, 2007). Brief
     treatments are found throughout NPS gray literature such as, with regard to Mission 66 era
     strategies for generating revenue, Mary Shivers Culpin, "'For the Benefit and Enjoyment of the
     People': A History of the Concession Development in Yellowstone National Park, 1872–1966,"
     [Washington, D.C.: National Park Service, 2003].

7   This time, though, the proposal originated not with the South Boston Citizens' Association,
     but rather with the Corporation Counsel of Boston, signaling the beginning of corporate
     sponsorship of the park concept, likely by the Chamber of Commerce. See advisory board
     catalog cards scanned and shared by NPS Bureau Historian John Sprinkle. Relevant minutes
     include VIII, 2 (2), August 15–18, 1938; XI, 9 (21), November 7–9, 1939; XII, 10 (2), March
     25–31, 1940); and XXIV, p. 14, April 26–27, 1951.

8   The March 17, 1951, memorandum of agreement was signed by Oscar Chapman, secretary of the
     interior, and John B. Hynes, mayor of Boston. See National Park Service Cultural Landscape
     Inventory, Dorchester Heights National Historic Site, BNHP-Dorchester Heights (2010),
     BNHP Archives, Charlestown, MA, 3, 38.

9   See advisory board catalog cards referencing minutes XXIV, p. 14, April 26–27, 1951, and
     XXVIII, Appendix, I (12), April 18–2, 1953; Memorandum of Agreement, March 17, 1951, 3, 38.

10   Rogers W. Young, "Preliminary Survey of Historic Sites in Boston and Vicinity in Connection
     with H.J. Res. 254, 1st Sess., 82nd Cong.," July 17, 1951, attached to Ronald F. Lee to Daniel
     Tobin, November 23, 1955, Folder VII, July–Dec 1955 Records, Box 2, Boston National Historic
     Sites Commission Records, 1956–1960, BNHP Archives, Charlestown, MA.

11   U.S. Congress, House of Representatives, Subcommittee on Public Lands, Committee on
     Interior and Insular Affairs, *Historical Commission for Boston and Vicinity*, 82nd Cong., 1st sess. (82
     H.J. Res. 254), August 15, 1951.

12   U.S. Congress, *Historical Commission for Boston and Vicinity*, August 15, 1951.

13   The report is cited in U.S. Congress, House of Representatives, Committee on Interior and
     Insular Affairs, *Boston National Historic Sites Commission*, 82nd Cong., 1st sess. (82 H.J. Res. 254),
     August 21, 1951, but not reprinted in whole.

14   U.S. Congress, *Boston National Historic Sites Commission*, August 21, 1951.

15   It is unclear whether Mills referred to his time as chair of the Public Lands and Land Office
     or as vice chair of Public Buildings and Grounds. U.S. Congress, *Boston National Historic Sites
     Commission*, August 21, 1951.

16   U.S. Congress, *Boston National Historic Sites Commission*, August 21, 1951.

17   U.S. Congress, House of Representatives, Committee on Interior and Insular Affairs, *Boston
     National Historic Sites Commission*, 83rd Cong., 1st sess. (83 H.J. Res. 122), February 17, 1953.

18   U.S. Congress, House of Representatives, Subcommittee on Public Lands, Committee on
     Interior and Insular Affairs, *To Provide for Investigating the Feasibility of Establishing a Coordinated
     Local, State, and Federal Program in the City of Boston, Massachusetts, for the Purpose of Preserving the Historic
     Properties, Objects, and Buildings in that Area*, 84th Cong., 1st sess. (84 H.J. Res. 207), May 4, 1955.

Of course, language associating preservation with urban problems would figure prominently in the preamble to the National Historic Preservation Act of 1966.

19   *Joint resolution to provide for investigating the feasibility of establishing a coordinated local, State, and Federal program in the city of Boston, Massachusetts, and general vicinity thereof, for the purpose of preserving the historic properties, objects, and buildings in that area,* Public Law 75, *U.S. Statutes at Large* 69, Stat. 136 (1955), 136–38.

20   U.S. Congress, *To Provide for Investigating the Feasibility of Establishing a Coordinated Local, State, and Federal Program in the City of Boston, Massachusetts,* May 4, 1955.

21   Figures based on Inflation Calculator, Bureau of Labor Statistics, United States Department of Labor, https://data.bls.gov/cgi-bin/cpicalc.pl.

22   The recommendations appear in NPS Director Conrad Wirth to Special Assistant Harry J. Donohue, July 7, 1955, Folder VII, July–Dec 1955 Records, Box 2, Boston National Historic Sites Commission Records, 1956–1960, BNHP Archives, Charlestown, MA.

23   Interestingly, it doesn't appear from correspondence that O'Neill and Bortman had a close relationship; in the records, Bortman addresses O'Neill as "Tom" rather than "Tip," as was the fashion with O'Neill's close associates.

24   Summary Minutes, Organizational Meeting of the Boston National Historic Sites Commission at Salem Maritime National Historic Site, September 12, 1955, Folder VII, July–Dec 1955 Records, Box 2, Boston National Historic Sites Commission Records, 1956–1960, BNHP Archives, Charlestown, MA.

25   The action on Sullivan is noted in Summary of Matters Voted on to Date by the Boston National Historic Sites Commission: March 6, 1957, Folder: Jan–Apr 1957, Box 1, Boston National Historic Sites Commission Records, 1956–1960, BNHP Archives, Charlestown, MA.

26   Daniel Tobin to Conrad Wirth, September 14, 1955, Folder VII, July-Dec 1955 Records, Box 2, Boston National Historic Sites Commission Records, 1956–1960, BNHP Archives, Charlestown, MA.

27   Crowninshield's comment was originally included in a letter to Superintendent Francis S. Ronalds of Morristown National Historical Park, though repeated in a letter from Tobin to Wirth, November 23, 1955, Folder VII, July–Dec 1955 Records, Box 2, Boston National Historic Sites Commission Records, 1956–1960, BNHP Archives, Charlestown, MA.

28   Walter Muir Whitehill to Conrad Wirth, January 3, 1956, Folder: US Government Misc., Box 28, Walter Muir Whitehill Papers, Massachusetts Historical Society, Boston, MA.

29   Summary of Matters Voted on to Date by the Boston National Historic Sites Commission: March 6, 1957.

30   Young shared pages 3–8. Summary of Minutes of Second Meeting, September 29, 1955, Folder VII, July–Dec 1955 Records, Box 2, Boston National Historic Sites Commission Records, 1956–1960, BNHP Archives, Charlestown, MA.

31   Alan W. Barton, "From Parks to Partnerships: National Heritage Areas and the Path to Collaborative Participation in the National Park Service's First 100 Years," *Natural Resources Journal* 56 (Winter 2016): 37.

32   Summary of Minutes of Second Meeting, September 29, 1955. On Moody, see Frederick S. Allis Jr., "Memoir of Robert Earle Moody" (July 1988), Colonial Society of Massachusetts, https://www.colonialsociety.org/node/1778.

33   For various materials related to this meeting, including participant forms and notes taken by Tobin, see Folder: BNHSC A2015 First Hearing 11/9/1955, Box 1, CRM Division Records, 1931–1955, Northeast Region, National Park Service, National Archives at Boston, Waltham, MA.

34   Emile Travel, "Bay Staters Plead for Historic Sites," *Christian Science Monitor,* February 7, 1956. Clipping included in Folder: Boston Nat'l Historic Site Commission: Correspondence 2 of 4, Box 188, Leverett Saltonstall Papers, Massachusetts Historical Society, Boston, MA.

35   Wirth's authorization appears in Wirth to Tobin, January 11, 1956, Folder: Jan–June 1956, Box 1, Boston National Historic Sites Commission Records, 1956–1960, BNHP Archives, Charlestown, MA.

36 Summary of Minutes of Second Meeting, September 29, 1955.

37 Bortman to F. Bradford Morse, December 9, 1955, Folder: Boston National Historic Site Commission Correspondence 3 of 4, Box 188, Leverett Saltonstall Papers, Massachusetts Historical Society, Boston, MA.

38 Tobin to Wirth, 6 March 1956, Folder: Jan–June 1956, Box 1, Boston National Historic Sites Commission Records, 1956–1960, BNHP Archives, Charlestown, MA.

39 It was Small, for instance, who was authorized as an agent of the Division of Disbursement to pay out salary checks and U.S. savings bonds to employees of BNHSC.

40 Evison, Oral History Interview of Edwin W. Small, 35.

41 Summary of Matters Voted on to Date by the Boston National Historic Sites Commission: March 6, 1957, Folder: Jan–Apr 1957, Box 1, Boston National Historic Sites Commission Records, 1956–1960, BNHP Archives, Charlestown, MA.

42 Summary of Minutes of Hearing of the Boston National Historic Sites Commission with State, City and Town Officials (and Others) of Massachusetts, February 6, 1956, Folder: Meeting Minutes, etc. Jan–June 1956, Box 1, Boston National Historic Sites Commission Records, 1956–1960, BNHP Archives, Charlestown, MA.

43 Summary of Minutes of Hearing of the Boston National Historic Sites Commission with State, City and Town Officials (and Others) of Massachusetts, February 6, 1956.

44 Summary of Minutes of Sixth Meeting, March 26, 1956, Folder: Meeting Minutes, etc. Jan–June 1956, Box 1, Boston National Historic Sites Commission Records, 1956–1960, BNHP Archives, Charlestown, MA.

45 Summary of Minutes of Sixth Meeting, March 26, 1956.

46 The complete list included (in order): the Old State House, Old North Church, Old South Meeting House, King's Chapel, Christ Church (Cambridge), Isaac Royall House (Medford), Shirley-Eustis House (Roxbury), Vassall-Craigie-Longfellow House (Cambridge), and Breed's Hill/Bunker Hill Monument (Charlestown). Other sites mentioned in passing included the Paul Revere House, the Moses-Pierce Hichborn House, the Stephen-Langdon House, the Dillaway-Thomas House (Roxbury), Dorchester Heights National Historic Site, the Old Ship Church (Hingham), and the Adams Mansion and Birthplaces (Quincy). A summary of Small's report and responses to it appears in Summary of Minutes of Sixth Meeting, March 26, 1956.

47 Summary of Minutes of Sixth Meeting, March 26, 1956.

48 Summary of Minutes of Sixth Meeting, March 26, 1956.

49 "Senate Approves $20 Million Plan for Market Place," *Boston Globe*, July 21, 1950, 7.

50 "South Bay Area Site for New Market: Authority Hopes to Start Building Within 6 Months," *Boston Globe*, November 11, 1951, C1.

51 "South Bay Area Site for New Market."

52 Earl Banner, "Consumer Gets More Bone, Fat," *Boston Globe*, May 13, 1951, C1. Regarding Boston laws made to manage meat market vendors, see Elijah Adlow, "Municipal Corporations," in *The Genius of Lemuel Shaw: Expounder of the Common Law* (Boston: Massachusetts Bar Association, 1962).

53 Earl Banner, "Boston Meat Dealers Pleased with OPS," *Boston Globe*, November 11, 1951, C25.

54 Lewis William, "Boston Artery Cuts Deep into Taxable Land: City May Lose $20,000,000 in Assessments," *Daily Globe*, February 10, 1952, C6.

55 Quote and visitation figures appear in Joan McPartlin, "Grasshopper Landmark Famous as Hall Itself," *Boston Globe*, October 10, 1953, 10.

56 Juan Cameron, "Faneuil Hall Market District Continues to Operate Successfully," *Boston Globe*, October 16, 1955, A39. This article includes a graphic portraying the city's network of food markets, along with a careful explanation of the various challenges confronting food distribution in postwar Boston.

57 For an overview of strategies used by developers during the 1950s to reimagine downtown shopping districts, see Alison Isenberg, *Downtown America: A History of the Place and the People Who Made It* (Chicago: University of Chicago Press, 2004), ch. 5.

58 "Why Faneuil Hall is a Market Place," *Daily Boston Globe,* February 12, 1956, C68.

59 G. Harris Danzberger, "A Sturbridge Village in Faneuil Hall," *Boston Sunday Herald,* January 15, 1956.

60 "Why Faneuil Hall is a Market Place." On the problem of replicas and the federal government's concerns about them—which date to the contest of authenticity at George Washington's birthplace—see John Sprinkle, *Crafting Preservation Criteria: The National Register of Historic Places and American Historic Preservation* (New York: Routledge, 2014), 95–98.

61 It is worth noting that Bortman also sat on the board of the Ancient and Honorable Artillery Company. Meeting Minutes, May 7, 1956, Folder 6, Meeting Minutes, etc. Jan–June 1956, Box 1, Boston National Historic Sites Commission Records, 1956–1960, BNHP Archives, Charlestown, MA.

62 Summary of Minutes of Sixteenth Meeting, September 24, 1956, Folder: Meeting Minutes July–Dec 1956, Box 1, Boston National Historic Sites Commission Records, 1956–1960, BNHP Archives, Charlestown, MA.

63 Summary of Minutes of Sixteenth Meeting, September 24, 1956.

64 Summary of Minutes of Sixteenth Meeting, September 24, 1956.

65 Summary of Minutes of Sixth Meeting, March 26, 1956.

66 Memo to Tobin, January 27, 1958, Folder IV, d. Faneuil Hall, Box 2, Boston National Historic Sites Commission Records, 1956–1960, BNHP Archives, Charlestown, MA. It is unclear who authored the memo; presumably it is from Small, though the document is signed "MHN."

67 Summary of Twenty-seventh Meeting, August 16, 1957, Folder: Meeting Minutes May 1957–Mar 1958, Box 1, Boston National Historic Sites Commission Records, 1956–1960, BNHP Archives, Charlestown, MA.

68 Letters appear summarized in Summary of Minutes of Twenty-eighth Meeting, November 20, 1957, Folder: Meeting Minutes May 1957–Mar 1958, Box 1, Boston National Historic Sites Commission Records, 1956–1960, BNHP Archives, Charlestown, MA.

69 Summary of Minutes of Twenty-eighth Meeting, November 20, 1957.

70 Proposed sketches, Folder: Duplicate Records (Mar. 1958–June 1959), Box 2, Boston National Historic Sites Commission Records, 1956–1960, BNHP Archives, Charlestown, MA.

71 "Historical Continuity versus Synthetic Reconstruction," *Athenaeum Items: A Library Letter from the Boston Athenaeum* 67 (January 1958), Folder IV, d. Faneuil Hall, Box 2, Boston National Historic Sites Commission Records, 1956–1960, BNHP Archives, Charlestown, MA.

72 Francis W. Hatch, "In the Name of Peter Faneuil, Beef Before Baubles," in "Old Landmark Doesn't Need Its Face Lifted," *Boston Globe,* February 1, 1958.

73 Lee to Regional Directors, Regions One, Two, Three, Four and Five, April 2, 1958, Folder IV, d. Faneuil Hall, Box 2, Boston National Historic Sites Commission Records, 1956–1960, BNHP Archives, Charlestown, MA.

74 Mentions of both of these appear in "The Let-it-Alone Club," *Athenaeum Items* 68 (March 1958), Folder IV, d. Faneuil Hall, Box 2, Boston National Historic Sites Commission Records, 1956–1960, BNHP Archives, Charlestown, MA.

75 Bortman's words appears in a summary of his April 11, 1958, telephone call with Lally—evidently compiled by Small—included in Folder IV, d. Faneuil Hall, Box 2, Boston National Historic Sites Commission Records, 1956–1960, BNHP Archives, Charlestown, MA.

76 These materials appear in Folder IV, d. Faneuil Hall, Box 2, Boston National Historic Sites Commission Records, 1956–1960, BNHP Archives, Charlestown, MA.

77 Small to Tobin, February 7, 1958, Folder: BNHSC Memos to Members 12/1957–12/1958, Box 2, CRM Division Records 1931–1955, Northeast Region, National Park Service, National Archives at Boston, Waltham, MA.

78 The park's newsletter, for instance, ran a story about meat merchants still working at Faneuil Hall in 1976. "Boston Historic Sites Still 'Living,'" *Broadside* 1, no. 3 (Winter 1976): 4. The meat markets did not leave entirely until completion of Faneuil Hall's rehabilitation in 1990, after which they were replaced by stylized colonial shops (see chapter six).

79 Summary of Minutes of 11th Meeting, May 28, 1956, Folder 7, Meeting Minutes July–Dec. 1956, Box 1, Boston National Historic Sites Commission Records, 1956–1960, BNHP Archives, Charlestown, MA.

80 Bortman's involvement with causes related to Paul Revere and his objects is well documented, for instance, in the Mark Bortman Papers, 1948–1967, P-856, American Jewish Historical Society, New York, NY.

81 Summary of Minutes of 15th Meeting, August 13, 1956, Folder 7, Meeting Minutes July–Dec. 1956, Box 1, Boston National Historic Sites Commission Records, 1956–1960, BNHP Archives, Charlestown, MA.

82 On Shurcliff and his Battle Road plan, see Zenzen, *Bridging the Past,* ch. 2. Shurcliff's role is also summarized in Boston National Historic Sites Commission, "The Lexington–Concord Battle Road, Interim Report of the Boston National Historic Sites Commission to the Congress of the United States," June 16, 1958, 19–20. Hereafter cited as "Interim Report."

83 Summary of Minutes of 13th Meeting, June 22, 1956, Folder 7, Meeting Minutes July–Dec. 1956, Box 1, Boston National Historic Sites Commission Records, 1956–1960, BNHP Archives, Charlestown, MA.

84 Zenzen, *Bridging the Past,* 37–43.

85 Summary of Minutes of 16th Meeting, September 24, 1956, Folder 7, Meeting Minutes July–Dec. 1956, Box 1, Boston National Historic Sites Commission Records, 1956–1960, BNHP Archives, Charlestown, MA.

86 Summary of Minutes of 16th Meeting, September 24, 1956.

87 Summary of Minutes of 17th Meeting, October 15, 1956, Folder 7, Meeting Minutes July–Dec. 1956, Box 1, Boston National Historic Sites Commission Records, 1956–1960, BNHP Archives, Charlestown, MA.

88 Evison, Oral History Interview of Edwin W. Small, October 19, 1971, 20.

89 Snow is incorrectly identified as "Sam Snell" in Small's oral history. Snow appears in "Interim Report," 20.

90 Evison, Oral History Interview of Edwin W. Small, October 19, 1971, 20–24.

91 "Interim Report," vii.

92 "Interim Report," 2–4, 7.

93 Public Law 86–321, 73 Stat. 590–592. Note that the park was initially established as Minute Man National Historic Site on April 14, 1959, by designation of the Historic Sites Act of 1935 covering federal property at Hanscom Airforce Base. See 24 F.R. 4987.

94 "Interim Report," 8, 10.

95 "Interim Report," 12.

96 Summary of 27th meeting, August 16, 1957, Folder 7, Meeting Minutes July–Dec.1956, Box 1, Boston National Historic Sites Commission Records, 1956–1960, BNHP Archives, Charlestown, MA.

97 Small to Director, December 11, 1957, Folder 4, May 1957–March 1958, Box 1, Boston National Historic Sites Commission Records, 1956–1960, BNHP Archives, Charlestown, MA.

98 Whitehill to Wirth, May 19, 1958, Folder 5, Admin Docs Mar 1958–June 1959, Box 1, Boston National Historic Sites Commission Records, 1956–1960, BNHP Archives, Charlestown, MA.

99 It is notable that although Whitehill sent Wirth, as he put it, a "confidential" letter, Wirth routed copies of his response to Small and Tobin, signaling his unwillingness to deal privately with Whitehill. Wirth to Whitehill, 11 July 1958, Folder 5, Admin Docs Mar 1958–June 1959, Box 1, Boston National Historic Sites Commission Records, 1956–1960, BNHP Archives, Charlestown, MA.

100 Small to Regional Director, July 31, 1958, Folder 5, Admin Docs Mar 1958-June 1959, Box 1, Boston National Historic Sites Commission Records, 1956–1960, BNHP Archives, Charlestown, MA.

101 Small to Tobin, January 29, 1959, Folder 5, Admin Docs Mar 1958–June 1959, Box 1, Boston National Historic Sites Commission Records, 1956–1960, BNHP Archives, Charlestown, MA.

102 Wirth to Assistant Secretary, Public Land Management, May 29, 1959, Folder 5, Admin Docs
    Mar 1958–June 1959, Box 1, Boston National Historic Sites Commission Records, 1956–1960,
    BNHP Archives, Charlestown, MA.

103 BNHSC, Final Report of the Boston National Historic Sites Commission, 87th Cong., 1st
    sess., March 15, 1961, H. Doc. 107, 7. Hereafter cited as "Final Report."

104 John H. Sprinkle Jr., "'Worthy Remains of a Beautiful and Historic Past': The National Park
    Service Recognizes Historic Districts," *Federal History* 11 (January 2019): 129–44.

105 Seth C. Bruggeman, *Here, George Washington Was Born: Memory, Material Culture, and the Public History
    of a National Monument* (Athens: University of Georgia Press, 2008), 182.

106 Brenda Barrett, "New National Parks in the 1990s: Thinning of the Blood or a Much Needed
    Transfusion?" (July 10, 1991), unpublished manuscript available at https://livinglandscape-
    observer.net/wp-content/uploads/2014/01/New-National-Parks-in-the-1990s.pdf. For an
    overview of National Heritage Areas and their antecedents, see Barrett, "Roots for the National
    Heritage Area Family Tree," *George Wright Forum* 20, no. 2 (2003): 41–49.

107 My overview of Cape Cod National Seashore's origin story is drawn from Francis P. Burling,
    The Birth of the Cape Cod National Seashore (Plymouth, MA: Leyden Press, 1979), reprinted in 2000
    by Eastern National. On the uniqueness of Cape Cod's establishing legislation in 1961, see
    Barrett, "Roots for the National Heritage Area Family Tree," 41–42.

108 For two views on changes ushered in by the Housing Act of 1954, see Alexander von Hoffman,
    "The Lost History of Urban Renewal," *Journal of Urbanism* 1, no. 3 (November 2008): 281–301;
    and Richard M. Flanagan, "The Housing Act of 1954: The Sea Change in National Urban
    Policy," *Urban Affairs Review* 33, no. 2 (November 1997): 265–86.

109 This area, though, given the integrity of its historic structures, did not figure in the BNHSC's
    final recommendation.

110 "Final Report," 7.

111 "Final Report," 14–15.

112 "Final Report," 15.

113 "Final Report," 9.

114 "Final Report," 27.

115 "Final Report," 16.

116 "Final Report," 19.

117 "Final Report," 20.

118 A cover letter introducing the document indicates "that the commission properly administered
    its activities and accounted for the funds under its control." Comptroller General of the United
    States, "Audit of Boston National Historic Sites Commission," April 1961, Folder: Audit of
    Boston National Historical Sites Commission [1961], Box 2, Resource Management Records,
    Early 1970s–1980s Park ("pre-park" generally), BNHP Archives, Charlestown, MA. Federal
    commissions had drawn increased scrutiny amid budget-minded Cold War congresses. See,
    for instance, Public Law 92–463, 92nd Congress HR 4383, October 6, 1972, also known as
    the Federal Advisory Committee Act. This law authorized the establishment of a system of
    governing the creation and operation of advisory committees in the executive branch.

119 Tape-recorded Draft of Meeting Minutes of 15th Meeting, August 13, 1956, Folder: BNHSC
    A2015, Box 1, Northeast Region New England Field Office—Boston, BNHSC 1955–66, National
    Archives at Boston, Waltham, MA. Note that this collection can be used to substitute for
    gaps in the Boston National Historic Sites Commission Records, 1956–1960, BNHP Archives,
    Charlestown, MA.

120 Tape-recorded Draft of Meeting Minutes of 17th Meeting, October 15, 1956, Folder: BNHSC
    A2015, Box 1, Northeast Region New England Field Office-Boston, BNHSC 1955–66, National
    Archives at Boston, Waltham, MA.

121 For an overview of nonprofit corporations and their function, see Paul Arnsberger, Melissa
    Ludlum, Margaret Riley, and Mark Stanton, "A History of the Tax-Exempt Sector: An SOI
    Perspective," *Statistics of Income Bulletin* (Winter 2008): 105–35.

CHAPTER 3: LOSING CONTROL OF THE AGENDA

1   Summary Minutes of the 43rd Meeting of the Advisory Board on National Parks, Historic Sites, Buildings, and Monuments, Isle Royale National Park, Michigan, September 17–22, 1960, 18–19, Advisory Board Files, National Register, History and Education (NRHE), National Park Service Washington Service Office, Washington, DC.

2   Denis Galvin, then NPS deputy director, quoted in David Foster, "'Park Barrel' Politics Seen as Redefining 75-Year-Old National System," *Los Angeles Times* (October 13, 1991).

3   See overview in Thomas H. O'Connor, *Building a New Boston: Politics and Urban Renewal, 1950 to 1970* (Boston: Northeastern University Press, 1995), 139–49; and Lizabeth Cohen, *Saving America's Cities: Ed Logue and the Struggle to Renew Urban America in the Suburban Age* (New York: Farrar, Straus, and Giroux, 2019), 151–52.

4   O'Connor, *Building a New Boston*, 163.

5   O'Connor, *Building a New Boston*, 173. For an overview of Logue's arrival in Boston, see Lizabeth Cohen, *Saving America's Cities*, 147–50.

6   See Cohen, *Saving America's Cities*, and for a review of Logue and second-phase renewal, see Lizabeth Cohen, "Liberalism in the Postwar City," in *Making Sense of American Liberalism*, ed. Jonathan Bell and Timothy Stanley (New York: Oxford University Press, 2012), 140; Mark Byrnes, "Don't Forget About Ed Logue," *Bloomberg CityLab* (March 15, 2017), https://www .citylab.com/equity/2017/03/dont-forget-about-ed-logue/519615; and Cohen, "Buying into Downtown Revival: The Centrality of Retail to Postwar Urban Renewal in American Cities," *Annals of the American Academy of Political and Social Science*, Vol. 611: *The Politics of Consumption/The Consumption of Politics* (May 2007): 82–95. On Collins and the Government Center, see Alejandra Dean, "Notes from the Archives: Urban Renewal and Government Center," *City of Boston Blog*, https://www.boston.gov/news/notes-archives-urban-renewal-and-government-center. O'Connor addresses Logue in *Building a New Boston*, 173–77, and the Government Center and matters of historic preservation throughout chapter seven.

7   "The 90 Million Dollar Development Program for Boston," reprinted from *City Record* (Boston city government newsletter), September 24, 1960, 1, Edward Joseph Logue Papers, Manuscripts and Archives, Yale University Library, New Haven, CT. Cohen notes the event's location in Old South Meeting House in *Saving America's Cities*, 151.

8   "The 90 Million Dollar Development Program," 2; italics in original.

9   "The 90 Million Dollar Development Program," 7.

10 Daniel J. Ahern, Manager, Urban Development Department, Greater Boston Chamber of Commerce, to Edward J. Logue, February 27, 1961, Folder 706, BRA Greater Boston Chamber of Commerce 1961, 1964, Box 169, Series VI, Edward Joseph Logue Papers, Manuscripts and Archives, Yale University Library. On the chamber's place in Logue's planning scheme, see Cohen, *Saving America's Cities*, 182–85.

11 "The 90 Million Dollar Development Program," 5.

12 Summary of Minutes of 16th Meeting, September 24, 1956, Folder 7, Meeting Minutes July-Dec. 1956, Box 1, Boston National Historic Sites Commission Records, 1956–1960, BNHP Archives, Charlestown, MA.

13 For correspondence detailing the response by NPS staff, including park planner Andrew Feil, to Boston's proposed Government Center, see Folder IV, Projects and Recommended Sites e. Boston Government Center, Box 2, Boston National Historic Sites Commission Records, 1956–1960, BNHP Archives, Charlestown, MA.

14 Summary of 27th Meeting, August 16, 1957, Folder 7, Meeting Minutes July-Dec.1956, Box 1, Boston National Historic Sites Commission Records, 1956–1960, BNHP Archives, Charlestown, MA.

15 Summary of 27th Meeting, August 16, 1957.

16 Small to Tobin, April 21, 1959, Folder 5, Admin Docs Mar 1958-June 1959, Box 1, Boston National Historic Sites Commission Records, 1956–1960, BNHP Archives, Charlestown, MA.

17   "The 90 Million Dollar Development Program," 6.

18   "The 90 Million Dollar Development Program," 7.

19   "The 90 Million Dollar Development Program," 7.

20   "The 90 Million Dollar Development Program," 9.

21   Cohen, *Saving America's Cities*, quotation 174. Cohen addresses Logue's relationship with Boston's preservationists on pages 200–6.

22   Draft letter written by Whitehill, intended for mayor to send to prospective committee members, sometime in 1961, Folder 726, BRA Historic Conservation Committee, 1961–66, Box 171, Series VI, Edward Joseph Logue Papers, Manuscripts and Archives, Yale University Library, New Haven, CT.

23   Whitehill to Charles A. Coolidge, President, Greater Boston Chamber of Commerce, January 13, 1961, Folder: Greater Boston Chamber of Commerce Tourist Committee 1961–62, Box 9, Walter Muir Whitehill Papers, Massachusetts Historical Society, Boston, MA.

24   Cohen notes their common club membership in *Saving America's Cities*, 166.

25   Whitehill discussed his role in this story in a talk titled "Neglected Assets," delivered at the fourth Citizens Seminar on the Fiscal, Economic, and Political Problems of Boston and the Metropolitan Community, Boston College, February 26, 1963, Folder: Historic Sites Committee, Box 148, Mayor John F. Collins Papers, Boston City Archives, West Roxbury, MA. See also, Joe Harrington, "Both the Old and New," *Boston Morning Globe*, December 28, 1961. Historic Boston, Inc. continues its preservation advocacy today; see "Our Mission," http://historicboston.org /about/.

26   John Crosby, "Cities Are for People," *New York Times*, November 17, 1960.

27   Logue to Whitehill, November 22, 1960, Folder 459, BRA Correspondence-Personal, Whitehill, Walter Muir 1960–61, Box 151, Series VI, Edward Joseph Logue Papers, Manuscripts and Archives, Yale University Library, New Haven, CT.

28   Whitehill wrote Logue, for instance, about rumors that the Charlestown Burial Ground was identified for removal. Whitehall to Logue, February 9, 1961, Folder 459, BRA Correspondence-Personal, Whitehill, Walter Muir 1960–61, Box 151, Series VI, Edward Joseph Logue Papers, Manuscripts and Archives, Yale University Library, New Haven, CT.

29   Frank L. Harvey, Chairman of the Mayor's Committee on North End Rehabilitation and Conservation, to Logue, January 9, 1961, Folder 970, North End 1960–66, Box 190, Series VI, Edward Joseph Logue Papers, Manuscripts and Archives, Yale University Library, New Haven, CT.

30   Barrett Williams, Secretary of the Bostonian Society and Representative of the Council of the Freedom Trail, to Logue, April 29, 1960; and Logue to Williams, May 6, 1960, both in Folder 723, BRA Historic Sites 1960–61, Box 170, Series VI, Edward Joseph Logue Papers, Manuscripts and Archives, Yale University Library, New Haven, CT.

31   The committee's BRA contact was W. J. Gurney. See Boston Historic Sites Committee Newsletter, 4 April 1962, Folder: Historic Sites Committee, Box 148, Mayor John F. Collins Papers, Boston City Archives, West Roxbury, MA.

32   Cover note by John Stainton, Project Planning Officer, Boston Redevelopment Authority, attached to Draft Proposal for Professional Services to Carry out an Inventory and Analysis of the Rehabilitation Potential of the Historic Buildings and Areas with the Charlestown Urban Renewal Project, Folder: Architectural and Topographic Survey of Charlestown, Mass 1962, Box 1, Resource Management Records, Early 1970s-1980s Park ("pre-park" generally), BNHP Archives, Charlestown, MA.

33   The Boston Historical Conservation Committee Survey team included J. Daniel Selig and Robert H. Nylander; Abbott Lowell Cummings advised. Folder: Architectural and Topographic Survey of Charlestown, Mass 1962, Box 1, Resource Management Records, Early 1970s-1980s Park ("pre-park" generally), BNHP Archives, Charlestown, MA. For a discussion of how Society Hill's gentrification was carefully orchestrated to consolidate whiteness adjacent to Philadelphia's new Independence National Historical Park, see Marcus Anthony Hunter,

Kevin Loughran, and Gary Alan Fine, "Memory Politics: Growth Coalitions, Urban Pasts, and the Creation of 'Historic' Philadelphia," *City and Community* 17, no. 2 (June 2018): 341–43.

34 Minutes of the Boston Historical Conservation Committee, December 14, 1961, Folder 728, Box 171, Series VI, Edward Joseph Logue Papers, Manuscripts and Archives, Yale University Library, New Haven, CT.

35 Details concerning the committee's early manifestations appear in Daniel J. Ahern to Logue, November 3, 1960; and Donald M. Graham, Planning Administrator, to Logue, February 24, 1961, both in Folder 723, BRA Historic Sites 1960–61, Box 170, Series VI, Edward Joseph Logue Papers, Manuscripts and Archives, Yale University Library, New Haven, CT. Records indicate that Lyons resigned as principal planner in December 1963. See BRA, Minutes of a Regular Meeting of the Boston Redevelopment Authority Held on Dec. 4, 1963, Boston Planning and Development Agency, http://www.bostonplans.org /getattachment/2e2b315f-19b7–49e2-8508-77ac9f989325.

36 Gladys Lyons, "Preliminary Report on Buildings Architecturally and/or Historically Significant within Boston's Downtown North GNRP, with Special Attention to the Proposed Government Center Area," n.d., Folder 610, BRA Government Center, Box 162, Series VI, Edward Joseph Logue Papers, Manuscripts and Archives, Yale University Library, New Haven, CT. On Logue's interest in staffing the BRA with young planners and his commitments to diversity—though not always gender diversity—see Cohen, *Saving America's Cities,* 169–70.

37 At this early point, Richard W. Hale Jr., who was appointed Archivist of the Commonwealth of Massachusetts that year, led the committee. Donald M. Graham, Planning Administrator, to Logue, February 24, 1961, Folder 723, BRA Historic Sites 1960–61, Box 170, Series VI, Edward Joseph Logue Papers, Manuscripts and Archives, Yale University Library, New Haven, CT.

38 The exchange is described in a memo from Lyons to Logue regarding the Union-Marshall Streets area, May 18, 1961, Folder 723, BRA Historic Sites 1960–61, Box 170, Series VI, Edward Joseph Logue Papers, Manuscripts and Archives, Yale University Library, New Haven, CT.

39 Small references Chapter 40C of the Laws of the Commonwealth. Small to Lyons, May 16, 1961, Folder 610, BRA Government Center, Box 162, Series VI, Edward Joseph Logue Papers, Manuscripts and Archives, Yale University Library, New Haven, CT.

40 Small to Lyons, May 16, 1961.

41 Martin Adler to Logue, May 17, 1961, regarding the meeting with Whitehill at the Boston Athenaeum, May 16, 1961, Folder 610, BRA Government Center, Box 162, Series VI, Edward Joseph Logue Papers, Manuscripts and Archives, Yale University Library, New Haven, CT. Lyons's concern with the confusion over preservation strategies peaked in June 1961, when the risks of indecision became powerfully evident. That month, the historic Old Howard Theater was inexplicably demolished, just as a grassroots preservation committee had formed to save it. See O'Connor, *Building a New Boston,* 199–200. Its destruction, along with a suspicious fire in the Bulfinch Home, prompted Lyons to plead with the BRA's director of administrative management to do something to encourage protection of Boston's historic sites. Lyons's memo activated Logue, who initiated the second part of his plan to monitor heritage matters. See Lyons to John P. McMorrow, June 20, 1961; and Logue to McMorrow, June 23, 1961, both in Folder 723, BRA Historic Sites 1960–61, Box 170, Series VI, Edward Joseph Logue Papers, Manuscripts and Archives, Yale University Library, New Haven, CT.

42 William J. Gurney, Research Analyst, to John P. McMorrow, Director of Administrative Management, 1962 (day and month omitted), regarding the Boston National Historic Commission Report (McMorrow's note is attached), Folder 723, BRA Historic Sites 1960–61, Box 170, Series VI, Edward Joseph Logue Papers, Manuscripts and Archives, Yale University Library, New Haven, CT.

43 "Small Williamsburg Envisioned to Help Hub Keep Individuality," *Boston Traveler,* March 9, 1961. Many more examples are included in scrapbooks, Edward Joseph Logue Papers, Manuscripts and Archives, Yale University Library, New Haven, CT.

44 Stephanie R. Ryberg, "Historic Preservation's Urban Renewal Roots: Preservation and Planning in Midcentury Philadelphia," *Journal of Urban History* 39, no. 2 (2012): 194.

45 The Eleventh District became the Eighth District in 1963.

46 U.S. Congress, House, *A Bill to Provide Federal Cooperation in a Program to Preserve Certain Historic Properties in the City of Boston, Massachusetts, and Vicinity, Associated with the Colonial and Revolutionary Periods of American History; to Authorize the Establishment of the Boston National Historic Sites and for Other Purposes,* H.R. 10836, 87th Cong., 2nd sess., introduced in House March 20, 1962.

47 Tobin to Director, NPS, April 1, 1963, Folder: Preliminaries, Memoranda from 1960s, Box 1, Resource Management Records, Early 1970s-1980s Park ("pre-park" generally), BNHP Archives, Charlestown, MA; and U.S. Congress, House, *A Bill to Provide Federal Cooperation in a Program to Preserve Certain Historic Properties in the City of Boston, Massachusetts, and Vicinity, Associated with the Colonial and Revolutionary Periods of American History; to Authorize the Establishment of the Boston National Historic Sites; and for Other Purposes,* H.R. 392, 88th Cong., 1st sess., introduced January 9, 1963.

48 See the park's copy of U.S. Congress, House, H.R. 10836, Folder: Preliminaries, Memoranda from 1960s, Box 1, Resource Management Records, Early 1970s-1980s Park ("pre-park" generally), BNHP Archives, Charlestown, MA.

49 The memo is unsigned thereby obscuring who the advisors are in this case. The memo arrived in Collins's office by way of O'Neill's office, which raises the possibility of O'Neill working against his own bill. "The attached copy of a memo has been sent to Henry A. Scagnoli at his request. Messrs. Jacoby and Lombard discussed this with him recently, and we were unable to locate the original memo in your files or Mary Callanan's. Attached is copy of memo to mayor dated 5 March 1963." James A. Travers, Youth Activities Bureau, to John H. O'Neill Jr., June 6, 1963, Folder: Historic Sites Committee, Box 148, Mayor John F. Collins Papers, Boston City Archives, West Roxbury, MA.

50 Tobin to Director, NPS, April 1, 1963.

51 John A. Conner Jr., Assistant Secretary of the Interior, to Wayne N. Aspinall, May 20, 1964, regarding H.R. 392, Folder: NPS Memos on Boston NHP Legislative Support Data, 1963–74, Box 1, Resource Management Records, Early 1970s-1980s Park ("pre-park" generally), BNHP Archives, Charlestown, MA. See also, Conner to Aspinall, May 20, 1964, Folder: Preliminaries, Memoranda from 1960s, Box 1, Resource Management Records, Early 1970s-1980s Park ("pre-park" generally), BNHP Archives, Charlestown, MA.

52 See Agenda, 51st Meeting, Advisory Board on National Parks, Historic Sites, Buildings and Monuments, Washington, DC, Shenandoah National Park, Blue Ridge Parkway and Great Smoky Mountains National Park, October 5–14, 1964, NPS Bureau Historian's Office, NPS Washington Service Office, Washington, DC. Thanks to John Sprinkle for sharing this. Note too that attached documents from the 1960 meeting include review of Theme X, "The War for Independence," which was included also to first round legislative materials in support of the bill.

53 E. Winslow Turner, Legislative Assistant to Sen. Edward M. Kennedy, to Frederick J. Bradlee, November 30, 1964, Folder: NPS Memos on Boston NHP Legislative Support Data, 1963–74, Box 1, Resource Management Records, Early 1970s-1980s Park ("pre-park" generally), BNHP Archives, Charlestown, MA.

54 Beninati to O'Neill, February 26, 1965, Folder 27, Box 6, Subseries D, Series 3, Tip O'Neill Papers, Burns Library, Boston College, Chestnut Hill, MA.

55 O'Neill to Beninati, March 1, 1965, Folder 27, Box 6, Subseries D, Series 3, Tip O'Neill Papers, Burns Library, Boston College, Chestnut Hill, MA.

56 O'Neill to Beninati, March 1, 1965.

57 Bortman, responding to "sources he has not revealed to us," convinced O'Neill to omit the BNHSC's recommendation that the Boston Historical Society's president be given a special role in the proposed advisory board. Small, now superintendent of Minute Man National

Historical Park, to Regional Director Ronald F. Lee, December 29, 1964, Folder: Preliminaries, Memoranda from 1960s, Box 1, Resource Management Records, Early 1970s-1980s Park ("pre-park" generally), BNHP Archives, Charlestown, MA; U.S. Congress, House, *To Provide Federal Cooperation in a Program to Preserve Certain Historic Properties in the City of Boston, Massachusetts, and Vicinity, Associated with the Colonial and Revolutionary Periods of American History; to Authorize the Establishment of the Boston National Historic Sites; and for Other Purposes,* H.R. 5607, 89th Cong., 1st sess., introduced March 1, 1965; and U.S. Congress, House, *To Provide Federal Cooperation in a Program to Preserve Certain Historic Properties in the City of Boston, Massachusetts, and Vicinity, Associated with the Colonial and Revolutionary Periods of American History; to Authorize the Establishment of the Boston National Historic Sites; and for Other Purposes,* H.R. 8391, 89th Cong., 1st sess., introduced May 24, 1965. The reason for the reintroduction is unclear, as both bills are identical.

58 McCormack to Ralph Rivers, January 31, 1966, Folder 27, Box 6, Subseries D, Series 3, Tip O'Neill Papers, Burns Library, Boston College, Chestnut Hill, MA.

59 Secretary of the Interior to Aspinall, March 11, 1966, included in transcript of hearings on U.S. Congress, House, H.R. 5607 and U.S. Congress, House, H.R. 8391.

60 Robert B. Phillips, Evergreen Park, IL., "A Tourist's Memories," *Boston Globe,* August 12, 1965.

61 O'Neill to Aspinall, April 25, 1966, included in transcript of hearings on U.S. Congress, House, H.R. 5607 and U.S. Congress, House, H.R. 8391.

62 The draft statement is in Folder 43, Box 6, Subseries D, Series 3, Tip O'Neill Papers, Burns Library, Boston College, Chestnut Hill, MA.

63 O'Neill to Aspinall, April 25, 1966.

64 Joan Zenzen, who authored an administrative history of Minute Man National Historical Park, explains that during planning for the Minute Man National Historical Park, the "NPS definitely experienced loud and vociferous reactions to NPS buying land . . . I interviewed one woman whose husband had built their house with steel supports. He had then been stricken with polio and worked out of their house. NPS wanted the land and forced them out . . . The woman, many years later, was still fuming." Joan Zenzen, email message to author, January 27, 2018.

65 Bortman's comments appear on pages 4–6 of the transcript of hearings on U.S. Congress, House, H.R. 5607 and U.S. Congress, House, H.R. 8391.

66 Elliot's comments, including the quotation, appear in his statement, which is included in the transcript of hearings on U.S. Congress, House, H.R. 5607 and U.S. Congress, House, H.R. 8391.

67 These exchanges, including the quotations, appear on pages 9–16 of the transcript of hearings on U.S. Congress, House, H.R. 5607 and U.S. Congress, House, H.R. 8391.

68 These exchanges, including the quotations, appear on pages 22–27 of the transcript of hearings on U.S. Congress, House, H.R. 5607 and U.S. Congress, House, H.R. 8391.

69 Daniel A. Gilbert, "'Why Dwell on a Lurid Memory?': Deviance and Redevelopment in Boston's Scollay Square," *Massachusetts Historical Review* 9 (2007), 130.

70 This is to say that neither the *Congressional Record,* nor the bill file associated with H.R. 5607, 89th Congress, at the National Archives indicates that a final vote was taken or that a formal committee report issued. My thanks go to Judith Adkins, archivist, Center for Legislative Archives, National Archives and Records Administration, for confirming this. Adkins, email message to author, January 19, 2018.

71 Whitehill had faded out, though, and his historic sites committee, it seems, had stopped meeting by 1964. The Boston Landmarks Commission was established in 1969 as an advisory group and then lodged within the BRA during 1973–74 with the purpose of establishing restoration policies. For further details, see Folder 37, Box 7, Mayor Kevin White Papers, Boston City Archives, West Roxbury, MA.

72 Summary of interview with Maurice L. Kowal, Chief of Area Services, Minute Man National Historical Park, January 20, 1981, contained within binder located in Box 1, 1989 Administrative History Records, MIMA 76679, Minute Man NHP Archives, Concord, MA.

73 Lee, Regional Director, Northeast Region, to Superintendent, Minute Man National Historic Park, August 28, 1964, cited in Pauline Chase-Harrell, Carol Ely, and Stanley Moss, *Administrative History of the Salem Maritime National Historic Site* (Boston: NPS North Atlantic Regional Office, 1993), 108.

74 Summary of telephone interview with George Hartzog, January 23, 1981, contained within binder located in Box 1, 1989 Administrative History Records, MIMA 76679, Minute Man NHP Archives, Concord, MA.

75 For more on the origins of Hartzog's urban commitments, see George B. Harzog Jr. *Battling for the National Parks* (Mt. Kisco, NY: Moyer Bell, 1988); and Kathy Mengak, *Reshaping Our National Parks and Their Guardians: The Legacy of George B. Hartzog* (Albuquerque: University of New Mexico Press, 2012), ch. 6.

76 Chase-Harrell, et al., *Administrative History of the Salem Maritime National Historic Site*, 108.

77 Stephen P. Carlson, *Charlestown Navy Yard Historic Resource Study*, v. 1 (Boston: Division of Cultural Resources, National Park Service, 2010), 313.

78 The events and circumstances leading to the navy yard's closure are expertly recounted in Carlson, *Charlestown Navy Yard Historic Resource Study*, ch. 2, especially 178–278.

79 The BRA had been planning diligently for Expo 76, in part owing to Mayor Kevin White's strong support for it. As conceived, Boston's Expo 76 would create a massive floating city connecting Columbia Point in Dorchester to Thompson Island. Key among its opponents was State Senator John Joseph Moakley, who worried about its environmental impacts. All of this is key context for the genesis of Boston Harbor National Recreation Area. For an overview of Expo 76 in Boston, see Mark Arsenault, "Dreams and Doubts Collided in Plans for Global 'Expo,'" *Boston Globe*, April 19, 2015. For a broad overview of relevant planning activities, see the David C. Harrison Papers, 1963–1975, State Library of Massachusetts, Boston, MA. Quotations are from Ian Menzies, "Role for Boston and Charlestown in Expo '76," *Boston Globe*, September 9, 1970.

80 Menzies, "Role for Boston and Charlestown in Expo '76."

81 By "perception centers," Warner meant to suggest kiosks from which visitors could variously perceive Boston's past. Robert F. Hannan, "Hub to Revise Historic Sites," *Boston Herald Traveler*, December 10, 1970.

82 Hannan, "Hub to Revise Historic Sites."

83 The BRA also sought to develop in and around Bunker Hill, including with plans related to the Library Archive Building on Monument Square. See two alternatives in Folder: Proposals for Boston NHP Prepared by Boston Redevelopment Authority [1970–1973], Box 1, Resource Management Records, Early 1970s-1980s Park ("pre-park" generally), BNHP Archives, Charlestown, MA.

84 The details of these early visions are examined at length in Carlson, *Charlestown Navy Yard Historic Resource Study*, v. 1, 194–203.

85 BRA Director Robert T. Kenney sent the BRA's plan for a national historical park to Admiral R. E. Rumble, commandant of the First Naval District. Rumble approved it but explained that the navy was already working in partnership with the NPS, adding that "at the same time I recognize that if we are to succeed in this endeavor we must also work closely with the City of Boston, principally through your agency, the BRA." Rumble indicated that he had already worked with BRA agents, including Phil Zeigler, Marcia Meyers, and Marc Older. He suggested that Kenney meet with Rumble and Albert Benjamin of the NPS to discuss the matter. R. E. Rumble to Robert T. Kenney, Director, Boston Redevelopment Authority, November 30, 1973, Folder: Navy Memos on Boston NHP Legislation 1973–74, Box 1, Resource Management Records, Early 1970s-1980s Park ("pre-park" generally), BNHP Archives, Charlestown, MA.

86 Carlson, *Charlestown Navy Yard Historic Resource Study*, v. 1, 197–99.

87 Representative Tip O'Neill reintroduced legislation in the House to authorize the establishment of the park in 1972, while Senator Edward Kennedy followed suit in the Senate. This legislation evidently died early on, though it is unclear from the *Congressional Record* why this was, and access to the Edward Kennedy archive was unavailable at the time of this research. U.S.

Congress, House, full title unavailable, H.R. 16745 (54), 92nd Cong., 2nd sess., introduced September 20, 1972; and U.S. Congress, Senate, full title unavailable, S. 4009, 92nd Cong., 2nd sess., introduced September 20, 1972.

88   Carlson, *Charlestown Navy Yard Historic Resource Study*, v. 1, 180.

89   Northeast Regional Director Brooks to Director, April 27, 1973, Folder: "NPS Letters and Memos RE: Legislation, 1964–1978," Box 1, Resource Management Records, Early 1970s-1980s Park ("pre-park" generally), BNHP Archives, Charlestown, MA.

90   Position paper titled "Boston Naval Shipyard," attached to Chester L. Brooks, Director Northeast Region to General Superintendent, Boston Group Chief, New England Field Office, May 2, 1973, Folder: Initial Transition Navy Yard to NPS/Planning Factors [1973–1976], Box 1, Resource Management Records, Early 1970s-1980s Park ("pre-park" generally), BNHP Archives, Charlestown, MA. This folder contains a range of documents relating to the transfer conversation. Included are materials demonstrating the BRA's eagerness to take over the navy yard and how the NPS and others insisted that it recognize provisions put forth in the National Historic Preservation Act regarding disposition of the yard in accordance with Section 106. Evident, too, is pressure exerted by the desire to prepare for the Bicentennial. The NPS had conducted a study of the shipyard in 1971, and so it had been considering this future. The NPS and the navy generally agreed on the disposition of the site, though encountered some friction regarding who would handle interpretation and how to conceive of the USS *Constitution* Museum Foundation. The larger concern, however, related to the challenge of managing the BRA and the Metropolitan District Commission (MDC), which both wanted a hand in developing the area.

91   U.S. Congress, House, *A Bill to Authorize the Establishment of the Boston National Historical Park in the Commonwealth of Massachusetts*, H.R. 7486, 93rd Cong., 1st sess., introduced May 3, 1973; and U.S. Congress, Senate, *A Bill to Authorize the Establishment of the Boston National Historical Park in the Commonwealth of Massachusetts*, S. 210, 93rd Cong., 1st sess., introduced January 4, 1973. The lead in Kennedy's office was Mary Murtagh, who prepared this S. 210 as "a holding action prior to the passage of the Boston National Park legislation." Chief, New England Field Office, Albert J. Benjamin, to Regional Director, May 4, 1973, Folder: Initial Transition Navy Yard to NPS / Planning Factors 1973–76, Box 2, Resource Management Records, Early 1970s-1980s Park ("pre-park" generally), BNHP Archives, Charlestown, MA.

92   Edward M. Kennedy to Rogers C. Morton, May 8, 1973, Folder: NPS Letters and Memos RE Legislation, 1964–1978, Box 2, Resource Management Records, Early 1970s-1980s Park ("pre-park" generally), BNHP Archives, Charlestown, MA.

93   Transcript of testimony from John Sears, Chairman of the MDC, Folder: Testimony Given before the Senate Committee of Insular Affairs [Robert T. Kenney, September 10, 1973], Box 2, Resource Management Records, Early 1970s-1980s Park ("pre-park" generally), BNHP Archives, Charlestown, MA.

94   Transcript of testimony of Robert T. Kenney before Senate Subcommittee on Parks and Recreation, Committee on the Interior and Insular Affairs, September 10, 1973, Folder: Testimony Given before the Senate Committee of Insular Affairs [Robert T. Kenney, September 10, 1973], Box 2, Resource Management Records, Early 1970s-1980s Park ("pre-park" generally), BNHP Archives, Charlestown, MA.

95   Statement of Witness for Department of the Interior before the Subcommittee on Parks and Recreation, Senate Committee on Interior and Insular Affairs, Regarding S. 210, Folder: Testimony Given before the Senate Committee of Insular Affairs [Robert T. Kenney, September 10, 1973], Box 2, Resource Management Records, Early 1970s-1980s Park ("pre-park" generally), BNHP Archives, Charlestown, MA.

96   Secretary of Interior Horton to Rep. Henry M. Jackson, Chairman, Committee on Interior and Insular Affairs, October 4, 1973, Folder: NPS Letters and Memos RE Legislation, 1964–1978, Box 2, Resource Management Records, Early 1970s-1980s Park ("pre-park" generally), BNHP Archives, Charlestown, MA.

97   Statement of John W. Sears, Metropolitan District Commissioner, on behalf of Governor
     Francis W. Sargent and the MDC of Massachusetts, to the Subcommittee on Parks and
     Recreation of the House Committee on Interior and Insular Affairs on H.R. 7486, the Boston
     National Historic Park Bill, January 28, 1974, Folder: NPS Letters and Memos RE Legislation,
     1964–1978, Box 2, Resource Management Records, Early 1970s-1980s Park ("pre-park" gener-
     ally), BNHP Archives, Charlestown, MA.

98   Statement of Robert T. Kenney, Director of the Boston Redevelopment Authority before the
     House Subcommittee on National Parks and Recreation, May 30, 1974, Folder: NPS Letters and
     Memos RE Legislation, 1964–1978, Box 2, Resource Management Records, Early 1970s-1980s
     Park ("pre-park" generally), BNHP Archives, Charlestown, MA.

99   Testimony presented by Thomas P. O'Neill Jr., Member of Congress, 8th District, Mas-
     sachusetts, to the Subcommittee on Parks and Recreation of the House Committee on Int-
     erior and Insular Affairs on H.R. 7486, May 30, 1974, Folder: NPS Letters and Memos RE
     Legislation, 1964–1978, Box 2, Resource Management Records, Early 1970s-1980s Park ("pre-
     park" generally), BNHP Archives, Charlestown, MA.

100 Kennedy introduced S. 2915 for himself and on behalf of fellow Massachusetts Senator Edward
     Brooke. U.S. Congress, Senate, *Bill to Authorize Establishment of the Boston Navy Shipyard Historic Site,* S
     2915, 93rd Cong., 2nd sess., introduced January 29, 1974; U.S. Congress, House, *Bill to Authorize
     Establishment of the Boston Navy Shipyard Historic Site,* H.R. 12359, 93rd Cong., 2nd sess., introduced
     January 29, 1974.

101 Richard C. Curry, Associate Director of Legislation, to Deputy Director, February 26, 1974,
     Folder: NPS Letters and Memos RE Legislation, 1964–1978, Box 2, Resource Management
     Records, Early 1970s-1980s Park ("pre-park" generally), BNHP Archives, Charlestown, MA.

102 Curry to Regional Director, February 27, 1974, Folder: NPS Letters and Memos RE Legislation,
     1964–1978, Box 2, Resource Management Records, Early 1970s-1980s Park ("pre-park" gener-
     ally), BNHP Archives, Charlestown, MA. Curry suggested another strategy would be to provide
     figures by a much earlier date for a less-than-full-park option, with the intent of doing it well
     rather than doing a full park poorly. His conviction was that there was no way to accomplish
     implementation of a reasonable park concept in time for the Bicentennial.

103 The plan and related materials appear in Folders: NPS Proposals for Parks [Management,
     Acquisition, 1974–75], and Legislative Support Data 1974 For Boston NHP, both in Box 1,
     Resource Management Records, Early 1970s-1980s Park ("pre-park" generally), BNHP Archives,
     Charlestown, MA.

104 Undated memo from Jerry D. Wagers, Director, North Atlantic Region, to Associate Director
     Legislation (this appears to be a draft with edits); revised memo sent on May 1, 1974. Both appear
     in Folder: NPS Letters and Memos RE Legislation, 1964–1978, Box 2, Resource Management
     Records, Early 1970s-1980s Park ("pre-park" generally), BNHP Archives, Charlestown, MA.

105 Assistant Secretary of the Interior to Chairman James A. Haley, May 28, 1974, Folder: NPS
     Letters and Memos RE Legislation, 1964–1978, Box 2, Resource Management Records, Early
     1970s-1980s Park ("pre-park" generally), BNHP Archives, Charlestown, MA.

106 Curtis Bohlen, Deputy Assistant Secretary for Fish, Wildlife and Parks, represented the
     Department of Interior, accompanied by Ernest Connally, NPS Associate Director for Pro-
     fessional Services; Richard Curry, NPS Associate Director for Legislation; and Jerry Wagers,
     NPS Regional Director, North Atlantic Region.

107 U.S. Congress, House, Subcommittee on National Parks and Recreation, Committee on
     Interior and Insular Affairs, *Boston NHP Archives,* 93rd Cong., 2nd sess., 1974, 8.

108 U.S. Congress, *Boston NHP Archives,* 20.

109 U.S. Congress, *Boston NHP Archives,* 11.

110 U.S. Congress, *Boston NHP Archives* 12.

111 U.S. Congress, *Boston NHP Archives,* 34–35.

112 U.S. Congress, *Boston NHP Archives,* 57.

113 U.S. Congress, *Boston NHP Archives*, 77—78.

114 Rumble to J. William Middendorf, Secretary of the Navy, June 18, 1974, Folder: Navy Memos on Boston NHP Legislation 1973—74, Box 1, Resource Management Records, Early 1970s-1980s Park ("pre-park" generally), BNHP Archives, Charlestown, MA.

115 For details regarding changes and compromises in final document, see U.S. Congress, House, *Mark-Up Session: HR 7486, To Authorize the Establishment of the Boston National Historical Park in the Commonwealth of Massachusetts*, 93rd Cong., 2nd sess., July 10, 1974.

116 U.S. Congress, House, *A Bill to Authorize the Establishment of the Boston National Historical Park in the Commonwealth of Massachusetts*, H.R. 7486, 93rd Cong., 1st sess., introduced May 3, 1973, *Congressional Record Daily Digest*, July 10, 1974, D497.

117 *An Act to Authorize the Establishment of the Boston National Historical Park in the Commonwealth of Massachusetts*, Public Law 93—431, 88 Stat. 1184 (1974).

118 Dorchester Heights was added by *National Parks and Recreation Act of 1978*, Public Law 95—625, *U.S. Statutes at Large* 92 (1978): 3467—550.

119 Quoted in David Foster, "'Park Barrel' Politics." See also, James M. Ridenour, *The National Parks Compromised: Pork Barrel Politics and America's Treasures* (Merrillville, IN: ICS Books, 1994).

120 Quoted in Charles Davies and Dennis Frenchman, "Boston National Historical Park: Images of a Planning Process," Slide-Tape Transcript, August 29, 1975, Folder: BNHP: Images of a Planning Process, Aug. 29, 1975, Box 2, Resource Management Records, Early 1970s-1980s Park ("pre-park" generally), BNHP Archives, Charlestown, MA.

CHAPTER 4: PLANNING A PARK FOR "MODERN BOSTON AND MODERN AMERICA"

1 Consider, for instance, that NPS units hosted just less than eight million recreational visits in 1970. By 1976, the number had climbed to nearly thirty-three million. National Park Service, "Visitation Numbers," https://www.nps.gov/aboutus/visitation-numbers.htm. That same year, the top-grossing independent film in the United States was *Grizzly*, which takes place in a fictional national park wherein uniformed rangers fight to protect young parkgoers from a bloodthirsty bear. Wikipedia, "*Grizzly*," https://en.wikipedia.org/wiki/Grizzly_(film).

2 Mary Holmes, "But Where's the Park?," *Broadside* (Boston National Historical Park Newsletter) (Summer—Fall 1977), this and all subsequent references to this publication are from the private collection of Stephen P. Carlson. For an overview of the agency's investment in urban parks, see Sarah J. Morath, "A Park for Everyone: The National Park Service in Urban America," *Natural Resources Journal* 56 (Winter 2016): 1—21.

3 Summary of Minutes of Sixteenth Meeting, September 24, 1956, Folder: Meeting Minutes July-Dec 1956, Box 1, Boston National Historic Sites Commission Records, 1956—1960, BNHP Archives, Charlestown, MA.

4 *Mission Hill and the Miracle of Boston*, directed by Richard Broadman, Boston: Cine Research, in cooperation with CD Film Workshop, 1982.

5 Thomas H. O'Connor, *Building a New Boston: Politics and Urban Renewal, 1950 to 1970* (Boston: Northeastern University Press, 1995), 234. O'Connor cites John Hull Mollenkopf, *The Contested City* (Princeton: Princeton University Press, 1983). For more on renewal in the South End, see Violet Showers Johnson, *The Other Black Bostonians: West Indians in Boston, 1900—1950* (Bloomington: Indiana University Press, 2006); and Russ Lopez, *Boston's South End: The Clash of Ideas in a Historic Neighborhood* (Boston: Shawmut Peninsula Press, 2015). For more on Roxbury, and particularly the BRA's privileging there of white, middle-class values, see John H. Spiers, "'Planning with People:' Urban Renewal in Boston's Washington Park, 1950—1970," *Journal of Planning History* 8, no. 3 (August 2009): 221—47.

6 O'Connor, *Building a New Boston*, 234.

7 O'Connor, *Building a New Boston*, 235; and Lizabeth Cohen, *Saving America's Cities: Ed Logue and the Struggle to Renew Urban America in the Suburban Age* (New York: Farrar, Straus, and Giroux, 2019), 244.

8   Lawrence Kennedy, *Planning the City upon a Hill: Boston since 1630* (Amherst: University of Massachusetts Press, 1994), 200–1, quoted in O'Connor, *Building a New Boston*, 235.

9   Jim Vrabel, *A People's History of the New Boston* (Amherst: University of Massachusetts Press, 2014), 40–43, 47–59.

10 It is worth noting that the debate over school desegregation in Boston had been raging since the 1850s and had always been tied to Revolutionary memory. See Hilary J. Moss, "The Tarring and Feathering of Thomas Paul Smith: Common Schools, Revolutionary Memory, and the Crisis of Black Citizenship in Antebellum Boston," *The New England Quarterly* 80, no. 2 (2007): 218–41.

11 Robert Levey, "N.E. Freedom Rallies," *Boston Globe*, April 27, 1964; Jane Harriman, "Exhibit Own 'Freedom Trail,'" *Boston Globe*, February 10, 1964; "300 Trek Hub's Freedom Trail to Protest War," *Boston Globe*, August 10, 1969; John Wood and Peter Cowen, "1500 antiwar protesters in Boston march to Navy Yard," *Boston Globe*, May 14, 1972; and Carmen Fields, "Baird's pro-abortion protest broken up at North Church," *Boston Globe*, December 31, 1973. Correspondence concerning the 1971 Bunker Hill incident is in Metropolitan District Commission, Folder: Bunker Hill Monument, Yellow Tab Subject Files, Secretary's Office, Department of Conservation and Recreation, Boston, MA.

12 Hugh Gurney, interview by Seth C. Bruggeman, September 1, 2017.

13 National Public Radio, "Life After Iconic 1976 Photo: The American Flag's Role in Racial Protest," September 18, 2016, https://www.npr.org/2016/09/18/494442131/life-after-iconic -photo-todays-parallels-of-american-flags-role-in-racial-protes. See also, Louis P. Masur, *The Soiling of Old Glory: The Story of a Photograph that Shocked America* (New York: Bloomsbury Press, 2009).

14 "The Bicentennial Blues," *Ebony* 31, no. 8 (June 1, 1976): 152. Thanks to Mitch Kachun for this reference.

15 Joe Harrington, "Gas Lamp Renaissance," *Boston Globe*, October 24, 1965.

16 In this way, Boston experienced the same waves of early gentrification documented, for instance, by Suleiman Osman in Brooklyn, New York. See Osman, *The Invention of Brownstone Brooklyn: Gentrification and the Search for Authenticity in Postwar New York* (New York: Oxford University Press, 2011).

17 Jim Vrabel, *A People's History of the New Boston*, 110. Vrabel's statistics appear throughout chapter ten.

18 For details concerning the Freedom Trail Foundation's organizational genesis, see unsigned letter (probably Robert F. Friedmann or someone else affiliated with Friedmann & Rose, Inc.) to Fred Davis, December 5, 1996, Freedom Trail Foundation Offices, Boston, MA.

19 Friedmann's comments appear in Minutes of the Meeting, July 15, 1965, Greater Boston Chamber of Commerce, Freedom Trail Foundation, Folder: Office Files: Freedom Trail 1965, Box 253, Mayor John F. Collins Papers, Boston City Archives, West Roxbury, MA.

20 Mrs. Jack Gold to Mayor John Collins, July 7, 1964, Folder: Office Files: Freedom Trail 1965, Box 253; Donald A. Armistead to Mayor John Collins, September 7, 1962, Folder: Office Files: Department of Public Works, Freedom Trail Commission, 1962–64, Box 80; and D. K. Benson to Mayor John Collins, July 19, 1965, Folder: Office Files: Department of Public Works, Freedom Trail Commission, 1962–64, Box 80, all in Mayor John F. Collins Papers, Boston City Archives, West Roxbury, MA.

21 See, for instance, Edgar J. Driscoll Jr., "Richard Berenson, 81; Civic Leader Who Guided City's Freedom Trail," *Boston Globe*, April 4, 1990.

22 Unsigned letter (possibly Robert F. Friedmann or someone else affiliated with Friedmann & Rose, Inc.) to Fred Davis, December 5, 1996, Freedom Trail Foundation Offices, Boston, MA.

23 *An Act Providing for an Official Designation and Delineation of a Freedom Trail in the City of Boston.* 1965 Mass. Acts 33, ch. 625 (January 1965).

24 Minutes of the Meeting, July 15, 1965, Greater Boston Chamber of Commerce, Freedom Trail Foundation; Cathleen Cohen, "Freedom Trail Booth a Multi-Purpose Room," *Boston Globe*, October 2, 1966; "Public Gets Chance to Buy Freedom Trail Shares," *Boston Globe*, July 16, 1965;

and Sara Davidson, "Ground-Breaking This Week: Plan Common Tourists Booth," *Boston Globe*, September 26, 1965.

25 Wilma Little to John A. Volpe, September 27, 1967, Folder: Department of Public Works Freedom Trail Commission 1965, Box 80, Mayor John F. Collins Papers, Boston City Archives, West Roxbury, MA.

26 Ken Botwright, "Those 'Blue' Sundays on the Freedom Trail," *Boston Globe*, July 9, 1966.

27 Display ad 152, *Boston Globe*, February 6, 1966.

28 Cohen, "Freedom Trail Booth a Multi-Purpose Room."

29 Barry Bluestone and Mary Huff Stevenson, *The Boston Renaissance: Race, Space, and Economic Change in an American Metropolis* (New York: Russell Sage Foundation, 2000), 59–66.

30 John Wood, "At the Yard, 'It's Too Late to Be Crying,'" *Boston Globe*, May 8, 1973.

31 O'Connor, *Building a New Boston*, 267–68.

32 According to Cohen, Logue imagined a "walk to the sea" from the Charles River to Boston Harbor. See Cohen, *Saving America's Cities*, 162.

33 O'Connor, *Building a New Boston*, 270–79, quotation 276. With regard to the problem of financing, see Cohen, *Saving America's Cities*, 185. On Rouse's vision for Faneuil Hall and its place within the broader landscape of American retail experience, see Alison Isenberg, *Downtown America: A History of the Place and the People Who Made It* (Chicago: University of Chicago Press, 2004), ch. 7, specifically 294–96 concerning the surprise success of Rouse's work in Boston.

34 Kevin White to Burgess & Blacher Architects, n.d. (ca. July 1973), Folder 6, Correspondence: BRA 1973 July -1974 December, Box 2, 0245.001 General Correspondence, 1969–1975 B, Mayor Kevin White Papers, Boston City Archives, West Roxbury, MA.

35 Chronology detailed in James I. F. Matthew, Deputy Director General Manager, to Henderson Supplee Jr., June 22, 1966, Folder 20, 1975 World Freedom Fair, Inc.—Weekly Reports September-December 1966, Box 2, David C. Harrison Papers, 1963–1975, State Library of Massachusetts, Boston, MA. Regarding BRA appointments, see Harrison's draft BRA report, February 24, 1967, Folder 27, 1975 World Freedom Fair, Inc., Box 2, David C. Harrison Papers, 1963–1975, State Library of Massachusetts, Boston, MA; and David C. Harrison to Walter Muir Whitehill, September 26, 1966, Folder 22, 1975 World Freedom Fair, Inc.—Correspondence June 1966-September 1967, Box 2, David C. Harrison Papers, 1963–1975, State Library of Massachusetts, Boston, MA. For the essay, see Walter Muir Whitehill, "Cerebration versus Celebration," *Virginia Magazine of History and Biography* 68, no. 3 (July 1960): 259–70.

36 For an overview of Expo 76 in Boston, see Mark Arsenault, "Dreams and Doubts Collided in Plans for Global 'Expo,'" *Boston Globe*, April 19, 2015; and Ian Menzies, "Role for Boston and Charlestown in Expo '76," *Boston Globe*, September 9, 1970. For a broad overview of planning activities, see David C. Harrison Papers, 1963–1975, State Library of Massachusetts, Boston, MA. Moakley's opposition to Expo 76 is discussed in Laura Muller, "The Contributions of Congressman John Joseph Moakley to Historical Preservation in Boston," (unpublished report), Moakley Archive and Institute, Suffolk University, Boston, MA. 2005, 1–2.

37 For the details of Boston 200's genesis, and an overview of its programs, see Boston 200 Corporation, *Boston: The Official Bicentennial Guidebook* (New York: Dutton, 1975), U.S. Government Documents, Boston Public Library, Boston, MA. Quotation appears on page 99.

38 According to NPS Bureau Historian John H. Sprinkle Jr., an earlier publicly funded Black History walking trail may have operated in Harlem beginning in the late 1960s.

39 Trail maps and route descriptions appear in Boston 200 Corporation, *Boston: The Official Bicentennial Guidebook*. On the two freedom trails, see Mary Meier, "Now There Are 2 Freedom Trails to Follow," *Boston Globe*, May 30, 1975.

40 M. J. Rymsza-Pawlowska, *History Comes Alive: Public History and Popular Culture in the 1970s* (Chapel Hill: University of North Carolina Press, 2017), 98–105.

41 Regarding the play, see materials in Folder 6, Festival American: Take a Look Around/National Park Service, Box 15, Boston 200 Collection, Boston City Archives, West Roxbury, MA. For feedback from students of Buckingham Brown and Nichols School following their November 12,

1974, tour of Charlestown, see Folder 8, Task Force Projects: Education: Walking Tours kids' reactions 1974, Box 6, Boston 200 Collection, Boston City Archives, West Roxbury, MA. John Bodnar discusses the play in terms of its framing of patriotism, citizen responsibility, and nation building in Bodnar, *Remaking America: Public Memory, Commemoration, and Patriotism in the Twentieth Century* (Princeton: Princeton University Press, 1992), 201–03.

42   Files concerning the Freedom Trail's dedication as a National Recreation Trail appear in Box 15, Boston 200 Collection, Boston City Archives, West Roxbury, MA.

43   Rymsza-Pawlowska, *History Comes Alive*, 139–42; Tammy S. Gordon, *The Spirit of 1976: Commerce, Community, and the Politics of Commemoration* (Amherst: University of Massachusetts Press, 2013), 76–77.

44   Ellen Goodman, "More than a Bicentennial Minute," *Ms.* (December 1976), 20, quoted in Gordon, *The Spirit of 1976*, 113.

45   Gordon, *The Spirit of 1976*, 114–15.

46   There are many overviews of the turn in Revolution historiography, including John Selby, "Revolutionary America: The Historiography," *OAH Magazine of History* 8 (Summer 1994), 5–8.

47   For a broad engagement with this problem and others concerning history in the NPS, see Anne Mitchell Whisnant, Marla R. Miller, Gary B. Nash, and David Paul Thelen, *Imperiled Promise: The State of History in the National Park Service* (Bloomington, IN: Organization of American Historians, 2011). On the 1970s job crisis, see Robert B. Townsend, "History in Those Hard Times: Looking for Jobs in the 1970s," *Perspectives on History: The News Magazine of the American Historical Association*, September 1, 2009, https://www.historians.org/publications-and-directories/perspectives-on-history/september-2009/history-in-those-hard-times-looking-for-jobs-in-the-1970s. On the confluence of progressive historians, the job crises, and NPS careers, see Cathy Stanton, *The Lowell Experiment: Public History in a Postindustrial City* (Amherst: University of Massachusetts Press, 2006), 8–16, 139.

48   Quoted in David Foster, "'Park Barrel' Politics Seen as Redefining 75-Year-Old National System," *Los Angeles Times*, October 13, 1991. See also, James M. Ridenour, *The National Parks Compromised: Pork Barrel Politics and America's Treasures* (Merrillville, IN: ICS Books, 1994).

49   Tammy Gordon summarizes this scenario in *The Spirit of 1976*, 105–7.

50   On NPS resistance to unit authorization and the succession of leadership, see Barry Mackintosh, *The National Parks: Shaping the System* (Washington, DC: U.S. Department of the Interior, 1991), 57–59.

51   Russell K. Olsen, *Administrative History: Organizational Structure of the National Park Service, 1917 to 1985*, (Washington, DC: National Park Service, September 1985), https://www.nps.gov/parkhistory/online_books/olsen/adhi-a.htm.

52   The Denver Service Center was established November 15, 1971. See chart 30 in Olsen, *Administrative History*. For details regarding individual service centers, see "Service Centers," in Harold P. Danz, *Historic Listing of National Park Service Officials*, May 1, 1991, https://www.nps.gov/parkhistory/online_books/tolson/histlist11.htm.

53   Master Plan Alternatives for BNHP, revised draft, June 23, 1975, Folder 1, Box 30, RG79, NPS Division of Interpretive Planning (entry P417); NARA, College Park, MD.

54   *Boston Beacon* (Boston National Historical Park newsletter), December 10, 1976, private collection of Stephen P. Carlson.

55   Acting Associate Director, Legislation, to Regional Director, North Atlantic Region, October 10, 1974, Folder: Boston NHP Resource Management Records, BNHP Legislation [Activation Memos, newsletters, 1974–1977], Box 1, Resource Management Records, Early 1970s-1980s Park ("pre-park" generally), BNHP Archives, Charlestown, MA.

56   The NPS invited local media to witness the meeting. See News Release, "Meeting Set to Begin Planning for Boston NHP Archives," November 18, 1974, Folder: BNHP Planning 1974, 1982, Box 1, Boston NHP Resource Management Records, Superintendent Files, Staff Meetings and Annual Reports, BNHP Archives, Charlestown, MA.

57 Meeting Minutes, November 21, 1974, Folder: BNHP Planning 1974, 1982, Box 1, Boston NHP Resource Management Records, Superintendent Files, Staff Meetings and Annual Reports, BNHP Archives, Charlestown, MA.

58 Meeting Minutes, November 21, 1974.

59 Meeting Minutes, November 21, 1974.

60 Meetings noted in Gurney to Regional Director, March 14, 1977, Folder: Boston NHP Resource Management Records, BNHP Legislation [Activation Memos, newsletters, 1974–1977], Box 1, Resource Management Records, Early 1970s-1980s Park ("pre-park" generally), BNHP Archives, Charlestown, MA.

61 Draft statement of objectives for planning and management, February 3, 1975, Folder: BNHP Planning 1974, 1982, Box 1, Boston NHP Resource Management Records, Superintendent Files, Staff Meetings and Annual Reports, BNHP Archives, Charlestown, MA.

62 Draft statement of objectives for planning and management, February 3, 1975.

63 Regional Director Jerry Wagers to "All those interested," February 3, 1975, Folder: BNHP Planning 1974, 1982, Box 1, Boston NHP Resource Management Records, Superintendent Files, Staff Meetings and Annual Reports, BNHP Archives, Charlestown, MA. Although it is unclear during what meetings they were taken, handwritten notes evidently compiled during discussion of alternatives appear in Folder: Boston National Historic Site, Box 30, Division of Interpretive Planning, Entry P417, RG 79 National Park Service, NARA, College Park, MD. Thanks to Jay Driskell for assisting with acquisition of these materials.

64 "Minimum Requirements for Operation of Boston National Historical Park", May 23, 1975, Folder: BNHP Planning 1974, 1982, Box 1, Boston NHP Resource Management Records, Superintendent Files, Staff Meetings and Annual Reports, BNHP Archives, Charlestown, MA.

65 My chronology of the review process is based on Gurney to Regional Director, March 14, 1977, Folder: Boston NHP Resource Management Records, BNHP Legislation [Activation Memos, newsletters, 1974–1977], Box 1, Resource Management Records, Early 1970s-1980s Park ("pre-park" generally), BNHP Archives, Charlestown, MA.

66 Master Plan Alternatives for Boston NHP, revised draft, June 23, 1975, i, Folder: Boston National Historic Site, Box 30, Division of Interpretive Planning, Entry P417, RG 79 National Park Service, NARA, College Park, MD.

67 Master Plan Alternatives for Boston NHP, revised draft June 23, 1975, ii.

68 Master Plan Alternatives for Boston NHP, revised draft June 23, 1975, 1–7.

69 Master Plan Alternatives for Boston NHP, revised draft June 23, 1975, 9–12.

70 Osgood was a senior trust officer at the State Street Bank and Trust Company and, though identified with the Paul Revere House during the park's first meeting, was also a stakeholder in the Old State House. Osgood was not the only individual who was involved with multiple sites. This quote, and the others that I've included in this paragraph, appear in James Corson, Chief of Interpretation North Atlantic Region, to the Park Master Planners, December 8, 1975, Folder: BNHP Planning, 1973–1978, Box 1, Boston NHP Resource Management Records, Superintendent Files, Staff Meetings and Annual Reports, BNHP Archives, Charlestown, MA. James Corson, Chief of Interpretation North Atlantic Region, to the Park Master Planners, December 8, 1975.

71 James Corson, Chief of Interpretation North Atlantic Region, to the Park Master Planners, December 8, 1975.

72 Boston National Historical Park Advisory Commission meeting minutes, December 8, 1975, Boston National Historical Park Advisory Commission Records, 1974–1986, BNHP Archives, Charlestown, MA.

73 Boston National Historical Park Advisory Commission meeting minutes, December 8, 1975.

74 Although various versions of the draft and revised alternatives exist, it is unclear which drafts are which—many are partial—thereby complicating possibilities for understanding

the evolution of this document. The most complete collection of materials is in Master Plan Alternatives for Boston NHP, revised draft June 23, 1975, Folder: Boston National Historic Site, Box 30, Division of Interpretive Planning, Entry P417, RG 79 National Park Service, NARA, College Park, MD. But even this version is incomplete and further complicated by handwritten corrections. Clarifying this record set is a top priority for understanding the genesis of the park's first management plan.

75   Gurney to Regional Director, March 14,1977, Folder: Boston NHP Resource Management Records, BNHP Legislation [Activation Memos, newsletters, 1974–1977], Box 1, Resource Management Records, early 1970s-1980s park ("pre-park" generally), Boston NHP Archives, Charlestown, MA.

76   Special Subcommittee of the Advisory Commission Statement of Support for Alternative Four, 1977, Folder: Boston NHP Resource Management Records, BNHP Legislation [Activation Memos, newsletters, 1974–1977], Box 1, Resource Management Records, Early 1970s-1980s Park ("pre-park" generally), BNHP Archives, Charlestown, MA.

77   Special Subcommittee of the Advisory Commission Statement of Support for Alternative Four, 1977.

78   Special Subcommittee of the Advisory Commission Statement of Support for Alternative Four, 1977. At their December 7, 1976, meeting, the commission agreed that formal public review of the Environmental Assessment was not necessary, given that "the Commission and the site owners had been given ample opportunity to express their views and since the Commission and those involved with the specific sites represented the interested public." Gurney to Regional Director, March 14,1977, Folder: Boston NHP Resource Management Records, BNHP Legislation [Activation Memos, newsletters, 1974–1977], Box 1, Resource Management Records, Early 1970s-1980s Park ("pre-park" generally), BNHP Archives, Charlestown, MA.

79   Charles Davies and Dennis Frenchman, "Boston National Historical Park: Images of a Planning Process," Slide-Tape Transcript, August 29, 1975, Folder: BNHP: Images of a Planning Process, Aug. 29, 1975, Box 2, Resource Management Records, Early 1970s-1980s Park ("pre-park" generally), BNHP Archives, Charlestown, MA. Note that Frenchman also had a role in planning at Lowell National Historical Park. See Stanton, *The Lowell Experiment*, 25.

80   Davies and Frenchman, "Boston National Historical Park."

81   Davies and Frenchman, "Boston National Historical Park."

82   Davies and Frenchman, "Boston National Historical Park." The NPS had done considerable outreach in and around Charlestown prior to authorization. For details, see Folder: Initial Transition Navy Yard to NPS / Planning Factors 1973–76, Box 1, Resource Management Records, Early 1970s-1980s Park ("pre-park" generally), BNHP Archives, Charlestown, MA. By way of comparison, consider the BRA's interests in and planning with Charlestown, discussed in O'Conner, *Building a New Boston*, 217–19.

83   Davies and Frenchman, "Boston National Historical Park."

84   Davies and Frenchman, "Boston National Historical Park."

85   For the conference report on H.R. 8773, wherein these negotiations are summarized, see U.S. Congress, House, Committee on Appropriations, *Making Appropriations for Department of interior and Related Agencies*, 94th Cong., 1st sess., H. Rept. 94–701, Washington: GPO, 1975.

86   For various appeals, see Folder 5, Appropriations Committee, Boston National Park, March-November 1975, Box 4, Subseries A, Legislative Files, Series III, Tip O'Neill Papers, Burns Library, Boston College, Chestnut Hill, MA. These include Joseph Fraser Conlan to O'Neill, February 27, 1975; Thomas F. Carty, Staff Advisor, and Andrew C. Hyde, Design Coordinator, Massachusetts Bay Transportation Authority, to O'Neill, March 3, 1975; Davis Taylor, Publisher, *Boston Globe*, to O'Neill, April 25, 1975; Mayor Kevin H. White to O'Neill, April 25, 1975; and Robert T. Kenney, Director BRA, to O'Neill, May 16, 1975.

87   Katharine D. Kane, Director, Boston 200, to O'Neill, March 12, 1975, Folder 5, Appropriations Committee, Boston National Park, March-November 1975, Box 4, Subseries A, Legislative Files, Series III, Tip O'Neill Papers, Burns Library, Boston College, Chestnut Hill, MA.

88 O'Neill to Sidney R. Yates, Chair Subcommittee on the Interior House Committee on App-ropriations, March 20, 1975, Folder 5, Appropriations Committee, Boston National Park, March-November 1975, Box 4, Subseries A, Legislative Files, Series III, Tip O'Neill Papers, Burns Library, Boston College, Chestnut Hill, MA.

89 *Department of the Interior and Related Agencies Appropriation Act,* Public Law 94–165, U.S. *Statues at Large* 89 (1975): 977–1001.

90 These figures are from house decision on H.R. 8773 (not final law), as reported by O'Neill to Kane, July 25, 1975, Folder 5, Appropriations Committee, Boston National Park, March-November 1975, Box 4, Subseries A, Legislative Files, Series III, Tip O'Neill Papers, Burns Library, Boston College, Chestnut Hill, MA. The transitional period reflected the change of the federal fiscal year from July 1 to June 30 to October 1 to September 30 starting with fiscal year 1977.

91 Hugh Gurney, interview by Seth C. Bruggeman, September 1, 2017.

92 Gurney had taken the tour and then, later, saw the vacancy notice for the new superintendent position. He applied and got the job, though it turned out he was a second pick after the top choice turned it down. Gurney thinks it may have actually been Benjamin. See Hugh Gurney, interview by Seth C. Bruggeman, September 1, 2017.

93 Nan Rickey, interview by Sarah Patton and Christine Arato, March 6, 2015, 43, Unprocessed Files, Longfellow House Washington's Headquarters National Historic Site Archives, Resource Management Records, John Fitzgerald Kennedy National Historic Site.

94 Hugh Gurney, interview by Seth C. Bruggeman, September 1, 2017.

95 Gurney's recollections of Maynard Spekin are recorded in my notes taken during an unrecorded conversation on July 12, 2017. Details regarding the queen's visit, and Spekin's role therein, appear in Hugh Gurney, interview by Seth C. Bruggeman, September 1, 2017. Thanks to Steve Carlson for his observations concerning Dave Rose.

96 Hugh Gurney, interview by Seth C. Bruggeman, September 1, 2017.

97 Hugh Gurney, interview by Seth C. Bruggeman, September 1, 2017.

98 Hugh Gurney, interview by Seth C. Bruggeman, September 1, 2017.

99 Gurney's recollections of Jason A. Aisner are recorded in my notes taken during an unrecorded conversation on July 12, 2017.

100 Meghan V. Doran, "Racial Remembering in Urban Politics," *American Journal of Cultural Sociology* 7 (2019): 29–53.

101 Osgood to Hugh Gurney, January 23, 1976, Folder: BNHP Planning, 1973–1978, Box 1, Boston NHP Resource Mgmt. Records, Supt Files, Staff Meetings and annual reports, BNHP Archives, Charlestown, MA.

CHAPTER 5: THE PROBLEM WITH HISTORY, THE PROBLEM WITH RACE

1 Peter Kadzis, "Black Group Attacked in Charlestown," *Boston Globe,* November 15, 1977.

2 Kadzis, "Black Group Attacked in Charlestown."

3 For broad context concerning this event and others like it, see Cameron McWhirter, *Red Summer: The Summer of 1919 and the Awakening of Black America* (New York: Henry Holt & Co., 2011).

4 Ronald P. Formisano, *Boston Against Busing: Race, Class, and Ethnicity in the 1960s and 1970s* (Chapel Hill: University of North Carolina Press, 1991), 123–24.

5 Kadzis, "Black Group Attacked in Charlestown."

6 Kadzis, "Black Group Attacked in Charlestown." See also, pages XXX–XX of this book.

7 Arthur Jones and Alexander Hawes Jr., "Byrne to Seek Indictments Today in Charlestown Attack on Blacks," *Boston Globe,* November 16, 1977.

8 James M. Hammond and George Croft, "Three Men Innocent in Charlestown Assault Case," *Boston Globe,* December 7, 1978; "Beating Investigations Should Continue," *Charlestown Patriot,* December 14, 1978, reprinted in *Boston Globe,* December 19, 1978; and "Charlestown Case Reopening Asked," *Boston Globe,* January 27, 1979. Battles is quoted in Timothy Dougherty, "Pottstown Students Not Surprised by Outcome of Boston Trial," *Philadelphia Tribune,* December 12, 1978.

9   Gurney cited in Boston National Historical Park Advisory Commission meeting minutes, May 26, 1978, Boston National Historical Park Advisory Commission Records, 1974–1986, BNHP Archives, Charlestown, MA.

10 "Bunker Hill Joins the National Park System," *Broadside* (Boston National Historical Park Newsletter) 2, no. 1 (April 1977): 2, this and all subsequent references to this publication are from the private collection of Stephen P. Carlson.

11 See, for instance, "Omnibus Parks Bill," *CQ Almanac 1978*, 34th ed., 704–07, http://library .cqpress.com/cqalmanac/cqal78–123690.

12 The legal transfer occurred on September 8, 1980. Anthony J. Yudis, "Park Service Due to Receive Historic Dorchester Heights," *Boston Globe*, February 19, 1980; and Thomas P. Winn, "A Proud Day for Heights," *Boston Globe*, March 9, 1980.

13 On Moakley's New Deal childhood, see Mark Robert Schneider, *Joe Moakley's Journey from South Boston to El Salvador* (Boston: Northeastern University Press, 2013), 61.

14 Laura Muller discusses the relationship between Moakley and McCormack in Muller, "The Contributions of Congressman John Joseph Moakley," unpublished paper in Congressman John Joseph Moakley Papers, Moakley Archive and Institute, Suffolk University, Boston, MA, 4–6. The Bicentennial designation is discussed in Muller, "The Contributions of Congressman John Joseph Moakley," 9.

15 1979 Annual Report, Folder: BNHP Annual Reports 1978–1989, Box 1, Boston NHP Resource Management Records, Superintendent Files, Staff Meetings and Annual Reports, BNHP Archives, Charlestown, MA.

16 *Boston Beacon* (Boston National Historical Park Newsletter), December 10, 1976, this and all subsequent references to this publication are from the private collection of Stephen P. Carlson.

17 Preservation Specialist Steve Carlson notes that Ed Locke and Frank Wilson also transferred to the NPS protection division from the navy yard and that both later ended up in the maintenance division aboard the USS *Cassin Young*. *Boston Beacon*, December 10, 1976.

18 *Boston Beacon*, December 10, 1976.

19 Steele held a BA from Yale University and MA in history museum studies from the Cooperstown Graduate Program. He began his NPS career as a curator in New York City and then at Sagamore Hill National Historic Site before coming to Boston. See "Park Names New Deputy Superintendent, Assistant Superintendent," *Broadside* (Winter 1991): 1.

20 Squad meeting minutes, September 8, 1981, Folder: Squad Meetings 01/1981–05/1982, Boston NHP Resource Management Records, Superintendent Files, Staff Meetings and Annual Reports, BNHP Archives, Charlestown, MA.

21 1978 Annual Report, Folder: BNHP Annual Reports 1978–1989, Box 1, Boston NHP Resource Management Records, Superintendent Files, Staff Meetings and Annual Reports, BNHP Archives, Charlestown, MA.

22 1979 Annual Report.

23 Harpers Ferry Center, "Our History," National Park Service, https://www.nps.gov/subjects /hfc/our-history.htm.

24 Boston National Historical Park Advisory Commission meeting minutes, May 19, 1977, Boston National Historical Park Advisory Commission Records, 1974–1986, BNHP Archives, Charlestown, MA.

25 Boston National Historical Park Advisory Commission meeting minutes, October 19, 1977, Boston National Historical Park Advisory Commission Records, 1974–1986, BNHP Archives, Charlestown, MA.

26 Boston National Historical Park Advisory Commission meeting minutes, May 5, 1981, Boston National Historical Park Advisory Commission Records, 1974–1986, BNHP Archives, Charlestown, MA.

27 1978 Annual Report.

28 1979 Annual Report.

29 Squad meeting minutes, November 24, 1981, Folder: Squad Meetings 01/1981–05/1982, Boston NHP Resource Management Records, Superintendent Files, Staff Meetings and Annual Reports, BNHP Archives, Charlestown, MA.

30 1981 Annual Report, Folder: BNHP Annual Reports 1978–1989, Box 1, Boston NHP Resource Management Records, Superintendent Files, Staff Meetings and Annual Reports, BNHP Archives, Charlestown, MA.

31 1978 Annual Report.

32 Boston National Historical Park Advisory Commission meeting minutes, October 19, 1977.

33 Boston National Historical Park Advisory Commission meeting minutes, May 19, 1977.

34 "What's Happening in the Park," Boston National Historical Park Newsletter, October 11, 1977, this and all subsequent references to this publication are from the private collection of Stephen P. Carlson; Ellen Fineberg, "HUES Program Now Underway," *Broadside* 3, no. 3 (Winter 1978): 6; and 1979 Annual Report. For more on HUES, see memos of agreement with Boston University's Human Environment Institute, Folder: COI NPS NARO/NERO, CRM Division Records 1931–1995, Box 18, RG 79 National Park Service, National Archives of Boston, Waltham, MA.

35 Boston National Historical Park Advisory Commission meeting minutes, May 5, 1981.

36 Boston National Historical Park Advisory Commission meeting minutes, December 2, 1982, Boston National Historical Park Advisory Commission Records, 1974–1986, BNHP Archives, Charlestown, MA.

37 Boston National Historical Park Advisory Commission meeting minutes, May 24, 1983, Boston National Historical Park Advisory Commission Records, 1974–1986, BNHP Archives, Charlestown, MA.

38 Boston National Historical Park Advisory Commission meeting minutes, April 12, 1984, Boston National Historical Park Advisory Commission Records, 1974–1986, BNHP Archives, Charlestown, MA.

39 Boston National Historical Park Advisory Commission meeting minutes, June 13, 1985, Boston National Historical Park Advisory Commission Records, 1974–1986, BNHP Archives, Charlestown, MA.

40 Mention of "People and Places" first appeared in Boston National Historical Park Advisory Commission meeting minutes, November 14, 1985, Boston National Historical Park Advisory Commission Records, 1974–1986, BNHP Archives, Charlestown, MA. For an early profile of the new program, see Paul Hirshson, "City Life: Taking Hold of History," *Boston Globe*, April 10, 1984, 17.

41 Quotations are from Hugh Gurney, interview by Seth C. Bruggeman, September 1, 2017.

42 Boston National Historical Park Advisory Commission meeting minutes, April and May 1976, Boston National Historical Park Advisory Commission Records, 1974–1986, BNHP Archives, Charlestown.

43 1981 Annual Report. Drafts of several cooperative agreements—with the CVB, the City of Boston, the Old South Association, the Bostonian Society, and the Paul Revere Memorial Association—appear in the appendix of the park's GMP. Boston NHP, *General Management Plan, Volume 1* (1980), report on file, National Park Service, Denver Service Center, Denver, CO.

44 Boston National Historical Park Advisory Commission meeting minutes, October 3, 1978, Boston National Historical Park Advisory Commission Records, 1974–1986, BNHP Archives, Charlestown, MA; and 1978 Annual Report.

45 1979 Annual Report.

46 1979 Annual Report.

47 Section 106 files, BNHP Archives, Charlestown, MA.

48 Squad meeting minutes, November 24, 1981.

49 Boston National Historical Park Advisory Commission meeting minutes, December 7, 1976, Boston National Historical Park Advisory Commission Records, 1974–1986, BNHP Archives, Charlestown, MA.

50 Boston National Historical Park Advisory Commission meeting minutes, October 27, 1981, Boston National Historical Park Advisory Commission Records, 1974–1986, BNHP Archives, Charlestown, MA.

51 Boston National Historical Park Advisory Commission meeting minutes, April 29, 1982, Boston National Historical Park Advisory Commission Records, 1974–1986, BNHP Archives, Charlestown, MA.

52 Squad meeting minutes, March 3, 1981, Folder: Squad Meetings 01/1981–05/1982, Boston NHP Resource Management Records, Superintendent Files, Staff Meetings and Annual Reports, BNHP Archives, Charlestown, MA.

53 Squad meeting minutes, April 6, 1982, Folder: Squad Meetings 01/1981–05/1982, Boston NHP Resource Management Records, Superintendent Files, Staff Meetings and Annual Reports, BNHP Archives, Charlestown, MA.

54 Boston National Historical Park Advisory Commission meeting minutes, May 24, 1983.

55 Boston National Historical Park Advisory Commission meeting minutes, November 29, 1983, Boston National Historical Park Advisory Commission Records, 1974–1986, BNHP Archives, Charlestown, MA.

56 Boston National Historical Park Advisory Commission meeting minutes, April 12, 1984.

57 Nan V. Rickey, Interpretive Planner, Division of Planning, Denver Service Center to Team Manager, Northeast Team, Denver Service Center, February 27, 1974, File: Boston National Historic Site, Box 30, RG79 National Park Service, NPS Division of Interpretive Planning (entry P417), NARA, College Park, MD.

58 Nan V. Rickey, Interpretive Planner, Division of Planning, Denver Service Center to Team Manager, Northeast Team, Denver Service Center, February 27, 1974. See also, David Wallace's (Harpers Ferry Center) summary of state of collections at various park sites, prepared for Rickey, in Harpers Ferry Center Manager to Denver Service Center Manager, March 5, 1975, Folder: Boston National Historic Site, Box 30, RG79 National Park Service, NPS Division of Interpretive Planning (entry P417), NARA, College Park, MD.

59 Boston National Historical Park Advisory Commission meeting minutes, December 7, 1976. Although it's not entirely clear to what group Berenson is referring, it is most likely the Boston Landmarks Commission.

60 Boston National Historical Park Advisory Commission meeting minutes, May 19, 1977.

61 "What's Happening in the Park," Boston National Historical Park Newsletter, October 11, 1977.

62 Boston National Historical Park Advisory Commission meeting minutes, May 19, 1977.

63 For an overview of this trend, see M. J. Rymsza-Pawlowska, *History Comes Alive: Public History and Popular Culture in the 1970s* (Chapel Hill: University of North Carolina Press, 2017).

64 Boston National Historical Park Advisory Commission meeting minutes, May 26, 1978.

65 Boston National Historical Park Advisory Commission meeting minutes, October 3, 1978.

66 Boston National Historical Park Advisory Commission meeting minutes, October 3, 1978.

67 "Sarah, A Proud Bostonian," *Broadside* (Spring 1979): 5.

68 "Summer 1979, A Special Summer," *Broadside* (Summer–Fall 1979): 2.

69 1979 Annual Report.

70 Boston National Historical Park Advisory Commission meeting minutes, November 29, 1983.

71 Hugh Gurney, interview by Seth C. Bruggeman, September 1, 2017.

72 For a detailed consideration of user access in the navy yard, including with regard to the Chelsea Street connector, see Stephen P. Carlson, *Charlestown Navy Yard Historic Resource Study*, v. 1 (Boston: Division of Cultural Resources, National Park Service, 2010), 215–22.

73 Richard Berenson, quoted from Boston National Historical Park Advisory Commission meeting minutes, April (or May) 1976.

74 See discussions regarding transportation and concessions in Boston National Historical Park Advisory Commission meeting minutes, May 19, 1977; and Carlson, *Charlestown Navy Yard Historic Resource Study*, v. 1, 222–24.

75 Gurney refers to it as the park's "YACC program." Boston National Historical Park Advisory Commission meeting minutes, October 19, 1977.

76 Boston National Historical Park Advisory Commission meeting minutes, December 7, 1976.

77 Boston National Historical Park Advisory Commission meeting minutes, December 7, 1976.

78 Boston National Historical Park Advisory Commission meeting minutes, October 19, 1977.

79 Berenson acknowledged several locals by name at this event, including Mary Colbert, Gus Charbonnier, Gloria and Jim Conway, and Vicki Olken. See Boston National Historical Park Advisory Commission meeting minutes, April 5, 1978, Boston National Historical Park Advisory Commission Records, 1974–1986, BNHP Archives, Charlestown, MA.

80 Boston National Historical Park Advisory Commission meeting minutes, April 5, 1978.

81 "Charlestown Navy Yard Public Response Form, Planning Issues and Concerns," packet of forms included with Boston National Historical Park Advisory Commission meeting minutes, April 5, 1978.

82 "Charlestown Navy Yard Public Response Form, Planning Issues and Concerns," packet of forms included with Boston National Historical Park Advisory Commission meeting minutes, April 5, 1978.

83 "Charlestown Navy Yard Public Response Form, Planning Issues and Concerns," packet of forms included with Boston National Historical Park Advisory Commission meeting minutes, April 5, 1978.

84 Boston National Historical Park Advisory Commission meeting minutes, May 26, 1978.

85 Boston National Historical Park Advisory Commission meeting minutes, May 26, 1978.

86 Boston National Historical Park Advisory Commission meeting minutes, May 3, 1979, Boston National Historical Park Advisory Commission Records, 1974–1986, BNHP Archives, Charlestown, MA.

87 Boston National Historical Park Advisory Commission meeting minutes, May 3, 1979.

88 Boston National Historical Park Advisory Commission meeting minutes, November 30, 1979, Boston National Historical Park Advisory Commission Records, 1974–1986, BNHP Archives, Charlestown, MA.

89 The Omnibus Bill of September 8, 1980, permitted the NPS to negotiate acquisition of the Ropewalk and Chain Forge, but did not allocate money for purchase. The NPS hoped that the BRA might donate the buildings.

90 Boston National Historical Park Advisory Commission meeting minutes, April 10, 1980, Boston National Historical Park Advisory Commission Records, 1974–1986, BNHP Archives, Charlestown, MA.

91 Squad meeting minutes, March 3, 1981. On the Ropewalk's long preservation saga, see Carlson, *Charlestown Navy Yard Historic Resource Study*, v. 1, 244–46.

92 Note that, within the advisory commission's minutes, the building is referred to as the "Chocolate Factory." The name was common then because the building's last owner had been a candy company, which used it for storage. Steve Carlson and Paul Weinbaum eventually succeeded in changing the name to the more historically appropriate "Hoosac Stores."

93 Boston National Historical Park Advisory Commission meeting minutes, April 29, 1982; and squad meeting minutes, June 2, 1981. Interior acquired the building on June 9, 1981, as reported in squad meeting minutes, June 23, 1981, Folder: Squad Meetings 01/1981–05/1982, Boston NHP Resource Management Records, Superintendent Files, Staff Meetings and Annual Reports, BNHP Archives, Charlestown, MA. For more information concerning the park's approach to Hoosac Stores, see Sean Hennessey, "Hoosac Stores Developers Sought," *Broadside*, no. 3 (1999): 10.

94 Boston National Historical Park Advisory Commission meeting minutes, May 29, 1986, Boston National Historical Park Advisory Commission Records, 1974–1986, BHNP Archives, Charlestown, MA.

95 National Park Service, *Final Revised General Management Plan*, Volume II: Charlestown Navy Yard (February 1987), 1.

96 On the siloing of history and interpretation, see Anne Mitchell Whisnant, Marla R. Miller, Gary B. Nash, and David Paul Thelen, *Imperiled Promise: The State of History in the National Park Service* (Bloomington, IN: Organization of American Historians, 2011).

97 "Digging at History's Grassroots," *Broadside* 3, no. 3 (Winter 1978): 1. On Dunning's work and life, see Ann Lage, "Remembering Judith Dunning, Oral Historian of the Richmond Community," *University of California Berkeley Library Update*, https://update.lib.berkeley.edu/2016/10/26/remembering-judith-dunning-oral-historian-of-the-richmond-community; and Paula Span, "Physician Aid in Dying Gains Acceptance in the U.S.," *New York Times*, January 16, 2007.

98 Michael Wurm, "Anatomy of a Navy Yard," *Broadside* 4, no. 3 (Spring 1978): 1.

99 Squad meeting minutes, June 30, 1981, Folder: Squad Meetings 01/1981–05/1982, Boston NHP Resource Management Records, Superintendent Files, Staff Meetings and Annual Reports, BHNP Archives, Charlestown, MA. Weinbaum reported for duty on August 23.

100 Squad meeting minutes, December 14, 1981.

101 Squad meeting minutes, September 21, 1982, Folder: Squad Meetings 09/1982–02/1983, Boston NHP Resource Management Records, Superintendent Files, Staff Meetings and Annual Reports, BHNP Archives, Charlestown, MA.

102 Paul O. Weinbaum, interview by Louis P. Hutchins and Lu Ann Jones, February 8, 2011, NPS History Program, Washington Service Office, Washington, DC.

103 These insights are variously represented in Paul O. Weinbaum, interview by Louis P. Hutchins and Lu Ann Jones, February 8, 2011; and Paul O. Weinbaum, telephone interview by Seth C. Bruggeman, July 1, 2020.

104 See Paul O. Weinbaum, *Hoosac Docks: Foreign Trade Terminal, A Case Study of the Expanding Transportation System Late in the Nineteenth Century*, Cultural Resource Management Study No. 11. (Boston: Government Printing Office, 1985).

105 See U.S. Department of the Interior, Office of Congressional and Legislative Affairs, "NPS Historic Leasing," https://www.doi.gov/ocl/nps-historic-leasing.

106 Paul O. Weinbaum, interview by Louis P. Hutchins and Lu Ann Jones, February 8, 2011, 12.

107 See Weinbaum, *Hoosac Docks: Foreign Trade Terminal*; and U.S. Department of the Interior, National Park Service, National Register of Historic Places Nomination Form, https://catalog.archives.gov/id/63796788.

108 Paul O. Weinbaum, interview by Louis P. Hutchins and Lu Ann Jones, February 8, 2011, 13.

109 Paul O. Weinbaum, interview by Louis P. Hutchins and Lu Ann Jones, February 8, 2011, 16.

110 Paul O. Weinbaum, interview by Louis P. Hutchins and Lu Ann Jones, February 8, 2011, 19–20.

111 Boston National Historical Park Advisory Commission meeting minutes, May 26, 1978.

112 Squad meeting minutes, January 1, 1981, Folder: Squad Meetings 01/1981–05/1982, Boston NHP Resource Management Records, Superintendent Files, Staff Meetings and Annual Reports, BHNP Archives, Charlestown, MA.

113 Boston National Historical Park Advisory Commission meeting minutes, May 5, 1981.

114 Squad meeting minutes, July 14, 1981, Folder: Squad Meetings 01/1981–05/1982, Boston NHP Resource Management Records, Superintendent Files, Staff Meetings and Annual Reports, BHNP Archives, Charlestown, MA.

115 Squad meeting minutes, December 14, 1981.

116 Gurney's quotations appear in Boston National Historical Park Advisory Commission meeting minutes, April 29, 1982. The Boston Committee consisted of various business and community leaders who gathered together, beginning in 1980, to address problems associated with racism in Boston. For more on the committee, see Rushworth M. Kidder, "Boston Fights Racism with the Tools of Academia," *Christian Science Monitor* (March 8, 1983). For more regarding the park's work with the Boston Committee, see Squad meeting minutes, December 14, 1981, Folder: Squad Meetings 01/1981–05/1982, Boston NHP Resource Management Records,

Superintendent Files, Staff Meetings and Annual Reports, BHNP Archives, Charlestown, MA; and Leslie McEwen, "Brush with Racism on the Freedom Trail," *Boston Globe*, December 30, 1986.

117 1979 Annual Report.

118 1979 Annual Report.

119 Boston National Historical Park Advisory Commission meeting minutes, October 30, 1980, Boston National Historical Park Advisory Commission Records, 1974–1986, BNHP Archives, Charlestown, MA.

120 Squad meeting minutes, April 28, 1980, Folder: BNHP Annual Reports 1978–1989, Box 1, Boston NHP Resource Management Records, Superintendent Files, Staff Meetings and Annual Reports, BHNP Archives, Charlestown, MA.

121 Squad meeting minutes, April 28, 1980.

122 Squad meeting minutes, January 27, 1981, Folder: Squad Meetings 01/1981–05/1982, Boston NHP Resource Management Records, Superintendent Files, Staff Meetings and Annual Reports, BHNP Archives, Charlestown, MA.

123 Squad meeting minutes, June 2, 1981, Folder: Squad Meetings 01/1981–05/1982, BHNP Resource Management Records, Superintendent Files, Staff Meetings and Annual Reports, BHNP Archives, Charlestown, MA.

124 Squad meeting minutes, June 30, 1981.

125 Squad meeting minutes, March 3, 1981.

126 Boston National Historical Park Advisory Commission meeting minutes, October 27, 1981.

127 Boston National Historical Park Advisory Commission meeting minutes, May 1981, Boston National Historical Park Advisory Commission Records, 1974–1986, BNHP Archives, Charlestown, MA.

128 Squad meeting minutes, January 12, 1982, Folder: Squad Meetings 01/1981–05/1982, Boston NHP Resource Management Records, Superintendent Files, Staff Meetings and Annual Reports, BHNP Archives, Charlestown, MA.

129 Luix Overbea, "Boston Wrestles with Racial Tensions as NAACP Convention Approaches," *Christian Science Monitor,* June 22, 1982.

130 Boston National Historical Park Advisory Commission meeting minutes, December 2, 1982.

131 Boston National Historical Park Advisory Commission meeting minutes, December 2, 1982.

132 Boston National Historical Park Advisory Commission meeting minutes, April 12, 1984.

133 Byron Rushing, interview by Laura Muller, November 18, 2005, John Joseph Moakley Oral History Project OH-062, John Joseph Moakley Archive and Institute, Suffolk University, Boston, MA, 3. Lizabeth Cohen notes Rushing's involvement with the Lower Roxbury Community Corporation and its campaign, beginning in 1966, to insist on affordable replacement housing. See Cohen, *Saving America's Cities: Ed Logue and the Struggle to Renew Urban America in the Suburban Age* (New York: Farrar, Straus, and Giroux, 2019), 222.

134 Byron Rushing, interview by Laura Muller, November 18, 2005, 4.

135 Byron Rushing, interview by Laura Muller, November 18, 2005, 4.

136 Boston National Historical Park Advisory Commission meeting minutes, May 26, 1978.

137 Boston National Historical Park Advisory Commission meeting minutes, April 10, 1980.

138 "A New National Park Comes to Boston," *Broadside* (June 1981): 1.

139 Boston National Historical Park Advisory Commission meeting minutes, April 10, 1980. The core of the site is the African Meeting House, which is the oldest Black church in New England. Other parts of the site included the Charles Street Meeting House (1876–1936), the Abiel Smith School, Saint-Gaudens 54th Regiment Monument, the home of abolitionist Lewis Hayden, the home of the nation's first published Black historian William C. Nell, the George Middleton House, the home of State Representative John J. Smith, the home of inventor and dentist George Grand (which though identified in the site's legislation, is actually a later building, as documented in the National Register nomination for Boston African American

National Historic Site), the Joseph Scarlett House, the Smith Court Residences, the John P. Coburn House and Coburn's Gaming House, and the Phillips School, which was integrated in 1855 only to be resegregated in 1880.

140 Byron Rushing, interview by Laura Muller, November 18, 2005, 8.

141 Hugh Gurney, interview by Seth C. Bruggeman, September 1, 2017.

142 NPS signed a cooperative agreement with the Afro-American museum in September 1981. See Squad meeting minutes, September 8, 1981, Folder: Squad Meetings 01/1981–05/1982, Boston NHP Resource Management Records, Superintendent Files, Staff Meetings and Annual Reports, BHNP Archives, Charlestown, MA.

143 Hugh Gurney, interview by Seth C. Bruggeman, September 1, 2017.

144 Squad meeting minutes, September 29, 1981, Folder: Squad Meetings 01/1981–05/1982, Boston NHP Resource Management Records, Superintendent Files, Staff Meetings and Annual Reports, BHNP Archives, Charlestown, MA.

CHAPTER 6: MANAGING MEMORY IN THE NEW ECONOMY

1 "USS Constitution Disgraced," *Boston Globe*, August 13, 1984.

2 Squad meeting minutes, August 14, 1984, Folder: Squad Meetings 03/1983–09/1984, Boston NHP Resource Management Records, Superintendent Files, Staff Meetings and Annual Reports, BNHP Archives, Charlestown, MA.

3 Squad meeting minutes, August 14, 1984.

4 His last day at the park would be September 14, 1984. Squad meeting minutes, September 11, 1984, Folder: Squad Meetings 03/1983–09/1984, Boston NHP Resource Management Records, Superintendent Files, Staff Meetings and Annual Reports, BNHP Archives, Charlestown, MA.

5 Preservation Specialist Steve Carlson recalls speculation within the park that Gurney's inability to please the USS *Constitution*'s various stakeholders prompted his departure. See Stephen P. Carlson, interview by Seth C. Bruggeman, March 1, 2019.

6 Alfred F. Young, "The Trouble with the Freedom Trail," *Boston Globe*, March 21, 2004.

7 See Jim Vrabel, *A People's History of the New Boston* (Amherst: University of Massachusetts Press, 2014), ch. 20, for an overview of these years.

8 Visitation figures appear in Boston National Historical Park Advisory Commission meeting minutes, December 2, 1980, Boston National Historical Park Advisory Commission Records, 1974–1986, BNHP Archives, Charlestown, MA. On Boston's ongoing decline, including the 1982 report and statistics, see Barry Bluestone and Mary Huff Stevenson, *The Boston Renaissance: Race, Space, and Economic Change in an American Metropolis* (New York: Russell Sage Foundation, 2000), introduction.

9 Data taken from http://worldpopulationreview.com/us-cities/boston-population/.

10 Bluestone and Stevenson, *The Boston Renaissance*, 1–16.

11 For examples of gentrification in Charlestown at this time and statistics concerning its impact, see various articles included in a special issue of the *Boston Globe*, January 4, 1982.

12 The Housing and Community Development Act of 1974 established the Community Development Block Grant program (CDBG), which began in earnest the focus on redevelopment of existing neighborhoods and properties, rather than demolition of substandard housing and economically depressed areas. On this, and concerning Flynn's positioning regarding race, see Vrabel, *A People's History of the New Boston*, ch. 20.

13 Documents and analysis concerning these changes appear in Lary M. Dilsaver, *America's National Park System: The Critical Documents* (Lanham, MD: Rowman & Littlefield, 1994), ch. 8, https://www.nps.gov/parkhistory/online_books/anps/anps_8.htm.

14 Boston National Historical Park Advisory Commission meeting minutes, May 5, 1981, Boston National Historical Park Advisory Commission Records, 1974–1986, BNHP Archives, Charlestown, MA.

15   Squad meeting minutes, January 1, 1981, Folder: Squad Meetings 01/1981–05/1982, Boston NHP Resource Management Records, Superintendent Files, Staff Meetings and Annual Reports, BNHP Archives, Charlestown, MA.

16   Staff meeting minutes, January 6, 1985, Folder: Staff Meetings 05/1985–06/1986, Boston NHP Resource Management Records, Superintendent Files, Staff Meetings and Annual Reports, BNHP Archives, Charlestown, MA.

17   Boston National Historical Park Advisory Commission meeting minutes, May 29, 1986, Boston National Historical Park Advisory Commission Records, 1974–1986, BNHP Archives, Charlestown, MA.

18   Staff meeting minutes, April 15, 1987, Folder: Staff Meetings 07/1986–07/1987, Boston NHP Resource Management Records, Superintendent Files, Staff Meetings and Annual Reports, BNHP Archives, Charlestown, MA.

19   For an explanation of how the change meant that "Parks have less control over handling of expenses," see Associate Director, Policy, Budget and Administration, to Field Directors, May 8, 1987, in Folder: Staff Meetings 08/1987–04/1989, Boston NHP Resource Management Records, Superintendent Files, Staff Meetings and Annual Reports, BNHP Archives, Charlestown, MA.

20   *National Parks for the 21ˢᵗ Century: The Vail Agenda,* NPS Report D-726 (Washington, DC: National Park Service, 1992). For an overview of these, see Janet A. McDonnell, "Reassessing the National Park Service and the National Park System," *George Wright Forum* 25, no. 2 (2008): 6–14.

21   Importantly, the NPS had also failed a federal audit during 1991, which set the stage for a byzantine structure of new spending guidelines.

22   Sandy Brue, "What's All this Talk about Restructuring?," *Broadside* (Boston National Historical Park Newsletter) (Autumn 1994): 14, this and all subsequent references to this publication are from the private collection of Stephen P. Carlson.

23   On the rise of interest in urban parks, see Barry Mackintosh, *The National Parks: Shaping the System* (Washington, DC: U.S. Department of the Interior, 1991), 71–78. The turn toward a concerted effort to think about interpretation in urban contexts is signaled in Assistant Director, Interpretation, to Regional Directors, September 10, 1987, at http://npshistory.com/publications/interpretation/urban-parks-interp-1987.pdf. In 1989, Burchill noted that "Boston's staff are sought after and competing very well for positions throughout the Service which is a sign of a healthy organization." See staff meeting minutes, September 12, 1989, Folder: Staff Meetings 05/1989–12/1989, Boston NHP Resource Management Records, Superintendent Files, Staff Meetings and Annual Reports, BNHP Archives, Charlestown, MA.

24   "Year-round Interpretive Duty Stations," attached to Gerald E. Swofford, Chief of Visitor Services, to Hugh Gurney, April 22, 1983, in Folder: Squad Meetings 03/1983–09/1984, Boston NHP Resource Management Records, Superintendent Files, Staff Meetings and Annual Reports, BNHP Archives, Charlestown, MA.

25   For an overview of the *Cassin Young*'s arrival in Boston, see Stephen P. Carlson, *Charlestown Navy Yard Historic Resource Study,* v. 1 (Boston: Division of Cultural Resources, National Park Service, 2010), 250.

26   Linda Canzanelli, "Welcome Aboard the U.S.S. Cassin Young," and "Dry Dock Number One Receives Landmark Status," *Broadside* (Winter 1979): 3–5.

27   Hugh Gurney, unrecorded telephone interview by Seth C. Bruggeman, July 12, 2017.

28   Hugh Gurney, interview by Seth C. Bruggeman, September 1, 2017.

29   Squad meeting minutes, November 17, 1981, Folder: Squad Meetings 01/1981–05/1982, Boston NHP Resource Management Records, Superintendent Files, Staff Meetings and Annual Reports, BNHP Archives, Charlestown, MA.

30   "Year-round Interpretive Duty Stations," attached to Gerald E. Swofford, Chief of Visitor Services, to Hugh Gurney, April 22, 1983.

31   Hugh Gurney, interview by Seth C. Bruggeman, September 1, 2017.

32 See *Broadside* for frequent mentions of the park's VIP program.
33 Boston National Historical Park Advisory Commission meeting minutes, April 29, 1982, Boston National Historical Park Advisory Commission Records, 1974–1986, BNHP Archives, Charlestown, MA.
34 Boston National Historical Park Advisory Commission meeting minutes, December 2, 1982.
35 Boston National Historical Park Advisory Commission meeting minutes, May 24, 1983, and November 29, 1983, Boston National Historical Park Advisory Commission Records, 1974–1986, BNHP Archives, Charlestown, MA.
36 Squad meeting minutes, January 12, 1982, Folder: Squad Meetings 01/1981–05/1982, Boston NHP Resource Management Records, Superintendent Files, Staff Meetings and Annual Reports, BNHP Archives, Charlestown, MA. See Mary Battiata, "GAO Says Watt Should Pay Part of Party Costs," *Washington Post*, February 25, 1982.
37 Boston National Historical Park Advisory Commission meeting minutes, April 29, 1982.
38 Boston National Historical Park Advisory Commission meeting minutes, December 2, 1982.
39 Squad meeting minutes, April 21, 1980, Folder: BNHP Annual Reports 1978–1989, Boston NHP Resource Management Records, Superintendent Files, Staff Meetings and Annual Reports, BNHP Archives, Charlestown, MA. These minutes include detailed instructions from Gurney about how to manage divisions.
40 Boston National Historical Park Advisory Commission meeting minutes, December 7, 1976, Boston National Historical Park Advisory Commission Records, 1974–1986, BNHP Archives, Charlestown, MA.
41 Squad meeting minutes, December 1, 1981, Folder: Squad Meetings 01/1981–05/1982, Boston NHP Resource Management Records, Superintendent Files, Staff Meetings and Annual Reports, BNHP Archives, Charlestown, MA.
42 Bob Norris (unclear who this is) to Superintendent's Squad, September 15, 1982, Folder: Squad Meetings 09/1982–02/1983, Boston NHP Resource Management Records, Superintendent Files, Staff Meetings and Annual Reports, BNHP Archives, Charlestown, MA. Note that the letter begins with "To the Squad, all hail!," which indicates the pervasiveness of squad culture at the park.
43 Squad meeting minutes, May 11, 1982, Folder: Squad Meetings 01/1981–05/1982, Boston NHP Resource Management Records, Superintendent Files, Staff Meetings and Annual Reports, BNHP Archives, Charlestown, MA.
44 Squad meeting minutes, May 11, 1982.
45 Squad meeting minutes, November 17, 1983. "A-76" refers to Office of Management and Budget (OMB) Circular A-76. For details, see https://www.whitehouse.gov/sites/whitehouse.gov/files/omb/circulars/A76/a076.pdf.
46 Squad meeting minutes, March 1, 1983, Folder: Squad Meetings 03/1983–09/1984, Boston NHP Resource Management Records, Superintendent Files, Staff Meetings and Annual Reports, BNHP Archives, Charlestown, MA.
47 Squad meeting minutes, January 24, 1984, Folder: Squad Meetings 03/1983–09/1984, Boston NHP Resource Management Records, Superintendent Files, Staff Meetings and Annual Reports, BNHP Archives, Charlestown, MA.
48 Squad meeting minutes, April 24, 1984, Folder: Squad Meetings 03/1983–09/1984, Boston NHP Resource Management Records, Superintendent Files, Staff Meetings and Annual Reports, BNHP Archives, Charlestown, MA.
49 I've argued throughout that much of this change in Boston related to the influence of urban renewal strategies on NPS management. There were certainty other catalysts. Beyond the NPS, some of the change owed to the shifting relationship between heritage work and the federal government, especially as it related to funding newly available from sources including the National Endowment for the Arts. See, for instance, Briley Rasmussen and Scott Winterrowd, "Professionalizing Practice: A [*sic*] Examination of Recent History in Museum Education," *Journal of Museum Education* 37, no. 2 (Summer 2012): 8. Others point to the rise of

professional training programs and the strained relationship between university historians and their public-facing counterparts. See, for instance, Bill Bryans, "Collaborative Practice," in *The Inclusive Historian's Handbook*, https://inclusivehistorian.com/collaborative-practice/. Cathy Stanton argues that heritage workers have always existed simultaneously at the periphery and at the center of industrial capitalism. See Cathy Stanton, "Displaying the Industrial: Toward a Genealogy of Heritage Labor," *Labor: Studies in Working-Class History* 16, no. 1 (2019): 151–70.

50 Squad meeting minutes, May 22, 1984, Folder: Squad Meetings 03/1983–09/1984, Boston NHP Resource Management Records, Superintendent Files, Staff Meetings and Annual Reports, BNHP Archives, Charlestown, MA.

51 Squad meeting minutes, July 17, 1984, Folder: Squad Meetings 03/1983–09/1984, Boston NHP Resource Management Records, Superintendent Files, Staff Meetings and Annual Reports, BNHP Archives, Charlestown, MA.

52 Sean Hennessey, "In Memoriam: John J. Burchill," *Broadside*, no. 2 (2002): 1.

53 Cathy Stanton, *The Lowell Experiment: Public History in a Postindustrial City* (Amherst: University of Massachusetts Press, 2006), 3.

54 Sean Hennessey, "In Memoriam: John J. Burchill."

55 Stanton, *The Lowell Experiment*, 115.

56 Note though Stanton's observation that Lowell's use of "celebratory ethnicity" to activate the voices of, say, Vietnamese and Cambodian immigrants nonetheless functioned within the economic logic of heritage tourism. Stanton, *The Lowell Experiment*, 94–96. On Boston's new Asian immigrants, see for instance, Karin Aguilar-San Juan, "Creating Ethnic Places: Vietnamese American Community-Building in Orange County and Boston" (PhD diss., Brown University, 2000), especially 144–48, for a discussion of memory and monument building in Dorchester.

57 Superintendent Report 1984, Boston NHP Resource Management Records, Superintendent Files, Staff Meetings and Annual Reports, BNHP Archives, Charlestown, MA.

58 Superintendent Report 1988, Boston NHP Resource Management Records, Superintendent Files, Staff Meetings and Annual Reports, BNHP Archives, Charlestown, MA.

59 Staff meeting minutes, December 9, 1985, Folder: Staff Meetings 05/1985–06/1986, Boston NHP Resource Management Records, Superintendent Files, Staff Meetings and Annual Reports, BNHP Archives, Charlestown, MA.

60 Superintendent Report 1984.

61 Debo had also recently trained in the Departmental Management Training Program in Washington, DC. See Staff meeting minutes, October 9, 1984, Folder: Staff Meetings 10/1984–05/1985, Boston NHP Resource Management Records, Superintendent Files, Staff Meetings and Annual Reports, BNHP Archives, Charlestown, MA. Debo stayed on until 1988, at which point he transferred to Cuyahoga National Recreational Area. See Staff meeting minutes, March 15, 1988, Folder: Staff Meetings 08/1987–04/1989, Boston NHP Resource Management Records, Superintendent Files, Staff Meetings and Annual Reports, BNHP Archives, Charlestown, MA.

62 The nature of Lowe's appointment is unclear insomuch as he arrived alongside Burchill but did not immediately receive a title. He had, however, received his title and began reporting at staff meetings by November 1984. Carlson recalls that Carter, although on the park payroll, worked primarily for the regional office until he replaced Dottie Powell at Boston African American National Historic Site. See staff meeting minutes, November 26, 1984, Folder: Staff Meetings 10/1984–05/1985, Boston NHP Resource Management Records, Superintendent Files, Staff Meetings and Annual Reports, BNHP Archives, Charlestown, MA.

63 Superintendent Report 1987, Boston NHP Resource Management Records, Superintendent Files, Staff Meetings and Annual Reports, BNHP Archives, Charlestown, MA. The NPS Northeast Region purchased a battery of Wang personal computers for its units. See, for instance, staff meeting minutes, August 12, 1985, Folder: Staff Meetings 05/1985–06/1986. The computer was installed in April 1983. Squad meeting, April 12, 1983, Folder: Squad Meetings 03/1983–09/1984. Implementation of the AFS Budget System involved struggles such as occurred when "we have

been plagued by an 'unknown bug' in the program and finally got an entire new disk from region yesterday which is working." Staff meeting minutes, February 28, 1989, Folder: Staff Meetings 08/1987–04/1989, Boston NHP Resource Management Records, Superintendent Files, Staff Meetings and Annual Reports, BNHP Archives, Charlestown, MA.

64 Staff meeting minutes, October 22, 1984, Folder: Staff Meetings 10/1984–05/1985, Boston NHP Resource Management Records, Superintendent Files, Staff Meetings and Annual Reports, BNHP Archives, Charlestown, MA.

65 Staff meeting minutes, November 26, 1984.

66 Staff meeting minutes, October 29, 1984, Folder: Staff Meetings 10/1984–05/1985, Boston NHP Resource Management Records, Superintendent Files, Staff Meetings and Annual Reports, BNHP Archives, Charlestown, MA.

67 He met, for instance, with Northeastern University's William Fowler, whom the park had engaged to write a visitor guide.

68 Staff meeting minutes, April 15, 1987.

69 Sean Hennessey, "In Memoriam: John J. Burchill," 1.

70 Nina Zannieri, interview by Seth C. Bruggeman, December 18, 2018.

71 Staff meeting minutes, March 31, 1987, Folder: Staff Meetings 07/1986–07/1987, Boston NHP Resource Management Records, Superintendent Files, Staff Meetings and Annual Reports, BNHP Archives, Charlestown, MA.

72 Nina Zannieri, interview by Seth C. Bruggeman, December 18, 2018.

73 Burchill hired Margaret Micholet, who, incidentally, was married to Curator Peter Steele. Boston National Historical Park Advisory Commission meeting minutes, November 14, 1985, Boston National Historical Park Advisory Commission Records, 1974–1986, BNHP Archives, Charlestown, MA.

74 On the establishment of cooperator meetings, see staff meeting minutes, July 11, 1989, Folder: Staff Meetings 05/1989–12/1989, Boston NHP Resource Management Records, Superintendent Files, Staff Meetings and Annual Reports, BNHP Archives, Charlestown, MA. During an August 16 cooperators meeting at Boston Marine Society, Peter Steele briefed the group on development, Debby Szarka commented on the CANA project, and John Piltzecker and Lee Heald discussed the People and Places program. They agreed to have meetings every two months. Staff meeting minutes, August 22, 1989, Folder: Staff Meetings 05/1989–12/1989, Boston NHP Resource Management Records, Superintendent Files, Staff Meetings and Annual Reports, BNHP Archives, Charlestown, MA.

75 In 1993, for instance, the board of managers at the Old South Meeting House appointed Emily Curran to the position of executive director. Curran had considerable experience in museums and had studied museum leadership at Bank Street College. "New Faces at Old South," *Broadside* (Spring/Summer 1993): 3.

76 Staff meeting minutes, January 12, 1987, Folder: Staff Meetings 07/1986–07/1987, Boston NHP Resource Management Records, Superintendent Files, Staff Meetings and Annual Reports, BNHP Archives, Charlestown, MA.

77 Staff meeting minutes, May 26, 1987, Folder: Staff Meetings 07/1986–07/1987, Boston NHP Resource Management Records, Superintendent Files, Staff Meetings and Annual Reports, BNHP Archives, Charlestown, MA.

78 Staff meeting minutes, June 14, 1988, Folder: Staff Meetings 08/1987–04/1989, Boston NHP Resource Management Records, Superintendent Files, Staff Meetings and Annual Reports, BNHP Archives, Charlestown, MA.

79 Staff meeting minutes, January 12, 1987.

80 Boston National Historical Park Advisory Commission meeting minutes, June 13, 1985, Boston National Historical Park Advisory Commission Records, 1974–1986, BNHP Archives, Charlestown, MA.

81 Staff meeting minutes, October 12, 1988; and staff meeting minutes, July 11, 1989.

82 A third option would be bus service from navy yard to downtown, using private funds and ticket sales. Staff meeting minutes, August 23, 1988, Folder: Staff Meetings 08/1987–04/1989,

Boston NHP Resource Management Records, Superintendent Files, Staff Meetings and Annual Reports, BNHP Archives, Charlestown, MA. The new service began on October 11. Staff meeting minutes, October 12, 1988.

83 For a detailed overview of the dispersal and consolidation of staff offices over time, see Carlson, *Charlestown Navy Yard Historic Resource Study*, v. 1, 224–25.

84 In 1978, for instance, the park acquired all of the equipment remaining in the navy yard's forge shop, which had previously belonged to the Smithsonian Institution. In 1984, accessioning began in preparation for the creation of new collections storage. Until that point, the navy yard artifact collection—which had first been assembled by the navy during shutdown—remained where the navy put it, in Buildings 125. See Superintendent Reports, 1978, 1984, and 1988, Boston NHP Resource Management Records, Superintendent Files, Staff Meetings and Annual Reports, BNHP Archives, Charlestown, MA; and Carlson, *Charlestown Navy Yard Historic Sites Report.*

85 Staff meeting minutes, December 2, 1987, Folder Staff Meetings 08/1987–04/1989, Boston NHP Resource Management Records, Superintendent Files, Staff Meetings and Annual Reports, Boston NHP Archives, Charlestown, MA.

86 Staff meeting minutes, January 17, 1989, Folder: Staff Meetings 08/1987–04/1989, Boston NHP Resource Management Records, Superintendent Files, Staff Meetings and Annual Reports, BNHP Archives, Charlestown, MA.

87 Staff Meeting, January 7, 1985, Staff Meetings 10/1984–05/1985, Boston NHP Resource Management Records, Superintendent Files, Staff Meetings and Annual Reports, BNHP Archives, Charlestown, MA.

88 "BNHP News Notes," *Broadside* (Spring 1991): 7.

89 "BNHP News Notes," *Broadside* (Winter 1991): 4.

90 Jorrin departed on May 3, 1985; Bob Pribula resigned January 4, 1986; Lou Venuto transferred to Edison National Historic Site on September 23, 1985; Wendell Simpson left in November 1986; and John Debo assumed the duties of the deputy superintendent. See staff meeting minutes, various, Boston NHP Resource Management Records, Superintendent Files, Staff Meetings and Annual Reports, BNHP Archives, Charlestown, MA. "Park Names New Deputy Superintendent, Assistant Superintendent," *Broadside* (Winter 1991): 1.

91 Staff meeting minutes, March 31, 1986, Folder: Staff Meetings 05/1985–06/1986, Boston NHP Resource Management Records, Superintendent Files, Staff Meetings and Annual Reports, BNHP Archives, Charlestown, MA; and staff meeting minutes, December 1, 1986, Folder: Staff Meetings 07/1986–07/1987, Boston NHP Resource Management Records, Superintendent Files, Staff Meetings and Annual Reports, BNHP Archives, Charlestown, MA.

92 Charles, who had previously worked at the Peabody Museum after graduating from Harvard in 1942 and serving abroad during World War II, invested himself especially in objects related to the Ropewalk and forge shop. Stephen P. Carlson, "Curator Arsen Charles Retires After 19 Years," *Broadside*, no. 3 (1995): 15.

93 Interestingly, conversations concerning Dorchester Height's revised GMP in 1985 involved the regional office's Terry Savage who, in about fifteen years, would become the park's third superintendent. Curatorial weekly report, June 14, 1985, Folder: Staff Meetings 05/1985–06/1986, Boston NHP Resource Management Records, Superintendent Files, Staff Meetings and Annual Reports, BNHP Archives, Charlestown, MA.

94 Another study useful for considering Burchill's influence on a rising generation of park managers trained at Lowell is Joan Zenzen, *Fort Stanwix National Monument: Reconstructing the Past and Partnering for the Future* (Albany: State University of New York Press, 2008). In chapter seven, for instance, Zenzen profiles Burchill's protégé Mike Caldwell and his approach to partnership with park stakeholders in Rome, New York.

95 Boston National Historical Park Advisory Commission meeting minutes, December 6, 1984, Boston National Historical Park Advisory Commission Records, 1974–1986, BNHP Archives, Charlestown, MA.

96 Carlson, *Charlestown Navy Yard Historic Resource Study*, v. 1, 246.

97 Superintendent Report 1987.

98 Superintendent Report 1988.

99 Squad meeting minutes, January 5, 1982, Folder: Squad Meetings 01/1981–05/1982, Boston NHP Resource Management Records, Superintendent Files, Staff Meetings and Annual Reports, BNHP Archives, Charlestown, MA.

100 Burchill indicated, too, that the park could expect to get architectural engineering money sometime in 1986, although the Gramm-Rudman Resolution then before Congress would limit further funds available to the NPS. Boston National Historical Park Advisory Commission meeting minutes, November 14, 1985.

101 Staff meeting minutes, February 10, 1987, Folder: Staff Meetings 07/1986–07/1987, Boston NHP Resource Management Records, Superintendent Files, Staff Meetings and Annual Reports, BNHP Archives, Charlestown, MA.

102 Muller, "The Contributions of Congressman John Joseph Moakley," unpublished paper in Congressman John Joseph Moakley Papers, Moakley Archive and Institute, Suffolk University, Boston, MA, 14–18.

103 Muller, "The Contributions of Congressman John Joseph Moakley," 19–20; Sean Hennessey (Public Affairs Officer, Boston National Historical Park), interview by Laura Muller, September 27, 2005, compact disc, in possession of Laura Muller.

104 Dan Rostenkowski to Joe Moakley, September 24, 1980, and drafts of Historic Preservation Tax Incentives Act of 1981 (ultimately introduced by Moakley to 97th Congress, 1st session), Folder 66, Box 7, Congressman John Joseph Moakley Papers, Moakley Archive and Institute, Suffolk University, Boston, MA.

105 Staff meeting minutes, February 3, 1986, Folder: Staff Meetings 05/1985–06/1986, Boston NHP Resource Management Records, Superintendent Files, Staff Meetings and Annual Reports, BNHP Archives, Charlestown, MA.

106 Staff meeting minutes, August 23, 1988. For a thorough detailing of the legislative process and Moakley's hand in it, see Muller, "The Contributions of Congressman John Joseph Moakley," 17–32.

107 "Funding for Park Project Advances," *Broadside* (Autumn 1990): 4.

108 Muller, "The Contributions of Congressman John Joseph Moakley," 31–32.

109 Staff meeting minutes, February 28, 1989.

110 Faneuil Hall and the Old State House were completed and reopened during July 1992, with a formal ceremony for the Old State House on July 10. Phil Bergen, Stephen P. Carlson, and John Manson, "Faneuil Hall, Old State House Projects Completed," *Broadside* (Summer 1992): 1.

111 Construction on Building 28 was set to begin in August 1989 with $4 million in federal funding. "The project includes structural stabilization and building work on Building 28 and the electrical sub-station building; construction of a connector structure, and site work. The NPS is responsible for building and site work, and the Constitution Museum is responsible for interior finishing, exhibits, and furnishings." Cost estimates rose to $7 million by 1993 when the project actually began. Plans now included conversion of Building 22, the old electrical substation, into a two-hundred-seat theater and public restroom, and connecting it with Building 28. All of this was planned to coincide with the 1997 bicentennial of the launching of the USS *Constitution.* Stephen P. Carlson and Dave Snow, "USS *Constitution* Museum Expansion Project to Begin," *Broadside* (Spring/Summer 1993): 1.

112 Leo Zani, "Secretary Lujan Visits Boston NHP," *Broadside* (Summer 1990): 1.

113 This summary based on Sean Hennessey, "In Memoriam: John J. Burchill," 2.

114 "Boston Architect Chosen for Faneuil Hall and Old State House Restoration Project," NPS press release, May 22, 1987, Folder: Staff Meetings 07/1986–07/1987, Boston NHP Resource Management Records, Superintendent Files, Staff Meetings and Annual Reports, BNHP Archives, Charlestown, MA.

115 Staff meeting minutes, February 16, 1988, and March 1, 1988, Folder: Staff Meetings 08/1987–04/1989, Boston NHP Resource Management Records, Superintendent Files, Staff Meetings and Annual Reports, BNHP Archives, Charlestown, MA.

116 Leo Zani, "Restoration Plans Unveiled for Old State House and Faneuil Hall," *Broadside* (Summer 1990): 2.

117 Sheila Cooke-Kayser and Vincent Kordack, "Harborfest Highlights Summer Interpretive Programs," *Broadside* (Summer 1994): 1.

118 Regarding Burchill's appointment, see "BNHP News Notes," *Broadside* (Summer 1991): 7.

119 Staff meeting minutes, December 2, 1987.

120 In coordination, of course, with the Department of Public Works. Staff meeting minutes, November 3, 1987, Folder: Staff Meetings 08/1987–04/1989, Boston NHP Resource Management Records, Superintendent Files, Staff Meetings and Annual Reports, BNHP Archives, Charlestown, MA.

121 Regarding costumed battle reenactments, Foley coordinated with Commander Robert Gillen and the Charlestown militia to plan the June 18 historic demonstration. Staff meeting minutes, June 14, 1988.

122 Richard W. Berenson, interview by Seth C. Bruggeman, August 1, 2017.

123 Regarding the nomination, see staff meeting minutes, May 17, 1988, Folder: Staff Meetings 08/1987–04/1989, Boston NHP Resource Management Records, Superintendent Files, Staff Meetings and Annual Reports, BNHP Archives, Charlestown, MA. Berenson received his award at a ceremony in Washington, DC, on September 13, 1988. "Mr. Berenson has helped shape and form the Freedom Trail concept here at Boston and was instrumental in seeking the establishment of the Boston National Historical Park and was the Chairman of the Park Advisory Commission from 1974–1986." Staff meeting minutes, August 23, 1988.

124 Edgar J. Driscoll Jr., "Richard Berenson, 81; Civic Leader who Guided City's Freedom Trail," *Boston Globe*, April 4, 1990.

125 Richard W. Berenson, interview by Seth C. Bruggeman, August 1, 2017.

126 Obituary for Warren Berg, *Boston Globe*, August 29, 2016. The organization's first executive director was Fred Davis.

127 Staff meeting minutes, January 12, 1988, Folder: Staff Meetings 08/1987–04/1989, Boston NHP Resource Management Records, Superintendent Files, Staff Meetings and Annual Reports, BNHP Archives, Charlestown, MA.

128 Staff meeting minutes, April 19, 1988, Folder: Staff Meetings 08/1987–04/1989, Boston NHP Resource Management Records, Superintendent Files, Staff Meetings and Annual Reports, BNHP Archives, Charlestown, MA.

129 Staff meeting minutes, March 21, 1989, Folder: Staff Meetings 08/1987–04/1989, and staff meeting minutes, May 9, 1989, Folder: Staff Meetings 05/1989–12/1989, Boston NHP Resource Management Records, Superintendent Files, Staff Meetings and Annual Reports, BNHP Archives, Charlestown, MA.

130 Staff meeting minutes, March 21, 1989.

131 "BNHP News Notes," *Broadside* (Winter 1992): 7.

132 People and Places reached a major milestone in 1991, when the Freedom Trail Foundation and the park won a two-year $150,000 National Endowment for the Humanities grant to sponsor local history workshops and an annual three-week institute for Boston teachers in the summer. Lee Herald, "People and Places Program Wins NEH Grant for Summer Teacher Institute," *Broadside* (Spring 1991): 1.

133 For Heald's biographical information, see her wedding announcement, *Boston Globe*, December 22, 1991. It is worth noting that Heald married William Fuchs, an NPS employee, thus demonstrating how closely the park and the foundation operated during these years.

134 John Piltzecker, "*People and Places Program* Welcomes a New Coordinator," *Broadside* (Spring/Summer 1993): 7.

135 The project was led by David Dixon/Goody Clancy, Planning and Urban Design, a division of Goody Clancy & Associates. Ruth Raphael, "Freedom Trail Planning Underway," *Broadside* (Summer 1995): 12.

136 Peter Steele, "In Memoriam: Congressman John Joseph Moakley," *Broadside*, nos. 2 and 3 (2001): 1–2.

137 Peter Steele, "Freedom Trail Plan Unveiled," *Broadside*, no. 2 (1996): 1–2.

138 David Dixon and Goody Clancy, *The Freedom Trail: A Framework for the Future* (Boston: The National Park Service, 1996), https://irma.nps.gov/DataStore/Reference/Profile/2190259.

139 Sheila Cooke-Kayser, "Hit the Trail! Passport Published," *Broadside*, no. 1 (1996): 1.

140 "BNHP News Notes," *Broadside*, no. 1 (1997): 7.

141 Stephen P. Carlson, "McConchie to Head Freedom Trail Foundation," *Broadside*, no. 5 (1997): 7.

142 "The Freedom Trail: A Framework for the Future," 4.

143 Richard Handler and Eric Gable, *The New History in an Old Museum: Creating the Past at Colonial Williamsburg* (Durham: Duke University Press, 1997).

144 John Manson, "A Decade of Collaboration," *Broadside* (Spring 1991): 3.

145 Squad meeting minutes, May 11, 1982.

146 Carter Lowe was detailed to Boston African American NHS as site manager in February 1988. "Carter will continue urban affairs responsibilities in the Region (NARO) on a limited basis. Superintendent welcomed the executive skills of Mr. Lowe to the Site noting the Site's significant program and growth recently, as well as excellent potential for the future." Staff meeting minutes, March 1, 1988.

147 Polly Welts Kaufman, Patricia C. Morris, and Joyce Stevens, "Boston Women's Heritage Trail," reviewed by Kimberly H. Brookes and Susan J. von Salis, *Public Historian* 15, no. 1 (1993): 125–28; The History Project, *Improper Bostonians: Lesbian and Gay History from the Puritans to Playland* (Boston: Beacon Press, 1998); Larry Kramer, "I Can't Believe You Want to Die," in *Documenting Intimate Matters: Primary Sources for a History of Sexuality in America*, ed. Thomas A. Foster (Chicago: University of Chicago Press, 2013), 186–88; and Nina Zannieri, "Report from the Field: Not the Same Old Freedom Trail—A View from the Paul Revere House," *Public Historian* 25, no. 2 (Spring 2003): 53.

148 Philip Bergen, "Bostonian Society Celebrates 'A Place in History,'" *Broadside* (Autumn 1992): 10; and Sean M. Fisher and Carolyn Hughes, eds., *The Last Tenement: Confronting Community and Urban Renewal in Boston's West End* (Boston: The Bostonian Society, 1992).

149 Superintendent Report 1984.

150 Paul Weinbaum, interview by Seth C. Bruggeman, July 1, 2020.

151 Martin Blatt discusses this tendency in Martin H. Blatt, interview by Seth C. Bruggeman, February 22, 2019.

152 Louis Hutchins, interview by Seth C. Bruggeman, June 30, 2020.

153 Paul O. Weinbaum, interview by Louis P. Hutchins and Lu Ann Jones, February 8, 2011, NPS History Program, Washington Service Office, Washington, DC, 24–25.

154 Paul Weinbaum, interview by Seth C. Bruggeman, July 1, 2020.

155 The one facet of operations beyond Boston African American NHS wherein critical history appears to have happened during the late 1980s concerns traveling Smithsonian exhibits. For instance, a Smithsonian exhibit concerning women in the industrial workplace during the nineteenth and twentieth centuries showed in the Preble Room from mid-July to mid-September 1988. "From Field to Factory," reserved for Black History Month in 1989, explored the Great Migration between 1915 to 1940. See staff meeting minutes, May 17, 1988. Staff meeting notes indicate that subsequent Smithsonian exhibits continued to be popular into the 1990s.

156 Curatorial weekly report, June 28, 1985, Folder: Staff Meetings 05/1985–06/1986, Boston NHP Resource Management Records, Superintendent Files, Staff Meetings and Annual Reports, BNHP Archives, Charlestown, MA.

157 Historian Perri Meldon recorded an October 8, 2019, oral history with former ranger John Manson, who pioneered interpretation for the hearing impaired at the park. The recording was still being processed by the NPS Oral History Program at the time of this writing. For more on interpretation and disability in the NPS, see Meldon, "Interpreting Our Disabled Heritage: Disability and the National Park Service," *History@Work* (March 16, 2021), https://ncph.org/history-at-work/interpreting-our-disabled-heritage-national-park-service/.

158 "Park Staff Appointments Announced," *Broadside* (Summer 1991): 4.

159 Louis Hutchins, interview by Seth C. Bruggeman, June 30, 2020.

160 Louis Hutchins, interview by Seth C. Bruggeman, June 30, 2020.

161 Louis Hutchins, interview by Seth C. Bruggeman, June 30, 2020. The park announced Hutchins's departure in "BNHP News Notes," *Broadside*, no. 4 (1995): 7.

162 Ellen M. Fusco, "Marty Blatt Joins Park Staff," *Broadside*, no. 2 (1996): 11.

163 Martin H. Blatt, interview by Seth C. Bruggeman, February 22, 2019.

164 Martin H. Blatt, interview by Seth C. Bruggeman, February 22, 2019.

165 Marty Blatt, "Hope and Glory: Shaw/54th Monument Centennial," *Broadside*, no. 3 (1997): 1. For materials relating to Shaw programming, see Folder: "Shaw/54th-Minutes Steering Comm," Box 1, Boston NHP Resource Management Records, Division of Cultural Resources, Chief Historian (Marty Blatt) Files, BNHP Archives, Charlestown, MA.

166 The symposium took place May 28–31, 1997. Martin Blatt, Thomas Brown, and Donald Yacovone, eds., *Hope and Glory: Essays on the Legacy of the Fifty-fourth Massachusetts Regiment* (Amherst: University of Massachusetts Press, 2001).

167 Marty Blatt, "Hope and Glory: Shaw/54th Monument Centennial," *Broadside*, 1.

168 John Manson, "Dorchester Heights Rededication Program," *Broadside*, no. 3 (1997): 2–3.

169 Martin H. Blatt, interview by Seth C. Bruggeman, February 22, 2019.

170 As examples of this type of work, Blatt cites the park's 2000 conference "Changing Meanings of Freedom: The 225th Anniversary of the American Revolution;" the "Patriots of Color" theme study prepared for the park by George Quintal Jr., in 2004; a partnership and exhibit project jointly sponsored by the NPS and the Gulag Museum at Perm-36 in 2006; the "Abolitionism in Black and White" symposium staged during 2009; and, in 2013, a historical pageant and conversation titled "Roots of Liberty: The Haitian Revolution and the American Civil War." Martin H. Blatt, interview by Seth C. Bruggeman, February 22, 2019. See George Quintal Jr. *Patriots of Color "A Particular Beauty and Merit": African Americans and Native Americans at Battle Road and Bunker Hill* (Boston: Division of Cultural Resources, Boston National Historical Park, 2004); and Blatt, "Reflections on 'Roots of Liberty: The Haitian Revolution and the American Civil War,'" *History@Work* (August 29, 2013), https://ncph.org/history-at-work/reflections-on-roots-of-liberty/.

171 Sarah J. Purcell, "Commemoration, Public Art, and the Changing Meaning of the Bunker Hill Monument," *Public Historian* 25, no. 2 (Spring 2003), 55–71.

172 Judy Rakowsky, "Charlestown Not Silent on New Movie, Art Project," *Boston Globe*, September 26, 1998. Purcell also discusses Conway's opposition in "Commemoration, Public Art, and the Changing Meaning of the Bunker Hill Monument," 67.

173 John Burchill, "Superintendent John Burchill Announces Departure," *Broadside*, no. 4 (1999): 1.

174 Stephen P. Carlson, interview by Seth C. Bruggeman, March 1, 2019.

AFTERWORD: LOST AND FOUND ON THE FREEDOM TRAIL

1 Byron Rushing, interview by Laura Muller, November 18, 2005, John Joseph Moakley Oral History Project OH-062, John Joseph Moakley Archive and Institute, Suffolk University, Boston, MA.

2 Martin Blatt, "Boston's Public History," *Public Historian* 25, no. 2 (2003), 16.

3 Blatt, "Boston's Public History," 11.

4 Blatt, "Boston's Public History," 15–16.

5 Nina Zannieri, interview by Seth C. Bruggeman, December 18, 2018.

6 Spencer Buell, "Hear Ye! The Freedom Trail's Tour Guides Have Had Enough," *Boston Magazine* (November 5, 2019), https://www.bostonmagazine.com/news/2019/11/05/freedom-trail-tour-guides-union-bellringers-guild/.

7 Martin H. Blatt, interview by Seth C. Bruggeman, February 22, 2019.

8 Abigail Feldman, "On Slavery's 400th Anniversary, a Day of Healing at Faneuil Hall," *Boston Globe*, August 25, 2019; Jennee Osterheldt, "Boston Was Robbed of a Slave Monument at Faneuil

Hall. Here's What Happened," *Boston Globe*, February 28, 2020; and Mark Pratt, "Faneuil Hall Name Change? Some Want It because of Slavery Ties," Associated Press, June 18, 2018.

9   Blatt discusses these changes in Tiziana Dearing, et al., "How Should Boston Address Its History of Slavery," *Radio Boston*, WBUR public radio, July 22, 2019. Abigail Feldman, "On Slavery's 400th Anniversary."

10 Haley E. D. Houseman, "Artists and Activists Trace Boston's Historic Red Line on the Streets," *Hyperallergic*, September 22, 2015, https://hyperallergic.com/238667/artists-and-activists -trace-bostons-historic-red-line-on-the-streets/.

11 On redlining specifically in Boston during the Logue years, see Lizabeth Cohen, *Saving America's Cities: Ed Logue and the Struggle to Renew Urban America in the Suburban Age* (New York: Farrar, Straus, and Giroux, 2019), 212–13. On redlining generally, as a national phenomenon, see Richard Rothstein, *The Color of Law: A Forgotten History of How Our Government Segregated America* (New York: Liverlight, 2017).

12 Cited in Sandra Larson, "National Park Service Aims to Engage Local Residents in Boston's Charlestown Navy Yard Planning," *Next City*, November 27, 2019, https://nextcity.org/daily /entry/national-park-service-aims-to-engage-local-residents-in-boston. The *Urban Agenda: Call to Action Initiative* (2016) is available at https://www.nps.gov/subjects/urban/upload /UrbanAgenda_web.pdf. For more on the Urban Agenda, see Sarah J. Morath, "A Park for Everyone: The National Park Service in Urban America," *Natural Resources Journal* 56 (Winter 2016): 14–16.

13 Nan Rickey, interviewed by Sarah Patton and Christine Arato, March 6, 2015, Unprocessed Files, Longfellow House Washington's Headquarters National Historic Site Archives, Resource Management Records, John Fitzgerald Kennedy National Historic Site, 43. For an early effort to document the experience of women in the parks, see Polly Welts Kaufman, "Women in the National Park Service," *Ranger: The Journal of the Association of National Park Rangers* 1, no. 4 (Fall 1984); and, more recently, Kaufman, *National Parks and the Woman's Voice: A History* (Albuquerque: University of New Mexico Press, 2006).

14 Anne Mitchell Whisnant, Marla R. Miller, Gary B. Nash, and David Paul Thelen, *Imperiled Promise: The State of History in the National Park Service* (Bloomington, IN: Organization of American Historians, 2011).

15 Whisnant, et al, *Imperiled Promise*, 55.

16 Consider, for instance, Max Page, *Why Preservation Matters* (New Haven: Yale University Press, 2016); and Stephanie Meeks, *The Past and Future City: How Historic Preservation is Reviving America's Communities* (Washington, DC: Island Press, 2016).

17 See, for instance, Oscar Beisert, "Wasting History in a World Heritage City," *Hidden City* (June 8, 2016), https://hiddencityphila.org/2016/06/wasting-history-in-a-world-heritage-city/.

18 See, for instance, Gareth Harris, "Vilified Statue of Abraham Lincoln and Kneeling Slave Removed from Park Square in Boston," *Art Newspaper* (December 30, 2020), https://www. theartnewspaper.com/news/vilified-statue-of-abraham-lincoln-and-kneeling-slave-removed -from-park-square-in-boston.

19 Paul Weinbaum, interview by Seth C. Bruggeman, July 1, 2020.

20 On the relationship between funding for public humanities and systemic racism, see GVGK Tang, "We Need to Talk About Public History's Columbusing Problem" *History@Work* (June 25, 2020), https://ncph.org/history-at-work/we-need-to-talk-about-public-historys -columbusing-problem/.

INDEX